SING SORROW

SING SORROW

Classics, History, and Heroines in Opera

Marianne McDonald

Contributions to the Study of Music and Dance, Number 62

GREENWOOD PRESS
Westport, Connecticut • London

Library of Congress Cataloging-in-Publication Data

McDonald, Marianne.
    Sing sorrow : classics, history, and heroines in opera / Marianne McDonald.
       p. cm.—(Contributions to the study of music and dance, ISSN 0193–9041 ; no. 62)
    Includes bibliographical references (p.) and index.
    ISBN 0–313–31567–1 (alk. paper)
    1. Classical literature—Musical settings—History and cricitism.   2. Operas—Literary themes, motives.   3. Opera—Classical influences.   4. Heroines in opera.   I. Title.
II. Series.
    ML2100.M34   2001
    782.1—dc21   2001023869

British Library Cataloguing in Publication Data is available.

Library of Congress Catalog Card Number: 2001023869
ISBN: 0–313–31567–1
ISSN: 0193–9041

First published in 2001

Greenwood Press, 88 Post Road West, Westport, CT 06881
An imprint of Greenwood Publishing Group, Inc.
www.greenwood.com

Printed in the United States of America

The paper used in this book complies with the
Permanent Paper Standard issued by the National
Information Standards Organization (Z39.48–1984).

10 9 8 7 6 5 4 3 2 1

To my children: Eugen, James, Bryan, Bridget, Kirstie, and Hiroshi
who taught me the meaning of music.

Contents

Photo essay follows page 114.

Acknowledgments

I am indebted to my mother, Inez Riddle McDonald, who, as a composer and concert pianist, surrounded me as a child with music. The nuns at the Convent of the Sacred Heart continued my life of music with their glorious hymns. Then, there were the many instructors—in harp, violin, and piano—who, in trying to teach me style and technique, also taught me theory and history. I single out Joy Huysak for her inspiration and patience.

I thank my teachers in both theory and musicology at the Chicago Musical College for teaching me while I was attending Chicago Latin School. I owe many thanks to my musical training from Sylvia Kenney and Horace Alwyne of Bryn Mawr College, where I continued my study of the Greek language and literature, and graduated with a joint degree in classics and music.

While opera may be considered an international language, I have tried not to ignore the contributions of particular people and nations. For expert attention to the many aspects of the music, I give heartfelt thanks to Karen Elaine and Richard Blackford. I particularly thank James Diggle, who spent many hours giving me his valuable critique. I am grateful to Athol Fugard, who patiently helped me with the entire manuscript. Also appreciated is the advice of Thomas MacCary on both the form and substance of my arguments. Michael Walton added his useful suggestions, as did his son Ben with his musical critique. Other readers who have been most generous are Perry Anderson, Alexander Cockburn, Phillip Gossett, George Huxley, Bernard Knox, Albert Liu, Francis Lovett, Bridget McDonald, Zeno Vendler, and the late John Sullivan, who gave valuable help on the *Elektra* chapter.

Prelude

Quand on est dans la merde jusqu'au cou, il ne reste plus qu'à chanter.
                                                                —Samuel Beckett

Rarely do critics or scholars mix fields without incurring the rancor of experts. There are many thousands of critical studies of opera, mainly by experts in musical subjects, whether of history, musicology, or of particular composers. Classicists occasionally add to these studies, as Michael Ewans did for the study of Wagner and P.E. Easterling for Richard Strauss's *Elektra*.[1] Many classicists, philosophers, and musicians attacked Nietzsche for writing *The Birth of Tragedy out of the Spirit of Music:* he invaded too many sacred precincts.[2] In her book on opera and feminism, Susan McClary complains that "musicology fastidiously declares issues of musical signification to be off-limits to those engaged in legitimate scholarship."[3] Alternatively, one can be criticized for not venturing into the new areas of theoretical work done on opera.

Nevertheless there is a need for such a work. Histories of operas have not done a systematic study of the operas based on classical themes and can make statements like "On the whole the preference for classical subjects is now much less pronounced than in former times," and single out Aeschylus for atypical use of his choruses, which "sometimes serve to narrate preceding events (*Agamemnon*) or take a direct part in the action (*Eurmenides*)."[4] In fact there are twice as many operas on classical themes in the twentieth century as in the nine-teenth, and more than in the seventeenth. Only the eighteenth century has more than any century. Given the fact that only thirty-three tragedies (including one Satyr play) survive from antiquity, and that is only one tenth of the tragedies that were composed and performed, it is difficult to say that anything is typical of the choruses. Aeschylus sets the pattern for the use of the chorus in Greek tragedy, and the two Aeschylean attributes of the chorus that Grout focuses on can be found in both Sophocles and Euripides. The citizens in the *Oedipus at Colonus* and the Bacchantes in the *Bacchae* both take a vital part in the action. I hardly know any chorus in Greek tragedy that does not narrate preceding events at some point. Euripides' *Trojan Women* is named for the chorus, and the chorus members tell the story of the taking of Troy that preceded the action of the play. On the other hand, classicists often omit opera in their discussion of later adaptations of Greek tragedy, or when the chorus members do speak about it, they omit much that interests musicians and musicologists.[5]

Since we are now supposedly living in a new geopolitical climate that disdains parochialism, its breezes can refresh critical territories cordoned off by their jealous guardians. Perhaps we can be allowed to think and reflect and apply more generally the knowledge we have gained from specialized education and experience. The theoretical field has expanded, and now we find much commentary on adaptation from linguists, philosophers, feminists, and experts from the world of theatre and of music. Language itself is understood differently. Ferdinand Sassure's work on linguistics and J.L. Austin's *How to Do Things with Words,* followed by the works of Barthes and Derrida, show us the sometimes tenuous connection between the signifier and the signified; music can sometimes bridge the gap. Barthes's study of the sculptor Sarrisine admiring the castrato La Zambinella broaches gender issues in opera and undermines essentialism, particularly fixed categories of male and female.[6] Julia Kristeva shows how language can shape society's attitude to gender issues. Music adds a new language. Susan Sontag has written on illness as metaphor, and Linda and Michael Hutcheon draw on this in their *Opera: Desire, Disease and Death.*[7] The gay voice is linked with opera as Wayne Koestenbaum shows in *The Queen's Throat: Opera, Homosexuality, and the Mystery of Desire.*[8] Michel Poizat in *The Angel's Cry: Beyond the Pleasure Principle in Opera* develops a theory of *jouissance* in opera, derived from Lacanian psychoanalysis.[9] The singing voice itself is related to Sappho in Elizabeth Wood's "Sapphonics" in *Queering the Pitch: The New Gay and Lesbian Musicology.*[10] Opera is a distinct locus for gender politics, we are told, in *En Travesti: Women, Gender, Subversion, Opera.*[11] Mary Ann Smart's edition *of Siren Songs: Representations of Gender and Sexuality in Opera* further refines these issues.[12]

Marxism, Colonialism, and other political issues influence the new interpretation. Theodor Adorno gives us a Marxist view, describing opera as "a bourgeois vacation spot," and further claiming that it had "little involvement in the social conflicts of the nineteenth century."[13] I disagree with Adorno here.[14] The ancients also saw the link between culture and politics, as Plato noted "Music never changes without radical political change" (*Republic,* 4. 424c). Edward Said modifies Adorno in his work on cultural imperialism.[15] Now there is much literature on history and opera, besides politics and opera. For example, useful models are provided by Paul Robinson's *Opera and Ideas: From Mozart to Strauss,* Jane Fulcher's *The Nation's Image: French Grand Opera as Politics and Politicized Art,* Anthony Arblaster's *Viva la libertà: Politics in Opera,* Herbert Lindenberger's *Opera in History From Monteverdi to Cage,* with many useful additions to and modifications of Joseph Kerman's earlier *Opera as Drama,* and Anselm Gerhard's *The Urbanization of Opera: Music Theater in Paris in the Nineteenth Century.*[16]

There is more interpretation from the point of view of the audience, that is, "reception theory" as put forward by Hans Robert Jauss in *Toward an Aesthetic of Reception.*[17] The study of intertextuality is important for understanding the transformation of an ancient text into an opera. There are many critical classics now in this area, including Herbert Lindenberger's *Opera: The Extravagant Art,* Peter Conrad's *A Song of Love and Death: The Meaning of Opera,* Gary Schmidgall's *Shakespeare and Opera,* and Robert Donington's *Opera and its Symbols: The Unity of Words, Music and Staging.*[18] One ignores their insights at one's peril.

If we try to analyze music's potential for meaning, we begin with its elusiveness: instrumental music has no immediately obvious message. Its sequence of notes, its organization into melody and harmony, its major and minor keys do not signify in the way a literary text does. Even in instrumental music, however, there are associative meanings: in Western music we associate certain keys and rhythms with certain situations. For instance, Don Giovanni, a noble, seduces Zerlina, a peasant girl, to music in the mode and rhythm of folk dance: by singing to her in ways that are familiar to her, he makes her feel secure (and therefore vulnerable to his proposal).[19] When we add the words of the vocal score and the action of the operatic stage, then there is a complex system of meanings: social, political, and economic.[20]

Some see tonality as reflective of society and, according to them, the hierarchy of the tonal order/key structure echoes social order and the class system, whereas atonality is democracy's correlative. For example, Edward Said implies that chromatics and fluid keys reflect the fluidity of modern society and a type of freedom, whereas the sonata form reflects the multiple constraints of the period when it flourished.[21] Rigid musical forms can indeed reflect the rigidity of societies and nations that created them. Peter Sellars is more practical in his approach to the social influence of opera: "Opera is a place where five hundred people learn how to get along together. If they don't they are dead meat." [22]

Geography can be linked with music. Rejecting Hegelian abstractions, Edward Said argues for consideration of the local, namely, "an alternative based on a geographical or spatial idea that is truer to the diversity and spread of human activity."[23] This provides a theoretical background for an opera like *Gospel at Colonus,* which combines the American Black gospel experience with Greek tragedy. So also a particular historical period provides a defining frame for artistic creations.

There are discussions in literature about music that add to our understanding of opera. Said mentions the uses to which Thomas Mann put Adorno's theories in *Doctor Faustus;* through intimate collaboration between the two exiles, living in Los Angeles in the 1940s, Mann developed for his central character a reading of Western musical history from 1800–1945 as an opposition between harmony and counterpoint, in which the latter finally triumphed: the poles are

Beethoven's "Hymn to Joy" and the last twelve notes of Berg's *Lulu*. This causes us to think about the many different levels on which musical history operates, indeed, how music has meaning. Adorno disparages Stravinsky's classicism because it is false to its age; he praises Schönberg for fulfilling the historically determined potential of musical form, to express the historically specific malaise of the twentieth century. Is this the era of dissonance? Nonsense? *Jouissance*?

Just as Adorno, following Hegel, sees history as driving the development of Western music, so I see the strange, contradictory role of women in western society as a powerful motor of modern opera. Many operas follow the time-honored ukase, "Torture the heroine." If the women are not killed, at least men try to control and limit their power. Nevertheless, even if they don't have Medea's dragon-drawn chariot, women can escape through the upper range of their voices. Sopranos and mezzos replace the mystical quality of the *castrati* with their avowed sensual and sexual presence. Brigid Brophy has spoken of this transition in dealing with Mozart's operas.[24]

The women in these operas suffer and die, kill their children and escape—do all manner of things—but they remain at the center of their operas. The men circle about them in frenzies of ambition and aggression, but the women are constant and secure in their own self-relevant nature. Their music defines them: they sing triumphantly in major keys, at the top of their soprano registers, and thus focus our attention on what is ageless and changeless in them and in the history of Western thinking about sexual relations. Hildegard von Bingen's *Ordo Virtutum* features triumphant female voices, culminating with their victory song. Perhaps as early as Homer's Penelope, but certainly beginning with Sophocles' Antigone, we have seen in men's writing about women a grudging respect for their grounding in nature, their assurance of constant values, their identities determined by some sense of inner strength unshaken by calamitous circumstance. It is the operas written about these women that I address, and I shall try to show how composers have used music to define and elevate their dominant roles.

The operas I have selected abound in heroines, and they can differ from their classical prototypes. Monteverdi's Penelope has as vital a struggle as Ulysses, and Purcell and Tate's Dido makes her own fatal choices, no longer the puppet of the gods as she is in Virgil. In Mozart's *Idomeneo*, the heroic and generous act of Ilia sets an example for the male heroes. Berlioz's Dido heroically defies Aeneas. Hofmannsthal and Strauss' Elektra becomes transfigured by her suffering and triumphs over her enemies; in Stravinsky and Cocteau's *Oedipus Rex*, the queen who is both mother and wife makes choices that show she has a strength that Oedipus lacks. In the *Gospel at Colonus*, Antigone is a strong guide for her father, contributing her strength to his. Finally Theodorakis' Medea is a heroine of Greece, one who suffers, yet fights for her freedom. In opera female heroism can flourish, both ideally and in reference to particular political and philosophical contexts.

Others, in writing about operatic heroines, have applied feminist theory. Catherine Clément and Susan McClary, for instance, see tonality and masculine cadences as tools to tame the chromatic female.[25] They talk about the reification of women as suffering creatures in opera. Sam Abel in his *Opera in the Flesh*: *Sexuality in Operatic Performance* claims, "Women find little encouragement to see themselves in opera, in either universalizing or minoritizing terms."[26] Ruth Padel follows in the footsteps of these authors:

It is a fundamental part of the male Western musical stage that the most large-scale, lavish, man-made performances should focus on one woman's self-abandoned, isolated voicing of pain. Dido, Ariadne, Butterfly abandoned—fine. Theseus, Heracles, Attila abandoned? No.[27]

I do not think these women are at all "self-abandoned"; rather, men have abandoned them. There are many counter-examples of women in opera who abandoned, rejected, or betrayed men: the husbands of the Danaids (except for one) in Angelo Tarchi's *Le Danaidi*, Haemon in Honegger's *Antigone*, Agamemnon in Theodore Antoniou's *Clytemnestra*, Theseus in Ildebrando Pizzetti's *Fedra*, José in Bizet's *Carmen*, the heroes in Massenet's *Werther*, and Berg's *Wozzeck*, and many men in *Lulu*. The men are left either weeping or silent. One can say that this is another way of "putting woman in her place" by demonizing her and warning the audience, but no one can take away her intrinsic power. These heroines are punished for what they do, but they first wreak havoc among the men. Suffering women certainly figure in opera, but there are also many who sing out their triumphs over men. Some theorists give tribute to their strength.[28] I think some of these earlier studies concentrated on nineteenth-century opera. Nineteenth-century operas tend to demonize or victimize women. I want to broaden the perspective. One should also look at Penelope, Ilia, Electra, and Medea, all of whom wield power and triumph unscathed, and significantly feature in seventeenth-, eighteenth-, and twentieth-century opera.

I shall begin with a "framing" chapter, "The Birth of Opera and the Use of Classics," discussing briefly how composers, singers, writers, and critics have dealt with the relations between the culture of classical antiquity and the emergence of the baroque opera as a crucial new aesthetic form, touching also on the theory of transmission. After that I will have chapters on eight operas that are based on ancient Greek and Latin epic and tragedy:

Claudio Monteverdi (1567–1643): *Il ritorno d'Ulisse in patria* (1640)
Henry Purcell (1659–1695): *Dido and Aeneas* (1689)
Wolfgang Amadeus Mozart (1756–1791): *Idomeneo, re di Creta* (1781)
Hector Berlioz (1803–1869): *Les Troyens* (1860)
Richard Strauss (1864–1949): *Elektra* (1909)
Igor Stravinsky (1882–1971): *Oedipus Rex* (1927)
Lee Breuer (1937–): *Gospel at Colonus* (1982)
Mikis Theodorakis (1925–): *Medea* (1991)

I begin each chapter with mythological and historical background, then analysis of the opera's relation to the original classic, and a discussion of what the music adds. I conclude with an appendix listing the operas I could find on this subject. The entire work concludes with an appendix of operas based on ancient classics—incomplete, as I hope it always will be, given the new operas to be written on these subjects.[29]

I start with the beginning of opera in the seventeenth century and end with the current scene in the twentieth. These operas also are examples from the major periods of opera. I have selected various countries: Italy, England, Austria, France, Germany, Russia, America, and, of course, Greece, which gave birth to tragedy. My study centers on Western opera, although I include a Japanese interpretation of Stravinsky's *Oedipus Rex* that takes elements from Noh and Kabuki.

I regret omitting Gluck and Handel. Both made brilliant contributions that I wish I could have considered, and certainly they were basically influenced by the classics. I chose instead Mozart's *Idomeneo, re di Creta* to represent the acme of *Opera Seria*.

I have omitted Wagner from this study because of the enormity of the task of including him, besides the fact that several works have already been written on the relationship between Greek mythical drama and Wagner.[30] Wagner theorized about the use of the classics, as did Nietzsche, and indeed about the use of mythology in general as a tool for opera. He was as important as the Florentine Camerata for shaping opera. Wieland Wagner claimed in 1965 that "The *Ring* constituted 'a return to mythical sources' and a revival of Greek tragedy."[31]

I chose Strauss instead of Wagner, and Strauss owed much to Wagner. Without the precedent of Wagner, Strauss would also probably have lacked the musical style he developed, as well as his entire philosophy of the nature of music drama. Strauss, also like Wagner, based many works on Greek mythology. Wagner resurrected and partially created a German mythology that both inspired and was inspired by the nationalistic drives of the time. It was his peculiar power both to redefine opera and to redirect German history that makes him a special and difficult case.

I shall touch on why certain topics were important in one age, rather than another: why, for instance, romance figures so clearly in nineteenth-century operas, whereas honor is more of a subject for the eighteenth. We often find clusters of operas on one subject or a favorite character, for example, Orfeo, Arianna, Didone, Lucio Vero, Alessandro, Achille, Arteserse, Circe, or Medea; the reasons are often historical and reflect the preferences of the time. Aeneas, for instance, is an obvious symbol for empire, and it is no accident that he is the hero of *Les Troyens*, composed in a nineteenth-century France that was creating its own empire.

I shall also investigate the way music fulfills the potential for meaning in the words. In the earlier periods there is more literal correspondence between words and music. We should also remember the attempts, through *recitativo secco* by Mozart right up to the *Sprechgesang* of Schönberg in *Moses and Aaron* and *Die glückliche Hand*, to render speech in a fluent and quasi-naturalistic way, which contrasts with the more florid or melismatic setting found in various aria or song forms. After the seventeenth century, music divorced itself more and more from the meaning of the text and became an end in itself. We see this in Schönberg's *Pierrot Lunaire,* also Stravinsky's *Oedipus Rex.* The contemporary English composer Harrison Birtwistle's *The Mask of Orpheus* is an opera in which barely a word is intelligible. Nevertheless, there are still other operas that are extremely programmatic; Richard Wagner and Richard Strauss spring immediately to mind.

Each of my chapters will touch on the notion of heroism—particularly that of the heroine—the role of religion, class and gender relationships, historical contexts, the relation of music to words, and most of all the relation of the modern work to the ancient one. I also discuss how musical creations can be political propaganda, as Plato noted in the *Republic.* It is obvious that each of these topics could entail a book in itself, but I hope that my limited use of them can help to elucidate the underlying theme of how a classic informs a modern work. As Verdi said, "Let us return to old times, and that will be progress."[32]

The Birth of Opera
and the Use of Classics

There were many precedents for opera throughout the ages, beginning with Greek tragedy itself with its danced and sung choruses and individual arias. Some would say the biblical *Song of Solomon* was the earliest opera.[1] It could be argued that Hildegard von Bingen (1098–1179) composed the first opera, *Ordo Virtutum*, a liturgical drama that recounts in song (soloists and choir) the story of a soul, Anima, struggling against the devil. Secular dramatic music also developed, and Adam de la Halle's *Le jeu de Robin et de Marion* (1283–1284) has been called the first *opéra comique*.

Renaissance courts entertained their guests with dramas in which stories were sometimes sung, danced, and acted. The sacred Mysteries were sung: for instance, "Jeu de Daniel" was performed in France in the thirteenth century, and "The Conversion of St. Paul" was performed in Rome in 1440.[2] These Mysteries often contained more spoken sections than the liturgical drama and were performed by the laity, which included professional actors from guilds.

There were other predecessors. Sixteenth-century masques (Italian *mascherata*, French *mascarades*, and English *masques*) were danced and sung, and featured figures from mythology, particularly abstractions like the sun, moon, and love. They were often used to honor kings or distinguished nobles. These masques contributed to the prologues to many early operas.

Ballets were both danced and sung. In 1581 Balthasar de Beaujoyeulx's *Circé ou Le Balet comique de la royne* (music by Lambert de Beaulieu and Jacques Salmon) was dramatically unified and on a mythological theme. *Intermedi* provided musical interludes to plays and showed how well music and text functioned together in performance. The *intermedi* were somewhat like Greek choruses in providing musical commentary on the plays. The dramatic madrigal also married music to text, as did Orazio Vecchi in his *L'Amfiparnaso* (1597). His work owed much to the *commedia dell'arte* of the time, which featured character types and domestic comedy.

Also in the sixteenth century one had dramatic pastorales, which were ballets and songs set in a peaceful countryside, with love as the main theme. Particularly notable were *La favola d'Orfeo* by Angelo Poliziano (1471–1480) and Agostino Beccari's *Il sacrificio d'Abramo* (1554). Pastorales were written on Torquato Tasso's *Aminta* (1573) and Battista Guarini's *Il pastor fido* (1581–1590). One can see that the first operas, *Dafne* and *Orfeo*, were also derived from pastoral themes.

In an auspicious moment for European culture at the end of the sixteenth century the Florentine Camerata wished to revive ancient Greek drama, with its rich mythology, in expanded musical versions.[3] Joseph Kerman points out that Andrea Gabrieli had earlier performed in 1585 a version of *Oedipus Tyrannus*.[4] His choral settings to this drama were particularly famous. The Greeks invented tragedy and comedy, but the Italians were the masters of the pastorale and opera.

Both the group of Giovanni de' Bardi and the followers of Jacopo Corsi are credited with the "invention" of opera around 1600, as a revival of ancient Greek drama.[5] Jacopo Peri and Jacopo Corsi's *Dafne*, based on a text by Octavio Rinuccini in 1597–1598, is arguably the first opera. The music does not survive, except for some brief excerpts. Peri and Giulio Caccini's *Euridice*, for which we have the music, followed in 1600. But it was Claudio Monteverdi who is considered the true father of opera because of the quality of his work. Joseph Kerman points out Monteverdi's debt to the past: "The first great opera composer was also the last great madrigalist."[6]

So the earliest opera was Italian and based on the classics. Other countries followed Italy's lead. Germany's first extant opera, by Heinrich Schütz, was also on *Dafne* (1627). The first Spanish opera whose music survives is by Juan Hidalgo: *Celos aun del aire matan* (1659, based on the myth of Cephalus and Procris) written to celebrate the marriage of Maria Theresa and Louis XIV. The earliest English opera is by Henry Cooke, Henry Lawes, Matthew Locke, and Charles Coleman, with a libretto by Sir William Davenant. It was called *The Siege of Rhodes* (1656), and its music has not survived. The music was probably added to Davenant's libretto / play simply to avoid Puritan censorship (see the chapter on Purcell's *Dido and Aeneas*). Davenant's sequel during the Restoration was simply a play. The earliest surviving English opera is by John Blow, *Venus and Adonis* (c.1683), and the first French opera is Robert Cambert's *Pomone* (1671). All except *The Siege of Rhodes* are based on mythological themes. In 1701 the first opera to be performed in the Americas (Lima, Peru) was *La púrpura de la rosa* by Tomás de Terrejón y Velasco; it was based on the mythological theme of Venus and Adonis.

Some claim that Monteverdi is the creator of modern music, whereas others say that he was simply talented at synthesizing the music available at the time.[7] He raised opera to the level of serious musical drama with *L'Orfeo*, first performed in Mantua in 1607. The earliest operas of the Florentine Camerata were failures because of the composers' inability to progress beyond turgid *arioso*. Monteverdi, on the other hand, showed in *L'Orfeo* that variation of musical form was essential for successfully building up and resolving dramatic tension.

The first themes were mythical and dealt with the gods or Orpheus, the musician who could make stones move or tame wild beasts. Operas about Daphne or Orpheus were also about Apollo, the god of music, who took over the lyre from Hermes and made it sing. Robert Donington shows well the symbolism of these early operas and their debt to Marsilio Ficino and his "Neo-platonism."[8] Donington goes on to show the symbolic content of all opera and how it resonates with archetypes.[9] Pierre de Ronsard gave instructions to a poet to "dissemble and conceal fables, fitly, and disguise well the truth of things with a fabulous cloak," so as to "make enter into the minds of ordinary people, by agreeable and colourful fables, the secrets which they could not understand when the truth is too openly disclosed."[10]

Other themes in opera included legendary figures who combined history with the supernatural (e.g., Ulysses). Great figures of Roman history appear in Italian opera as if they were deities, as Nero in Monteverdi's *Poppea*. History can be treated as myth in the way it is reworked for an opera text. History still influences opera, as we see, for example, in Iain Hamilton's *The Royal Hunt of the Sun* (1977), John Adam's *Nixon in China* (1987), and *The Death of Klinghoffer* (1991).

Ancient texts fueled opera, and their modern adaptations make opera particularly rich. We see the conjunction of the ancient and the modern as we picture ourselves in the ancient characters. Our individual problems may be insoluble, but we appreciate their resemblance to the problems others have always had, and thereby translate ourselves to a higher plane of experience. Superficially we seem to have even less in common with Agamemnon, Clytemnestra, and Electra than the original Greek audience did. We do not believe in their gods. We do not live in small, integrated city-states. We rarely share their values and aspirations. But for this very reason, our response, as a modern audience, may be even more complex than that of the original audience two and one-half millennia ago, because we combine our modern perceptions with an enhanced knowledge of the ancient period, in the perspective of the history that followed.

If the modern performance is not just a translation of the original Greek text presented in spoken form by actors on a stage, but rather an operatic adaptation, with music and dance supplementing the text, then our experience is again enriched and elevated. Ancient Greek tragedy was originally presented in alternating passages of spoken and sung verbal exchanges. Generally, the action moves forward in the dialogue sections spoken by the actors. The chorus provides commentary and meditation in its lyrics, and is sometimes choreographed and accompanied by the *aulos*—a pipe (usually played in pairs) with a reed mouthpiece (probably double in the classical period) somewhat akin to the oboe or clarinet.[11]

Greek literature began with epic and progressed through introspective lyric to the more ironic modes of drama, and finally philosophy—following the development of Greek thinking from mythic to religious to analytical.[12] One can trace a similar progression in the development of opera. Opera was the creation of the baroque, when men seem to have lost intimacy with the transcendent.

Adam is touched by God, and both appear in human form in Michelangelo's ceiling of the Sistine Chapel, emblems of the high renaissance conviction of the complete inter-penetration of human and divine. But Caravaggio, Guido Reni, and other artists of their generation split the world into mutually exclusive realms; Monteverdi's pagan gods and personified abstractions have the appearance of the ruins of a lost faith. Joséphin Peladan claimed, "Besides religions as such, a new religiosity comes into being in all decadent times, and this religiosity is aesthetic."[13] Peter Conrad notes that "the art of opera has itself been established as a religion."[14]

Walter Benjamin spoke of the baroque as the ruins of history.[15] There is a terrible nostalgia for former intimacy, a yearning for the abundance and instant gratification of childhood. Monteverdi's Ulisse is ministered to by Athena; Nero, a secular god, is adored by Poppea, a secular goddess. Apollo restores Eurydice to Orpheus, not in her physical form, but as an image to be contemplated in the stars. The ending in Striggio's libretto, which featured bacchantes rending apart our hero, was rewritten by Monteverdi to show Orpheus transported to heaven by his father Apollo. He has failed in virtue, but his father offers him a paradise beyond suffering. The baroque thus hypostatizes human suffering, turning it into art. Monteverdi also learned quickly in his career that secular deities such as the Gonzagas (his employers) wanted happy endings, and certainly since *L'Orfeo* was written for a marriage celebration it *had* to have a happy ending.

In Monteverdi's operas and in many others of the time, the systematic undercutting of the serious drama by humor and parody leads to a curious ironic distancing that encourages audacious interrogation by the audience. The art of the time often depicts a tortured saint looking off to a remote point in the heavens, while in the foreground his suffering is thrust upon us and some bestial onlooker with a savage grin on his face intervenes between him and us. The focus is now on suffering and human corruption instead of the divine promise of salvation.

Rome, Venice, Mantua, and Florence struggled among themselves for political and artistic supremacy. Art served politics, and a musical victory was often the equivalent of one achieved in the field. Monteverdi was not removed from this struggle, and, in addition, after the establishment of the first commercial opera house in Venice, he had to write opera that would be popular, sell tickets, and could be produced within a limited budget. Amid such constraints, his works were masterpieces of drama, illustrating the text in ways that had become popular through the art of the solo song. He defended the priority of the text by citing Plato, who describes *melos* as consisting of *logos, harmonia,* and *rhythmos* (*Rep.* 3.398D). *Logos* ("word/text") came first, as treatises by the Florentine Camerata pointed out.[16] His enemy Artusi used the same passage from Plato to illustrate the opposite point, namely that conventional rules of harmony should have priority over the text. The classics provided not only subjects for the operas but also material for the debates. They were ancient, noble, open vessels to be filled with the ideas of the baroque. Our aesthetic response is then based on this recycling: we see the Homeric and classical elements re-arranged, always aware of their fragmentation.[17]

The process of adaptation from classical sources into the earliest operas is both direct and yet difficult to follow. Since Greek tragedy was poetic, and one is aware of the problem of translating poetry, an opera in a language other than Greek is bound to complicate the problem. Nevertheless, music can be a bridge to understanding a poetic text. Roland Barthes well elucidates this problem: opera can translate the narrative, even though the poetry may at times elude translation.[18] Sometimes sound itself conveys meaning, as Pietro Bembo (1525) asserted.[19]

While there was a clear intention to recreate ancient Greek tragedy, it was restricted by a set of cultural and artistic circumstances completely different from the original. Similarly, we moderns, who try to appreciate this difference, have little in common with the audience of Claudio Monteverdi, either the audience at the court of Duke Vincenzo Gonzaga of Mantua or the more popular one in the Republic of Venice. To complicate matters further, this baroque music had neither the complete notation of contemporary music, nor was it played on modern instruments. Only the bass line was given along with the vocal parts; in the *sinfonia* (overture and interludes) the instrumentation is fuller. We are, however, delighted by its performance, whether in the more traditional renderings, such as by Nikolaus Harnoncourt, or in those that use modern instruments and orchestration, such as the version of *Il ritorno* by Hans Werner Henze.

Like both Greek tragedy and epic, early opera tells of the exploits of gods and heroes. Baroque opera owed allegiance to noble patrons, and the subject matter reflected this. It was "the age of absolutism."[20] The masque was more democratic than opera, since it included the antimasque, but even here it was clear who was to be taken seriously and who was an object of derision. We might compare the amusements offered the courtiers by their underlings in Shakespeare's *Love's Labors Lost* ("The Seven Worthies") and *A Midsummer Night's Dream* ("Pyramus and Thisbe"). It is only later opera that deals with all the classes, the most obvious being John Gay's *The Beggar's Opera* (1728), but other examples are Puccini's *La Bohème* (1896), Bizet's *Carmen* (1875), and operas from the Italian *realismo* or *verismo*, like Pietro Mascagni's *Cavalleria Rusticana* (1890) and Leoncavallo's *Pagliacci* (1892).

The twentieth century continues to present us with a realistic portrayal of all social classes, although the very medium of opera is theatrical and unrealistic. We think of Alban Berg's *Wozzeck* (1925), George Gershwin's *Porgy and Bess* (1935) and Benjamin Britten's *Peter Grimes* (1945). Modern opera sometimes introduces new figures of authority, namely the politician, as in John Adams' *Nixon in China* (1987).

Although the Florentine Camerata claimed Greek tragedy as its inspiration, epic and folk tales were predominant themes throughout the seventeenth and eighteenth centuries. There is modern obeisance to the origin of opera as a revival of Greek tragedy: for instance, Francesco's Cilea's *Adriana Lecouvreur* (1902) recounts the story of an actress who plays Phaedra. She calls herself *l'umile ancella* ("humble handmaid") of the classical heroines that she portrays. Greek tragedy can be revived in other ways; for instance, Peter Conrad says, "*Cavalleria Rusticana*, set in Sicily, is a Greek tragedy restaged by peasants."[21]

Monteverdi's operas changed after his move to Venice (a public theatre instead of a royal court): it is interesting to compare the type of drama that directly revolved around royalty with the operas he composed when he went to Venice. *Orfeo* is still in the courtly tradition. One thinks of the masques of James I and the tradition of Florentine *intermedi* (short episodic musical interludes popular in the fifteenth and sixteenth century). Masques featured dance more than song, and the nobles "played" the parts. They were often conceived for events, such as marriages. They contained themes from classical antiquity as evolved in the Italian Camerata.

The Masque of Oberon (1611), with a text by Ben Jonson as well as innovative lighting supplied by Inigo Jones and—if we are to believe accounts—a polar bear, was planned to end as the sun rose. In order to "disappoint" the rising sun, the Masque concludes that its own sun, James I, must make haste away to bed. This "interactive" music drama, which had become extinct more or less by the opening of San Cassiano in 1637, clearly delineated social ranks. The rulers were always a factor: the opening toccata of *Orfeo*, which was repeated three times, was written for the entrances of the Duke and his family.

In some musical performances the rulers played the gods, or themselves. This transition from courtly dramas to opera in a public opera house involved many changes, and obeisance to the nobles became less important.[22] Different audiences had different needs. Instead of a simple story with lyrical flourishes (*Orfeo*), Monteverdi could afford to develop themes that sometimes questioned the role of the nobles (*Il ritorno*, and *Poppaea*).

Human emotion figures prominently in opera from the beginning. The earliest operas were based on mythological stories of love (Dafne, Euridice, Cephalus and Procris, Venus and Adonis). Love is featured in all opera in some way or another until the twentieth century, when there are exceptions (e.g., Philip Glass's *Einstein on the Beach*). World wars strangle love. Some ancient myths contributed love stories to the first operas, but ancient Greek tragedy rarely featured erotic love, and then only to show the disasters to which it could lead. It was New Comedy in the fourth century B.C., and later the Greek novel that presented love stories with happy endings. The twentieth century shows a return to the beginning (early epic and Greek tragedy) when it presents tragic stories without the component of erotic love (e.g., Strauss's *Elektra*).

Many early laments were for absent or lost loves. Monteverdi's *Arianna* (1608, the year following *Orfeo*) was based on another mythical theme, and although the opera itself has not survived, the lament does, and is considered one of the masterpieces of world music. *Arianna* was written after his wife's death, and one tends to think his genius for emotive expression was enhanced by this tragic experience.

The sorrows of loss and love are main themes of Monteverdi's operas, with love personified in the last two. *Orfeo* also expresses some of the neoplatonic themes current at the time, so human love in this case is construed as something impermanent, to be rejected in favor of the eternal: "immortal life . . . and the eternal god."[23]

Monteverdi and Mozart took over the structure of Greek tragedy in dividing their libretti between aria, or *arioso* sections, and recitative. The action moves forward in the recitatives, and we learn from the characters in their arias how they feel about these developments. A verbal text set to music is by nature more abstract and more philosophical—indeed, more idealized—than a simple spoken utterance. Again, it is further from our own everyday experience and we receive it differently. A musical setting simultaneously invites us into the character's own peculiar emotional range and universalizes these emotions.

Two dimensions—the profound response of the modern audience to the seemingly alien matter of ancient Greek tragedy, and the elevating and universalizing effect of music—make the experience of a modern opera based on Greek tragedy an extraordinarily demanding and rewarding one. The *Elektra* of Strauss and a few other masterpieces of that genre involve us in an almost religious ritual: we worship not some god, or even some philosophical concept, but rather the essence of human emotion. We hear ourselves in elevated song.

The apotheosis of human suffering implicit in Greek tragedy is best expressed in opera, or as a Behan put it: "You might as well sing grief as cry it."[24] Opera achieves the same elevation and concern for the ideal that tragedy did, and this lends a heroic quality to the protagonists. Like the tragic hero, they are larger than life, and in opera the hero is often a heroine.[25]

History often shapes transmission. Operas in the baroque period were influenced first by the needs of the nobles and then by the public. Religion colored the way things and people were interpreted: Penelope is seen in the light of the Marian cult and shares attributes with the Virgin. In the eighteenth century there is a new emphasis on rationalism and humanity. This is also the time of the "enlightened monarch," something reflected in Mozart's *Idomeneo*. The nineteenth century shows us the era of nationalism and rising imperialism, which led to orientalist overtones in Berlioz's *Les Troyens*. This is the time when the operatic heroine is often sacrificed, something that delights the audience (described by Clément in her *Opera, or the Undoing of Women*). Is this power exerted over women another type of imperialism? The twentieth century shows that women have more power, and Medea may kill her children and escape without penalty. In some cases there is a return to religion, some order imposed on perceived chaos (Stravinsky's *Oedipus Rex*). The experience of slavery is reflected in *The Gospel at Colonus*, an expression of the joys and sorrows of those blacks who suffered from oppression in America.

The political use of myth and the classics is well documented. Jacques Attali says, "Music is more than an object of study: it is a way of perceiving the world."[26] It also can be used as a tool for power. Attali traces "three strategic usages of music by power": one which makes "people forget the general violence"; another "to make people believe in the harmony of the world"; and finally "one in which it serves to silence."[27]

The use of art to further politics may be traced to the birth of tragedy in the fifth century B.C., when Athens staged dramatic festivals to impress foreigners and their allies. At the beginning of opera, rulers liked to have opera composers as well as armies to display their power. Greek tragedy has had particular popularity in the twentieth century. The Irish have staged more than fifty modern versions of Greek tragedy, mainly dealing with the question of human rights. *Antigone* has often been played when there is political unrest, as when Jean Anouilh staged his *Antigone* (1944) during the Nazi occupation of Paris; his seemingly even-handed presentation of both Creon's and Antigone's positions got it past the German censors. Bertolt Brecht's *Antigone* (1948) showed Creon overtly as Hitler. Athol Fugard's *The Island* (1973) featured prisoners of apartheid playing out *Antigone* in protest. In 1984, *The Island* was also staged in Ireland along with four other *Antigones* and was revived in London at the Royal National Theatre in 2000. Perhaps this is the appropriate restoration of ancient Greek tragedy that Schelling dreamed about when he spoke of the debasement of ancient Greek tragedy in opera.[28] I, for one, am grateful for both types of revivals.

Time brings about many changes. Monteverdi's instruments were different from Berlioz's. Modern composers can use street sounds. Attitudes change. An eighteenth-century audience enjoyed the same lighting as the performers, and there was a relaxed interchange between the two. A post-Wagnerian audience is supposed to watch lighted proceedings in a darkened room in silence. Operas change in response to their conditions, their resources, and differences in historical perspective.

Monteverdi's *Il ritorno d'Ulisse in patria:* Heroism at Home

INTRODUCTION

Throughout his life, Monteverdi faced a constant struggle for property, free time, and recognition. It was only after the death of Vincenzo de Gonzaga and Monteverdi's appointment as the director of music at San Marco in Venice in 1613, that he could count on receiving a regular salary. He still maintained relations with the court of the Gonzagas and wrote many major works for them.

Monteverdi lived in turbulent times. Many of his works were lost in the sack of Mantua following the death of Vincenzo II (1630). This was followed by a year of plague, which affected performances. It was also a time of political upheaval, since Spain, France and the Holy Roman Empire (as Germany would like to call itself) were vying for control in Italy.

Il ritorno d' Ulisse in patria was probably produced in Venice in 1640, at the first opera house, Teatro San Cassiano, built in 1637. There was possibly an earlier performance at Bologna, although some say the opera was first performed at Teatro SS. Giovanni e Paolo in Venice. Finally, *L'incoronazione di Poppea* was presented in 1642 at Teatro SS. Giovanni e Paolo.[1]

I have found more than one hundred operas either about Ulysses or in which he appears. Ulysses is always popular, but at no point more so than in the eighteenth century, when he became a symbol of the investigative spirit of the Enlightenment. It is typical of opera that the titles of over half of these operas refer to a heroine (Penelope, Circe, or Calypso).

Operas on classical themes abound in the eighteenth century, but this figure from epic—with his adventurous mind—was particularly popular in this period. Penelope is also a heroine who is celebrated in these operas; her fidelity becomes an active virtue. She intervenes in the lives of the people around her. Ulysses must prove himself worthy of her. This is a shift from the original epic, in which her cleverness was a trait she shared with Ulysses. In Monteverdi's opera she borrows strength from the Virgin Mary, both musically and in her virtue. Ulysses, by contrast, is more of a cipher. He is someone to sing duets with Penelope, if he behaves.

It seems that for every opera about Penelope, there is also one about Circe or Calypso. Like Dido, they are abandoned, or, as was often the case in the seventeenth century, their stories were rewritten with happy endings. They are seductive women who challenge marriage and its values. Their theme of unlawful love provides counterpoint to the theme of marital fidelity. Their stories are varied for each century's needs. In the seventeenth century Penelope is most popular: she is the chaste ideal. She represents what society expected from women. In the eighteenth century, both Penelope and her rivals are seen to have their merits. The basis for the rules in the former century is questioned. Nevertheless good is still rewarded and evil punished: Reinhard Keiser has Penelope applauded and Circe punished in his *Ulysses* (1722). In the nineteenth century, both Penelope and Circe/Calypso appear in opera, but Circe and Calypso suffer more, like the romantic heroines they are. In the twentieth, Circe/Calypso is preferred; when women gain legal rights (e.g., the vote), the wayward female is celebrated. Nevertheless another approach is seen in Dallapicolla's *Ulisse* (1968): the soprano singing Penelope's role often doubles as Calypso. In the twentieth century one can accept and endorse a complex woman.

By the time Monteverdi composed *Il ritorno* and *Poppea* he had taken Holy Orders. Some might consider *Poppea* incomprehensible in this context, given its dissolute thesis of virtue defeated by fortune and love. It has been suggested that *Il ritorno* and *Poppea* take the two sides of a debate popular at the time about the superiority of chaste over unchaste love.[2]

Monteverdi is traditional, transitional, and original, which one could also say of Mozart and other geniuses. Monteverdi's is "a highly elaborate type of music, employing new extremes of chromaticism, word painting, coloristic effects, declamatory monody, virtuosity of the vocal soloist and dramatic effects."[3] Such musical characteristics can be shown to have broader social implications. Susan McClary's dissertation on *The Transition of Modal to Tonal Organization in the Works of Monteverdi* emphasizes "a brand of tonality that emerges at this time: a surefire method for inciting and channeling expectations that easily supplants the less coercive procedures of modality."[4] In his free use of older modal harmonies and dissonance, McClary sees Monteverdi as giving more freedom to female characters in his operas. She writes: "For despite the fact that aristocratic patrons had extensive control over the subject matter of their entertainment, the works themselves often appear—at least at first glance—to undercut assumed social hierarchies and call into question the authority of patriarchy and nobility."[5] This tendency developed further when the operas were performed in opera houses, as noted above. Particularly in the operas following *Orfeo*, the female character now expresses herself: "Not only is the role of seductive orator often reassigned to female characters in later opera, but similarly most of the women who lament and are celebrated in dramatic works after *Orfeo* (Arianna, Penelope, and Ottavia) are female: all women who have been betrayed by treacherous, absent, or ineffectual male authority and who express their righteous indignation in tirades as blistering as any present-day feminist critique."[6]

Catherine Clément tends to reduce the role of the female in opera and would see Monteverdi's "abandoned nymph" as simply another sacrifice on the altar of male desire.[7] It should be obvious that I agree more with McClary than with Clément: I think Monteverdi's Penelope is a woman who is more a victor than a victim.

Monteverdi incorporated elements that we associate with the baroque, such as surface display and form for its own sake.[8] Another is the juxtaposition of the humorous and the grotesque, and finally also the clear division between divine and human spheres, with an increased emphasis on the secular. The interaction of the divine and the human expresses a type of nostalgia for something lost.

Monteverdi is a great artist with a fine sense of form. He reduces Badoaro's libretto from five to three acts and adds a prologue that ties into Penelope's lament, so we can immediately see its relevance. Then the first act is balanced by the third: both begin with a lament, contain a scene among the gods, and finally an attempt to sway Penelope from her adamant fidelity. Of course, by finally giving in, Penelope remains faithful, since Ulisse is her only love. The first and third acts concentrate on love and the reconciliation of Penelope with Ulisse, whereas the second focuses on vengeance. We might say the second act is Homeric in contrast to the courtly ones.

Monteverdi was fortunate in finding good librettists: Alessandro Striggio for *Orfeo*, Giacomo Badoaro for *Il ritorno*, Francesco Busenello for *Poppea*. Yet he followed none of them slavishly and made many cuts in Badoaro's libretto— for example, a scene where the suitors' ghosts are swallowed by hell; also, a moralizing chorus at the end. The chorus of the Nereids and Sirens (Act I, Scene iii) and the Chorus of the Naiads (Act I, introduction to Scene ix) also lack music.

Sometimes Monteverdi accepts Badoaro's repetition of phrases, though juxtaposition with what precedes and follows can create nonsense of the phrase. For instance, Badoaro, for the sake of repeating *O fortunato Ulisse*, has our hero ignore what is being said as he congratulates himself. Minerva tells him that he will see the terrible excesses of the rival suitors who are robbing him, and he bursts out with *O fortunato Ulisse*, which suits the next line better, where he is told that he will see Penelope again and that she has remained faithful to him. In this case, obviously, formal musical and poetic concerns predominated, despite Monteverdi's stated preference for the text's meaning. Monteverdi also alters Badoaro's text by eliminating what he considers material extraneous to the opera, as in the excision of the second scene in Act 3, in which Mercury leads the shades of the suitors to the underworld. The text is filled with moralizing that Monteverdi rightly considered undramatic. For instance, the text includes ponderous lines like, "A hard and unfortunate exchange it is of a butterfly of joy for a Phoenix of suffering."[9]

The librettists Badoaro and Busenello were both members of a society called the *Accademia degli Incogniti*, which was characterized as "cynical and libertine."[10] If we look at Monteverdi's time, with its corrupt secular and religious leaders, *Poppea* accurately reflects the historical situation, although the story is located in the past. It is well known that performances of some versions of the classics have been used to mask criticism of the present.

Gods figure prominently in all these musical dramas. They soar over the stage or look on with varying degrees of interest. Just as in Homer, they wrangle as much as the humans. They direct human affairs, but their own impulses are rooted in human psychology. Monteverdi's opera uses them as external motivations or explanations of human affairs, and we feel there a great yearning for order and authority. Like *Orfeo*, *Il ritorno* is replete with divine manifestations, which include not only Giove, Nettuno, and Minerva, but also the abstractions Time, Fortune, and Love, instead of Badoaro's original Fate, Power and Prudence; man himself appears abstracted as Human Fragility. But by the end of the opera the hero and heroine of *Il ritorno* usurp the musical expression, with its lyrical flares and colorful ornaments that had been used exclusively by the gods. There is an acknowledgment of the gods' power, but at the same time an intimation of how human virtue can allow man access to divinity. Does this subtlety suggest that Monteverdi's genius allowed him access to a power equal to the Gonzagas, albeit aesthetic in nature?

Monteverdi—critical and satirical by disposition—had inevitably to capitulate to powerful regimes, both secular and ecclesiastical. He wrote glorious music none the less. At times one glimpses criticism and satire. He celebrates himself as the artist in *Orfeo* and also in the characters of Ulisse and Penelope: Ulisse weaves endless stories and Penelope an endless tapestry; above, there is even the resourceful goddess Minerva, outmaneuvering her father Jove. Nature is hostile. Monteverdi's heroism is exemplified by Ulisse's bravery and Penelope's shrewd chastity. Her shrewdness itself must be overcome as a final victory, to allow her to be reunited with Ulisse.

There has been some question whether Monteverdi was indeed the composer of *Il ritorno*. Gary Tomlinson, however, in his study of Monteverdi, echoes the prevailing opinion: "It seems clear on stylistic grounds that most of the music of both operas not called into question by the sources could have been written by no one but Monteverdi; it is, in its variety, its versatility, and especially its gestural distinctiveness, unrivaled by any other mid-century idioms."[11]

Music at this time is at an interesting point of transition before major and minor scales, resolutions, and fixed tempi come to dominate later baroque music, setting the pattern which continues well into the nineteenth century. As Nikolaus Harnoncourt puts it, "During the intervening 33 years [between *Orfeo* in 1607 and *Il ritorno* in 1640], an historical and musical transition from the Renaissance to the Baroque occurred."[12] The final two operas have benefited from the motets and madrigals that Monteverdi had written over the years. Not only does his *Orfeo* have a barely disguised religious theme (Orpheus is wafted off to heaven at the end), but the music resembles the earlier religious music that had formed Monteverdi. *Il ritorno* is more secular, but still retains some religious elements to color certain sections where the subject matter derives from Christianity, such as those that speak of Heaven's mercy. The reward for the protagonists, however, is found in *earthly* love.

IL RITORNO D'ULISSE IN PATRIA

I will illustrate these points through specific analysis of the opera, and make still others.[13] I shall use the Italian names when I refer to characters in the opera, and the Greek names (transliterated into English) when I am referring to them in Homer. The *Iliad* and the *Odyssey* are the main sources for *Il ritorno*, *Odyssey* 13–22 in particular, but the opera departs from Homer's epic in many ways. The libretto of Giocomo Badoaro shows additions and cuts from Homer's epic; joyful sections alternate with melancholy ones.

The *Odyssey* has a complicated structure, introducing us to Odysseus' son Telemachus first, and then to the main hero only in Book 5; thereafter Homer indulges in elaborate flashbacks until Book 13. *Il ritorno* is straightforward, comparable to Odysseus' arrival in Ithaca in Book 13, until Penelope and Odysseus are reunited in Book 23, but it also incorporates elements from the earlier books, such as Telemachus' return and the suitors plotting his death. The new emphasis is on love and vengeance, leading to the reunion of Penelope with Odysseus: from a *chanson de geste* to a *chanson d'amour*.

Badoaro and Monteverdi applied principles derived from Aristotle's *Poetics*. Aristotle discusses the differences between epic and drama. The epic has narrative that is expansive and descriptive, whereas drama is "the imitation of an action, heroic and complete and of a certain size, with a language pleasing in variations appropriate to each section, by means of action rather than narration, through pity and fear effecting a *katharsis* of those emotions" (*Poetics* 1449b). The structure of opera followed that of drama and Aristotle's categories of plot, characterization, thought, language, music, and spectacle. Opera was the perfect locus to develop these ideals, although the priorities (if there are priorities) might be different.

Opera, too, has differences from the stories it adapts. Opera's expansiveness was in song, but a limited dramatic structure contained these moments of emotional expressiveness. Monteverdi felt that music was the perfect illustrative medium for an emotional text. There is a movement in Homer's epics from the *aristeia* (heroic deeds) of heroes in the *Iliad* to the romance of the *Odyssey*, and it is romance that dominates early opera. There are more fantastic creatures in the *Odyssey*, more fairy-tale adventures (including a descent to the underworld), and it concludes with love reconsummated and a promise of further adventures to come. The final distillation is into an operatic tale of love. The wanderings found their home in Badoaro's *Ulisse errante*, published in 1644, with music by Sacrati.

The prologue features Human Fragility buffeted by Time, Fortune, and Love, an apt theme of this work, illustrating through their heroic constancy the triumph of man and woman. When replayed at the end as Ulisse and Penelope are reunited, it is particularly poignant: the immortal gods cause change in the world, but lovers at least can remain the same, achieving thereby a secular divinity. The myth also endows them with this constancy.

In this prologue, man appears and is assailed by lame, blind, and deaf forces, as Time, Fortune, and Love claim they will make him fragile, wretched, and tortured. This is an addition to Homer: only in the late fourth century B.C. do we find statues dedicated to forces such as *Tyche*, "Chance," who is then worshipped as a type of goddess. The personification of Time is also a late addition. *Tempus*, *Fortuna*, and *Amor* were more popular in Rome. *Eros*, or love, played a greater role in Virgil's *Aeneid* than in Homer's epics, but held a firm place in art and poetry from that point on. Cherubs derived from *erotes* flitted across many a baroque ceiling, not simply to fill space, but as constant reminders of their domination over human lives.[14] Perhaps some of the popularity of these divine figures in artistic works produced for the court lay in the way that they duplicated royal rule. The divine right of the ruler was externalized in these moving icons.

In *Il ritorno*'s prologue, Time's theme is ponderous, staccato, and limping, but then it soars to accompany Time's claim that though he is lame, he can fly. He has the lower brass associated with him. Blind and deaf Fortune is true to character, not heeding the rhythms of the orchestra, singing in a triplet-figured ornamentation against the orchestra's constant duple division. This is Monteverdi's playfulness, making a musical device represent a title and a theme. Triplets also characterize the songs and dances of the lower classes, servants and shepherd—and even Ulisse in his role of an aged beggar.

Time claims that he makes man weak, Fortune that she makes him wretched, and Love that torments him; each negative claim is expressed in a descending figure. A descending tetrachord (four notes descending), which was associated with laments, is part of this motif. Time, Fortune, and Love all say that man will suffer their effects, and the opera illustrates this. Man's victory is in surviving the assault of time and fortune, and ultimately triumphing in love.

The main opera opens with Penelope singing a song about time and fortune and love: her song relates more to the prologue than to Homer. It is a song of mourning, a studied lamentation in a minor mode without much ornamentation. Her lament is worthy of comparison with Arianna's lament (1607), or the *Lamento della Ninfa* (1638). She sings in the style called *recitar cantando*, a style that typifies the noble heroes. The figure accompanying the word for grief is a descending second. This is the same figure that Orpheus used when he is told of Eurydice's death, to accompany the word *Ohime* ("Alas").

Penelope concludes with a lyrical plea for return, a charming interlude speaking about all things returning, a frequent motif in ancient Greek poetry.[15] This arioso section is the only purely lyrical section that Penelope sings until her final duet with Ulisse, in which, with florid ornamentation, the couple's lyricism resembles the gods'. Pure song here is indeed divine, and a sign of human triumph. In her opening lament Penelope speaks of time limping, but concludes here with a soaring vision of victorious love.

Badoaro's Penelope makes an anachronistic reference to the soul's return to heaven. Christianity inevitably suffuses his libretto, as it did the period. The theme of this aria is return: the flowers return in spring, the soul returns to God; why does Ulisse not return to me? Return is a natural pattern, and the opera follows this in bringing Ulisse home. Art wins a victory over nature in which the song is a sort of incantation that will work.

The most dramatic alteration from the epic to the opera is in the character of Penelope. Penelope is also now the "modern" woman, a goddess who controls her suitors and her entire household, including her son. She rebukes the latter when his worship of her wavers for an instant as he admires Helen's power. All the suitors pay tribute to Penelope with elaborate poetry, finally praising her as a goddess. Ulisse's fidelity to her in the opera is additional tribute.

Ulisse has only one main confrontation, and he has been assured by Minerva that he will win. Penelope is constant without the help of the gods; thus waiting is a challenge for her and contributes to her heroism. Several modern studies show Penelope's complexity in Homer. Marilyn Katz, for instance, has said, "even when Penelope speaks her mind, it is hard to know what is on it."[16] In Homer, Penelope's character can be seen to be as devious and cold as Odysseus'. In Badoaro some of this complexity is elided and romance colors both the hero and heroine in their steadfast devotion to each other and their ideals. Monteverdi's music restores some of the complexity by giving additional commentary on the text (e.g., a dissonance indicating doubt). In contrast to the Homeric epic, most issues are now clear-cut, written big in opera: we see virtue rewarded and vice punished.

Penelope here is not only a goddess, but also the Virgin Mary, and finally one who will share her power when she is courted on her own terms. She does not test Ulisse as she did in the *Odyssey* with a riddle and identification of their bed constructed around an old olive tree (this Penelope will not lower herself to deception), but Ulisse proves his identity by describing the pattern on their bed's cover, made by Penelope herself: chaste Diana, a good symbol for both Penelope and the Virgin Mary, who shared in art many of the attributes of Diana/Artemis (e.g., with the moon at her feet). This symbolism derives from both the Courtly Love tradition and the Marian cult.

Monteverdi mixed the secular and the sacred in his music. For instance, he used the same opening toccata for *Orfeo* as for the *Vespers* in honor of the Virgin Mary composed in 1611. It is easy to see how Badoaro in his libretto also mixes the sacred and secular, since that seems part of the Zeitgeist. Penelope benefits by partaking of divine virtues through an identification with Mary, while also possessing the acme of human virtues.

In Homer we are impressed with Odysseus' prowess in constructing the marriage bed. It is fitting in this opera that we instead marvel at Penelope's prowess in weaving and in her choice of subject matter (the chaste Diana, a doublet for her). Also, whereas Ulisse lies and deceives, our divine Penelope does neither.

In her own way, Penelope is a heroic predecessor for Poppea and yet is the opposite of Poppea in being a model of virtue. Penelope's task is to fight so that her virtue is not so overwhelming as to become a vice, as in the case of Euripides' Hippolytus. She must overcome her habits and doubts, and learn to share rule with another, her newly rediscovered husband.

In this opera, Penelope is more heroic than Ulisse: she has more songs to sing, more contests to fight; she protects her honor, which is constantly assailed by both her maid and the suitors. Monteverdi's *Eighth Book of Madrigals* features one by Ottavio Rinuccini called "Every Lover is a Warrior," *Ogni amante è guerrier*. Penelope is as much a warrior as Ulisse, and the new field of combat is love. This new emphasis on love we find in Sappho, who applies Homeric terms of combat to the situation of love (fr. 16), and in Latin poetry, for instance, *omnia vincit Amor: et nos cedamus Amori* ("Love conquers all, so let us cede to Love," Virgil's *Eclogues*, X. 69). The evolution continues in Petrarch's sonnets, where lovers confront each other as opposing armies on the battlefield.

A debt is owed to Ovid's *Heroides*, which feature the laments of many prominent women, Penelope included. There are obvious parallels between *Heroides* 1 and Homer's *Odyssey*: from complaints about the protracted absence of her husband to condemnations of Helen's adultery. In both *Heroides* 1 and the opera it is said that guilty Troy was taken, but Penelope, the innocent woman suffers. In both, she also fears that Ulysses may be faithless (true certainly to Homer), and in both, three main suitors are mentioned.

There are other lyric touches, and we see the influence not only of Roman elegy but of Greek tragedy, such as in Penelope fearing that Ulisse may resemble Jason in his infidelities. Penelope complains about Ulisse as Medea complains about Jason and love in general, in her first speech to the women of Corinth (E. *Med.* 213 ff and 330); love is a great evil for man (*Med.* 330).

Homer is also reshaped by cultural changes, such as the way women were viewed in the Courtly Love tradition. The suitors presenting their gifts along with elaborate praises have no precedent in Homer. The libretto at this point reminds one of the songs of the troubadours, since Penelope is offered divine worship. Thomas MacCary speaks of the period as the time "When God Became Woman": a woman was worshipped as God and His powers attributed to her.[17] She thus becomes inaccessible, the embodiment of the idealized woman we find in Dante, Petrarch, Tasso, Marino, and Ariosto, all poets used in Monteverdi's madrigals.[18] She is also the Mary adored so often in Monteverdi's motets and *The Marian Vespers* (1611): that her main virtue is chastity makes this parallel all the more apt. Her main beauty is spiritual.

In Homer, Odysseus is pleased to see Penelope tricking the suitors into giving her gifts, "but her heart was elsewhere" (*Od.* 18. 281–283). Monteverdi's Penelope inspires the suitors to bring her gifts without the use of a ruse.

In Badoaro's text, Penelope is shown as having authority over her son Telèmaco. In Homer the relationship is the reverse: as Penelope greets the returned Telemachus, saying he is sweeter to her than sunlight, he says, "Not now," and sends her off to bathe (*Od.* 17. 41–51). Earlier in the *Odyssey*, Telemachus tells his mother not to blame the minstrel for a sad song, and he orders her off to her room, saying speech is the concern of men, and most of all for him who has the power in the house (346 ff). There is a parallel in the *Iliad* where Hector tells Andromache to go home and look to her spinning and weaving but leave war to men, for that is their business, and most of all his (*Il.* 6. 490–493). When the disguised Odysseus is about to try the bow, Telemachus tells his mother that he can give it to whomever he likes, and then orders his mother to go to her room and supervise her spinning and her servants: the bow is for men and for him as head of the house (*Od.* 21. 343–353).

Monteverdi shows us a different Penelope, one clearly in charge, and possibly one that will send Ulisse away if in fact she continues to doubt his story. This polite Telèmaco would not speak to his mother in the way he does in the *Odyssey*.

The praise of Helen also resembles courtly praise: this woman, who is the source of death for so many men, is a paradigmatic *belle dame sans merci*. And ironically Penelope functions in the same way for the suitors: she allows herself to be adored, but gives them no quarter and will ultimately be the source of their death.

Eurìmaco, instead of being one of the suitors as in Homer, has become a servant who courts Melanto. She is invoked as a goddess by her lover; so too will Penelope be invoked by her suitors. The charming love duet contrasts with Penelope's solitary lamentation. It is filled with dance-like figures in triple time appropriate to their joy. Eurìmaco tells Melanto for the sake of their own love to kindle love in the breast of Penelope. Romantic interest of this sort is hardly Homeric.

Melanto is not the villainous slave who was punished severely in Homer's *Odyssey*, but is transformed into a fun-loving and love-advocating companion to Penelope. She is the typical *soubrette*, like Susanna to the countess in *Marriage of Figaro*. In telling Penelope she should not reject the suitors, Melanto also resembles the nurse who urges Phaedra to yield to love in Euripides' *Hippolytus*; or Anna, who tells Dido that she should love again. So also Eurìmaco is Melanto's devoted lover rather than an evil, calculating suitor as he is in the *Odyssey*. Melanto adds a love interest, and this alteration is in line with the greater emphasis on love in the opera. There is only a slightly darker side to Melanto in the opera: she assails Penelope's chastity by continually urging her to take a new husband, and thus she becomes a female equivalent to the suitors.

A scene of majesty is provided by the interchange between Nettuno and Giove, and both are announced by gongs, dramatic brass flourishes, and timpani as Nettuno emerges from the ocean. This is particularly dramatic in the modern orchestrated version of this opera by Hans Werner Henze, first performed in Salzburg in 1985. Brass announces him, a typical flourish used by Monteverdi to introduce gods or people of importance. Nettuno confronts Giove, and his musings are rather like Zeus' at the beginning of the *Odyssey* (1. 32–35): Men blame the gods, but they themselves are responsible for their own excesses. Nettuno asks for vengeance for wrongdoing, concentrating now on the Phaeacians rather than Ulisse, who blinded his son, the Cyclops. This latter concern seems forgotten in this text. Giove says that mercy inspires him, and this addition seems clearly part of Christian teaching. But Nettuno gets his vengeance and turns the Phaeacian ship to stone. Nettuno's oceanic majesty is manifested not only in his florid recitative, but also in his deep bass voice. Giove is a lighter baritone, conveying majesty along with the light of heaven.

Ulisse is washed up on his native soil, but does not recognize it. He sings a song of despair. Minerva appears as a shepherd boy and tells Ulisse that he is in Ithaca. She sings a charming shepherd song in a dance-like meter. She claims for youth that, whereas time limps, love flies to the young, thus carrying on the theme of the prologue and affirming again time's defeat by love.

When the shepherd asks Ulisse who he is, he lies. The libretto condenses the characterizing comment by Athena, who, in Homer, as she reveals herself in her true form as a goddess, chides Odysseus on lying simply for the fun of it, even when the situation does not warrant deception: "It seems you will not give up deception and lies, which are so dear to you, even when you are in your own land" (*Od.* 13. 293–295). She goes on to say they are both clever, he surpassing other men in plans and speech, but she among the gods has a reputation for wisdom and craft (*Od.* 13. 296–299). Badoaro succinctly condenses the latter: "Ulisse may be clever, but Minerva is wiser." Her song is now a dramatic recitative, showing the change in her station.

There is a charmingly naive reaction on the part of Ulisse in the libretto, when he addresses the audience, asking them "Who would believe this transformation?" and "Are there such masquerades in heaven?" This is hardly Homer's hero, who is used to seeing and speaking with the gods. In this reaction on Ulisse's part, perhaps Monteverdi is calling attention to his own craft and skill in making the gods appear before the audience.

As mentioned, a clear attribute of divine beings is their lyric capacity. Following her meeting with Ulisse, Minerva has a solo scene, and her song is distinguished by coloratura flourishes. This shows us another difference between the gods and mere man. In the most florid passage Minerva warns man of his limitations and not to meddle in the affairs of the gods, citing the punishment of Troy as an example of divine might, a sacred vendetta. Brass accompanies the mention of Troy, and we see that brass is used not only to accompany the appearances by the gods; its flourishes can also signify a battle. This passage is written in the *stile concitato* with its rhythmically stressed repeated notes that were meant to signify fights and warlike states, a style for which Monteverdi was famous.[19] In *Orfeo* its harsh tones were used to advantage to convey the underworld with its hostile spirits. Minerva's florid style was called *cantar passaggiato* (filled with vocalises), and regarded as archaic.

Melanto urges love on Penelope, singing the gay *ama dunque* aria, which will be cleverly developed later by the suitors. Penelope answers by singing that love is an empty idol; she voices her fears that Ulisse may be transformed into inconstant Jason.

The faithful shepherd Eumete appears and is brutalized by Iro the beggar. Baroque history was certainly violent, but baroque art sublimated and transformed it, while modern times enjoy an art form that literally replicates violence.

Ulisse appears as an old man, in the disguise Athena has given him. He assures Eumete that Ulisse will return soon. His introductory recitative wanders around tonalities in a way that evokes his own wanderings since Troy. Monteverdi was criticized for his harsh innovations. For instance, the contemporary Bolognese music theorist Giovanni Maria Artusi claimed of the opening of the madrigal "Era l'anima mia" that Monteverdi's dissonant phrases "have by nature no sweetness or softness; rather they cause an effect of unbearable harshness."[20] The dissonance does not grate on a modern ear. One instance in which dissonance is used effectively in this opera is when the disguised Ulisse wishes that he will die if his prediction is not true (that Ulisse will return), and when he speaks of death again, a few bars later, we hear another dissonance. Death is well expressed through dissonance in contrast to the life-affirming harmonies when love is described. Monteverdi's music well illustrates the text, even abstractions like death. The frequent mention of heaven in this opera is often accompanied by a rising figure, earth, and the tomb with descending figures. Monteverdi uses mimetic figures in the music, not only for the abstractions of joy and sorrow but for the sound of waves, bleating animals, laughter and tears, and even a character's stammer.

Telèmaco returns, transported by Minerva, in another fascinating stage effect: he flies onto the stage in a cloud chariot. Eumete and Ulisse greet him, and Telèmaco is anxious to bring the news to his mother of his father's return home. Eumete's first song praising the life of the country over life in the court is based not only on the ancient pastoral, but also resembles the speech by Euripides' Ion, who prefers his service to Apollo in his sylvan mountain retreat, Delphi, to a precarious life at court (*Ion*, 585 ff). Ulisse's music has lost the characteristics of noble recitative and now sounds like Eumete's simple and rustic style of lyric.

Eumete is dispatched to the court. One sees a flash and Ulisse disappears, to reappear in his former shape. Telèmaco blames the heavens for this prodigy, as Ulisse mistakenly had earlier blamed the Phaeacians. Soon Telèmaco welcomes his transformed father. Again this is hardly Homer. In the *Odyssey* (16. 172 ff), Athena touches Odysseus with a wand so that he reappears in his younger form before Telemachus, and the effect is very subtle, almost as if Telemachus had only rubbed his eyes. In Monteverdi, the earth splits and fire leaps out, a theatrical effect one might think typically baroque. The libretto takes the occasion for a song urging man to hope, for anything is possible with heaven's blessing. This resembles the more sober comment in the *Odyssey* that the gods can easily honor a man or send evil to him, but the ancient work contains no reference to hope (16. 211).

The suitors have the most elaborate madrigal sections for pursuing their courtship. Whereas they court Penelope in a playful canonic round and celebrate her beauty in a madrigal-like form, with a descending figure on the word for weeping, she answers them in solo monodies, with simple instrumental accompaniment. These monodies resemble the madrigals in Book 6 by Monteverdi, almost exclusively devoted to lamentations. Her fidelity extends to the musical form, discords, and simple lamentation, in contrast to the more harmonious and elaborately joyful music of the suitors.

Compared to the hundred and eight suitors of the epic, only three appear in the opera. These are aptly named Anfinomo ("disputing law"), Pisàndro (Peisander: "one who persuades men") and Antinoo ("against reason"). Each implies rhetorical proficiency, or unreliability, in contrast to Penelope, whose rhetoric and music are both emblems of her fidelity. The first is usually a high tenor (or even countertenor), the second somewhat lower, and the third a baritone.

A dance and chorus of Moors urging love recall the theme of *Il ballo dell' ingrate* (1608), a ballet about the "ungrateful souls" in the underworld, "women and girls who in their earthly lives foolishly refused the favors of Amor."[21] These light interludes resemble those found in Gluck's *Orfeo*. The suitors then sing a round to happiness that has suggestions of the *stile concitato*. Now the contest is one of love.

In the opera, there are three separate realms—heaven, the palace, and the country—with a clear hierarchy: Giove rules in the heavens, Penelope in the palace, and Eumete in the country. Giove's space is invaded by Nettuno, Penelope's by the suitors, and Eumete's by Iro. Each prevails over the invaders, through crucial alliances. Ulisse's alliance is with Penelope. This form of maneuvering was common in the politics of the time, as evidenced by the marriages of Vincenzo Gonzaga with Eleonora de Medici in 1584 and of Henri IV of France with Maria de Medici in 1600, a ceremony attended by Vincenzo Gonzaga. Monteverdi accompanied Vincenzo Gonzaga on a military campaign in Hungary in 1595, and the success of such campaigns depended on funding from the alliance of these powerful families. Monteverdi wrote his *Arianna* for the wedding of Prince Francesco Gonzaga with Margherita of Savoy. Both *Il ritorno* and *Poppea* are celebrations of marriages that reflect alliances made between powerful families, which were necessary in order for them to survive in Monteverdi's dangerous time. In this period, the marriage alliance is as important as war.

Monteverdi uses different styles that vary in accordance with the three realms: the gods are expressed by elaborate coloratura, the peasants by rhythmic melodies and simple songs, the main hero and heroine by *cantar parlando,* until their final lyrical transformation (the humans can finally share divine music, transformed by love). The nobles also often sing in a complicated contrapuntal form, with delayed fugal entries, whereas simpler music is given to Eumete. When Minerva pretends to be a shepherd boy, she sings a rustic song, which is the musical equivalent of her disguise. So also does Ulisse join Eumete in an unrefined madrigalesque duet, singing music untypical for him to complete *his* disguise. The popular style is also illustrated by the love song associated with Melanto and the pastoral *canzonetta* of Eumete. The lower classes in this opera are given folk motifs, and their music has a simpler and more constricted structure than the unfolding lyrical recitativo passages given to the nobles and gods. Here complex music conveys the freedom that comes with power.

The three suitors and Eurìmaco illogically plot to kill Telèmaco when they hear that Ulisse is returning, hardly an act that would endear them to Ulisse. The ambush of Telemachus in the *Odyssey* was placed more logically at a point when there is no hint of Odysseus' return. Instead, Antinous suggests it is because Telemachus has gathered together men and sailed away; Antinous thus felt Telemachus himself was a force to be reckoned with (see *Od.* 4. 663 ff). In Monteverdi and Badoaro the emphasis is more on Ulisse.

Badoaro has the eagle of Giove appear and the suitors cede to divine will; the music has cadences reminiscent of sacred motet, with a subdominant-tonic (IV-I) resolution. The suitors give up their bloody plan. In Homer's version the eagle appears in omens interpreted by Theoclymenus.[22] Two eagles fly over the assembly and fight each other. Halitherses says that these foretell the bloody return of Odysseus (*Od.* 2. 146 ff). His interpretation is rudely dismissed, a contrast to the opera's suitors heeding heaven's warning. In the opera we have vivid dramatic effects that resemble those that appear in the Jacobean masque.

The suitors plot to win Penelope with gifts. As would be expected, the suitor's song, which speaks of harmony, is a glorious study in harmonies: "Love is a harmony whose songs are sighs, but the song is not appreciated without the sound of gold." This was certainly an experience familiar to Monteverdi, who left his position with the Gonzagas because they paid him so poorly.

In both Homer and Monteverdi we see men's greed: the suitors' for the kingdom, the beggars' for food, Eurìmaco's for power in court; violence is an undercurrent, and the gods are not immune: Nettuno, for instance, desires vengeance. The modern enters with the word *vendetta*, which punctuates the main battle scene and is a word that sums up much of the politics both of antiquity and Monteverdi's time. Ulisse claims that Giove calls for *vendetta*, and this should suggest a holy war, as well as a family feud. Greed, power, and vengeance were popular themes.

Badoaro has Minerva appear to Ulisse and tell him that she will have Penelope suggest a trial with his bow. Minerva commands him to kill all the suitors. At the beginning of *Odyssey* 21, Athena inspires Penelope with the thought of the contest. Minerva's solo scene, following her first appearance, becomes the model for many florid displays in opera, and one thinks inevitably of the Queen of the Night in *The Magic Flute*, or Turandot in her opera. A difference here, however, is that whereas the Queen of the Night is defeated by the forces of the day, Sarastro and his Masonic crew, Minerva shares power with her father Giove and is not defeated.

Telèmaco tells Penelope of Helen's beauty. His poetic admiration of beauty resembles much in the poetry of other madrigals by Monteverdi. It also reminds us of Homer: when Priam asks Helen to identify the Greek heroes, the old men marvel at her beauty, saying, "It is no wonder that the well-greaved Achaeans suffered so long for her, since she is so like the immortal goddesses" (*Il.* 3. 150–158). Penelope rebukes Telèmaco for praising the faithless Helen.

Antinoo blames Eumete for introducing a new beggar into the household. At least he does not brutally throw a stool at Ulisse's head, as in the *Odyssey.* This baroque piece favors noble sensitivities.

Ulisse has a comic contest with Iro the beggar, who in this libretto stammers. His defects bring him into line with Thersites, the lower-class, physically ugly buffoon who is beaten by Odysseus for daring to speak out the truth against someone who is higher in rank (*Il.* 2. 225 ff). In both Homer and Badoaro, Odysseus easily defeats Irus. Monteverdi uses *stile concitato* to help define Ulisse as the hero. He is the one who struggles and conquers as a mortal. For fragile man life is a constant fight against adversity, and the contest makes him more heroic than the gods, who do not risk their lives. Ulisse must fight first to remain at the court and then to reclaim it as his. The assertive music in the major and bold chords augments his success. We hear this type of music when Minerva speaks of the Trojan War, and it indicates Ulisse's domestic heroism in his fight with Iro and the suitors.

Monteverdi used *stile concitato* often, with particular success in *Il combattimento di Tancredi e Clorinda* (1624), based on a poem by Torquato Tasso, from the *Eighth Book of Madrigals.* He said he was inspired by Plato to develop this style, citing Plato's third book of the *Republic* 399A, and felt that it replicated the "utterances and the accents of a brave man who is engaged in warfare."[23] Certain modes were said to give rise to corresponding emotions (cf. Plato, *Laws*, II. 668 a, b).

The suitors bring gifts and Anfinomo and Pisàndro offer their crowns and kingdoms; Antinoo claims he will honor Penelope as a goddess. In Homer their gifts were solicited by Penelope and hardly so grand; in Monteverdi we see the courtly tradition again invoked. Here is a chance to praise beauty and urge love, recalling the theme of the omitted Moors' chorus and dance.

This "nobility" of the man physically defending his Lady's honor is part of a later tradition that did not appreciate the Homeric emphasis in the *Odyssey* on using deception and craft instead of force.[24] Both Odysseus and Penelope in the epic use clever lies to get what they want. Achilles on the other hand hates lying and would rather use force than a lie. He claims that more hateful to him than the gates of Hades is the man who says one thing and hides something else in his heart (*Il.* 9. 312–313). The operatic hero is quite different from the Homeric hero, who loves lying (*Od.* 13. 293–295). Monteverdi refashions Odysseus and makes him more like Achilles: more absolute in his heroism, less clever and deceptive.

After the suitors offer gifts, Penelope suggests a contest with Ulisse's bow. In the opera, there are several reflective moments: Ulisse marveling at Athena, a goddess appearing to him; Penelope wondering why she suggested the contest of the bow and immediately regretting it. This adds a baroque touch, with artifice becoming a conscious part of the performance.

Each prefaces his attempt with an invocation. Anfinomo calls on Love to help him, Pisàndro on Mars, and Antinoo on Penelope's beauty; in the priamel form, the third element is best. In this case Penelope is placed above the gods, her beauty more powerful than divinity. There is no such courtly beginning to the attempts on the bow in the *Odyssey*.

In the opera, before the contest the suitors claim there will be an end to their torment, and each enters with a tetrachord, parodying the standard lament. Every suitor fails at the attempt, and Antinoo blames witchcraft, concluding that even the bow remains faithful to its master. Mentioning witchcraft is another departure from Homer, but appropriate for the time. Ferdinando di Gonzaga accused Isabella Gonzaga di Novellara of witchcraft and had her imprisoned.[25] This was also the time of the Inquisition and the execution of witches. Monteverdi's own son was imprisoned for reading the wrong books, and he himself dabbled in alchemy, though he never challenged the religious authorities.[26]

The suitors return to *recitativo* when they cannot draw the bow, and finally even their *recitativo* becomes monotonal. Lyricism departs with defeat. Ulisse suggests he try, and when he is successful Minerva appears to all. Ulisse then kills the suitors and the unfaithful servants.

Iro kills himself in a burlesque scene, prefacing his suicide by a parody of heroic poetry. He laments the absence of food and wine in the same way that Penelope lamented the absence of Ulisse, and the music reflects this. The same descending figures predominate, with the final descent of a third on the words "the tomb": he claims he feeds the tomb instead of food feeding him (one thinks of the etymology of "sarcophagus," "that which eats flesh"). The music is a parody of the lament, with descending staccato figures replicating the lumbering awkwardness of the ponderous Iro. This parody of heroism and the lament suggests a breakdown of the older values. Perhaps survival itself is to be prized: man has learned his lesson from his sufferings at the hands of unjust nobles and whimsical Nature (see the Prologue to the opera). The aristocratic code may be good for the aristocrats, but not for common man.

Monteverdi refashions characters and types; for instance, Iro hardly follows his Homeric prototype, but becomes a comic figure, even in his suicide. In Homer, Irus did not get off so easily. Before his fight with Odysseus, Antinous said,

> If this man wins, and bests you in the fight,
> I'll ship you off to that shore on a black boat,
> To Echetos the king, who carves up every man.
> With his brutal knife, he'll cut off your nose and ears,
> And feed your genitals raw to the dogs for a feast.[27]

After the fight, Antinous reaffirms that he will put this threat into effect. And this is the last we hear of Irus in Homer. In this opera, Antinoo earlier has begged Ulisse to be merciful after his fight with Iro. Mercy is a theme, along with beauty and love, which also departs decisively from the Homeric epic. In the *Odyssey*, Odysseus leaves Irus bleeding in the courtyard, and the only reason he does not kill him is that he does not want to give himself away.

Before his burlesque suicide, Iro claims his belly has defeated him. This comic element underlines his unheroic attitude. Homeric heroes recognize the value of food, but Achilles has to be told by Odysseus to eat and to let the others eat before battle, "since in food and wine there is strength and force," (*Il.* 19. 160–161). Achilles urges Priam to eat, in the midst of their sorrows, claiming that even Niobe in her mourning still had thought of food (*Il.* 24. 602), and Odysseus himself makes similar claims in *Od.* 7. 215 ff., 15. 344, and 17. 286–289.

Iro's occasional lyric *arioso* parts undercut the seriousness of his *recitativo*. The earlier *arioso* passages were generally in the context of love; here the love is for food. One need only compare this music with Penelope's opening lament to realize how much this is parody.

We also find traces of Archilochus. Iro, in saying that he who escapes the enemy has great glory, paraphrases the antiheroic verse of Archilochus, which claims that it is better to save oneself than one's shield.[28] But in a last ironic twist, for Iro, this escape will be suicide.

Ellen Rosand claims Iro's role is tragic in this opera, but in my view the comic element overrides the tragedy.[29] Iro is based on the parasites from Greek New Comedy, Plautus and Terence, and the commedia dell'arte. He is definitely a figure of fun, although dire things happen to him—or, following the classical model of new comedy, *because* dire things happen to him. Monteverdi describes his role as a *parte ridicola*, and this gives us a clue about his intent.

The scene in which Giunone and Minerva try to persuade Giove that Ulisse has suffered enough is reminiscent of Monteverdi's *Orfeo* in which Persephone tries to convince Pluto that he should help Orfeo. Nettuno agrees to set aside his anger, since at least he had his vengeance on the Phaeacians. There is another reference to heaven's mercy, and Christianity once again intervenes.

In accordance with Giove's and Nettuno's agreement, an impressive chorus, religious in timbre, sings that the heavens will be merciful, and man can rely on the grace of the gods through prayer. The words that are notable are ones that speak of heaven and piety and the conclusion is: "Pray, Mortal, oh, pray, for a god may be won over through prayer."

The use of religious music shows another shift from Homer, and also conflates the ancient gods with the Christian tradition, abetting the transformation of Penelope into someone resembling the Virgin Mary. When the chorus invokes the gods in prayer, asking for mercy, these could be words from the sacred music that Monteverdi had written at the beginning of his career and was still writing now as Maestro di Cappella at the Cathedral of St. Mark. This chorale would be suited for a mass—an interesting resolution for the pagan gods. No longer do we hear the flourishes of Minerva, warning about *vendetta*, but the cause of a merciful god being urged. The Queen of the Night has been tamed by

Sarastro, and the pagan gods are defeated by Christ. This endorsement of the merciful qualities of the gods could also be intended for the ears of the nobles on whose generosity Monteverdi constantly depended.

Minerva is also Penelope's divine counterpart. Both are clever females. The difference is that in the opera Penelope relies not so much on her wit as on her virtue. Minerva is not defeated, but is rather the conqueror at Troy. She knows how to get what she wants by making alliances with the males in power. And a word with the queen (Giunone) is not in vain. Giunone in the libretto and Minerva in the score persuade Giove as easily as Proserpine did Pluto in *L'Orfeo*. True to the baroque world, it is good to have friends in both high and low places.

From the heavenly reconciliation of divine powers we descend to an earthly farce. Ericlèa debates telling Penelope a secret she swore to keep. If we know our Homer, we are aware that she has seen Ulysses' scar and recognized him before his conflict with the suitors. Without such knowledge, her ruminations are obscure. This debate with herself adds another element of humor to the opera. All try to convince Penelope. Ulisse enters, and, after his bath, is restored to his youthful appearance. This makes Ericlèa's dilemma even more ridiculous. What need of secrecy *after* the suitors have been killed? Did she bathe him when he first arrived, although it is first mentioned here? One can see the hazards of adapting an epic for opera. Ericlèa adds her evidence to the other claims, all of which are rejected by Penelope. She dismisses Ulisse's transformation by calling him a sorcerer. This is another allusion to magic in a period that took magic seriously. Ulisse is finally only successful when he identifies the coverlet that she made depicting Diana surrounded by her virgin retinue.

In his final plea for recognition, following Penelope's claim that she is only wife to Ulisse and no charm will shake her fidelity, Ulisse makes the ridiculous claim that he has been faithful to her all these years. He says that he has punished adulterers and thieves and never himself committed either crime. Did he not steal the Cyclops's property? Although Odysseus may not have equaled Don Giovanni, a combined list of his thievery and amorous adventures would at least evoke the list of Giovanni's seductions recited by Leporello to Donna Elvira. It is true that Odysseus chose mortality, rather than the immortality that Calypso offered him, so that he could return to Penelope. Nevertheless, he remained with Calypso for seven years and with Circe for one. For the Homeric man the question of sexual fidelity would not arise. By emphasizing it in opera, we see an additional infidelity, namely to the Homeric text and its realism.

Penelope is the property and honor that Odysseus would not give up for immortality. He chose instead immortal fame over immortal life, and that fame entailed his overcoming the suitors and securing his property. Badoaro and Monteverdi give us a chaster, courtly variation. We hear nothing about Circe or Calypso, and for all we can tell from the libretto, Ulisse has been engaged in an undeflected struggle to return. This also adds to Penelope's glory: she was worth waiting for. Two faithful lovers struggling against dire opposition is a theme worthy of romance, the Hellenistic novel, and Roman elegiac poetry, but not Homer.

In contrast to the ending of the *Odyssey*, it is significant that in this opera the final resolution is domestic. Ulisse yields to Penelope's gentler virtues. Monteverdi's Penelope has a new heroism, and it is that of resistance. She is an anti-Phaedra, Euripides' heroine who was cursed by Aphrodite with an adulterous passion. Man may be a victim of his passions, but not Penelope. We can see Ulisse as an example of Human Fragility, buffeted by time, fortune, and love; Penelope, although she too is assailed, shows heroic strength in her refusal to succumb.

In the final duet, the two reunited lovers apply to each other the image of sunlight and life that Homer had Penelope use to communicate her love for Telemachus. This joyful aria is comparable to the conclusion of *L'incoronazione di Poppea,* and the final words of each opera refer to their loves as "life." Both stories have tragic sequels, but the operas celebrate a moment of bliss.

This opera's brilliant ending and the displays of the gods were typical of the baroque. We think of the ending of Molière's *Tartuffe*, when the messenger from Louis XIV comes on resplendent, like the sun god. The gods were associated with royalty's power, and this was the age of absolutism. The masque and the pastoral tradition were also associated with court diversions, and we see elements of that here with the disguised Ulisse and the scenes with Eumete.

Monteverdi concludes his opera with a glorious hymn to joy and love. A joyful pathetic fallacy is created by having the heavens shine and the earth bloom in response to Ulisse's and Penelope's happiness. The beginning showed man's weakness, but the conclusion is an affirmation of his capacities and ends on the affirmative word "Si" ("Yes") and the final chord of C Major. The brass of the gods now endorses man.

In the concluding song by Ulisse and Penelope, the final flourish is secular. Penelope finally gains the lyrical exuberance that had been confined to Minerva and on a smaller scale to Melanto. The final madrigal is an endorsement of human power, and it is a duet, on a *chaconne* base. Monteverdi is well on the way to *bel canto* style. Penelope will no longer sing alone. Ulisse does not invoke Penelope as a goddess, as her suitors did. He knows the difference between a goddess and his wife, and he chose the latter. And she accepts this role.

Ulisse performs the ultimate heroic act of Courtly Love: he offers his soul to a woman. He is not Homeric man desiring exclusively his own kingdom and property, his wife figuring prominently among the latter. He is a post-Marian product, a man of the Counter-Reformation. The Marian cult inspired Courtly Love, and love became the salvation of man. Even Giove is addressed by the chorus as "Jove the amorous," and Giunone is seen to have obtained mercy for Ulisse by inspiring Giove with love.[30] Penelope is called "harbor of Ulisse's soul"; her eyes inspired him to reject immortality; she is his sun. She is the courtly goddess, but not *sans merci*, and she is Ulisse's wife, not his mistress; in many ways she offers the comfort of a mother. Ulisse is the wandering soul come home to bliss, and the suggestion of salvation is clear. This is a marriage made in heaven, and the price is the human soul. Penelope will sell herself for no less. The love of the prologue is triumphant here as it is in *Poppea*, but in *Ulisse* we find transcendent Courtly Love, different from the love in *Poppea*, which is tarnished by the crimes in the opera and the history that followed. Nevertheless, in Monteverdi's music, both Penelope and Poppea are earthly goddesses transformed by love. Only love allows access to divine musical flourishes.

The music conflates god and human. The mystery is a reversal of that in the Catholic mass: instead of God becoming man, a woman has merged with a goddess and the Blessed Virgin: Penelope's heroic struggle against her own doubt was as important as Ulisse's struggle against the suitors. Human suffering and endurance is a heroism that elevates this woman to the divine, and even more, shows how she surpasses the gods by acknowledging and overcoming her limits as a human being.

CONCLUSION

A popular classical epic has been adapted to suit the needs of Monteverdi's period. Now the emphasis is on the return of Ulisse and the domestic situation, filled with amorous complications and conflicts that are finally surmountable. The danger of the male-oriented Homeric world has been translated into the courtly baroque world. The latter had its threats, but not at this time in opera, where happy endings prevailed; noble men were gallant, and important women shared traits with the Virgin Mary.

Monteverdi was constrained to a life of work in which he was exploited, but he attained freedom in that limited context which he could call his own kingdom: the church, opera, and music. Orpheus, Penelope, and Poppea are his models; they are constrained by superior forces, but they are masters in their particular spheres. Through these figures he himself obtains freedom. Orpheus achieved a stellar deification, and Penelope added the virtues of Mary to her already admirable assembly of talents—from weaving tapestries to weaving words to make effective riddles. Poppea shared in Nero's earthly deification.

Monteverdi took the language of his oppressors and used it to enchant and enslave; his most skillful rhetoric was in his music. He can say, as Music did at the beginning of *Orfeo:*

> Singing on my golden lyre
> I enchant the ears of men;
> Harmony does their souls inspire
> To seek the notes of heaven's lyre.

Monteverdi offers paradise to others in the shape of his music. His is the ultimate power and victory: he is the creator. We do not long for the harmonies of heaven's lyre, because we have found them incarnate in Monteverdi's music, and love's triumph in his case is the love of music. Music's heaven offers escape

from earthly hell, a theme that is recurrent in this study of operatic transformations.

APPENDIX
OPERAS ABOUT ULYSSES (or in which he appears)

Claudio Monteverdi (1567–1643) (b. Cremona, Italy)
Il ritorno d'Ulisse in patria (1640)

Francesco Sacrati (1605–1660) (b. Parma, Italy)
L'Ulisse errante (1644)

Pietro Andrea Ziani (1616–1684) (b. Venice, Italy)
Circe (1665)

Jacopo Melani (1623–1676) (b. Pistoia, Italy)
Il ritorno d'Ulisse (1669)

Domenico Freschi (c.1630–1710) (b. Bassano del Grappa, Italy)
La Circe (1679/80)

Antonio Draghi (c.1634–1700) (b. Rimini, Italy)
Penelope (1670)
Il Telemaco (1689)

Bernado Sabadini (b.?–1718) (b. ?Venice, Italy)
Circe abbandonata da Ulisse (1692)

Carlo Pallavicino (c.1640–1688) (b. Salò, Italy)
Penelope la casta (1685)
Circe abbandonata (1692)

Marc'Antonio Ziani (1653–1715) (b. Venice, Italy)
La finta pazzia d'Ulisse (1696)

Carlo Francesco Pollarolo (c.1653–1723) (b. ?, Italy)
Circe abbandonata di Ulisse (1697)
L'Ulisse sconosciuto (1698)

Giovanni Porta (c.1655–1755) (b. Venice, Italy)
Ulisse (1725)

Henry Purcell (?1659–1695) (b. London, England)
Incidental Music for Plays:
Circe (1685)

André Campra (bap. 1660–1744) (b. Aix-en-Provence, France)
Télémaque (1704)

Alessandro Scarlatti (1660–1725) (b. Palermo, Italy)
Penelope la casta (1694)
Telemaco (1718)

Henry Desmarets (1661–1741) (b. Paris, France)
Circé (1694)

Giacomo Antonio Perti (1661–1756) (b. Bologna, Italy)
Penelope la casta (1696)

Jean-Féry Rebel (bap. 1666–1747) (b. Paris, France)
Ulysse (1703)

Jean-Claude Gillier (1667–1737) (b. Paris, France)
Circé (1705)
Télémaque (1715)
La Pénélope moderne (1728)

Giuseppe Boniventi (?1670–1727) (b. Venice, Italy)
Circe delusa (1711)

Georg Caspar Schürmann (1672/3–1751) (b. Idensen, Germany)
Telemaque (1706)

Carlo Agostino Badia (1672–1678) (b. ?Venice, Italy)
La costanza d'Ulisse (1700)
Gli amori di Circe con Ulisse (1709)

André Cardinal Destouches (1672–1749) (b. Paris, France)
Télémaque et Calypso (1714)

Reinhard Keiser (1674–1739) (b. Teuchern, Germany)
Circe, oder des Ulysses erster Theil (1696)
Penelope, oder des Ulysses anderer Theil (1696)
Ulysses (1722)
Circe (1734)

Giuseppe Porsile (1680–1750) (b. Naples, Italy)
Il ritorno di Ulisse alla patria (1707)

Georg Philipp Telemann (1681–1767) (b. Hamburg, Germany)
Calypso (1727)

Francesco Bartolomeo Conti (1681–1732) (b. Florence, Italy)
Circe fatta saggia (1713)
Penelope (1724)

Christoph Graupner (1683–1760) (b. Kirchberg, Saxony, Germany)
Telemach (1711)

Andrea Stefano Fiore (1686–1732) (b. Milan, Italy)
La casta Penelope (1707)

Fortunato Chelleri (1686–1757) (b. Parma, Italy)
Penelope la casta (1716)

John Ernest Galliard (1687–1749) (b. Celle, Germany)
Calypso and Telemachus (1712)

Giovanni Verocai (c.1700–1745) (b. Venice, Italy)
Penelope (1740)

Giuseppe Carcani (1703–1778) (b. Crema, Italy)
Alcuni avventimenti di Telemaco (1749)

Baldassare Galuppi (1706–1785) (b. Burano, Italy)
Penelope (1741)

Antonio Orefice (fl.1708–1734)
Circe delusa (1713)

David Perez (1711–1778) (b. Naples, Italy)
Il ritorno di Ulisse in Itaca (1774)

John Christopher Smith (1712–1795) (b. Ansbach, England)
Ulysses (1733)

Cristoph Willibald Gluck (1714–1787) (b. Ersbach, near Weidenwang, Austria)
Telemaco, ossia L'isola di Circe (1765)

Gregorio Sciroli (1722–after 1781) (b. Naples, Italy)
Ulisse errante (1749)

Ferdinando Bertoni (1725–1813) (b. Saló, Italy)
Telemaco ed Eurice nell'isola di Calipso (1776)

Pasquale Anfossi (1727–1797) (b. Taggia, Italy)
La maga Circe (1788)

Tommaso Traetta (1727–1779) (b. Bitonto, Italy)
Telemaco (1777)

Giacomo Insanguine (1728–1795) (b. Monopoli, Italy)
Calipso (1782)

Niccolò Piccinni (1728–1800) (b. Bari, Italy)
Pénélope (1783)

Tommaso Giordano (c.1730–1806) (b. Naples, Italy)
Calypso, or Love and Enchantment (1785)

Giuseppe Carcani (1703–1778) (b. Crema, Italy)
Alcuni avvenimenti de Telemaco figliuolo di Ulisse, re d'Itaca (1749)

Bernardo Ottani (1736–1827) (b. Bologna, Italy)
Calipso (1776)

Josef Myslivecek (1737–1781) (b. Prague, Czechoslovakia)
La Circe (1779)

Giuseppe Gazzaniga (1743–1818) (b. Verona, Italy)
Circe (1786)
L'isola di Calipso (1775)
Gli errori di Telemaco (1776)

João de Sousa Carvalho (1745–1798) (b. Estremoz, Portugal)
Penelope nella partenza da Sparta (1782)

Felice Alessandri (1747–1798) (b. ?Rome, Italy)
Il ritorno di Ulysse a Penelope (1790)

Joachim Albertini (1748–1812) (b. Pesaro, Italy)
Circe und Ulisses (1785)

Theodor Schacht (1748–1823) (b. Strasbourg, Alsace)
Calypso abbandonata (1784)

Domenico Cimarosa (1749–1801) (b. Aversa, Italy)
La Circe (1783)
Penelope (1795)

Mathias Stabinger (c.1750–1815) (b. Germany)
Calipso abbandonata (c.1777)

Giuseppe Giordani (1751–1798) (b. Naples, Italy)
Il ritorno d'Ulisse (1782)

Ferdinand Kauer (1751–1831) (b. Klein-Thaya, Austria)
Telemach Prinz von Ithaka (1801)
Der travestirte Telemach (1805)
Antiope und Telemach (1805)

Franz Anton Hoffmeister (1754–1812) (b. Rothenburg am Neckar, Austria)
Der Königssohn aus Ithaka (1795)

Peter Winter (1754–1825) (b. Mannheim, Germany)
Circe (1788)
La Grotte di Calipso (1807)

João Cordeiro da Silva nell'isola di Calipso (fl. 1756–1808) (b. Portugal)
Telemaco (1787)

Antonio Calegari (1757–1828) (b. Padua, Italy)
Telemaco in Sicilia (1792)

Jean-François Le Sueur (1760–1837) (b. Drucat-Plessiel, France)
Télémaque (1796)

Simon Mayr (1763–1845) (b. Mendorf, Germany)
Telemaco nella isola di Calipso (1797)
Il ritorno di Ulisse (1809)

Franceso Basili (1767–1850) (b. Loreto, Italy)
Il ritorno di Ulisse (1798)

Bernard Heinrich Romberg (1767–1841) (b. Dinklage, Germany)
Ulysses und Circe (1807)

Antoine Reicha (1770–1836) (b. Prague, Czechoslovakia)
Télémaque (1800–1801)

Ferdinando Paer (1771–1839) (b. Parma, Italy)
Circe (1792)

Josef Triebensee (1772–1846) (b. Wittingau, Bohemia)
Telemach auf der Insel Ogygia (1824)

François-Adrien Boieldieu (1775–1834) (b. Rouen, France)
Télémaque (1806)

Sir Henry Rowley Bishop (1786–1855) (b. London, England)
Telemachus (1815)

Saverio Mercadante (1795–1870) (b. Altamura, Italy)
Le nozze di Telemaco ed Antiope (1824)

Hervé (Ronger, Louis Auguste Joseph Florimond) (1825–1892) (b. Paris, France)
Le retour d'Ulysse (1862)

Gabriel Fauré (1845–1924) (b. Parmiers, Ariège, France)
Pénélope (1913)

August Bungert (1845–1915) (b. Mülheim an der Ruhr, Germany)
Die Odyssee:
Kirke (1898)
Odysseus' Heimkehr (1896)
Nausicaa (1901)
Odysseus' Tod (1903)

Gaston Salvayre (1847–1916) (b. Toulouse, France)
Calypso (1872)

Raoul Pugno (1852–1913/14) (b. Montrouge, France)
Le retour d'Ulysse (1889)

Alexander Zemlinsky (1871–1942) (b. Vienna, Austria)
Circe (1939)

Reynaldo Hahn (1874–1947) (b. Caracas, Venezuela)
Nausicaa (1919)

Henri Tomasi (1901–1971) (b. Marseilles, France)
Ulysse, ou Le beau périple (1962)

Werner Egk (1901–1983) (b. Auchsesheim, Germany)
Circe (1945)

Lennox Berkeley (1903–1989) (b. Boars Hill, England)
Castaway [on Odysseus and Nausicaa] (1967)

Luigi Dallapiccola (1904–1975) (b. Pisino d'Istria, Italy)
Ulisse (1968)

Inglis Gundry (1905–) (b. London, England)
The Return of Odysseus (1938)

Elisabeth Lutyens (1906–1983) (b. London, England)
Penelope (1950)

Rolf Lieberman (1910–) (b. Zurich, Switzerland)
Penelope (1954)

Peggy Glanville-Hicks (1912–1990) (b. Melbourne, Australia)
Nausicaa (1961)

Gerard Victory (1921–) (b. Dublin, Ireland)
Circe (1971–1972)

Karel Kupka (1927–1985) (b. Rychvald, Czechoslovakia)
Opus Odysseus (1984)

Raymond Pannell (1935–) (b. London, England)
Circe (1977)

Henry Purcell's *Dido and Aeneas:* Witches and Weddings

INTRODUCTION AND BACKGROUND

An English newspaper contemporary with Purcell said, "Opera is all very well for other nations, but experience hath taught us that [the] English will not relish that perpetual singing." Henry Purcell proved this critic wrong. His tercentenary is just past. He was born in 1659 (shortly after Monteverdi's death in 1643) and died in 1695. Monteverdi brought early opera to unsurpassed heights, and Purcell has been called the father of English opera. Gustav Holst rightly claims that Purcell wrote "a perfect opera—the only perfect English opera."[1]

Purcell spent much of his life composing for the theatre. From 1682, Purcell held an appointment at the Chapel Royal conjointly with a position as organist at Westminster Abbey. Purcell may have been a counter-tenor, and one account has it that he sang the role of Belinda in the first performance of *Dido and Aeneas.*[2]

There are six main works that can be called semi-operas.[3] *Dido and Aeneas* is Purcell's sole complete opera (with instrumental and vocal score throughout), but he contributed music to forty-three plays. *Dido and Aeneas* was used as a masque in an adaptation by Charles Gildon of Shakespeare's *Measure for Measure:* the corrupt Angelo sees himself in the role of Aeneas, as a seducer who enjoys the fruits of conquest and then abandons the woman. *Dido and Aeneas*, about an hour long, was also used as an epilogue to different plays. This seems to cater to English taste; the English were impatient with an evening devoted exclusively to pure opera, in other words, a continuously sung text, without spoken interludes.[4] The English preferred words over music, in contrast to the Italians (in spite of Monteverdi's protestations to the contrary).

Opera did not take hold in England as quickly as it did on the continent. The earliest English opera, called *The Siege of Rhodes* (1656), is by Henry

Cooke, Henry Lawes, Matthew Locke, and Charles Coleman with a libretto by Sir William Davenant, but its music has not survived. Possibly Davenant had his libretto set to music only to avoid the restrictions of the Puritans against plays following the death of Charles I. The first English opera that has survived is John Blow's *Venus and Adonis* (1683). Very likely these two operas compare with Purcell's as Peri and Caccini's work compared with Monteverdi's: the latter was clearly the master. Now Britten and Tippett allow English opera to hold its head high, but I do not believe Purcell's prototype has been surpassed.

Besides Nahum Tate's *Brutus of Alba* (discussed below) there are several dramatic precedents for *Dido and Aeneas.* Christopher Marlowe wrote a *Dido and Aeneas* in the 1580s, with Iarbas, Dido's suitor, in a sub-plot. Iarbas kills himself when Dido dies, and Anna commits suicide for love of Iarbas. This is a tragedy typical of the time, which demanded as many deaths as Shakespearean comedy did marriages. There were also plays on the theme: George de Scudéry, *Didon* (1635), and Antoine-Jacob de Montfleury, *L'ambigu comique, ou Les amours de Didon et d'Aenée* (1673). Dryden wrote *All for Love* (1678), an adaptation of Shakespeare's *Antony and Cleopatra*, another story of a man tempted to give up empire for the love of a foreign queen. (Virgil makes the comparison between Dido and Cleopatra in *Aeneid*, Books 4 and 6.)

There were about three operatic versions of Dido before Purcell's.[5] The subject of Dido continued to be popular in opera. Most of the seventy-some operas I have located on Dido come from the eighteenth century. The suffering Dido does not appeal to the twentieth century as much as the powerful, vengeful Medea, a potent symbol not only of women's liberation but of the moral chaos of modern times.

The original score for *Dido and Aeneas* is lost, so one must rely on later scores and scholarly reconstruction. Dido and Aeneas was performed at Mr. Josias Priest's Boarding School for Young Ladies, with a libretto by Nahum Tate, but the date is in question. The first performance may have taken place sometime between 1685 and 1689, the year of William and Mary's coronation, following the Glorious Revolution of 1688.[6] This might account for the lavish prologue featuring Phoebus Apollo and Venus, who share a mutual luster comparable to that of William and Mary: "When Monarchs unite, how happy their state, / They triumph at once o'er their foes and their fate" (p. 11).[7] Nevertheless it would be an odd tribute to the new couple. I am more convinced by Andrew Walkling's claim that this is political allegory referring to the reign of James II, his rise and fall.

The political allusions have been the topic of much speculation: for example, if this is a celebration of the union of William and Mary, then there may be an implied warning to William to be sure that he shares his rule properly.[8] Tate wrote a poem in 1686 in which he calls James II, Aeneas, and says that he has been led astray by witches (i.e., Catholicism, which Curtis Price says was "a common metaphor at the time").[9] There was a Whig pamphlet that also identified James with Aeneas.[10] England feared James' Catholicism, so if this opera is an allegory, then Dido is probably England. Such allegories were common throughout the seventeenth century.

Ellen Harris interprets *Dido and Aeneas* as a morality play to instruct the young ladies of Priest's school. Yet when she presents earlier precedents to disprove Buttrey's ("marriage") and Price and Walkling's (anti-Catholicism) theories, these same precedents can be mustered to refute her. For instance, the play *Brutus of Alba, or The Enchanted Lovers*, written by Nahum Tate in 1678, has a similar plot. It tells the story of Dido and Aeneas, but Tate changed the names and period out of modesty, so as not to challenge "the incomparable Virgil." In the intervening years he overcame his scruples about challenging Virgil.

John Blow's *Venus and Adonis* also recounts the story of a frustrated love, and that tragic story is alluded to in Tate's version (Venus is also Aeneas' mother). Since Blow was Purcell's teacher, it must have influenced him. The structures of *Venus and Adonis* and *Dido and Aeneas* are similar, with three acts and an allegorical prologue. Dance is used in both, and the chorus also alternates roles, turning from courtiers into witches, huntsmen, Cupids, and sailors. Both use the *arioso* recitative. Purcell's opera, however, has many more arias than Blow's. *Venus and Adonis* was first performed privately for Charles II and then adapted for Priest's school for girls about a year later, and it is said that Adonis was sung by Priest's daughter (the role was transposed up an octave). Curtis Price suggests that *Dido and Aeneas* may *first* have had a *royal* performance and this "would help explain several discrepancies between the libretto printed for the Chelsea amateur production ('perform'd by young gentlewomen') and the earliest surviving score, which includes a baritone Aeneas as well as a countertenor, tenor and bass chorus parts; these could hardly have been executed by Priest's young pupils."[11] A Royal performance might explain the elaborate effects in the Chelsea libretto, such as "Phoebus Rises in the Chariot"; "Venus Descends in her Chariot"; "Cupids Appear in the Clouds o'er [Dido's] Tomb." These effects would hardly suit a girls school, with its limited resources.

There are seventeenth-century theatrical precedents for suicide following sexual disgrace, and these may have influenced Tate. Such "morality plays" tread nimbly among entertainment, voyeurism, and edification. (A classical precedent is Livy's quasihistorical account of Lucretia, who commits suicide after she has been raped by Tarquin; she provides the subject of Shakespeare's *Rape of Lucrece*, also Benjamin Britten's *The Rape of Lucretia*.) John Fletcher wrote *Valentinian* in 1612, and its revised version was performed in London with music by Louis Grabu in 1693. Valentinian rapes Lucina, who dies from the shame. So too there is Philip Massinger's *The Unnatural Combat* (1624–1625), in which a ravished maid dies almost spontaneously after she is raped. Dido, of course, is not raped, but only abandoned.

Dido and Aeneas also draws on the masque tradition, popular on the English stage throughout the seventeenth century. As already mentioned in connection with Monteverdi, these masques occasioned a lavish mixture of short dialogue with dancing, in which the nobles themselves took part. The lower classes—sometimes actors disguised as monsters—were represented in the antimasque that came after the masque proper, as a parody of the more formal presentation. The antimasque was a way for the lower classes to be neatly incorporated into the kingdom, an amusing diversion comprised of people who were not to be taken seriously. Witches could also appear in the antimasque. There were other Restoration operas that featured magic, for example Matthew Locke's *Psyche* (1675) and Charles Davenant's *Circe* (1677).

It is thought that Purcell himself wrote music for the sacrificial scene in *Circe*, which featured a chorus of magicians; Circe was, of course, a famous witch from antiquity, Medea's aunt, and the Circe in this opera calls on infernal powers. Circe may be called the Ur-witch. The plot was a reworking of the story of Euripides' *Iphigenia in Tauris*, with a love interest between Ithacus, Circe's son, and Iphigenia.[12]

The addition of the witches to Virgil's tale may be seen as the personification of what might threaten organized society, an element of the satyric antimasque tradition. They also replace the force of fate and the intervention of the gods. This reflected the taste of the period, and the evil acts of the witches justified their punishment.[13] Showing us evil witches conveys their threat and makes us feel better about persecuting them; once again, art is enlisted in the service of the dominant male power. It is estimated that "Between the 15th and the 17th centuries, more than 30,000 people, mostly women, were executed for witchcraft in Britain."[14] Witches were also scapegoats for the evils of the time, such as the great London fire of 1666 and the Great Plague. In Protestant England, witches could symbolize the "Catholic threat."

The most notorious witches are those in Shakespeare's *Macbeth*, made into opera by Matthew Locke (?1621–1677). Ben Jonson's *Masque of Queens* (1609) featured an antimasque of witches (with music probably by Robert Johnson). Thomas Middleton wrote a play, *The Witch* (1610). Purcell himself wrote a song on the meeting between Saul and the Witch of Endor.[15]

Purcell in all of his other semi-operas (primarily spoken acts with musical interludes) introduced a supernatural element comparable to the witches. Instead of gods, so beloved by the Greeks in their *ex machina* appearances, the Elizabethan, Jacobean, and Restoration playwrights added ghosts and evil spirits. Perhaps these ghosts and witches provide a simple explanation for the existence of evil. Besides this, witches are a creation of misogyny ("We punish women because they deserve it"; "Every woman has the potential for becoming a witch"). It is interesting, however, that "on the Restoration stage witches and sorceresses were almost always acted by men," and in the Chelsea libretto the part of the sorceress was marked baritone/mezzo-soprano.[16] A bass-baritone took the part in the adaptation as an interlude for *Measure for Measure*. Does this imply a sharing of responsibility for evil? More likely that a woman was a witch if she usurped male prerogatives.

Tate and Purcell reworked their predecessors' efforts to come up with their own tragedy. *Dido and Aeneas* owes much to manners derived from the Courtly Love tradition. Virgil himself has a "baroque" quality in that he interrupts his narrative to allow his characters to expose their inner conflicts; in comparison with Homer, he is more delicate, more focused on mood and emotions. Purcell's genius is well matched to Virgil's.[17] The introduction of several ballets is consistent with the masque tradition; Josias Priest, at whose school this was performed, was a noted dancing master.

In spite of a rigid frame, Purcell is able to let his genius flourish. He creates a Dido who outshines Aeneas in nobility, much like Monteverdi's Penelope, who surpasses Ulisse in the way she meets her challenges. Both differ herein from their classical predecessors. The Courtly Love tradition, with its elevated view of women, has influenced this change. *Dido and Aeneas* offers not a simple lesson in morality, but an illustration of a noble, heroic woman meeting her challenges with dignity. Although politics may have influenced this presentation, it primarily allows the depiction of heroic ideals, and nobility coping with overwhelming passion. This Dido is committed to her ideals as a noble being for whom continued life can only mean a diminution of honor (like Sophocles' Ajax, or Euripides' Phaedra).

Purcell's music is the perfect vehicle for transmitting these ideas. It has the same literal quality as Monteverdi's in attempting to interpret words. And, like Monteverdi, Purcell goes beyond the literal and offers interpretation and development. He expands language through the musical and enhances the noble. As he said himself, "Musick is the exaltation of poetry. Both of them may excel apart, but surely they are most excellent when they are joyn'd, because nothing is then wanting to either of their proportions; for thus they appear like wit and beauty in the same person."[18]

DIDO AND AENEAS

We lack the music for the prologue, which showed the interaction of Phoebus Apollo and Venus, the god of music and light and the goddess of love, appropriate choices for an opera dealing with love. The opera concludes with an Ode to Spring, probably reflecting the time of the performance; the music for this is also missing from the scores we have.

The surviving opera begins with an overture divided into two parts, the first a somber musical statement announcing the tragedy, followed by a quicker movement sweeping us directly into the passionate play of the opera. It is written in the French style and is characterized by simplicity in harmony and rhythm rather than contrapuntal complications. The music is scored for a string ensemble plus harpsichord. Without the prologue the action can be divided among six scenes, each mainly in one key: C minor, C Major, F minor-major, D minor-major, B flat major, and G minor. The earliest versions had three acts, which begin respectively, "Shake the cloud," "Wayward sisters," and "Come away, fellow sailors."

The overture and the first scene establish the somber mood, but alternate with a lighter one, and both elements are present throughout the opera. Dido refutes Belinda's optimism by her lament on a descending *ostinato* played by the *basso continuo*. This bass line (from middle C to C an octave lower) is an ominous foreshadowing of the postlude to Dido's lament at the end. The instrumental postlude and the chorus both consist of descending figures, as does Dido's own lament, which concludes with an octave descent from G. There is a ring structure or arch form: the opera begins and ends with a lament.

The descending tetrachord was commonly used at the time to indicate woe. The *Lamento della ninfa* by Monteverdi also had a descending figure played by the *basso continuo*, and his *Arianna's Lament* is another precedent for this figure being used to express sorrow. It is interesting how laments are often written over an *ostinato* that repeats itself until the lament concludes. It is as if violent sorrow has to be contained by the formality of the *continuo*. This allows the freedom of dissonance and rhythmic variation in the melody over a regular accompaniment (for instance, the "Ah!" in Dido's first lament occurs on the weak beat). This type of interplay was typical of the period, but also evinces the timeless proclivity of art to impose order upon chaos. The line of the lament probably comes from the Italian tradition, whereas the orchestral and choral sections derive much from the French.

The poetry is different from Virgil's; he used the hexameter, which is more flexible than Tate's rhymed verse. Virgil could concentrate on the poetry alone, whereas Tate had to be concerned about how it would fit the music. (This was the case for Dryden also: he collaborated with Purcell in *King Arthur* and wrote in a style adapted for music, more succinct and to the point, so that it could be understood over the music). Purcell's music adds another dramatic dimension to this piece. He balances the irregular with the regular, and takes rhythmic and tonal liberties within the constraints of a rigid frame.

Belinda, Dido's advisor (Virgil's Anna), begins by urging Dido to cheer up. The chorus urges the same, but Dido answers in a moving aria, claiming "Ah, ah, ah! Belinda, I am prest with torment. Peace and I are strangers grown." "Prest," "torment," and "strangers" are the words that have descending figures calling attention to her plight.[19]

The opera begins, as does Book 4 of the *Aeneid*, with Dido uncertain about her love for Aeneas. Dido's sister and passionate ally Anna has been transformed by Purcell and Tate into the reasonable counselor Belinda. In the *Aeneid* Dido speaks of Aeneas' nobility and his strength. The opera adds, "How soft in peace, and yet how fierce in arms." *The Aeneid* does not show us much of Aeneas' softness; the opera turns this into his flaw.

Belinda guesses the cause of her sorrow, namely love for Aeneas, the Trojan guest: she urges a union of their two kingdoms. Dido delicately confirms Belinda's guess. In the opera Belinda says that such sufferings as he underwent "might melt the rocks as well as you." Virgil's Dido says, *Non ignara mali miseris succurrere disco*, "Not ignorant of suffering, I have learned to help the wretched" (*Aen.* 1. 630). The *Aeneid*'s Anna assuages Dido's fears about her vow to a dead husband and tells her of the political advantage of such a union. The Tate and Purcell Belinda is more concerned with love itself, although she does counsel Dido to encourage Aeneas' suit: "The greatest blessing Fate can give, / Our Carthage to secure, and Troy revive."

There are strong programmatic elements in the music, and it illustrates and expands the meaning of the words. Ellen Harris has an excellent analysis of the musical declamation of "Whence could so much virtue spring," pointing out that on the word "storms," "[Purcell] makes the line leap down a fifth and tear back up through an octave," and for "valour" "he uses the pomp of dotted notes in a turn figure," and "'Fierce' calls upon a rising line similar to 'storms' but ascends a fifth higher and is pitted against a resolutely descending bass."[20] She goes on to note, "Venus's charms are reflected by the flat and minor chords; Aeneas's might and Anchises's valour by the sharp and major chords."[21] In her final aria, "When I am laid in earth," Dido herself uses flat and minor chords (but not F minor, the key that is used by the witches and suggests horror). These chords and keys are softer than the harsh major keys.

The chorus tries to reassure Dido, singing, "Fear no danger to ensue, / The hero loves as well as you." The key now is C major, signaling a happier mood. Purcell also cleverly uses music against word accents to suggest more than the text itself could. As Belinda and the second woman reassure Dido, we find the same rhythmic "Scottish snap" as in the faithless sailors' chorus later. The assurance at the beginning becomes the disaster at the end, and the link between the rhythms gives further proof. Aeneas' love for the queen is seen to be as brief as his sailors' for their "nymphs on the shore." The main notes also clash with the text; for instance, "hero" is musically accented on the second syllable. Here rhythm wreaks havoc with the text, as Aeneas will with Dido.

Aeneas appears and verifies what Belinda and the chorus has claimed, namely that he loves Dido and would welcome a political union. Dido complains, "Fate forbids what you pursue," but Aeneas counters, "Aeneas has no fate but you." Whereas Dido sings in C Major, Aeneas begins in G major and ends in E minor. He is wandering all over the place in the keys he uses, just as he himself will wander away. Belinda sings a lovely aria urging the union, "Pursue thy conquest, love." The word "pursue" is conveyed by a quick rising figure, literally rendering the chase. The chorus sings a song, also filled with programmatic tropes, celebrating the triumphs of Love and Beauty. It begins, "To the hills and the vales" in C major, but modulates to G minor for "and the cool shady fountains." The minor key augments the coolness as described in the text. The word "triumph" shows a clear return to C major, the key of celebration, and is sung to a gay rhythmic figure.

Beauty, nobility, and happiness are repeated themes: "Grief should ne'er approach the fair," and "When monarchs unite how happy their state." Aeneas calls Dido, "Royal fair." Likewise there is a chorus that sings, "Let the triumphs of Love and of Beauty be shown." These celebrations are often juxtaposed with something ominous—the appearance of the witches, for instance. Triumphal music alternates with the forbidding; lighter music with the more serious. Purcell and Tate have a fine sense of dramatic structure. The witches will see that nobility falls and that love and beauty will be destroyed as they clarify their motive for destroying Dido, "The Queen of Carthage, whom we hate, / As we do all in prosp'rous state." There is no god in the *Aeneid* who hates Dido; her death is only incidental to the sequence of events started by Juno's hatred of Aeneas and all things Trojan.

A dance of triumph concludes the first act. We can assume that Dido and Aeneas consummate their union. This action may all have taken place during one evening.

Act 2 begins with a prelude for the witches. A sorceress calls to her helpers, "Wayward sisters," to "share in the fame of a mischief shall make all Carthage flame." Her key is F minor, Purcell's "horror key."[22] The witches' chorus that follows is in F major: "Harm's our delight and mischief all our skill." The key is major as the chorus members laugh together. Gloating over what they are doing seems even more sinister because the key is major: their wickedness is an unadulterated source of joy for them. In this opera, filled with sharp contrasts, these laments of the hero and heroine are balanced by the rejoicing of the witches in the "laughing chorus" that rises more than it falls, comparable to the progress of their own power. So also the joyous sailors' hornpipe, celebrating their "boozy short leave" from the women they have deceived, is an ironic anticipation of Aeneas' own parting to come. It draws a parallel that we cannot miss, and neither does Dido. She considers him as faithless as his sailors. The sailors' chorus is as hybristic in its way as the chorus of Phaeacian sailors in Monteverdi's *Il ritorno d'Ulisse in patria*.

Here the witches are active in bringing about the fall of the hero and heroine. In the *Aeneid* one has more the sense of an inevitable fate. Nevertheless, the witches keep the story on track and force Aeneas to be faithful to his well-known destiny. We see another precedent for the witches of the opera in Virgil's Dido herself, who claims she will use magic given her by a Massylian priestess. The Dido of the *Aeneid* deceives her sister Anna by saying that she will muster magic arts to rid herself of Aeneas' love. She asks her sister to build a pyre on which she will burn all of Aeneas' possessions (including his sword, on which she secretly intends to fall). Virgil's Dido is comparable to Euripides' and Apollonius' Medea, and again we see a connection with witchcraft, although Dido is the victim rather than the perpetrator. Purcell displaces onto the witches the supernatural that Virgil associates with Dido. We can call this a metathesis of demonization, another survival of the ancient in the modern.

The witches also derive in part from Virgil's *Fama,* a monster who slanders the lovers (*Aen.* 4. 174 ff.). She is small at first, but soon reaches heaven as she walks on the earth, a huge monster with as many eyes as she has feathers, and as many tongues, as many speaking mouths and erect ears. Iarbas, Dido's former suitor, hears *Fama*'s rumors about Dido and Aeneas and prays to Jupiter. Jupiter sends Mercury in response to Iarbas' prayer. So Virgil's *Fama* is as effective as Purcell's witches in destroying Dido, but *Fama* acts in response to a prayer, whereas the witches are impelled by their own malevolence.

The head sorceress uses an elf in the form of Mercury to tell Aeneas to leave the queen. This is a strange transposition of a Virgilian device: Virgil has Cupid take the place of Aeneas' son Ascanius so that Dido will fall in love with the child's father. Mercury delivers two scathing denunciations of his behavior to Aeneas, calling him uxorious. The witches will first make a storm for the lovers as they hunt. The hunt is indicated by strings imitating a hunting horn, and this is in the key of D major, the key of the hunting scene. Purcell is creating tonal links between the two. There is also an extended, wild, descending figure on the word "storm," suggesting a powerful wind. An echo chorus is made up of dark tones: the key has returned to F major but alternates with C minor. The text speaks of a "deep vaulted cell," necessary to conceal their "dreadful practice." The scene ends with an echo dance of Furies. Its solemn, slow quality seems to sanction their enterprise.

When this chorus begins, "In our deep vaulted cell," it blackly anticipates "In these hallowed halls" from Mozart's *Die Zauberflöte*, conveying dignified and sacred majesty.[23] This resembles a Protestant chorale. The gods determine Aeneas' departure in the *Aeneid*, but here the witches do it, and Purcell lets them take over the function of the gods through a musical endorsement. It is balanced by a chorale in the last act, "Great minds against themselves conspire." It is as if the witches were symbolic of the inner evil human beings can create, and they are musically equated with inner demons. The text is especially ironic since it plays upon the idea of the union of monarchs: "When monarchs unite how happy their state, / They triumph at once o'er their foes and their fate." This is also a stately chorale. It is shown that rulers can both triumph and bring ruin on themselves. Monarchs, in this music, are elevated to the stature of the divine, but as their rise is great, so is their fall precipitous.

Scene 2, which alternates between D minor and major, begins with the hunt, and a song by Belinda that speaks of Diana frequenting these woods. There is a bass musical line that suggests walking, as Diana is described in "Oft she visits." There is an ominous allusion to the story of Actaeon, and when the chorus sings "Diana's self might to these woods resort," one can ominously think of the gods hunting man. Repetition of themes sheds new light on the progress of the drama. The theme of the hunt suggests the pursuit of love is a deadly sport, dangerous for both hunter and hunted: "Pursue thy conquest love"—and the hunt of sport—"so fair the game, so rich the sport."

The women dance to entertain Aeneas. He appears with his hunting prey on his spear and also makes a grim allusion to Adonis' hunting prowess. *Dido and Aeneas* has two warnings from mythology for the lovers: Actaeon and Adonis. The chorus speaks of Diana frequenting the forest where the royal party goes hunting. They add ominously that this is the place Actaeon "met his fate" because he had gazed on the goddess Diana as she bathed. She turned him into a stag who was then torn apart by his own hounds, a wonderful figure for the self-lacerating effects of prurient interest. Aeneas also boasts that he has killed a boar with "tushes [sic] far exceeding / Those did Venus' huntsman tear." Diana also killed this hero, Adonis, beloved of Venus, by having him gored by a boar. Blow's *Venus and Adonis*, which owed much to Shakespeare, probably influenced Purcell and Tate's choice here. In Euripides' *Hippolytus*, Artemis alludes to this vengeance on Aphrodite. The choice of Artemis, a virgin goddess, who not only shuns sensuality but actually attacks it, is appropriate for the opera. By sleeping with Aeneas, Dido has violated the rule of chastity. The *Aeneid* is explicit about this, and Dido's lapse is all the more serious because she has made a vow to be faithful to her husband's memory. Virgil says that Dido is no longer moved by reputation or appearance, nor does she think any more of a furtive love: "She calls it marriage, and with this name she covers her fault" (*Aen.* 4. 170–172).

The storm begins, and the violins imitate thunder with repeated notes that do not rise and fall as did the earlier repeated notes that indicated a horn. All return to court except Aeneas; he is detained by Mercury, who tells him that he must leave this night. Aeneas consents.

Aeneas' reaction to the spirit's command to leave Dido is expressed by a short lament, prefaced by a groan rendered on the word "Ah!" which has a comparable rhythm and figure (a three-note rise and descent) to Dido's "Ah!" in her lament at the end ("When I am laid in Earth"). Purcell draws a parallel between Aeneas' expression of sorrow at leaving Dido and Dido's own expression of sorrow. This gives us a dramatic anticipation, which we recall when we hear Dido's lament. Nevertheless Aeneas has no aria of his own, and this further adds to the depiction of him as a weak character. As mentioned above, witches' roles were commonly sung by men, and the voice of the Sorceress (the leader of the witches) may have been pitched lower than the singer playing Aeneas, which would have added to her authority and further diminished Aeneas.

In this opera Aeneas is hardly *pius*, the epithet that Virgil gave to his hero, indicating his devotion to the gods and his destiny. Purcell's Aeneas is willing to throw over his fate for his queen, and then, at the first command of Mercury, embrace it again. When he confronts the angry queen, he changes his mind once more, and she has to get rid of him by threatening suicide before his eyes. Aeneas is further diminished by being deceived simply by the false construction of witches. Virgil had the god Mercury himself appear to call him away. The Virgilian Aeneas is tempted by Dido, but does not lose sight of his original goal, Italy. He is more honest with her.

Yet Tate's Aeneas is more sympathetic on a human level; he shows more concern for Dido's feelings. This is in contrast with Virgil's Aeneas, who causes the death of Dido and finally kills Turnus with little concern or mercy, heedless of the maxim that his father gave him, *parcere subiectis* ("spare the subdued," *Aen.* 6. 853). Virgil sensitively conveys the ambiguity of Rome—and perhaps every empire—by not sparing us the brutality and carnage that conquest entailed. Perhaps Tate and Purcell give a comparable warning in showing us the disaster that follows from a conquest that sets no limit on itself ("Pursue thy conquest love").

Cupid's dart is comparable to the spear that Actaeon used when hunting and the horn that impaled Adonis. The hunt itself is another motif shared with the epic. There the hunt was the site of consummation that Dido called "marriage"; in the opera it is the occasion for the appearance of the false Mercury, and the beginning of the lovers' separation.

A sailor's hornpipe begins the second scene, plus a rollicking song by the sailors, who are glad to leave, urging, "Take a boozy short leave of your nymphs on the shore, / And silence their mourning / with vows of returning, / But never intending to visit them more." This song begins on the weak beat and its rhythm (a short note followed by a longer one) illustrates the "Scottish snap," for which Purcell was famous. The key is B flat major both for this song and the next, linking Aeneas' thoughtless crew with the callous witches. There is also a link in the structure that features a descending tetrachord, the same figure that will occur in Dido's lament and symbolize her destruction. The witches' dance and the boozy sailors' hornpipe are ominous; the witches celebrate their evil acts and the sailors laugh at the lies they tell the women they abandon. Only fifty years earlier the Puritans banned dance itself. Dance in this opera becomes an act of *hybris* or triumph of evil.

The witches sing a song of triumph. They say that they will cause a storm to overtake Aeneas when he sails. They conclude, "Elissa bleeds tonight, and Carthage flames tomorrow." They dance. Virgil uses the symbols of the fire and the snake to express love, death, and perverted fertility.[24] They become recurrent themes in the epic. Tate also has recurrent themes in his text, as does Purcell in his music. Fire is one such a motif. Belinda notes of Dido, "Her eyes confess the flame her tongue denies."[25] On the word "flame" we find a quick descending figure of sixteenth notes that matches Aeneas' descent on the words "hopeless fire" and "fall" when he speaks of his love: "Ah! Make not in a hopeless fire, a hero fall, and Troy once more expire." The ominous parallel of the flames of love and the flames of Troy show how destructive Aeneas will be for Dido, and this is well expressed by the music. This flame will be disastrous for Carthage. Other Dido operas show the spurned "barbarians" setting torch to the city at the end (e.g., Pietro Metastasio's libretto, which was altered for stages that could not accommodate the conflagration). Carthage's flames are not only from her pyre, but are symbolic of the future conflict with Rome. Aeneas saw the dire flames of Elissa's pyre, and Virgil drew there the analogy with love—the pain that comes from a thwarted love (*Aen.* 5. 1–6). Those flames would also signal the flames of future wars. Our opera's Dido speaks of "The injur'd Dido's slighted flame." In this opera, war leads to love, then love leads to war.

The second scene is all in G minor: sorrow prevails. Belinda still tries to reassure her mistress of Aeneas' love, although she is aware he is planning to depart. Aeneas confirms that he will leave, using the god's decree as an excuse. Dido accuses him of hypocrisy: "Thus on the fatal banks of Nile, / Weeps the deceitful crocodile." Aeneas changes his mind, "In spite of Jove's commands, I'll stay." Dido urges him to leave and threatens him with her suicide if he stays. When he leaves she says she will die anyway.

Like the Sophoclean Ajax and Euripidean Medea, Dido cannot forgive dishonor. She responds to Aeneas' pleas to stay by saying, "For 'tis enough, whate'er you now decree, / That you had once a thought of leaving me." This uncompromising nobility is absent from the Virgilian Dido, who will do anything to prevent Aeneas from departing, to the point of burning his ships.

Both Dido and Aeneas are radically changed from the way Virgil depicts them. In the *Aeneid* Dido is characterized by *furor*, or ungovernable passion, disastrous to herself and her country. Tate and Purcell make her rational and dignified instead. In contrast to Virgil's devout hero (*pius Aeneas*), Purcell's is weak and vacillating. One wonders if Purcell was influenced by Monteverdi, who showed this same shift of emphasis from the male to the female in his *Il ritorno d'Ulisse in patria*, in contrast with Homer.

Purcell observes "Aristotelian unities," namely the unities that Aristotle suggested and Lodovico Castelvetro (1505–1571) engraved in stone for Italian and French drama: unity of place, time, and action. Dryden says he also followed these unities in *All for Love* (1678), his adaptation of Shakespeare's *Antony and Cleopatra*, and predecessor of Purcell's *Dido and Aeneas* (1689). This distinguished drama from epic. By contrast, Virgil shows us the story of Dido and Aeneas unfolding over many days, and they conduct their love "over the long winter, reveling in luxury, forgetting their realms as they are slaves to their base passion" (*Aen.* 4. 193–194). Tate and Purcell claim the time they enjoyed together is one night,

> No sooner she resigns her heart
> But from her arms I'm forced to part;
> How can so hard a fate be took?
> One night enjoy'd, the next forsook (p. 57).

Dido's and Aeneas' lovemaking seems to fit the unities also. The opera begins one evening and ends the next with Aeneas' sailing and Dido's death, so the unity of one day is observed. The action all takes place in Carthage and is centered exclusively on their love, so the unities of place and action are similarly maintained. From the unities and the addition of a chorus, we see that the story now follows the contours of tragedy rather than epic. Many critics have called *Aeneid*, Book 4, "The Tragedy of Dido."

In the opera the attraction is more clearly mutual. The Virgilian "marriage" is sealed on the day of a hunt, when Juno and Venus stir up a storm to get rid of the curious. Aeneas and Dido take shelter in a cave. Earth and Juno give a sign: fires gleam and heaven is witness to their nuptials. The nymphs ululate on the mountain top (*Aen.* 4. 166–168). This ululation serves the same function as the allusions to the myths of Actaeon and Adonis in the opera. It is hardly an auspicious beginning for the marriage. From the start the notes of wildness and unlawfulness are struck. In the opera the storm is a prelude to the false vision of Mercury, and both the storm and vision are the work of the witches.

There is also a note of human responsibility in the chorus: "Great minds against themselves conspire, / And shun the cure they most desire." This applies most to Dido in that she is unforgiving, and will take her life to prove her point. But we remember comparable words in Greek tragedy: Creon describes Oedipus, "Such natures are rightly most painful to themselves" (S. *OT.* 675); and Medea's nurse asks, "What will be done by that lofty mind, so difficult to stop when bitten by evils?" (E.*Med*. 108–110). Both analogies show that Purcell's Dido shares in a similarly heroic, if misdirected, virtue. Great minds are their own worst enemies.

This is followed by Dido's moving aria, "When I am laid in earth, / May my wrongs create / No trouble in thy breast; / Remember me, but ah! forget my fate"—noble cries delivered over an *ostinato* in the bass. The beauty of this song is difficult to convey. There is a descending figure on the word "laid." The repetition of "am laid" is in a major key following the minor at the beginning. The change of key conveys her own translation: death will be transcendent. There is no resolution in Dido's song from the key of G minor until the end, when, it may be assumed, Dido departs from this life. She expires, as if spontaneously, from her disappointed love and crushed honor. She does not curse Aeneas in her final breath but is a noble lady to the end.

Dido's beautiful lament is a chaconne with a descending chromatic bass. The repeated descending pattern contains the descending tetrachord. We might construe this as not only death itself, with relentless repetition showing its inevitability, but the tears shed on its account. This is sorrow distilled. When she repeats, "Remember me," the repetitions in performance often become fainter and fainter as her life ebbs away.

Dido's final song, containing the words "Remember me," alludes to the memory that was so valued by the ancient Greeks, the *kleos aphthiton*, "immortal fame," prized by Achilles. Dido is in this way close to the Homeric hero, wishing to be remembered for the nobility of her choice. One recalls the repeated words of Hamlet's father's ghost demanding vengeance.

Darkness and death are closely aligned: "Thy hand, Belinda, darkness shades me." This is another image from Virgil, derived from Homer. Homer expresses life in terms of light, and death in terms of darkness: a hero dies when darkness shades his eyes.[26] It is also a frequent image in Greek tragedy, which this opera so closely resembles. Euripides' Iphigenia bids farewell to the beloved light, as she goes to meet her death (*IA* 1509) and Sophocles' Ajax, who welcomes death, addresses the darkness as his only light (*Ajax*, 394). He claims death is his only salvation, as he bids farewell to the light and the lands dear to him, just before his death (*Ajax,* 859–863). The bright Mediterranean sun makes such an image understandable, and Tate and Purcell knew their classics.

The chorus concludes, "With drooping wings, ye Cupids come, / And scatter roses on her tomb." As we might expect, the word "drooping" is conveyed by a descending figure—indeed spanning an entire octave. The final lines are an invocation to the Cupids to "keep here your watch, and never, never, never part." The Cupids will be loyal to Dido in death, a contrast with Aeneas, who is disloyal in life. Like a work of art, death is a way to crystallize the transient. Music itself best suits the transient since, in contrast to visual arts, it vanishes after it is produced. The reprise is taken up by the instruments alone as the Cupids perform their slow, stately dance of mourning.

In the opera Dido is persuaded by Belinda and her followers that she should pursue her love. Cupid throwing a dart in the opera is comparable to the

Aeneid's Cupid being sent by his mother Venus to make Dido fall in love. He takes the form of Ascanius, Aeneas' son, and Dido fondles him, "ignorant of how great a god sits there" (*Aen*. 1. 718–719). In the opera the Cupids who scatter roses on Dido's tomb call to mind Boucher and Fragonard. The violence of the original is sentimentalized into rococo delicacy.

The Cupids who shoot their arrows at the beginning are invoked at the end to scatter roses on Elissa's tomb. Cocteau had the image of a gun that shoots roses. A missile of love turns into a weapon, and finally a rose: what was active and mobile becomes soft, still, and will fade. The chorus sings of the Cupids scattering roses at the end, "Soft, and gentle as her heart." These Cupids are invoked to keep watch "and never part." They will not be like Aeneas; instead, they will be a tribute to Dido's earned everlasting fame.

Purcell has a two-note descending figure that predominates in the conclusion of the chorus, invoking the Cupids at the end over the words "soft." This takes over the two-note descending figure in the chorus beginning "Great minds against themselves conspire." It seems the conspiracy is over, and now lamentations begin in earnest.

The two-note descent denoting sorrow was also used by Monteverdi in Penelope's lament at the beginning of *Il ritorno d'Ulisse in patria*, and it prefigures the *Wehe* ("woe") motif from Wagner's *Ring*. The final chorus calling on the Cupids to keep their watch and never part is also punctuated by rests. It is as if phrases are delivered in sobs, and silence takes over where music is inadequate. This is the silence of death. "The rest is silence."

Book 4 of the *Aeneid* is only a small part of Virgil's twelve-book epic. Even the action of this love story takes place over a long period. Aeneas sees Dido not only in Carthage, but also in the underworld. The epic action fits the broader picture of the history of Rome. Dido is symbolic of Carthage and the long history of hostility between Carthage and Rome, which culminates in the destruction of Carthage. Cato demanded *Carthago delenda est* ("Carthage must be destroyed"), and Virgil shows us Dido as interchangeable with Carthage: Jove's command to Mercury that Aeneas sail to Italy was Dido's death sentence. She represented the oriental *femme fatale* that Romans had recently confronted in the form of Cleopatra. Antony gave up his empire to her, and Caesar had been tempted: as souvenir he left her his child Caesarion, the very gift that Virgil's Dido says she wished Aeneas had left her. The Romans had enjoyed seeing the downfall of this "Asiatic" woman in Virgil's epic. As John Sullivan says, "Put bluntly, Woman—the Other—whether Creusa, the disheartened Trojan women in Sicily, Dido or Cleopatra, should be construed as an obstacle to the fulfillment of Man's creative vision and goals, whether political, artistic or moral."[27]

Virgil's Dido was a threat to Rome's manifest destiny, and the poet did not spare her. She curses Aeneas, foretells an evil future (half wish and half prophecy), and even when he visits Hades she turns her face from him. This is the way that Aeneas learns the truth of the story he has heard, namely that she had died by her own hand, using his sword. (One thinks of the Sophoclean Deianeira killing herself with Heracles' sword, on their own marriage bed.) In the underworld,

Virgil's Aeneas asks himself if he was the cause. He swears that he did not want to leave her, but that he was forced by the gods' command. This differs from his earlier harsh words to Dido, that he did not promise marriage, and that his love lies in Italy, his promised "fatherland" (*hic amor, haec patria est, Aen.* 4. 347). In Virgil's *Aeneid*, the imperial goal is offered by the fatherland, love, whereas Dido's motherland offers a stifling love. The shade of Dido in the underworld justifiably turns away in her anger and walks to Sychaeus, her former husband, who returns her love (*Aen.* 6. 467–474). She is still Aeneas' enemy (*inimica, Aen.* 6. 472).

Virgil's Dido curses Aeneas, prophetic of the bloody future for Rome and Carthage. First she calls the gods to smash his ship and threatens that she will become an *Erinys* (a Fury), pursuing him with dark fire. She will follow him as a ghost and will relish hearing in the underworld about her fulfilled vengeance (*Aen.* 4. 380 ff). Dido refines her curse later, saying that if the gods allow Aeneas to reach his land, she wishes him war, and when finally he makes an "unjust peace," she wishes him unhappiness and a premature death, lying un-buried on the sand. The reference here for the ancient audience was no doubt the murdered Pompey the Great. Dido follows this with a curse for the future, that all the Tyrians wage untiring war for all generations (*Aen.* 4. 612 ff). This vengeful queen is a far cry from Purcell's demure Dido, whose worst accusation is that Aeneas is a liar.[28]

Virgil's Dido teeters on the verge of madness, unlike Purcell's Dido. In her dreams Virgil's Dido is pursued by a wild Aeneas. This Dido is like a character from Greek tragedy, from Aeschylus' *Oresteia* or Euripides' *Bacchae*. Euripi-des' Medea also helped form Virgil's Dido: passionate barbarian princesses capable of both love and hate in excess. Like Pentheus she sees Furies, a double sun, and double Thebes; she also is compared to Orestes, who is pursued over the stage by his mother, who is carrying torches and snakes while the Furies lurk on the threshold (*Aen.* 4. 465–473). This is not the world of Purcell with a chorus giggling over its mischief (the "Ho ho ho" chorus).

Dido's *furor* has been transformed by Tate and Purcell. Dido is, as it were, split in two. Her negative side and, perhaps, the misogyny of the age are turned into witches in this opera, and they are—alas—trivialized. By contrast, Virgil gave us Allecto, the fury sent by Juno, whom we shall never forget. Juno says that if she cannot influence the gods, she will move hell (*flectere si nequeo superos, Acheronta movebo, Aen.* 7. 312). The Allecto she sets loose on Italy to stir up war is an avatar of Dido and a fulfillment of her curse.

In the opera, the gods are barely mentioned, and when they are, the allu-sion is ominous, from Cupids, who become caretakers of a tomb, to Diana, who destroyed Actaeon, and Venus, who lost her lover Adonis. Monteverdi and the Italian baroque stage welcomed the appearance of gods in elaborate machinery. In general, however, Tate and Purcell seem to have taken a secular stance: no pagan gods (replaced by witches and a false Mercury) and no parallels drawn between the pagan gods—or the characters in the opera—with a Christian god or the Virgin Mary of the kind we saw in Monteverdi's operas, even on the classical themes he chose. Such omissions are understandable now after the Restoration, which saw a relaxation of the morality of the Puritan Commonwealth, but which remained Protestant and fiercely anti-Catholic. The English did not have that comfortable, rich exchange with Catholicism that the Italians did. Monteverdi and Badoaro's Penelope may have paralleled the Virgin Mary, but hardly Purcell and Tate's Dido. Some of the difference is built into the characters: one was a paragon of chastity, and the other was not. We see a parallel drawn more between Dido and Venus. This is ominous, like the later parallel between Adonis (Venus' beloved) and Aeneas. Association with this goddess can be particularly dangerous (unless one is her son). At the same time it elevates Dido by putting her on a par with the goddess Venus.

Ellen T. Harris reports an Epilogue by Thomas D'Urfey, originally delivered by Lady Dorothy Burke, which corroborates her theory of the Dido legend as "suitably adapted as a morality for the girls of Josias Priest's boarding school who acted the drama":

> All that we know the angels do above,
> I've read, is that they sing and that they love,
> The vocal part we have tonight perform'd
> And if by Love our hearts not yet are warm'd
> Great Providence has still more bounteous been
> To save us from those grand deceivers, men.[29]

Mark Goldie discovered a letter (1691) in which a woman tells her friend (in the context of selecting a school) that "Priests att Little Chelsey was one which was much commended; but he hath lately had an opera, which I'me sure hath done him a great injurey; & ye Parents of ye Childern not satisfied with so Publick a show."[30] It is possible that the Whigs were offended at what they might see as Tory propaganda, showing James as simply deluded by his Catholic advisors. But the theme itself of love and abandonment, crudely expressed by sailors at one point, could be sufficient reason for disapproval. Arguments for the allegory and earlier date include the unsuitability of this opera either for praising monarchs or edifying young women. The majority of scholars now doubt that this opera was written expressly for a girl's school.

We see messages in both Virgil's epic and in Tate and Purcell's opera. The former warns of the temptations that might distract from the path of destiny, a type of *Pilgrim's Progress*. The *Aeneid*'s Dido is possessive (although certainly more appealing than *pius* Aeneas); the opera's Dido is the opposite: she is recklessly willing to allow Aeneas to go, even though he pleads to stay. Neither Dido nor Aeneas in the opera indulges in the soul searching of their classical prototypes.

What we have is a brilliant opera with all the trappings of Greek tragedy, and with the *megalopsychia* ("great-mindedness") of the hero, now a heroine. Love may not triumph in the end, but Dido does. Her death, as spontaneous as Elektra's in the Hofmannsthal and Strauss version, is her noble choice.

CONCLUSION

Dido as a heroic queen contrasts with the faithless Aeneas. Tate and Purcell contradict Virgil's "A woman is changeable and an unreliable creature," *varium et mutabile semper femina (Aen. 4. 569–570)*. They have also inverted the accusation against Aeneas' uxoriousness, suggesting Aeneas should listen to Dido. Perhaps Aeneas is urged to resemble Monteverdi's Ulisse. Like Ulisse, Aeneas ought to stop wandering and heed a wise woman. Dido, like Penelope, dominates her opera. Dido, also like Penelope in relation to Ulysses, sings more than Aeneas and is more steadfast. She makes the heroic decisions, whereas Aeneas succumbs to each pressure, not the least of which is his own whim. Obviously Dido's heroism is not that of either a Homeric or Virgilian hero; it is that of a baroque queen so ordering her life that she is master of the limited choices she is given. The new heroics are in the domestic sphere, and the emphasis is on love, not on power. In this way the opera differs from Greek epic and tragedy, which are more concerned with subjects other than love. So, too, in the baroque there is a shift towards the individual from the more public concerns that characterized the Renaissance.

The Restoration encouraged music that made order out of chaos.[31] This is art that leads to social pacification and a homogeneity in taste. According to one allegory suggested for *Dido and Aeneas*, England can hold its head high (at least morally) in spite of the vagaries of James II.

Dido and Aeneas extols the calm after the storm with a peaceful choral commentary following Dido's impassioned final aria. Cupids are instructed to scatter roses on her tomb. This contrasts with the ending of Virgil's Book 4 and the beginning of 5, where Dido's pyre is burning, an ominous message for Aeneas. Purcell's Dido, in refusing to curse Aeneas, shows British restraint. There are times that we long for the passionate Mediterranean Virgilian Dido, but Purcell did not choose to make *this* fiery queen immortal in opera. English *politesse* and *noblesse oblige* replace Mediterranean passion; nevertheless, the marriage of the ancient text with Purcell's music is a happy one.

It is no accident that the most beautiful music is Dido's, not Aeneas'.[32] Dido springs from the Courtly Love tradition and does it honor. She is not, however, simply a passive heroine as in much Renaissance love poetry, but in her rejection of Aeneas when her honor is slighted she comes closer to the more lively heroines of Shakespeare.

Purcell's Dido knows the risks of love and she pays the price. She is an Achilles of love, claiming her honor, even if the communal good suffers. She creates an image of beauty and elegance, and Purcell makes it lasting: "Forever wilt thou love and she be fair."

Purcell has illustrated Tate's text with music that adds a new dimension. It is also faithful to the text. Both Purcell and Tate have learned from Shakespeare and exhibit a dramatic sophistication that is lacking in many other operas. In this case the English respect for the word and text pays off. There is a succinctness and dramatic drive that impels us to the tragic end. One never feels impeded by musical meditations.

Purcell creates commentary that goes beyond the text, using dissonance and different keys in a subtle way to add to the characterization and elucidation of the plot. At the same time he is never simply or naively programmatic. His music can stand on its own, and the final lament is marvelous in its expressive quality. At the same time one is impressed by the dramatic quality. Throughout the ages Purcell has earned the admiration and respect of fellow musicians. Benjamin Britten said, "I had never realised, before I first met Purcell's music, that words could be set with such ingenuity, with such colour."

Purcell's epitaph in Westminster Abbey is a truthful one: "Here lies Henry Purcell, Esq, who left this life and is gone to that Blessed Place where only his harmony can be exceeded."

APPENDIX
OPERAS ABOUT DIDO AND AENEAS

Francesco Cavalli (1602–1676) (b. Crema, Italy)
Didone (1641)

Andrea Mattioli (c.1620–1679) (b. Faenza, Italy)
La Didone (1656)

Carlo Pallavicino (c.1640–1688) (b. Salò, Italy)
Didone delirante (1686)

Henry Purcell (?1659–1695) (b. London, England)
Dido and Aeneas (1689)

André Campra (bap. 1660–1744) (b. Aix-en-Provence, France)
Énée et Didon (1714)

Alessandro Scarlatti (1660–1725) (b. Palermo, Italy)
La Didone delirante (1696)

Henry Desmarets (1661–1741) (b. Paris, France)
Didon (1693)

Johann Christoph Pepusch (1667–1752) (b. Berlin, Germany)
The Death of Dido (1716)

Tomaso Giovanni Albinoni (1671–1751) (b. Venice, Italy)
Didone abbandonata (1725)

Domenico Natale Sarro (1679–1744) (b. Trani, Apulia, Italy)
Didone abbandonata (1724)

Christoph Graupner (1683–1760) (b. Kirchberg, Saxony, Germany)
Dido, Königin von Carthago (1707)

Nicola Porpora (1686–1768) (b. Naples, Italy)
Didone abbandonata (1725)

Giovanni Alberto Ristori (1692–1753) (b. ?Bologna, Italy)
Didone abbandonata (1737)

Leonardo Vinci (c.1696–1730) (b. Strongoli, Calabria, Italy)
Didone abbandonata (1724)

Pietro Auletta (c.1698–1771) (b. San Angelo, Italy)
Didone (1759)

Gaetano Maria Schiassi (1698–1754) (b. Bologna, Italy)
Didone abbandonata (1735)

Johann Adolf Hasse (1699–1783) (b. Bergedorf, Germany)
Didone abbandonata (1742)

Andrea Bernasconi (1706–1784) (b. ?Marseilles, France)
Didone abbandonata (1741)

Baldassare Galuppi (1706–1785) (b. Burano, Italy)
Didone abbandonata (1740)

Egidio Duni (1708–1775) (b. Matera, Basilicata, Italy)
La Didone abbandonata (1739)

Giovanni Battista Lampugnani (1708–1788) (b. ?Milan, Italy)
Didone abbandonata (1739)

Thomas Augustine Arne (1710–1778) (b. London, England)
Dido and Aeneas (1734)

Rinaldo da Capua (c.1710–c.1780) (b. Capua or Naples, Italy)
Didone abbandonata (1741)

Ignaz Holzbauer (1711–1783) (b. Vienna, Austria)
La morte di Didone (1779)

David Perez (1711–1778) (b. Naples, Italy)
La Didone abbandonata (1751)

Giuseppe Bonno (1711–1788) (b. Vienna, Austria)
Didone abbandonata (1752)

Paolo Scalabrini (1713–1803) (b.?)
Didone (1746)

Domènech Terradellas (1713–1751) (b. Barcelona, Spain)
Didone abbandonata (1750)

Niccolò Jommelli (1714–1774) (b. Aversa, Italy)
Didone abbandonata (1747)

Gennaro Manna (1715–1779) (b. Naples, Italy)
Didone abbandonata (1751)

Ignazio Fiorillo (1715–1787) (b. Naples, Italy)
Didone abbandonata (1751)

Antonio Mazzoni (1717–1785) (b. Bologna, Italy)
Didone abbandonata (1752)

Antonio Ferradini (?1718–1779) (b. Naples, Italy)
Didone (1760)

Vincenzo Ciampi (?1719–1762) (b. Piacenza, Italy)
Didone (1754)

Andrea Adolfati (1721–1760) (b. Venice, Italy)
Didone abbandonata (1747)

Ferdinando Bertoni (1725–1813) (b. Saló, Italy)
Didone abbandonata (1748)

Pasquale Anfossi (1727–1797) (b. Taggia, Italy)
Didone abbandonata (1775)

Tommaso Traetta (1727–1779) (b. Bitonto, Italy)
Didone abbandonata (1757)

Giacomo Insanguine (1728–1795) (b. Monopoli, Italy)
La Didone abbandonata (1770)

Niccolò Piccinni (1728–1800) (b. Bari, Italy)
Didone Abbandonata (1770)
Didon (1783)

Giuseppe Sarti (1729–1802) (b. Faenza, Italy)
Didone abbandonata (1762)

Giuseppe Colla (1731–1806) (b. Parma, Italy)
Didone (1773)

Ignazio Celoniati (c.1731–1784) (b. Turin, Italy)
Didone abbandonata (1769)

Franz Joseph Haydn (1732–1809) (b. Rohrau, Lower Austria)
Dido (1776)

Gian Francesco de Majo (1732–1770) (b. Naples, Italy)
Didone abbandonata (1770)

Bernardo Ottani (1736–1827) (b. Bologna, Italy)
La Didone (1779)

Francesco Zannetti (1737–1788) (b. Volterra, Italy)
La Didone abbandonata (1766)

Antonio Boroni (1738–1792) (b. Rome, Italy)
Didone (1768)

Johann Gottfried Schwanenberger (c.1740–1804) (b. Wolfenbüttel, Germany)
La Didone abbandonata (1765)

Francesco Piticchio (fl.1760–1800) (b. ?Palermo, Sicily)
Didone abbandonata (1780)

Giovanni Paisiello (1740–1816) (b. Roccaforzata, Italy)
Didone abbandonata (1794)

Giuseppe Gazzaniga (1743–1818) (b. Verona, Italy)
La Didone (1787)

Gennaro Astarita (c.1745–1803) (b. ?Naples, Italy)
La Didone abbandonata (1780)

James Hook (1746–1827) (b. Norwich, England)
Dido (1771)

Joseph Schuster (1748–1812) (b. Dresden, Germany)
La Didone abbandonata (1776)

Louis Joseph Saint-Amans (1749–1820) (b. Marseilles, France)
La mort de Didon (1776)

Michele Mortellari (c.1750–1807) (b. Palermo, Sicily)
Didone abbandonata (1772)

Gaetano Andreozzi (1755–1826) (b. Aversa, Italy)
Didone abbandonata (1784)

Joseph Martin Kraus (1756–1792) (b. Miltenberg am Main, Germany)
Aeneas i Cartago eller Dido och Aeneas (1782)

Stephen Storace (1762–1796) (b. London, England)
Dido, Queen of Carthage (1792)

Franz Danzi (1763–1826) (b. Schwetzingen, Germany)
Dido (1811)

Valentino Fioravanti (1764–1837) (b. Rome, Italy)
Didone abbandonata (1810)

Ferdinando Paer (1771–1839) (b. Parma, Italy)
La Didone (1810)

Saverio Mercadante (1795–1870) (b. Altamura, Italy)
Didone abbandonata (1823)

Karl Gottlieb Reissiger (1798–1859) (b. Belzig, Germany)
Didone abbandonata (1824)

Hector Berlioz (1803–1869) (b. Paris, France)
Les Troyens (1856–59)

Dionyssios Lavrangas (1860/4–1941) (b. Argostolion, Greece)
Dido (1909)

George W.L. Marshall-Hall (1862–1915) (b. London, England)
Dido and Aeneas (?before 1890)

Benjamin Britten (1913–1976) (b. Lowestoft, England)
Realization of Henry Purcell—*Dido and Aeneas* (1951)

Mozart's *Idomeneo, re di Creta:* The King of the Day

INTRODUCTION AND BACKGROUND

Karl Barth thought that angels played Mozart for themselves, and then the "Lord listens with special pleasure."[1] Goethe called Mozart an incomparable genius; Chopin's last request was that Mozart be played in his memory.

At twenty-one, Mozart told his father, "You know my greatest desire is to write operas." He fulfilled this desire, and his operatic voice sings from all his scores, both instrumental and vocal. The same expertise in the lyric line shines through his instrumental works, and his violins—even his piano—rival the human voice in expressing his melodic genius.

Throughout the seventeenth century, Italian operas contained both comic and serious elements. A "reform" was initiated by the poets Apostolo Zeno (1688–1750) and Pietro Metastasio (1698–1782), although some librettists like Silvio Stampiglia (1664–1725) refused to give up the tragicomic mixture.[2] Nevertheless, for the most part, Italian operas came to be classified as either *opera seria* or *opera buffa*. Most critics claim that *opera seria* represented the old regime, whereas *opera buffa* represented change and showed a shift towards modern, more democratic ideals. A quick look at the two genres shows us how this argument works. *Opera seria* often derives its material from mythology: it is tragic; it features dissonance, complicated rhythms, and is distinguished by complicated vocal figures that demand special expertise; it favors the *prima donna* and sophisticated *castrati* and singers with a higher *tessitura;* it often had problems resolved by a *deus ex machina;* it deals with lofty virtues and ideals; a recitative is followed by a *da capo* aria—action, with lots of reflection. *Opera buffa,* on the other hand, took its themes from everyday life and showed every-day figures (some from the *commedia dell'arte*); it was comic; there could be bass singers; problems were solved by the humans rather than a god; there was often some moral lesson, but peccadilloes were acknowledged with grace and favor, along with the characters who committed them; the vocal line was simple, with fewer formal divisions; the rhythms were often dance-like, the harmony clear, and action was favored over reflection. One can see that the representations of the nobles, thinly disguised as gods and furnished with vocal expertise (the nobles could afford paying for these virtuosi), were a part of *opera seria*. It flourished during the first half of the eighteenth century. *Opera buffa* gained in popularity after 1750 as we enter the time of revolution, notably the American and the French. In *The Marriage of Figaro*, Da Ponte with his subversive libretto based on Beaumarchais was using the *opera buffa* to convey the new values.

It was probably because his patrons preferred *opera buffa* that Mozart produced so many masterpieces in this genre.[3] But he transformed the *buffa*, and not one of the operas written in that genre is without *seria* elements. *Seria* elements even in a *buffa* production add important characterization. For instance, in *Don Giovanni* we remember Donna Anna as a *seria* character as opposed to Zerlina, a clearly *buffa* character, each with her own distinguishing music; Don Giovanni himself is a mixed character. The themes also always have something of the tragic. Mozart understood human nature and life, and did not eliminate the tragicomic mixture that is fundamental to the human condition. Christian Gottfried Körner wrote to Friedrich Schiller: "Mozart was perhaps the only one who could be equally great in the comic as in the tragic."[4]

Idomeneo is the supreme example of *opera seria* and investigates themes important to both Mozart and the Enlightenment.[5] It was commissioned at Munich by Count Seeau and performed in the Residenztheater there in January of 1781. The libretto is by Giovanni Battista Varesco. Mozart made another version in German, and here Idomeneo is a bass rather than a tenor, and Idamante a tenor rather than a *castrato*. He rewrote ensembles, eliminated Arbace's arias, and reduced the recitative, besides making other alterations. Richard Strauss has yet another version (published in a vocal score) in which we can find more of Strauss than Mozart. He replaces Elettra with a Cretan high priestess Ismene, who—even more than Elettra—has racist and nationalist concerns. Strauss added music by Mozart from other sources, also his own.[6] He retained, however, a soprano for the role of Idamante, preferring the higher *tessitura* first chosen by Mozart, who had access to a *castrato*.

Despite the constraints imposed by aristocratic patronage, even in *Idomeneo* Mozart was able to convey some politically subversive themes. For instance, he stressed egalitarian principles over those that supported an absolute monarchy. We find Idamante freeing the prisoners at the beginning of the opera: his clemency and democratic leanings prevail over the aristocratic values of an Elettra who, by the end of the play, chooses a death she sees as inevitable. She realizes her world has ended, and a new one is beginning that has no place for her. The old Idomeneo who made a self-serving vow is punished and must hand over the reins of power to his democratic son.

First performed in 1781, *Idomeneo* appealed to the eighteenth-century interest in classical antiquity, particularly Greek classics, and also to the ideals shaping the new age. There are eight operas that I have located on this subject: five are in the eighteenth century, two in the nineteenth, and one in the twentieth (the reworking by Richard Strauss of Mozart's opera). Only two of these operas were composed before Mozart's.

Idomeneus is not a popular character for opera. Even the appeal that the son and the heroines add is not enough to redeem him. The obscurity of the myth that entered the classical canon at a late date may be a contributing factor. In both the seventeenth and the eighteenth century the question of serving the king or serving one's own ideals—country vs. conscience—was a lively one. Pierre Corneille's *Le Cid* (1637) comes to mind, as also Schiller's *The Robbers* (1781). One remembers the classical precedent in Sophocles' Antigone, who supported the "unwritten laws of the gods" against the laws of the city that forbade her to bury her brother. The other main but related theme, namely the intellectual implications of inadvertently vowing to kill one's child, is more properly a topic for debate than the subject for an opera.

Many ancient stories inspired the libretto. We have the obvious parallel with the biblical tale of Jephthah (*Judges* XI) in which a father vows to sacrifice to Jehovah whatever or whomever he first encounters after he returns from victory over the Ammonites. There was *Jephté, tragédie en musique* by Michel Pignolet de Montéclair, performed in 1732; it is the first to be performed at the Opéra on a biblical theme; the theme of sacrifice is now a popular one. In 1751 Handel began to compose *Jephtha*, but was prevented from completing it because of blindness.

In the biblical story the daughter is sacrificed, and she is grateful that her death can help her father win a battle. Simon-Joseph Pellegrin wrote a happy ending for Montéclair to suit his time (we remember Nahum Tate's happy ending for Shakespeare's *King Lear*). This biblical tale is closely paralleled by the story of Iphigenia, and Iphise's name seems to resemble hers. There are obvious comparisons between Idomeneo and Agamemnon. Iphigenia was sacrificed by her father Agamemnon so that he could gain favorable winds for the sake of the Trojan War. Euripides in *Iphigenia at Aulis* does not give the reason for the oracle, simply saying Agamemnon must sacrifice his daughter to Artemis: if he does he will sail and be victorious, if not, he will do neither (*IA* 88–93). This version of Iphigenia we have by Euripides has a happy ending, although that ending was added by a much later writer.[7] But there is some evidence that the original Euripidean ending may have referred to the salvation of Iphigenia by Artemis' substitution of a hind for her at the moment of sacrifice as recounted in earlier epic.[8] According to Sophocles in his *Electra*, Agamemnon killed a stag in a grove of Artemis and boasted about his prowess. Presumably to teach him humility and respect for the gods, an angry Artemis kept him and his fleet at Aulis by sending adverse winds (according to some interpretations). To get favorable winds, he had to kill his daughter.

Euripides' *Iphigenia in Tauris* follows a myth closer to the opera: Iphigenia tells of the storms that arose in Aulis as her father waited with the Greek army to sail to Troy. Calchas said her father would sail only when he had made the appropriate sacrifice to Artemis. He had vowed to sacrifice the fairest thing born each year: Artemis claimed Iphigenia *(IT* 15–33).

There were many closer precedents. We find the story of Idomeneus recounted in Fénelon's novel *Télémaque* (1696). This was followed in 1705 by a spoken tragedy *Idomenée*, by Prosper Jolyot de Crébillon. Racine also recounts the story of Iphigenia in a play. Among the operas on the subject we have two settings by Gluck. Goethe also wrote an *Iphigenie*, which he bases on Euripides' *Iphigenia among the Taurians.*[9] Giambattista Varesco made an Italian libretto from Antoine Danchet and André Campra's *tragédie en musique* (*Idomenée*) performed in 1712, with elements from Fénelon and Crébillon. The work was distinguished by its depiction of a storm and by an offstage chorus of the shipwrecked people. For *Idomeneo*, Varesco rejected the tragic ending in which Idomeneus goes mad (driven insane by Nemesis) and kills his son, but is prevented from killing himself; he also eliminated the love rivalry that Danchet added between Idomeneo and his son, a punishment inflicted by the goddess Venus. We see a shift from the immoral pagan gods to a moral god who embodies some of the aspirations of the Enlightenment. Also eliminated was Elettra's revelation to the high priest of Idomeneo's plan to save his son.

Classics in the eighteenth century were interpreted in accord with the preoccupation of the age. Those who saw the classics as balanced and simple praised them for those virtues. Johann Joachim Winckelmann, the great German classicist and art critic, described classical art as exhibiting *edle Einfalt und stille Grösse*, "noble simplicity and silent grandeur." Gotthold Ephraim Lessing refuted him in his *Laokoön, or On the Limits of Painting and Poetry*, claiming that the statue of Laocoön (a Hellenistic statue that emphasizes the contorted agonies of the victims) itself should be refutation enough. Sophocles' *Philoctetes* and Homer should illustrate the depths and heights of passion and suffering, hardly *stille Grösse*. Both used the classics to further their politics: Lessing's thoughts were revolutionary, whereas the conservative Winckelmann expressed a hope for the peaceful retention of the status quo.

Earlier, in the seventeenth century, the excesses of Greek tragedy were eschewed by Racine and Corneille, who revised the violent classics lest they offend royal sensibilities. The beginning of opera, coinciding with the dawn of the seventeenth century, was dedicated to a revival of Greek tragedy, but, out of deference to the refined taste of noble patrons, much of the violence was avoided. Monteverdi's *Orfeo* does not show the poet torn apart by Bacchantes, as Striggio had first intended; it was revised to show Apollo, his father, inviting Orpheus to heaven to contemplate his beloved Eurydice in the stars and the sun. Avoiding this spiritual ending, Gluck goes further and shows Orpheus physically reunited with his Eurydice. Gluck emphasizes the emotional power of music and endorses bourgeois values over aristocratic spirituality. Mozart walks the same tightrope and wishes to obtain royal patronage, while endorsing some of the new values of the Enlightenment. He uses the classics for both.

Now the classical sources for *Idomeneo*: we find Idomeneus throughout ancient literature, beginning with Homer (?eighth or seventh century B.C.) in both the *Iliad* and the *Odyssey*. He also appears in Pseudo-Apollodorus (second century B.C.), Diodorus Siculus (first century B.C.), Virgil (70 B.C.–19 A.D.), Pausanias (second century A.D.), Quintus Smyrnaeus (fourth century A.D.) and many of Virgil's later commentators. Idomeneus' father was Deucalion, and his grandfather Minos. Idomeneus was one of Helen's unsuccessful suitors, but instead married Meda. He said he would send a hundred ships to Troy if Agamemnon would send at least the same number. He went to Troy and volunteered to fight Hector alone, was one of the warriors hidden in the Trojan Horse, and also later one of the judges who awarded Achilles' arms to Odysseus. The earliest appearance of the myth about Idomeneus' vow and sacrifice is in Servius' commentary on Virgil (fourth century A.D.) According to most versions, the vow was carried out. Idomeneus was banished for his cruelty, and settled in southern Italy. There is a story that Idomeneus judged a beauty contest between Thetis and Medea, and he chose Thetis. Medea said in rebuke, "All Cretans are liars," and this was the origin of the proverb.

Other myths shape this libretto, including Oedipus with its father/son conflict. In its own way, *Idomeneo* is a compendium of Greek tragedy: nobility and sacrifice, with final salvation by the gods who reward human virtue. We also find the theme of love, something rare in Greek tragedy, where, if love is dealt with at all, as in Sophocles' *Trachinians* and Euripides' *Medea* and *Hippolytus*, it spells disaster for all involved. The tragicomedy *Alcestis,* in the place of a satyr play, may deal with love and have a happy ending, but the ironies ensure an unquiet life between the rejoined couple, much like Menelaus with Helen in Euripides' *Helen* or Homer's *Odyssey.* There is just so much one can forgive and forget.

Whereas there are no classical precedents for Electra joining Idomeneus, one can see the obvious parallel with the *Oresteia*: the theme of vengeance, and the sacrifice of Iphigenia. In the opera we have two women at first lusting after vengeance; Electra can be found in the *Oresteia,* and Ilia parallels Cassandra as a captured prisoner from Troy. The unforgiving Elettra comes from classical myth with its ethic of an eye for an eye; she often invokes the Furies who share her bloodthirsty approach. On the other hand, Idamante embodies a new political outlook and suggests a type of progress such as we see at the end of the *Oresteia.* Just as in the *Oresteia,* the gods are the ultimate judges. Nettuno functions here as Athena does there.

Another source for Elettra is Dido. Just as Dido curses Aeneas and commits suicide, so in this opera Elettra curses Idamante and Ilia, and the inference is that she also commits suicide. She certainly speaks of joining Orestes in the underworld. Elettra says the Furies are in her heart: in her first "angry" aria she harnesses them to aid her in her vengeance; in the second they are within. She says Aletto's torch is killing her. Virgil's Dido imagined Aeneas pursuing her, and, comparably Clytemnestra and the Furies menaced Orestes. We remember that Electra helped Orestes, and once again various lines cross: the law of curse and vengeance must cede to rational arbitration. Love must serve the new order.

The Magic Flute also shows the new spiritual aspect of love, and we see the parallel between Ilia and Pamina.

Now Nettuno represents the just law of nature, after imposing a test on his subject. Because he failed the test, Idomeneo must cede his throne to Idamante. By freeing the prisoners, Idamante expresses the thinking of the period. Joseph II, an enlightened ruler who enjoyed music, succeeded to the throne of Austria after the death of his mother Maria Theresa in 1780. Joseph II himself said, "All men are equal at birth: we inherit from our parents no more than animal life, hence there is not the slightest difference between King, Count, bourgeois and peasant. I find nothing in divine or natural law to contradict this equality."[10] Under Joseph II's laws, nobles, if convicted of wrongdoing, would sweep streets like commoners; besides this nobles were subject to the same taxation as the lower classes. Serfdom was abolished and censorship reduced.[11]

We see some of the period's misogyny in the way that the compliant Ilia is considered superior to the passionate and vindictive Elettra. Ilia shows what is expected of a woman, and Elettra the consequences of excess. Women are not trusted to make their own decisions, but should be guided by men. As Goethe said of a woman seeking education, "If she wants to read, surely she can choose a cookbook." According to many savants of the Enlightenment, women are qualified to cook, manage servants, but hardly to be educated or occupy positions of power. The Masons are notorious in this respect, and we know that Mozart joined this movement. Some see this misogynist influence in Schikaneder's libretto for *The Magic Flute*, added to the obvious racism in the way Monostatos is treated. Beaumarchais provided an exception to this misogyny and in his *Figaro* gave a wonderful speech to Marcelline on the emancipation of women. It is often omitted in performance.

Mozart's *Idomeneo* celebrates the triumph of human virtue and the force of intellect over religious superstition. Reason triumphs. Good vanquishes evil. Idamante and Ilia represent pure innocence and goodness, whereas Elettra personifies evil. She is a model for another virtuoso dramatic soprano, the Queen of the Night in the *Magic Flute*, to come ten years later. That Queen of the Night is overcome by the force of light as represented by Sarastro. In a sense both Elettra and the Queen of the Night are overcome by male power; Ilia is one who simply sacrifices herself to the male will. This is another example of opera raising the spectre of a powerful woman, but also providing male restraint and control. In this view I differ from that of McClary and Clément who place more emphasis on the dynamic of the victim.[12]

Order is often represented by the paternal figure of Idomeneo, but he is not the patriarch of the Old Testament, rather, the benign and protective father depicted by Voltaire and Rousseau, and Mozart's own father.[13]

Mozart's opera endorses love, a favorite theme for opera in the late eighteenth century and throughout the history of opera until the twentieth century. Love, with the sacrifices it could entail, was adopted—along with the figure of the benevolent father—as a new ideal.[14] *Fraternité* was an ideal of the French

Jacobins. Love could benefit society with its healing quality (see Locke's political theory). The good and loving father was endorsed by Diderot in *Le père de famille*. Familial harmony was praised by Rousseau, who like Aristotle saw the family as the natural basis for society (*Du contrat social*). The opposite is unruly love driven by egotistic passion rather than social concern, and, in contrast to the self-sacrificing Ilia, Elettra embodies this. We see a criticism of aristocratic sexual license again in the figure of Count Almaviva in the *Marriage of Figaro* and in *Don Giovanni*.

As seen from his letters, Mozart had respect and love for his father, but he also felt dominated by him. He had to conceal his mother's death for several days before he dared reveal the truth to his father. She had been on a tour with Wolfgang in Paris to help him with his career, and no doubt he felt guilty that she fell sick there and died. *Idomeneo*, written shortly after his mother's death (1778), may in part be a working out of some of the problems between father and son. This ideal ending, which included the cession of paternal authority to an enlightened son, may have represented Mozart's own aspirations. Fathers at this time had much power over their sons, as Diderot learned to his dismay when his father committed him to prison with a simple *lettre de cachet*. These tensions are reflected in *Idomeneo*, Mozart's version of *Le père de famille*.

Mozart put music first, over text. He spoke of the wretchedness of the Italian librettos, but acknowledged that they were successful "because in them music rules and compels us to forget everything else. All the more must an opera please in which the plot is well carried out, and the words are written simply for the sake of the music and not here and there to please some miserable rhyme, which God knows, adds nothing to a theatrical representation but more often harms it."[15] This differs from Monteverdi and Gluck, who put poetry first. Mozart had a great dramatic sense, marrying music to drama in a way that marred neither. He made his arias flow into the drama and eliminated Metastasian stasis, where an aria marked the end of a scene.[16] Thus Mozart sometimes eliminated the final cadence so that an aria flows naturally into the subsequent action.

Mozart never abandoned Italian lyric; rather he married it to the text so that it made dramatic sense. In a letter to his father, speaking of *Die Entführung aus dem Serail* but applying the principles to opera in general, he said, "The best thing of all is when a good composer, who understands the stage and is talented enough to make sound suggestions, meets an able poet, that true phoenix; in that case no fears need be entertained as to the applause even of the ignorant."[17]

This opera is a magnificent combination of French, German, and Italian influences in the chorus and ballet, orchestral mastery, and contrapuntal and dramatic finesse, in addition to the mellifluous arias. The themes of Greek tragedy are enhanced by the music, and if one is faithful to the Greek original, then music is essential for conveying, accenting and commenting on the drama. Music is as important as the Greek chorus. Emotional expressions cannot be fully conveyed by words, but they can be through music.

IDOMENEO

Idomeneo has three acts and combines both French and Italian elements: ballet, ensembles, choruses, and orchestrated passages besides arias. Both Gluck and Jommelli shaped Mozart's thinking, particularly Gluck in *Idomeneo*'s religious passages, which resemble many from Gluck's *Alceste* and *Orfée*.

The choice of casting Idamante as a *castrato* may have been influenced by Antoine Danchet's Idamante as *haute-contre* in André Campra's *Idoménée*, mentioned above. Perhaps the higher range of the voice merely conveyed the idea of youth. In late baroque and early classical music, there was a tradition of using high virtuoso voices in male *opera seria* roles. The mingling of *castrato* and soprano voices in the roles of Idamante and Ilia leads to some of the most glorious vocal work in this opera, not only in their duets, but in the quartet with Idomeneo and Ilia.

The opera begins with an overture that lays out the major themes.[18] It is in a brief sonata form, in D major, and conveys majesty and conflict. We have a hint of a storm in the sweeping strings that surge underneath the themes. The overture is marked by the ascending *arpeggio,* which is inverted in the aria *Fuor del mar*, and returns again in the finale (the chorus); both are in D major. The minor conclusion leads into Ilia's recitative, followed by an aria (she is a soprano, which in a sense establishes her moral superiority to Elettra, who is a mezzo). The scene is in Crete after the Trojan War, which Greece waged successfully. We see Ilia, the captured Trojan princess, lamenting the conflict between her loyalty to her father and her love for Idamante, the prince of Crete. She fears he may love Elettra, the Greek princess, instead of her. She mentions vengeance, but concludes she is incapable of hate. Characteristically, her aria is in a moderate tempo and tone, but we find an *agitato* jumping figure in the first violins that expresses her inner conflict. This aria is in sonata form, in G minor, one of Mozart's favorite keys for portraying this emotion.

Idamante enters and says that he will free the prisoners, claiming he is the only prisoner left—of love. He blames the gods for his plight, and his aria, including a fast tempo *allegro*, is more forceful than Ilia's; it recollects the majesty of the beginning of the overture. At least he knows his own mind, and this is conveyed by the music.

Along with the Cretans, the chorus of freed Trojans sings their thanks. Arbace enters to say that the king has been shipwrecked. A mournful scene follows. Elettra now thinks that Idamante will be able to marry Ilia instead of herself; his father might have coerced him into loyalty to the Greeks and thus forced him to marry her, since she was Greek rather than a hated enemy. She sings an impassioned aria that begins in one key (D minor) and ends in another (C minor). This aria, which moves around its tonal center, is shocking in its effect, and its whole-tone descent foreshadows Elettra's impending fall into despair and madness by the end of the opera. Her passionate outburst is the emotional equivalent of two storms: the one that accompanied Idomeneo home and the one that prevents Idamante's departure when his father orders him to leave Crete. As she invokes the Furies to embody her cruel vengeance on the two lovers, Elettra shows herself as proud and jealous. She exits.

The inner storm in Elettra is externalized in the storm at sea before our eyes, just as the words of Idomeneo's aria (*Fuor del mar*) describe the sea within him as more deadly than the sea itself.[19] Mozart does musically what Varesco does in his libretto. Comparably, in *Die Entführung*, Mozart ends Osmin's vengeance aria in a different tempo and key. As Mozart claims, "This is bound to be very effective, for, just as a man in a towering rage oversteps all the bounds of order, moderation and propriety, and completely forgets himself, so too will the music forget itself."[20] We find another wrenching use of the change of keys at the appearance of the sea monster when the storm is in progress: B-flat minor is substituted for the expected C minor. Mozart musically links the vindictive rage of Elettra with that of the sea monster. Strings, harsh brass, and timpani characterize Elettra more than Ilia. There is nothing "giving" or gentle in Elettra's nature.

Ilia, in contrast, is predictably harmonic in her arias. Wind instruments characterize her, and we can see the association with the peaceful breezes that she invokes to carry a message to her beloved. She is the typically redemptive female illustrating what Goethe claimed: "Man aspires for freedom, woman for morality." Men in opera are driven by their individual ambitions, but women by what they know to be absolute right. Remember Creon and Antigone, Jason and Medea. The Enlightenment was preoccupied with individual freedom; there is a consequent desire for the universal good that is lost in the disparagement of church and state. Brophy points this out in the opposition between Don Giovanni and the Commendatore: "When Mozart chose to re-animate this incredible old legend in which the re-animation of a stone memorial was turned to the greater glory of GOD, he was re-animating the GOD whom he and the enlightenment had considered stone cold dead."[21]

We hear a storm in the music and a double chorus of sailors both nearby and in the distance, invoking the gods. Four horns are used and in their way prefigure the trombones that will later signify the divine oracle's presence. They intermingle, displaying all of Mozart's contrapuntal craft.

Idomeneo enters and dismisses his men. He sings his anguish as he recounts his dire vow to sacrifice whomever he first met. The calm he now sees is refuted by the music's counterpoint describing the storm raging in his heart. He imagines the ghost of the victim haunting him. As Idamante approaches, Idomeneo curses the gods, rather than blaming himself. We begin to understand why he will be punished.

Idamante appears. A recognition scene follows, which ends with the rejection of his son by Idomeneo. We hear the theme again from the overture, showing Idomeneo's suffering in relation to Idamante and the sacrifice. Idamante wonders if it is his guilt for loving a Trojan that is to blame. A joyous march follows, in contrast with the sorrow we have witnessed. The chorus sings a hymn to Nettuno. It is religious and celebratory. The first act has ended joyously, with a march and choral dance, a *chaconne*, but the audience senses the tragedy lurking in the background. The families are reunited. The royal family is about to be divided.

Mozart indulges the contemporary taste for marches, having no fewer than three: first, a joyous march concluding the first act to show the return of Idomeneo's sailors; an embarkation march just before the storm that concludes the second act; and, finally, a somber march of the priests near the end of the third. Each is placed in a prominent position and shows the progression of the tragedy, from joy to sorrow and solemnity. The priests march to a Largo in A flat using the strings in a low register, doubled with the bassoons, which Mozart used, like the trombones, in a way to suggest some kind of association with the church.

The second act begins with Idomeneo confessing to Arbace that his son is pledged to Nettuno. Arbace suggests sending the boy away. He sings an aria pledging his fidelity, and (alas) one can see the problem with having two good tenors, and not enough plot to sustain the second. Both of his main arias could be the Abbé's and Mozart's gestures to Joseph II. The first is about a loyal subject's fidelity to his ruler, and the second is a prayer for peace for the ruler and in his kingdom.

One rather glaring anachronism occurs. Idomeneo says here that he will send his son to Argos and have him restore Elettra to her paternal throne, but why is she alive and Orestes dead at this point? Electra in Scene 4 says that soon the rebels will be put down. What rebels? Was Aletes, along with Erigone (according to some mythical accounts the children of Aegisthus and Clytemnestra) in power after Aegisthus and Clytemnestra were killed? Are they, or the people who support them, rebels? Where is Pylades, Electra's husband-to-be?

In her final aria Elettra says she will join Orestes in Hades. Orestes, according to most mythological accounts, lived to be about ninety. Which brings us to the first question, what is Elettra doing in Crete? It would seem she and her brother have killed their mother Clytemnestra and Aegisthus, her lover, who ruled after she killed Agamemnon, following his successful return from the Trojan War. At the end of the war, Orestes was still young. It took some years for him to grow up and join Electra to avenge their father. In this opera, Idomeneo has just returned from the Trojan War. Something is wrong with this chronology unless Idomeneo has been absent for at least ten or twenty years. Ilia seems just to have come from Troy with the other prisoners. They are waiting for Idomeneo to return. Classics and chronology did not mean much to this librettist. Perhaps with music as glorious as this, one should simply accept the fact that a new version of the old myth has been created to suit this opera. Elettra hypothetically will return to Argos and put down a rebellion, presumably because of the crime she committed with her brother. Her presence in Crete seems to be explained by her need for a refuge. In this hypothetical version, she will become queen in Argos, I assume along the lines of Maria Theresa. Aeschylus, Sophocles, and Euripides would have been amused.

Ilia enters to say that she has found another home, here in Crete, and another father in Idomeneo. This is expressed in a beautiful aria (*Se il padre perdei*), which Mozart liked his wife Constanze to sing. This concludes with scales and trills that suggest heavenly bliss.

The few arias we find in this opera contribute to the dramatic realism. Generous Ilia is clearly distinguished from grasping Elettra. In *Se il padre perdei* Ilia accepts her changed circumstance, her loss of her father and country, and takes Idomeneo as her new father, with all the duties and loyalty that that entails. Elettra on the other hand wants to be in control of her circumstance and others; if she cannot be she would prefer to die (*D'Oreste, d'Aiace*). In one case the music is gentle, soothing, melodic and unified; in the other it is abrupt, violent, wandering over a large range and rhythmically driven. Each augments its text and characterizes the singer.

Idomeneo realizes that his son and Ilia probably love each other: Nettuno has destroyed all three of them by demanding Idamante's life. Idomeneo thinks he has found the reason why Idamante is being punished: he should not have released the Trojan prisoners. Idomeneo sings his most outstanding aria *Fuor del mar*, which expresses the madness of the sea, echoed in his own heart. Mozart calls it "the most splendid aria in the opera."[22] Both literally and figuratively (one hears the *mare funesto* and *minacciar* through the music), it conveys menace. The aria conveys a defiant king, railing against the gods, passionate and distraught.

Elettra has a recitative and aria that contrast with her other two arias of vengeance. *Soavi Zeffiri* is an aria of peace and calm, and features an orchestral figure that presents the same inversion of the "Idamante" theme as in Ilia's aria, and in a way she sees herself as Idamante's lover and supplanting Ilia. The music conveys a wish. Nevertheless, the aria seems to concentrate as much on Ilia as Idamante: overcoming her rival is as important as gaining Idamante's love. The aria is accompanied by lyrical strings, a contrast with the way the strings are used in her other two wrath-filled arias. Elettra's words are peculiar, but typical: "My idol! Although another lover yields you reluctantly to me, you cruel man, this does not offend me; / this difficult love attracts me all the more."[23] She finds his withdrawal from her even more pleasing than if he were readily available: the challenge excites her. She invokes the wind, soon to become a tempest. There is no formal end, but the aria merges into a march, featuring winds, brass and drums, typical of the military. It is also typical of Elettra's approach to things: force instead of gentle persuasion.

A peaceful hymn-like farewell follows with the popular *Placido è il mar, andiamo*. Idomeneo, Idamante, and Elettra join in a trio of farewell. But a storm comes up, which we hear in the orchestra as the strings race back and forth in chromatic patterns, the music conveying the roar of the wind and the surge of the waves. There are repeated notes, such as Monteverdi used for his *stile concitato*. A monster should appear at this point, depending on the production (we hear him appear in "a burst of imposing B Flat minor, and [he] is recognized as Nettuno's emissary)."[24] Wind instruments underline the question, "Who is guilty?" Idomeneo rails against Nettuno's injustice. As peace ended the first act, so a storm ends the second, with the people scattering in fright.

The third act begins with Ilia confessing her love. To the accompaniment of flutes, clarinets, bassoons, horns, and strings, she asks the winds to bring tales of her love to Idamante (*Zeffiretti lusinghieri*). A motif suggests light breezes, as the instruments have a melody flowing back and forth, doubling Ilia's voice. Elettra also appealed to the *Soavi Zeffiri*; in Elettra's case it was to enable the ship to take her off with an unwilling lover, whereas for Ilia it is to bring messages of love *to* her lover. Idamante enters. He says that Ilia and his father have rejected him and that a monster menaces. He should wait no longer to meet his destiny. Ilia asks him to stay and confesses her love. They sing a charming duet, concluding with the words that love conquers all. We hear a clash of the two notions: war and love.

Mozart's use of dance is as significant as his use of counterpoint, one conveying the secular and the other the religious element, and, in his operas, he would freely intermingle the two. His first love duet, with its waltz-like rhythm resembling a *Ländler*, conveys the youthful innocence of the hero and the heroine. There are also several ballets, paying tribute to the French tradition already established by Lully and Gluck. The entire opera ends with a ballet that includes a chorus and the coronation of Idamante.

The ensembles show Mozart's drive for the reconciliation of diversity. Elettra and Idomeneo join the lovers, Elettra to express her habitual wrath, and Idomeneo to order his son to depart. Ilia asks to go with Idamante. In the quartet that follows, all express their personal tragedies. Constanze reported that, because he was so moved, Mozart, who was playing the role of Idamante, once left in tears when he was singing this quartet with his family (herself, his father, and his sister).[25] In its agonizing beauty, it expresses the utter distillation of sorrow. Each character in this quartet is clearly differentiated by the music, which ends with Idamante's halting sobs and farewell. Mozart himself answered when his singer Raaff wanted it changed: "My dear friend, if I knew of a single note in this quartet that could be altered, I would do it at once. But there is nothing in this opera that I like so much as this quartet."[26]

The scene shifts from the garden to the palace, with Idomeneo holding court. There is another gratuitous aria for Arbace, which does not dramatically advance the action, although the music is appealing. He offers his life for Idamante, and this offer is ignored. Crowds make their appeal and the High Priest enters to deliver his stern declaration.

Fear and trembling are conveyed by the use of strings in the High Priest's recitative (*tremolando*) and in *O voto tremendo* as a percussive response to the muted trumpets, and a harp-like pizzicato when Nettuno is called upon in the last scene. The harmonies, daring for their time, also seem to partake of the divine.

Metastasio had dispensed with the supernatural in his *opera seria*, but Mozart reinstated it, which may be an affirmation of his own spiritual beliefs. In his letters he expressed belief in the Catholic Church and his immortal soul. Mozart's Masonic lodge *Zur Wohltätigkeit* was the Catholic one, as opposed to the more liberal and deist-inspired *Zur wahren Eintracht*. The choice of a *basso-*

profundo for the voice of the god adds to the divine authority, as also the typical church cadences (plagal, IV-I) in the recitative reinforce the religious quality. The minor progressions give a hint of the sternly authoritarian nature of this god.

Swayed, like Oedipus, by the suffering of his people, the king confesses. He says the victim is Idamante, and we hear a reprise of Idamante's theme (which some also call the sacrifice theme) from the overture. A dignified march follows as the scene is set for the terrible sacrifice.

Themes can be associated with various characters. The way that these themes are developed and used in various contexts adds to the musical commentary on the drama. When the priest demands to know what can be done to save the people, and when Idomeneo says the victim demanded is Idamante, we hear a theme we associate with Idamante: it resembles a sigh. Repeated themes function somewhat as a Greek chorus in tragedy, providing commentary for a given text. It is interesting that as Gluck used the solo oboe to represent the sacrificial victim, so also Mozart features a mournful song played by the oboe as Idomeneo names Idamante the intended victim. This melody is followed by the chorus commenting on this terrible vow. The bleak chorus *O voto tremendo, spettacolo orrendo* is in C minor over stately triplets such as Mozart uses for the Commendatore's death in *Don Giovanni;* later Beethoven would make use of this in the funeral march of the *Eroica*.

Perhaps the prime issue investigated here, making this opera decisively of the Enlightenment, is the issue of human sacrifice. It probably existed in ancient Greece, although it characterized the civilizations of the Ancient Middle East more than the Greeks. Along with the precedent of Jephthah, and Abraham and Isaac, another example comes from the *New Testament:* God himself offered his own son for sacrifice on the cross to expiate the sins of mankind. Ivan Nagel tells us that "the opera devotee and skeptic" Baron Grimm, in his review of Lemierre's play *Idomenée*, expressed "the rudest scorn for God 'who must sacrifice his son because he once allowed an apple to be eaten.'"[27] The Enlightenment questioned the authority of religion for commanding man to commit what he must rationally know to be a crime. As Walter Burkert has said, "With human sacrifice, religion and morality part company."[28]

The idea of making a vow to a god was regarded with suspicion in the Enlightenment. Voltaire satirized the idea of an irrational vow in a story called *Le taureau blanc*, telling of a father making a vow to kill his daughter if she mentions the name of her lover. Voltaire provides a happy ending, but underlines the idiocy of the vow, particularly one going against nature and society. Hobbes and Locke also focused on this problem, and Diderot investigated it in his *Encyclopédie*. Hobbes says explicitly, "They that Vow anything contrary to any law of Nature, Vow in vain."[29] Kant was also critical of God's command to Abraham to sacrifice Isaac.

Mozart's *Idomeneo* reflects a just god who alters his unjust command, inspired by Ilia's vow of love and offer of self-sacrifice. The emphasis in the libretto is on the intransigence of the priest rather than the god, and this may go along with the general anticlerical feeling of the period, as evidenced in

Voltaire's writings. In 1762, Jean Calas was convicted of killing his son lest he become a Catholic (falsely, it seems, since his son was probably a suicide); he in turn was tortured and executed for this act.[30] Voltaire used this story to illustrate religious excesses. As Gotthold Ephraim Lessing asked, "What is the good of having the right beliefs if we do not live rightly?"[31]

Voltaire and others blamed the priests for corruption. As Voltaire said, "From Calchas, who murdered the daughter of Agamemnon, sacerdotal power has been disastrous to the world."[32] Mozart, who had bad relations with the Archbishop of Salzburg, Hieronymus Colloredo, was ready to blame priests. Joseph II reduced the rights of the clergy and the influence of the Pope by refusing to allow publication of new papal bulls. Joseph II issued his Edict of Toleration in the same year that *Idomeneo* was performed (1781).

Various critics who write about this opera, like Daniel Heartz, blame the priests, and emphasize that it is a priest who demands that the sacrifice be performed. I see rather a concerned priest relaying the complaints of the people, who demand that a solution be found to the destruction caused by Nettuno's monster.[33] Dramatically the crisis echoes the plague inflicted on Thebes: Oedipus must sacrifice himself. Like many idealists of the period, Mozart, who joined the Masonic movement, probably believed more in God and Goodness than in organized religion, but, despite his association with corrupt clergy, he was conservative about religion. In the opera, Mozart, along with Varesco, blamed Idomeneo more than the priest or the god. Johann Pezzl claimed that Varesco's words showed "the sort of wit that we associate with the breviary and hagiography, and with the school and monastery."[34] It is not likely that such a man would write like Voltaire, or overtly question the validity of the priesthood.

Friedrich Melchior von Grimm, an important opera critic contemporary with Mozart, saw this opera as anticlerical: "What I want to see painted in the tragedy of Idomeneo is that dark spirit of uncertainty, of fluctuation, of sinister interpretations, of disquiet and of anguish, that torments the people and from which profits the priest."[35] The music certainly underlines the dark spirit, but, as mentioned above, I do not share Grimm's view of the corrupt priest, which seems more a symptom of Enlightenment's anticlericalism than Mozart's own intention.

Euripides flourished during the period of the sophists, in the late fifth century B.C. His lost play *Bellerophon* raised some of the questions that we find in *Idomeneo*, as is shown by the fragment, "If the gods do evil, they are not gods."[36] Elsewhere in this play the existence of the gods is called into question because of the existence of evil in the world and the thriving of the wicked (fr. 286). We find other indictments of the gods in Euripides' plays (e.g., *Helen*, *Bacchae*). Iphigenia says that gods do not do evil: the goddess does not ask for human sacrifice, but bloodthirsty humans themselves are responsible, (*Iphigenia among the Taurians*, 385–391), and Heracles says he does not believe the stories about the gods saying they commit evil, for gods, if truly gods, are deficient in nothing: it is poets that lie (*Heracles*, 1341–1346). These echo many speculations of the period, such as the famous statement given by Protagoras about the gods: "On the subject of the gods, I cannot know whether they exist or do not exist, nor what form they have, because there are so many things that hinder this investigation: the obscurity of the question and the shortness of man's life."[37] Idomeneo accuses Nettuno in terms resembling Bellerophon's: "If you demand another victim because of my mistake, I cannot hand over to you someone who is innocent; this demand itself proves you are unjust." Sacrilege is added to sacrilege as Idamante kills the monster sent by Nettuno. Idomeneo says, "O terrible, now Nettuno, angry at this new offense, will oppose us." Nevertheless, the slaughter of the monster is a heroic act. Idamante is also heroic in offering his life to his father and for his country. He goes to his death willingly with words that resemble Iphigenia's: both had devotion to *Pater* and *Patria*.[38] Mozart and Varesco would be familiar with this text from Racine, Goethe, Gluck, Danchet, if not Euripides directly.[39]

There are classical precedents for dire consequences following the killing of animals, such as Agamemnon's killing a deer sacred to Artemis and having to sacrifice his child in repayment. One thinks of the bull that Minos, another Cretan king, son of Europa and Zeus and grandfather of Idomeneus, did *not* sacrifice to Poseidon, as he should have done. In consequence Pasiphae was cursed so that she developed a strange love for the bull and Daedalus created a contraption whereby she might mate with it; the Minotaur was born, another Cretan monster that took its share of human offerings. The opera draws on the entire ominous heritage of Crete with Idomeneo, besides Mycenae and both Atreus and Agamemnon through Elettra.

Neither Mozart nor Varesco question the *existence* of the gods: at all points Idomeneo believes in the existence of Nettuno. What he questions is the justice of the vow: he also calls fate barbaric. The ending, which shows a just god, underlines human error, and Idomeneo himself is punished. Ilia's love and self-sacrifice are what finally win over the god, and these "virtues" are quite different from their ancient classical predecessors, although we find hints in Euripides. In Sophocles, Ajax fought for his own honor rather than serve the community. In Euripides this was a new type of heroism, namely that of the victim, or the power of the powerless.[40] Ilia now renounces self, for a greater good, much as Iphigenia did when she agreed to give her life for Greece. Devotion and self-sacrifice are praised. Christianity also endorsed these qualities, which are exemplified by our heroine. We see a strange and interesting mixture of the ancient with what was, for Mozart, modern.

Trumpets interrupt the solemnity to announce that Idamante has slain the sea-monster. Idamante freely offers his life to his father, saying that if his father and country will be saved, he does not fear death. His father asks for a last kiss, rather like Andromache in the *Trojan Women* asking her son Astyanax to kiss her for the last time just before he is killed because the Greeks considered him a threat (761). This is a dramatically poignant scene, and naturally Idomeneo hesitates, but then resolves to fulfill his vow. Ilia enters and offers to die in his place, saying that it is fit that an enemy of Greece die rather than a friend, she being Trojan.

One of the main issues involved here is the one that Sophocles raised in *Antigone*. When do personal or familial values override those of the state? Antigone went to her death defending the former, and Creon was destroyed because he was intransigent in his defense of the latter. Idomeneo must either serve his people and kill his son, or protect his own family and not fulfill the vow. There have already been innocent deaths in Crete because he did not carry out his promise. So there is another issue here: keeping a promise to a god, particularly to a god who demands a human sacrifice.

Kant bypassed the moral problem of Abraham and Isaac by questioning whether it was God who issued the command that a father kill his son.[41] Ilia says something comparable: "The gods are not tyrants; you have misinterpreted what the gods want." She in turn echoes Iphigenia in Euripides' *Iphigenia among the Taurians,* who could not blame the sacrifice of humans on the gods, but said rather that it is man who attributes to the god his own sin, for she thinks no god evil (*IT* 380–391).

Introduced by trombones, which usually heralded the supernatural, the Oracle/Nettuno speaks, the only basso-profundo. (Trombones are typical of the underworld: in Monteverdi's *Orfeo*, they herald Charon, a bass.) Mozart used trombones in a comparable way in *The Magic Flute* to indicate the supernatural. Both musically and thematically, the final scenes of *Idomeneo* have much in common with the final scenes of *The Magic Flute*: through their love, after undergoing severe tests, the two lovers overcome all.

Mozart shared Gluck's appreciation for simplicity, particularly for the sake of the drama, but he added his own contrapuntal complications. He borrowed freely from Gluck where needed; for instance, the divine voice, the *deus sub terra*, that resolves the action at the end of *Idomeneo*, was certainly influenced by Gluck's *Alceste*, and both divine voices played against trombones. One tends to associate brass with enlightened authority.

Wind instruments accompany *recitativo* passages preceding the two final arias, as if god were present to endorse the final summation. It was in *Idomeneo* that Mozart first introduced clarinets in an opera. The horns, flutes, oboes, bassoons, and trumpets are also striking. When the god speaks, trombones add to the unearthly quality, and this unearthly quality through the use of winds will be found again in *The Magic Flute*; the supernatural quality of the Commendatore's invitation to supper in *Don Giovanni* is also comparable.

The oracle announces that love has saved Idamante and Ilia, but Idamante must replace Idomeneo as King since retribution must be exacted for *il gran trascorso*, not living up to promises. Such a transgressor is not fit to be king. Idamante will rule in his place with Ilia as his wife. As Idomeneo announces that Idamante will be king, the theme associated with Idamante and sacrifice is reversed and rises instead of descends. Idamante's fortunes are on the rise. The Oracle says love has conquered (*ha vinto amore*), carrying this theme of the play to the proper conclusions.

Mozart eliminated some of the best arias in the first performance because he thought the last act too long: Idamante's *No, la morte io non pavento*;

Elettra's magnificent *D'Oreste, d'Ajace / Ho in seno i tormenti;*[42] and finally Idomeneo's *Torna la pace al core.* We are fortunate that most modern productions retain them all, but this shows how sensitive Mozart was to what he thought was dramatically proper, even if it meant sacrificing his own music. He also cut Varesco's speech for the oracle, and it is worth quoting his letter to his father, written on November 29, 1780:

Tell me, don't you think that the speech of the subterranean voice is too long? Consider it carefully. Picture to yourself the theater, and remember that the voice must be terrifying—must penetrate—that the audience must believe that it really exists. Well, how can this effect be produced if the speech is too long, for in this case the listeners will become more and more convinced that it means nothing. If the speech of the Ghost in Hamlet were not so long, it would be far more effective. It is quite easy to shorten the speech of the subterranean voice, and it will gain thereby more than it will lose.[43]

We can see from this how Mozart is not only familiar with Shakespeare, but developed his own aesthetic theory of dramatic effectiveness accordingly.

The theme of love satisfies the taste of the period, which emphasized love as much as philosophy.[44] Nicholas Till quotes Norman Bryson on Watteau's *Meeting in a Park*: "An attempt is being conducted by a small group of highly civilized people, to take the greedy, raw material of *eros* and transform it into a principle of social harmony."[45] Much eighteenth-century thought claims that love had to be sublimated to make civilization run smoothly. The ancient classical world felt the same. Untamed, *eros* could lead to disaster. De Laclos' *Les Liaisons Dangereuses*, 1782, a year later than *Idomeneo*, and de Sade illustrate the excesses.

Most of Mozart's operas have a sentimental undercurrent. By means of their love and self-sacrifice, from Ilia to the Countess Almaviva and Pamina, women exhibit this quality and save their men. Even in *La Clemenza di Tito* the "evil" Vitellia saves her hero: her reformed character implies that Elettra and the Queen of the Night could also be tamed by love. Nevertheless, Elettra and the Queen of the Night, precisely because they are not tamed (their voices run all over the scale), remain as threats to the order imposed by the gods through benevolent male rulers (Idomeneo and Sarastro). By the end of their operas both Elettra and the Queen of the Night have been overcome by male authority, but they do not admit defeat in their musical virtuosity.

Elettra has a final fury-filled aria and asks to join her brother Orestes in death. She says that she endures the torments of Orestes and Ajax in her breast and sees the torch of the Fury Aletto. She begs the serpent monsters to kill her; or that she be given a sword. She either falls here—with the implication that she dies on stage—or she leaves the scene, never to be heard from again, after expressing her wish to die. A tour de force, this aria makes the storm visible in Elettra's rage. She is the obvious scapegoat and all miseries depart with her.

Forgiveness was a theme of the "Catholic" Enlightenment in Austria, and in *Idomeneo* we find forgiveness by an "enlightened" god. Elettra was not so enlightened, and her intransigence and her wrath are unrelenting. In her vengeance aria, which features a recapitulation, the return to the first theme, which was in D minor, is now in C minor (D minor is the primary key of *Don Giovanni* and the *Requiem*).[46] D minor is also the key of the Queen of the Night's vengeance aria in *The Magic Flute*; she exhibits the same unrelenting wrath as Elettra. Elettra's madness is conveyed by the strongly unrelated key relationship of C minor and D minor. Just as the themes cannot be reconciled, neither can she. This is a brilliant musical comment, because it is the same key as the complaint of the sailors in their C minor chorus. The key is also that of Elettra's final angry aria.

Elettra dies as she does in Strauss's opera, *Elektra*, but in the latter she dies spontaneously in triumph. Here she dies in defeat and, like Dido, she will not live longer in a world that does not suit her. These heroines set the stage for future spontaneous deaths: Isolde in her *Liebestod* in Wagner's *Tristan and Isolde*, and Elsa at the end of *Lohengrin*. These women are not killed by others, but choose their own exits. If they cannot fashion their lives the way they would like, then at least they can choose their deaths. This spontaneous operatic death is neither that of men, nor classical in origin.

Ilia expresses her love for Idamante and Idomeneo in a final aria that speaks of peace returning. It is filled with brilliant figures and is a good vehicle for virtuoso display: the main melodic figure descends and then rises on the tonic, in contrast to the simple rise on the tonic in the overture. The music conveys peace and reconciliation, wisdom attained through suffering. Idamante's coronation follows with a ballet, and the chorus concludes with an invocation to Love (*Amor*), the god of marriage (*Imeneo*) and Juno (*Giunone*). This brings us home to the key of D major with which the opera began.

CONCLUSION

Mozart's genius allows us a glimpse of evil, and the darkness in human nature is effectively conveyed by his music and by the symbolism of the drama. *Opera seria*, like Greek tragedy, shows us a battle of humans with the evil within them: Idamante and Ilia win; Idomeneo and Elettra lose. The storm is seen to be internal as well as external. Death is the definer, and because the two are willing to give their lives for others, they achieve not only self-definition, but heroism.

Mozart was a product of the Enlightenment. We find that, particularly in the Lorenzo da Ponte operas, Mozart had in mind social criticism and themes that spoke of change along humanitarian lines. *Idomeneo* prefigures this. Da Ponte says in his preface to *Le nozze di Figaro* (1786) that it was "a new kind of spectacle" that showed the "dynamics of the social classes," and we see this in Beaumarchais' *Le mariage de Figaro* and Schiller's *Kabale und Liebe*, which circulated in 1784.[47] We find revolutionary suggestions in Figaro's song, *Se vuol ballare Signor Contino*, from *Le Nozze di Figaro*; and we remember the quintet celebrating liberty, *Viva la libertà*, from *Don Giovanni*: it is a sinner who is singing this.[48] The least overtly moral operas by Mozart seem to be those with the strongest social conscience. This was the time of change, as Beaumarchais claimed in the finale of Salieri's *Tarare* (1787): "*Homme, ta grandeur sur la terre, / N'appartient point à ton état: Elle est toute à ton caractère.*" After quoting this Pestelli goes on to note, "In musical terms, unisons, sforzatos and minor keys in a *Sturm und Drang* mould have been given revolutionary significance."[49] It is arguable that the *Sturm und Drang* period begins before the French Revolution and can be traced to Goethe's *Götz von Berlichingen* (1773) and *Die Leiden des jungen Werthers* (*The Sorrows of Young Werther*, 1774). In both cases we have a young man who opposes society, and we can see this same type of young man in Idamante, with his democratic ideas of freeing slaves.

Political ideals of the Enlightenment for society can be seen alongside Gothic excesses in the individuals, and we think again of *Don Giovanni*. *Idomeneo* shows Locke's political philosophy in action, to say nothing of Kant and Descartes. These philosophies all believed that happiness and government either are, or should be, based on the good. God was closely linked with goodness, and one learnt through empiricism, because God could create a man with an inquiring mind. Even Nettuno learns the force of love and overturns the ruler who has not lived up to his mandate to provide good government for the people. Idomeneo's reckless vow brought disaster on everyone.

Freemasonry with its egalitarian attitudes influenced Mozart. Idamante's liberation of the prisoners shows some of this enlightened attitude. The benevolence of Pasha Selim in *Die Entführung aus dem Serail* is comparable: he frees Belmonte even though he is the son of an old enemy.

There were three major social groups vying for power at this time: absolutists, aristocrats, and the bourgeoisie. The absolutist group often aligned itself with the bourgeoisie and effected reforms of the former feudal systems. Louis XIV tamed his nobles by keeping them busy at Versailles; Frederick the Great made his Junkers into bureaucrats, and in Sweden Gustavus III also took privileges away from his aristocrats. Mozart and Varesco were not unaware of these currents, and endorsed the reforms. Maria Theresa died in 1780, a year before this opera, and it is not too far-fetched to see Idamante embodying the new ideals of Joseph II—as Mozart would wish them to be. In this case we can see Elettra as representative of feudal nobility: one who arrogates rights by virtue of her birth. Both Elettra as feudal aristocrat and Idamante as enlightened monarch are apt representatives of the conflicting class roles of this period.

We can see other significance abstracted from the myth: Idomeneo sacrifices his son, as all countries sacrifice their young when they go to war or pursue their own collective power. Idamante is heroic in sacrificing himself for the common good and the restoration of peace. Just as Odysseus, with his skill at negotiation, was symbolically awarded the arms of Achilles over Ajax, the paradigmatic warrior—because after the war the skills of peace were more important than the skills of war—so Idamante, by his act of self-sacrifice, is working for peace. He says, "No, I am not afraid of death, O gods, if it brings your love and the beautiful tranquility of peace to my country and my father." Ilia also endorses peace and by offering her life shows her ultimate commitment; she joins the ranks of women who risk their lives for the sake of their loves. As Ilia says, "Heaven wishes Greece to be free of its enemies, not to lose its children." She calls herself an enemy (claiming her Phrygian ancestry makes her "enemy by nature to the Greek name"), but as a result of her act shows herself as a friend to the country and beloved of Idamante, and the source of new children. Idomeneo sings of peace returning in his final aria (*Torna la pace al core*), and characteristically refers to himself, whereas Idamante refers to the public good. The proper ruler is in place, and the proper woman at his side, both endorsed by God and the people: rulers for an enlightened age.

The classic predecessors here are a mélange of epic, various myths, and tragedies. One can understand why the librettist was taken seriously at this time, since he was creating the bulk of the textual narration. By contrast, Mikis Theodorakis in his *Medea* will simply translate.

Mozart's genius would not allow him merely to replicate what had gone before; he incorporated it, varied it, and transformed it. His librettists reflected the times, and Mozart's daring humanitarian choices show him flirting with a liberalism that flew in the face of the conservatism that he knew and constantly defied.

It is difficult not to see in Idamante's struggles some of Mozart's with his demanding father. Ilia is a blending of his mother and Constanze: loyal and supportive. He adored women. The women in this play are touchstones for good and evil. Elettra is the monstrous woman who seeks to slake her own desires, even when they will be destructive for the man. Ilia will lay down her life for her beloved. Ilia displays enlightened love, which played so great a role in the literature and philosophy of the time. This love is beneficent and good for society, whereas Elettra's was destructive. The music reflects this difference, and Ilia's flowing and lyric arias win out over her rival's jagged and tempestuous songs. Harmony enhances Ilia: her generous act qualifies her to be an enlightened queen, fit to rule with her enlightened husband, who freed the prisoners at the start. Idamante also offered his life, but it was his life that Nettuno was demanding; Ilia's generosity can be regarded as the more heroic, because it was freely offered. Thus Ilia, as many of our other heroines, shows *arete* or "virtue," which elevates her above all others in this opera.

Mozart also shows us the face of death and evil, and allows us to approach the sublime by the terror that such contemplation inspires in us. The quartet that caused Mozart to weep anticipates the late quartets of Beethoven. This, if anything, shows disparate personalities unified in enlightened harmony. Mozart does not abandon us to the abyss; rather we are rescued by the formal sublimity of his art.

Leviathan smiles in the music of Mozart: life is affirmed after death has threatened. In this opera, it is also the son, the child who knows more than the parent, who brings the promise of a new world, one tempered by mercy and love. A daughter and wife advance this dream. The humanity of man prevails over the inhumanity of gods, and the gods themselves endorse the process, as

Joseph II himself so often gave his approval to Mozart. Mozart, the eternal child genius, leaves us the sun, not the night; in contrast to the powers of darkness, he is truly an enlightened king of the day.

APPENDIX
OPERAS ABOUT IDOMENEO

André Campra (bap. 1660–1744) (b. Aix-en-Provence, France)
Idomenée (1712)

Baldassare Galuppi (1706–1785) (b. Burano, Italy)
Idomeneo (1756)

Giuseppe Gazzaniga (1743–1818) (b. Verona, Italy)
Idomeneo (1790)

Wolfgang Amadeus Mozart (1756–1791) (b. Salzburg, Austria)
Idomeneo, re di Creta (1781)

Vincenzo Federici (1764–1826) (b. Pesaro, Italy)
Idomeneo (1806)

Giuseppe Farinelli (1769–1836) (b. Este, Italy)
Idomeneo (1811)

Ferdinando Paer (1771–1839) (b. Parma, Italy)
Idomeneo (1794)

Richard Strauss (1864–1949) (b. Munich, Germany)
Idomeneo (Mozart) (1931)

Berlioz's *Les Troyens:*
Making the Romans Romantic

Hector Berlioz has both irritated and pleased his fellow musicians. Rarely has a composer met with such love and such hate. Mendelssohn claimed, "Without a spark of talent, he gropes in the dark while he thinks he is the creator of a new world."[1] Paganini admired him, whereas Wagner claimed he was out for money and lacked depth. Rimsky-Korsakov admired his rhythm, and said, "Berlioz is the only indisputable genius in all music."[2] Busoni saw his music pointing the way for future generations. Stravinsky said, "Berlioz's reputation as an orchestrator has always seemed highly suspect to me. He was a great innovator. But the music he had to instrumentate was often poorly constructed harmonically."[3] Both Wagner and Stravinsky said about Berlioz negative things that were often said about them. Although Paul Robinson has claimed, "*Les Troyens* is incomparably the most important French opera of the nineteenth century," critics are still divided.[4]

This splendid example of French grand opera was conceived in 1856 and finished around 1858. It was considered too difficult because of resources it required—and inordinately long. Nevertheless Berlioz estimated that even at four hours and twenty-six minutes, "it was shorter than the uncut *Tristan*."[5] Only the second half of the opera was performed in the first production in 1863 at Paris' *Théâtre lyrique,* and there were other extensive cuts. Budgetary and physical disasters plagued the opening. Berlioz agreed to the cuts because he wanted his opera performed, even in truncated form. But a great disservice was done to the subtle details that bind the two great parts together, and to the overall conception. Berlioz never heard the entire opera in his lifetime. Only after his death in 1869 was the work performed in its entirety, first in 1890, in Germany (Karlsruhe). Colin Davis' recording of the work still has the reputation for being the most expensive recording ever made. Only in 1969 was the full score published.[6]

Berlioz wrote *Les Troyens* at the peak of his creative powers. He began it around 1856, at the urging of Princess Carolyne Sayn-Wittgenstein, a close friend of Lizst. Berlioz had been entranced by Virgil from his early youth and quoted him frequently in his memoirs and letters. His father, a doctor, was his major tutor, and in addition to naming his son Hector, he encouraged his son to read and translate Latin. When the young Hector was working on Book 4 of Virgil's *Aeneid*, which recounts the tragedy of Dido, he wept and was so moved that his father had to stop him. Berlioz also describes his Virgilian obsession in a letter that he wrote to the Princess:

As for the principal object of the work, the musical rendering of the characters and the expression of their feelings and passions, it was always the easiest part of my task. I have spent my life with this race of demi-gods; I know them so well that I feel as if they must have known me. And this recalls to me a boyhood experience which will show you how fascinated I was from the first by these splendid creatures of the ancient world. . . . One Sunday I was taken to Vespers. The sad persistent chant of the psalm *In exitu Israel* had the magnetic effect on me that it still has today, and plunged me deep in the most real and vivid day-dreams of the past. . . . I heard the great palaces of Laurentium ring with lamentation—and I was seized by an overwhelming sadness. I left the church, sobbing uncontrollably, and cried for the rest of the day, powerless to contain my epic grief. Is that not a strange and marvelous manifestation of the power of genius? A poet dead thousands of years shakes an artless ignorant boy to the depths of his soul with a tale handed down across the centuries, and with scenes whose radiance devouring time has been powerless to dim.[7]

Berlioz (1803–1869) lived through the epoch after the French Revolution that saw the successive accessions to the throne of Napoleon, Louis XVIII, Charles X, Louis-Philippe, formerly Duc d'Orléans (called the "citizen king"), and finally, Napoleon III. He had sympathy for the ideals of the Revolution, but also expressed respect for royalty. He had an artist's approach to politics and did not let the contradictions bother him: he admires Aeneas, and all he stands for, as much as Dido.[8] Many times he wrote pieces in support of his ruler, as for example his "Emperor Cantata" for Napoleon III. But he was also well known for his lavish orchestral setting, with double chorus, of *La Marseillaise,* and received an enthusiastic letter from its author, Rouget de Lisle, who wanted to collaborate with him on an opera (*Othello*). He adored marches, and his inspiration could be musical as much as political; there are three marches in *Les Troyens*. The entire opera ends with a march, in contrast to the quiet, tragic ending of Purcell's *Dido and Aeneas*.

This was an age of imperial expansion. In 1798 Napoleon launched his Egyptian campaign. France was establishing itself in Africa: Algeria (1830), then Morocco (1844), Guinea (1849), and Madagascar (1860s). How appropriate for Berlioz to write an opera based on a work that addressed the very problem of imperialism, while at the same time supporting it![9]

Virgil was in a comparable position, dependent on the emperor Augustus for his support, but also sensitive to the devastation wrought by imperial conquest. One of the differences between Virgil and Berlioz is that Berlioz seems more seduced by the pomp he saw, and contributed to it himself with stirring marches that glorified the establishment of imperial order. His opera ends with a vision of Imperial Rome that seems uncritically the final word, although fresh in our memory are the victims sacrificed on its altar. He orchestrated like a painter, mixing colors and hues, and masterfully varying the intensity. A poet of music, he was daring in the use of rhythm, keys, harmonies, form, melodies—and of course, orchestration. Politics were secondary to music and emotions, but the interweaving informed the final text.

This was indeed a time of extravagant operas in support of empire. Meyerbeer's *L'Africaine*, which was performed two years after Berlioz's *Les Troyens* in 1865, enjoyed a great success. The critic G. Spada said of Meyerbeer's opera that it "bears the stamp of that proud genius who has left such a bright mark on contemporary musical art."[10] The stories of the heroine in *L'Africaine* and of Dido are parallel. The *Africaine* is an "oriental" female (Sélika), who tries to divert Vasco da Gama from his imperialist mission. He flees her embrace, and as he sails off she kills herself by inhaling the poisonous fumes of a flower (*mancinilla*).

For the death of Cassandra, Berlioz was also probably influenced by Gioachino Rossini's *Le siége de Corinthe* (1826) with its tragic end. Félicien David's *La perle du Brésil* (1851) and his comic masterpiece *Lalla-Roukh* (1962) carry on the Orientalist agenda, and his *Herculanum* (1859) showed the destruction of an ancient city with the eruption of Vesuvius. Berlioz's own teacher Jean-François Le Sueur respected the mythological past, as shown in his opera *Ossian* (1804). These in their own way may have contributed to the conception of *Les Troyens*, if only to correct what Berlioz saw as their mistakes: except for *Ossian*, the operas of these composers were reviewed by Berlioz.[11]

Berlioz owes much to Meyerbeer, but did not enjoy Meyerbeer's popular success. It was only *Les Troyens* that freed Berlioz financially so that he could give up his thankless job as a critic, six years before his death.[12] Lindenberger claims that Berlioz's opera "spells out its imperial theme even more explicitly than Meyerbeer's opera."[13]

Berlioz was continually on the move physically and emotionally, never as appreciated in France as he was in Germany, England, and the United States. He understood the life of an exile, and he sympathized with the displaced while simultaneously harboring a strange nostalgia for the conquerors.

Berlioz had sympathy for his characters. Dido is a Phoenician from Tyre (in modern Lebanon) who sailed to North Africa and came to rule the land given her by the Gaetulian Iarbas; she is also a woman abandoned in love.[14] Berlioz's Énée may not be as gallant as Purcell's, but he is certainly more passionate, and ostensibly more heroic (Purcell's Aeneas seems to get more excited about hunting boar than pursuing Dido, let alone empire.) It is likely that Berlioz identified with his hero, forced to carry out his duty while being shredded emotionally. He was fond of quoting Victor Hugo in lines like *Je marchais tout vivant dans mon rêve étoilé* (*Ruy Blas*, Act 3, Scene 4, slightly paraphrased); he grew up nurtured on heroism and romanticism.

Berlioz would not allow his beloved Virgil to be translated by anyone who, in his estimation, did not understand the poet or the composer's own music. He did the libretto himself, and through elaborate alexandrines and florid vocabulary revived a classical diction that Hugo was working to eliminate. But the musical quality of Berlioz's words works.

Les Troyens comprises *La prise de Troie* in two acts, and *Les Troyens à Carthage* in three acts. The first half is based on Book 2 of Virgil's *Aeneid*, and the second on Books 1 and 4, but Berlioz takes freely from other books, such as Aeneas' comment to his son about learning bravery from him, but happiness from others (*Aen.* 12. 435–436). In the libretto this becomes, "Others will show you how to be happy, I shall only teach you the warrior's virtue, and to respect the gods.[15] Énée adds a note of piety ("respect for the gods") whereas the original *pius Aeneas* speaks only of warfare and heroism (*Aen.* 12. 436–440).

It is obvious that Berlioz used the story of Dido to provide commentary on things he was witnessing politically. He also was psychologically drawn to her. Many operas were written about Dido. There are fewer on Aeneas and the Trojan War. The sufferings of the Trojan Women provide an apt subject for the twentieth century; the Polish composer Joanna Bruzdowicz (1943–) composed *Les Troyennes* (1972) as a protest against war. Likewise Cassandra often fascinated modern composers because she was someone who revealed the true horror of war but was never believed.[16] She also predicted vengeance. Theodore Antoniou's *Cassandra* (1969) provides political commentary on Greece. These uses differ from Berlioz's. He was interested more in the artistic balance between Cassandra's death and Dido's: the dramatic and emotional potential was enormous.

Aeneas is a character only in operas that include Dido. Achilles is a more popular subject for opera than Aeneas, who is a more passive hero; it is perhaps only in Berlioz's opera and Johann Wolfgang Franck's *Aeneas der trojanischen Fürsten Ankunft in Italien* (1680), that Aeneas is fully appreciated as a hero. In their literature and in the school curriculum, the English in the nineteenth century showed preference for the *Aeneid* over the *Iliad*, perhaps precisely for its endorsement of empire; since they did not have as strong an operatic tradition as the French, Germans, or Italians, Aeneas was not lauded in opera.

In the epic, the main action at Troy is recounted by Aeneas when he is in Dido's court. Both stories are trimmed to an artistically manageable form for Berlioz's opera.

Berlioz used other sources, for instance, a painting by Guérin of Aeneas recounting his sufferings to Dido, which led to a comparable scene in the opera. Gluck's *Orfeo ed Euridice* may have inspired the scene with the bard Iopas. The dialogue between Lorenzo and Jessica from Act 5 of Shakespeare's *Merchant of Venice* lies behind the love duet between Dido and Aeneas, and the words match well. Berlioz admired Shakespeare as well as Virgil. He said, "I am quite transported by some words of old Nestor in Shakespeare's *Troilus and Cressida*. I have just reread this amazing parody of the *Iliad*, where none the less Shakespeare makes Hector even greater than Homer did."[17]

Harriet Smithson, Berlioz's first wife, with their son Louis inspired the tableau of Andromache and her son—one the wife of Hector, the Trojan hero, and the other the son of Hector, the composer. However, we also find Andromache mentioned in Virgil: Aeneas climbs to the roof of the palace by a gate that Andromache used when she brought Astyanax to visit his grandfather Priam (*Aen.* 2. 453–457). Aeneas again meets her in Buthrotum in Epirus where she has founded a new "little Troy" (*Aen.* 3. 349).

Louis, who pursued the profession of a sailor, was the model for Hylas. Berlioz's own life and his desire for romance, besides his dedication to duty, give *Les Troyens* its unique character.

We see at the outset that empire is the major theme of *Les Troyens*; in fact, the cry *Italie!* echoes throughout the opera, as does the Trojan March itself, which appears in various altered forms in both parts and at the conclusion of the opera during the spectacular tableau of Rome. Berlioz was much impressed by Aeneas' remark when he saw the Trojan battles depicted on Dido's palace walls: *Sunt hic etiam sua praemia laudi, / sunt lacrimae rerum, et mentem mortalia tangunt* (*Aen.* 1. 461–462: "There are even here prizes appropriate for praise; there are tears in the world, and mortal suffering touches the heart"), words almost impossible to translate.[18] Aeneas here is viewing people who staked their lives, and lost, but who won everlasting fame. He weeps in sympathy with the dead, and personal loss, but his tears are mingled with nostalgia for their heroism. This had double meaning for Berlioz, for he had both sympathy for others who suffered like himself and respect for the glory (*le jour de gloire*) that he had witnessed in the struggles that France was undergoing.

Berlioz composed several operas in his lifetime, besides brilliant symphonic works like the *Symphonie fantastique*, *Roméo et Juliette*, *Harold in Italy*; various overtures, such as *Roman Carnival*; and religious works, such as his operatic *Requiem*, and *L'enfance du Christ*. He also composed works for special occasions, like the *Grande symphonie funèbre et triomphale*. He is a most prolific and innovative composer. His operas are on various subjects: *Estelle et Némorin* (lost), *Les francs-juges* (fragmentary), *Benvenuto Cellini*, *La nonne sanglante* (fragmentary), *La damnation de Faust*, *Les Troyens,* and *Béatrice et Bénédict*. The last three are his particular masterpieces, and are based on Berlioz's three loves: Goethe, Virgil, and Shakespeare. He is also famous for his theoretical work, *Grand traité d'instrumentation*, which is still taken seriously by composers interested in orchestrating well, and for his *Mémoires*, in addition to essays on various composers such as Beethoven, Gluck and Wagner. Musicians worship his work; Paganini asked Berlioz to write a solo for him, saying, at least as Berlioz recalled, "I have no confidence in anyone but you for such a work."[19]

LES TROYENS: LA PRISE DE TROIE

Berlioz dedicated his opera to the divine Virgil, *Divo Virgilio*. Both shared a melancholy, an acute sense of the tears that life exacted.[20] Berlioz was more faithful to the events and the text than Nahum Tate, in his version for Purcell. The French composer gives us a fiery Mediterranean Didon, with love and its frenzy turned to hate. But neither she nor Énée rises—or sinks—to the coldness of the Virgilian originals. This is grand opera, not epic. Like Tate, Berlioz added rhymes and adapted the metrical structure so that it could be more easily set to music. The rhymes and alexandrines suit their operatic context and lend themselves to song, whereas Virgil's driving unrhymed hexameters lead to a forceful narrative less amenable to musical settings.

Both Virgil and Berlioz build an intricate formal structure. Nevertheless Virgil's work, like Homer's, leaves many open ends, whereas Berlioz's work is more complete. The tragic love story has its conclusion; Énée gains his Italy, which even though faced with threats will prevail. Virgil leaves us at the end of Book 12 with Aeneas vengefully killing Turnus, hardly the glorious vision of an apotheosis of empire that Berlioz gives us at the end of his opera. Aristotle says this completeness is typical of tragedy, whereas epic is more open-ended. Virgil also uses flashbacks, whereas Berlioz's presentation is linear. And, whereas the goal of Italy is revealed and obscured and revealed again in the *Aeneid*, the opera is more straightforward. Many things only implied in the epic are made explicit in the opera.

A quotation from Berlioz tells us how he regarded his music, and we can note the imperial accents:

May Virgil's gods come to my aid; otherwise I am lost. The hardest task is to find the musical *form*, this form without which music does not exist, or is only the craven servant of speech. That is Wagner's crime; he would like to dethrone music and reduce it to "expressive accents," exaggerating the system of Gluck, who, fortunately, did not succeed in carrying out his ungodly theory. I am in favor of the kind of music you call *free*. Yes, free and proud and sovereign and triumphant, I want to grasp and assimilate everything, and have no Alps nor Pyrenees to block its way; but to make conquests music must fight in person, and not merely by its lieutenants; I should like music if possible to have fine verses ranged in battle order, but it must itself lead the attack like Napoleon, it must march in the front rank of the phalanx like Alexander. Music is so powerful that it can sometimes conquer on its own, and has a thousand times the right to say, like Medea, "Moi, c'est assez" [Corneille's *Médée*]. To want to tie it down to the old kind of recitation of the ancient *choros* is the most incredible, and mercifully, the most fruitless folly ever recorded in the history of art. How to find the means to be *expressive* and *truthful* without being any the less musician, and how to give the music new means of action, is the problem. Another pitfall in my way is that the feelings I have to express move me too strongly. That is no good. One must try to do fiery things coolly.[21]

It is obvious that Berlioz has joined Mozart against Monteverdi and Wagner in putting the music first. He gives it imperialist overtones.

He uses his orchestra like a Greek chorus for additional commentary. He uses musical themes that recur throughout the opera in various restatements to convey the author's ideas about the text. The most obvious are the Trojan March, and the repeated *Italie!* (even in such strange contexts as, for instance, the pantomime of the hunt and storm, and after Didon's and Énée's great love scene). These themes reiterate the main thrust of this opera. He also had access to a greatly expanded orchestra, which would include the newly invented saxophone (its inventor Adolphe Sax came from Brussels and lived in Paris), many harps, the ophicleide (a type of horn), the English horn, and other interesting wind instruments.

Many have noted the sequence of keys and their symbolic use. Berlioz described what tonalities meant for him in his *Grand traité*. In this opera, B flat predominates and has a range of associations, particularly those that have to do with empire, since it is the key of the Trojan March. In its major variations it signifies triumph; in its minor ones, suffering. It seems that "E major suggests an otherworldly purity; B major, fiery resolution; A minor, grief; F major, pastoralism."[22] Julian Rushton analyzes the melodic, harmonic, rhythmic, timbral, and textural images.[23] Violin harmonics in the ghost scenes were also put to dramatic use. Sweeping arpeggios and the diminished seventh generally convey agitation and crisis, but Berlioz is too great a composer for there not to be exceptions. For instance, the diminished seventh is often used for its simple coloring effects, not only during crises.

La prise de Troie begins with a short prelude in the winds and brass that launches us *in medias res*, rather like the beginning of Virgil's *Aeneid*, which plunges us into the storm that scatters the Trojan fleet after the fall of Troy. Berlioz puts us at the *kairos*, the critical moment when the Trojan Horse holding the Greeks is wheeled into the citadel. We are plunged amid jubilant Trojans: they think the war is over and that the Greeks are gone. The woodwinds and brass change keys giddily and convey an ominous wild ecstasy of delusion. Peter Conrad has said, "Énée proves his leadership by drilling the mass to make music, calling for the trumpet and lyre to accompany the wooden horse through the gates, [and later] or cementing a new alliance of Trojans and Tyrians by setting a march tempo in which all are compelled to join."[24]

There is a very short orchestral opening to the opera, so we are truly thrust *in medias res*. The gay short phrases, without strings, with little support from the bass, illustrate the deluded excitement of the Trojans who think the war is over. Cassandre is introduced by passionate violins that have been hitherto mostly muted. She knows the truth, clearly foreseeing the fall of Troy, and, more immediately, the death of her lover Chorèbe. Because she rejected Apollo after enticing him, she is forever condemned to prophesy the truth, but not be believed. She tries to persuade Chorèbe to flee. The ardent strings that accompany Cassandre's pleas illustrate her passion and intimate access to the truth. Chorèbe answers her with an optimistic, clueless *cavatina*, showing how divorced he is from that reality: he chooses a musical form that suggests rustic celebration.

Their music clashes, like their perspectives. Recitative alternates with aria and duet. She accepts that he will not escape.

The royal court enters to a march, which wantonly changes keys, underlining the optimistic madness of the Trojans. A ballet of wrestlers (*Combat de Ceste/Pas de lutteurs*) follows, which cedes to a sad pantomime of Andromaque and her son, who will be killed by the Greeks; she has already lost her husband Hector, the greatest Trojan warrior. The music for the scene with Andromaque features a sorrowful solo clarinet that contributes to the poignancy of her mourning and contrasts with the full brass display in the march. Once more Cassandre laments the blindness of the Trojans.

It is interesting that there is no mention of Helen, nor does she appear in this court gathering. This is true to Virgil who only mentions Helen twice, once to identify the veil that Ascanius gives to Dido (1. 650) and the other in a complaint that Amata makes to Latinus about giving their daughter to Aeneas and breaking a promise to Turnus (7. 363–64).[25] Both are ominous contexts. As mentioned in the chapter on *Il ritorno d'Ulisse*, Homer has the old Trojans admiring Helen's beauty, and saying that they understand why a war could have been fought over her (*Il*. 3. 150–158). In the opera, during this opening scene, one might consider having Helen silently enter before the ballet. Then when Andromache appears this would draw the same poignant contrast that Euripides made between these two women in his *Trojan Women:* the faithless wife, the cause of the war, and the faithful one who must suffer the consequences; the same contrast exists between Helen and Penelope.

After the lament of Cassandra, Aeneas rushes in to tell of the horrible fate of Laocoön, the priest of Neptune, who, along with his sons, has been killed by two snakes sent by Minerva, the goddess on the side of the Greeks. We hear in the music the clash of arms that Laocoön's thrown spear evoked from the horse; but the people ignore the obvious. We also hear the rhythmic theme of fate, "short repeated notes recurring on down beats preceded by upbeat of same value."[26]

Priam urges that the horse be drawn into the city and Minerva appeased. Cassandre goes again into her mournful chant. We hear for the first time the Trojan March, from a distance, and it gradually approaches until it is heard in all its brilliant splendor. It becomes a symbolic theme for these people and their fortunes. The march begins with the rhythmic figure that conveys death, "two-four very short notes usually upbeat to a longer note."[27] The march appears in its strong variation when they are strong, and weak when they are weak. Its key, B flat major, is the dominant key of the opera. Ian Kemp has pointed out that the three major decisions ("rush out of the city, give thanks to the gods, and to bring the wooden horse into the city") in this act are expressed by the three tonalities of G, C, and F leading to B flat, a descending cycle of fifths: "a symbol, it may be deduced, of inexorable descent into destruction and, of course, with destruction, into rebirth."[28] As the fortunes wane, the tonality descends too. We shall see that Didon is finally caught up in this descending tonal cycle. Berlioz's music is often characterized by programmatic elements.

Minerva is vainly invoked. The chorus stops, disturbed because a clash of arms has been heard, but it sings again, even more loudly, as if to drown out its own fears. As the march again wanes, Cassandre warns once more. Her cry of "unhappiness" provides tonal counterpoint to the optimistic chorus. Cassandre's B minor cancels the triumphant B major. The chorus sings a hymn to Pallas, and then a great crash is heard in the orchestra: again the arms, but the chant is sung even louder.

Act 2 begins with fitful music, and we hear night sounds mingled with distant fighting. The orchestra reproduces the din of the fatal night when the Trojan horse was taken into the city, and disgorged the Greek warriors to let in their comrades and lay waste to the city. We hear music suitable for the night— quiet punctuated by crashes. Énée tosses in his sleep until he is awakened by an orchestral fortissimo; he sees the ghost of Hector before him. Eerie music accompanies the appearance of Hector's ghost, who warns Énée to flee. The violin harmonics show us Énée's hair standing on end, a good musical translation of *arrectaeque horrore comae, Aen.* 4. 280.[29] In the *Aeneid*, Aeneas' hair stands on end at the appearance of Mercury, but here it is Hector's ghost. The ghost himself is well conveyed by the strange sound of pedal tones, stopped horns, and pizzicato strings, besides the harmonics. The ghost here speaks in monotones in contrast to the wandering line of Énée's responses. These repeated monotones are what has been called the fate theme.

Hector's warning is in B minor, and we hear the death theme with the words "The enemy has breached our walls." The fate theme underlines the words "incessant fate." Énée is told to leave, immediately, to save himself and a few others, and to found "a powerful empire." He specifies Italy, whereas Virgil left the goal for a new Troy ambiguous. Berlioz eliminates this doubt, which will create a new problem later. How can Énée think he will escape his destiny by staying with Didon? In the opera Aeneas is awake when he sees the ghost of Hector, whereas in Virgil he only sees him in a dream. Virgil allows more ambiguity, but Berlioz locks his Aeneas into his destiny from the start. Opera seems to demand more precision from its texts, since more ambiguity can be added by the music.

Énée does not leave at once, but continues to fight to save the citadel. The music is excited, with abruptly changing tempos and keys to simulate the confusion of the night fatal to Troy. Énée quotes Virgil's *una salus victis nullam sperare salutem (Aen.* 2. 354: "the only refuge for the defeated is not to hope for refuge"), singing against descending thirds, the opposite of the rising fanfares of the marches.

This scene of action, violence, and heroism is balanced by the next scene, with the women assembled in a room in Priam's palace, which has an altar to Cybèle and Vesta. A hymn to Cybèle follows, which shows us Berlioz's talent for religious music. Cassandre tells the women that Chorèbe is dead. She says she will join her young husband and die rather than be shamed in captivity. Most of the women join her resolve, but some hesitate, and Cassandre prophetically calls them slaves. Cassandre's song shows us that she has been successful in convincing the women. She exudes confidence that they shall win eternal glory in the memory of the founders of a new Troy in Italy. The others sing songs to reinforce their resolve. The women's hymn to death goes from A flat minor to A major as the women accept their glory.

The Greeks enter and hesitate in amazement at the beauty of these women holding their lyres. They ask the women to deliver up the treasure. Cassandre stabs herself and hands the dagger to Polyxena, who follows her example. The other women kill themselves either with knives or by leaping off a parapet. Cassandre boasts to the soldiers that the treasure is safe with Énée, who has escaped. The scene is emotively brilliant and all hearts soar in admiration of these women, who are as strong as, if not stronger than, the men defending their future.

Cassandra's last word is *Italie*, and with this word the whole opera will end. So also the entire opera will end with a vision of Rome. *Italie* is sung to the rhythmic phrase that suggests death because it appears so often when death is being discussed. By associating *Italie* with this ominous rhythmic phrase, we are perhaps meant to think about the many who must die to build an empire by seizing others' land. The final chord is in C minor, the melancholy key Beethoven made famous in his Symphony no. 5, op. 67.

Virgil did not show us a heroic Cassandra, but Berlioz does. His Cassandre resembles more her Euripidean model in the *Trojan Women*, both in her recognition of the heroism of the Trojans and the vengeance that will come on the Greeks. But in that play she is carried off to fulfill her role—as shown in Aeschylus's *Oresteia*—as the prize concubine of Agamemnon, murdered at his side by Clytemnestra. This is the traditional tale of Cassandra, but not one told by Berlioz.

The last scene of Act 1 may have been suggested by the ending of Shakespeare's *Antony and Cleopatra*. Proud Cleopatra and her handmaidens refuse to be subjected to domination by the conquering Octavian, later the emperor Augustus. Instead they choose to end their lives themselves. Rome's imperialism colors both that play and this opera.

LES TROYENS: LES TROYENS à CARTHAGE

Some of the limitations that Aristotle considers characteristic of drama in relation to epic apply also to opera. Whereas *La prise de Troie* observes the unities of day, theme, and place, *Les Troyennes à Carthage* is looser but takes place only in North Africa; the theme is unified, although the action must occur over several days, as indeed does Virgil's narrative. With the addition of the section on the *Siege of Troy*, there are more complex allusions possible in the second half of the opera. We compare the simpler version by Purcell, which concentrates on the relation of Dido with Aeneas. Berlioz wants us to see this relationship in the context of empire, a reborn Troy. Besides being more passionate than Virgil's Aeneas, Berlioz's Énée is more committed to the dream of Italy, though mourning its human cost.

Les Troyens à Carthage begins as the reverse of the ending of *La prise de Troie*. The opening notes are in a major key and convey the success that Didon and her people have achieved. Its optimistic music in major keys conveys the prosperity of Didon's people and her success as a queen. The opera will end in darker musical colors for the Carthaginians.

It is again indicative of women's roles in opera that Didon, the queen of Carthage, has more positive music and greater praise in this second act in comparison with the praise accorded to Priam, the king of Troy, in the first act. The opening positive march associated with Carthage also contrasts with the march of the Trojans, which wanders over various keys, suggesting the vicissitudes of empire.

Ballets feature prominently in both sections of the opera and provide light interludes to the darkness of the other sections. The music is bright with lively rhythms suitable for dancers.

Light sections alternate with dark, and the words are enhanced by the music. The moments of comedy, as when Ascagne hesitates to wake his father, and the complaints of the watchmen, are conveyed by the music. There are short phrases that show Ascagne's hesitation, and the watchmen also do not speak in extended lyric phrases; their comments have a marching bass that describes the activity they are engaged in.

Didon enters to a march that features the usual fanfare of rising thirds which then descend, and we hear the ominous death rhythm. All empire, it seems, entails death, a characteristically Virgilian theme. This music accompanies the entry of Queen Didon, who, having escaped from Tyre with some of her people, now enjoys the fruits of a reestablished kingdom. Trophies of agriculture, commerce, and the arts are displayed. Besides praising those who raise crops, Didon sounds the note of empire again by urging the people to give another example to the world: "[those who are] Great in peace, become in war a nation of heroes" (p. 10).

The queen tells her history: the flight from Tyre after the murder of her husband by her ambitious and ruthless brother. Her dead husband had told her to flee and also confided to her the whereabouts of his treasure; in these myths ghosts often function as saviors or emissaries of fate. Iarbas, the Gaetulian king, sold Dido land in Africa, but she rejected Iarbas' offer of marriage, so now he threatens to attack.

There is a procession of builders, sailors, and farm workers. Cérès, the goddess of grain, is invoked. Anna, Didon's sister, rejoices at her sister's success, calling her the queen of a young empire, but again we hear the death motif. Didon communicates her uneasy feeling, and expresses herself in roaming chromatics; her sister immediately recognizes the desire for a new love. Didon swears by the ring given her by her dead husband that she should be cursed if she ever gives it up.

Iopas, a poet from Tyre, enters to announce the arrival of a fleet. Didon welcomes the emissaries, paraphrasing *Aeneid*, l. 630, *non ignara mali miseris succurrere disco*, "knowing suffering myself, I have learned to help the unfortunate." The "Trojan March" is heard as the soldiers enter, with Énée in disguise and his son Ascagne asking for asylum and presenting gifts. They tell Didon of their quest for Italy. Narbal, her minister, enters with dire news: Iarbas is attacking and laying waste her fields. Énée reveals himself and pledges Trojan support. Didon accepts.

Iarbas' attack is an addition by Berlioz to show Énée's virtues and is based on a comment by Anna in the *Aeneid*, who tells Dido that she should marry Aeneas to have an ally as protection against Iarbas, whom she has refused in marriage. Anna's conversation with Didon comes before Énée's entry, whereas in the *Aeneid* it is later. It is a lyrical duet that characterizes both Didon and Énée in the opera. It also prefaces Didon's state of mind, whereas we had a longer prelude in the *Aeneid*, with Aeneas' giving an account of the war at a banquet with Dido (something covered by *La prise de Troie* in the opera).[30]

Énée uses imperialist rhetoric when he refers to the enemy as the "vile [literally filthy] horde of Africans," which he asserts will be scattered like sand by the wind, and the enemy will be driven back to the burning deserts; the chiefs then speak of exterminating this black army.

Énée entrusts his son to Didon's care. She says she will guard him with a mother's love. Berlioz returns again to the *Aeneid* for this farewell of the hero to his child: to learn happiness he should look to others, but his father will teach him the courage of a warrior (*la vertu guerrière*) and respect for the gods (a paraphrase of *disce, puer, virtutem ex me verumque laborem, fortunam ex aliis, Aen.* 12. 435–436, itself a paraphrase of Ajax's farewell to his son Eurysaces, "May you be happier than your father, but in all other things like him," Sophocles, *Ajax* 550–551).[31] The soldiers call for arms and repeat that they will march against the filthy horde of Africans. The act ends.

Act 4 begins with the pantomime and overture, which suggest a hunt: Didon is dressed as Diana (*Aen.* 1. 496–504). Both Berlioz and Purcell place the hunt in lush forests in contrast to Virgil, who evokes the rocky landscape of North Africa. We have here the same ominous suggestion that we find in Purcell's *Dido and Aeneas* during the hunt: "So fair the game, so rich the sport, Diana's self might to these woods resort." There is mention of Actaeon, one of Diana's victims, followed by the allusion to Venus and Adonis, an ominous myth, since Adonis is Diana's victim. Didon is violating the goddess of chastity's commands; she also will soon be a victim.

During the Operatic Interlude we see and hear the nymphs crying out, as ominous as the ululation of their Virgilian predecessors (*Aen.* 4. 168), but they prove more articulate and we hear the word *Italie!* repeated. Their shrieks may have provided a model for Wagner's Valkyries. There is a storm, waterfalls mingle with the rain, and a tree, struck by lightning, catches fire. Nymphs pick up the flaming branches and run about. (At the first performance the waterfall was painted and fire was forbidden because of the danger.)

The scene shifts to Didon's gardens. Narbal and Anna discuss the queen and Énée—Anna defending their love, and Narbal fearing it. Anna, like her original in Virgil (and Belinda in Purcell's opera), advocates love, even to

Didon's detriment. We do not see the gods in either opera, except for a brief visit from Mercure in *Les Troyens*.

The queen enters to the national march. It is a curious rendition, which begins hesitantly and ominously in the minor before launching into a major reprise. There are ballets for Egyptian dancing girls, male slaves, and female Nubian slaves. Then the Nubians sing a type of manufactured language, mixing nonsense words.[32] Flaubert was more thorough and did exhaustive research for his Carthaginian novel, *Salammbô* (1862, a year before *Les Troyens* was performed for the first time). It is likely that these two Frenchmen, obsessed with empire, were engaged on these works at the same time. In contrast to Flaubert, Berlioz, either by preference or prejudice, scorns such research about "natives," whom he uses as dramatic oddities to amuse his audience. Delibes' *Lakmé* (1883) and Puccini's *Madame Butterfly* (1904) carry on the idea of the foreign female who must die because her union with a Caucasian male is unthinkable. The western hero must simply occupy the land, hardly mix with the locals.

Berlioz uses what he considers the barbaric music of North Africa. He adds a tambourine, tarbuka (possibly the tarabouk, or darabukka, a goblet-shaped drum from North Africa), and ancient cymbals, to the flutes, English horns, and the strings. The melodic line is simple—if not simplistic—and its musical basis is primarily percussive. Berlioz makes no rhythmic differentiation in the percussive part, which keeps up a constant droning rhythm. The babble of the words extends to the music. It is what Berlioz considers barbaric. Such lack of appreciation for "foreign" music is not unique; Berlioz did not have an open ear. He treats Chinese music with the same condescension.[33]

Didon dismisses the musicians and dancers, but asks her bard Iopas to stay and sing about the fields. That is different from Iopas' song in the *Aeneid*, which is about the movement of the stars. Is this Berlioz's homage to Virgil's *Georgics*?[34] It is a fitting feminine shift, from the cold stars to the fertile land and the earth-goddess Ceres, offering fruits that Dido herself promises. This aria to the goddess Ceres features a rising figure and a rhythm not unlike *Celeste Aïda*, which Radames sings about his beloved: she is addressed like a goddess. Verdi's *Aida* was performed in 1871, less than ten years after Berlioz's *Troyens*. Both are set in Egypt and are about women who lead men astray from their nationalist commitments.

Didon is restless while Énée recounts some of the events in the fall of Troy. He addresses the fate of the women, telling Didon that Andromaque at first mourned Hector but, married next to the son of the man who murdered her husband, ruled jointly with him (an operatic variation from Euripides' sequel, which shows her *not* married to Neoptolemus, but a slave concubine who is persecuted by his lawful wife, Hermione). This operatic Andromaque is an obvious model for Didon, who comments that everything is conspiring to overcome her scruples.

Ascagne plays the role of Cupid (he is explicitly said to look like Cupid) and steals the ring Didon wears in memory of her deceased husband Sichée; she retrieves it but later leaves it on the couch: these are human actions that imply

Didon's consent. In the *Aeneid*, Cupid himself takes the place of Ascanius (657–660), but the theft of the ring is a specific addition by Berlioz and is based on a painting by Pierre Narcisse Guérin (1774–1833), *Énée racontant à Didon les malheurs de Troie*; Berlioz probably saw it hanging in the Louvre. The staging is often based on the painting, with Didon reclining on a couch. Actually, aside from the theft of the ring, this also follows Virgil: *aulaeis iam se regina superbis / aurea composuit sponda mediamque locavit* (*Aen.* 1. 697–698). The ring episode could also have been suggested by Shakespeare: in *The Merchant of Venice* the loss of a ring is symbolic of a threat to the relationship between the lovers.

More ominous images are brought up by Didon and Énée as they plight their troth: Didon mentions Venus and Anchises, and Diana and Endymion. These lovers were ultimately separated. Venus could not stay with a mortal; Diana, the goddess of chastity, was more a source of death for young men than of love; it was Selene who was associated with Endymion, and perhaps Berlioz is here identifying Diana as a goddess of the moon with Selene. Endymion chose eternal sleep as a gift from Zeus, so he remained eternally young, but more an object of desire rather than as an active lover. Diana is also ominously associated with Didon, who is said to be dressed like the goddess during the pantomime of the hunt that opens Act 4. This pantomime obviously parallels Virgil's hunt, storm, and flight to the cave (*Aen.* 4. 160–172). The opera is much more complicated in its ominous allusions, including the appearance of nymphs bearing torches, a grim reminder that the women in *Aeneid*, Book 5, set fire to the Trojan ships because they wish to remain in Sicily and thus, like Dido, seek a type of security (an end to their voyaging). We also see the image of love as flame, an all-consuming passion, but whereas this is a feminine disease in Virgil, in Berlioz's opera it is shared by the men, both Énée and his sailors, who are attached to the local women.

In the *Aeneid* Dido is said to resemble Diana with her Oreads as she moved through her people (*Aen.* 1. 498–501). The ominous suggestion is there: as long as she remains a "virgin goddess" she will retain her power. She is also a source of disaster for men, and the gods warn Aeneas of Dido's power over him, telling him to hasten his departure, warning that *varium et mutabile semper femina* (*Aen.* 4. 569–570).[35] The danger increases with goddesses and queens: both enjoy great power. Diana, the goddess of the hunt, as identified with Dido, also suggests the game of love, which could have fatal consequences for the victim. Indeed it did, but the victim was the heroine: in this case the goddess must die.

There is peace before the storm. A septet describes the peace of the evening (Act 4, sc. 2, no. 36). The sweetness of the music conveys the charm of the stillness, and there is a suggestion of a lullaby in the graceful descending figures. This section is filled with woodwinds, and the strings mostly stay on a single note. It is quite programmatic, and we can hear crickets in the music and the slow rolling of the sea. This is a beautiful interlude, followed by a duet alone between Didon and Énée, the climactic romantic aria they share, as filled with passion as the last septet was with peace. Seething violins dominate the soothing winds.

In this major love scene, Berlioz uses allusions from Shakespeare's *Merchant of Venice* to the thwarted love of two figures from the Trojan War: Cressida's abandonment of Troilus parallels Aeneas' of Dido. What appears to be bliss has an ominous undercurrent:

Lorenzo: The moon shines bright: in such a night as this,
When the sweet wind did gently kiss the trees
And they did make no noise; on such a night
Troilus methinks mounted the Troyan walls
And sigh'd his soul toward the Grecian tents
Where Cressid lay that night.
(Act. 5, sc. I, 1–6)

In such a night
Stood Dido with a willow in her hand
Upon the wild sea banks, and waft her love
To come again to Carthage.
(Act. 5, sc. I, 9–12)

How sweet the moonlight sleeps upon this bank!
Here will we sit and let the sounds of music
Creep in our ears: soft stillness and the night
Become the touches of sweet harmony.
Sit, Jessica. Look how the floor of heaven
Is thick inlaid with patines of bright gold:
There's not the smallest orb which thou behold'st
But in his motion like an angel sings,
Still quiring to the young-eyed cherubins;
Such harmony is in immortal souls;
But whilst this muddy vesture of decay
Doth grossly close it in, we cannot hear it.
(Act 5, sc. I, 54–64)

This is roughly echoed by:

Only peace and charm surround us.
The night spreads its veil and the sleeping sea
Murmurs its sweetest harmonies as it rests.

and the duet:

Night of intoxication and infinite ecstasy,
Blond Phoebe, great stars of her court,
Shine on us your blessed light,
Flowers of heaven, smile on an immortal love . . . .

On such a night, mad with love and joy,
Troilus waited under the walls of Troy
For his beautiful Cressida.[36]

Berlioz's love scene features the high romance of Shakespeare and grand opera. He makes explicit what Virgil only suggests. There are hardly such vows exchanged between the classical lovers. Virgil pities Dido's grand passion for Aeneas, but never treats it as anything but an aberration. The ancients generally considered love a disease. Only in the twelfth century with the rise of the Courtly Love tradition did love come to be treasured, elevating the lover above the mundane.[37] In this sense Shakespeare can be said to be "romantic": he invokes the Courtly Love tradition. However, his romanticism differs from that of Berlioz, who is interested more in the suffering and deprivation attendant upon an impossible love.

Berlioz told his sister Adèle that he "stole from Shakespeare and Virgilianized."[38] The imagery is enhanced by the music, conveying both the peace of night, with images of calm water, and the passion and fire of the lovers, reflected in the light of the stars. These "flowers of heaven" suggest fertility and blossoms that should be plucked. Shakespeare links music, night and the heavens shared by two lovers through his verbal imagery, and Berlioz adds music to Shakespeare's words.

Shakespeare refers to the "music of the spheres" in the verses quoted above, with the idea that the planets in their orbits create a harmony to which sensitive souls respond. In Berlioz the stars are invoked to smile on an eternal love, though it is more likely that they wept at the tragedy. In Virgil love is a disease; in Shakespeare it can lead to transcendence; in Berlioz love causes exquisite pain: three views of love in classical epic, Elizabethan tragedy, and nineteenth-century opera.

The lovers complete their duet in the wings and consummate their love. This duet features the full strings, as does also Cassandre's love song. The duet soars with passion, as Mercure appears, strikes the shield of Énée with his messenger's staff, and repeats *Italie* three times. Like the ghosts, the god speaks in a monotone.

There is another peaceful song, which again resembles a lullaby, and indeed the singer falls asleep at the end, suggesting Virgil's navigator Palinurus, who falls asleep at his post and is drowned. This sailor (called Hylas) laments his absence from his homeland in Phrygia. The refrain is a true *berceuse*, with a rocking melody. The beginning of the refrain of Hylas' song covers only four notes and rocks back and forth between them. The B flat major / G minor keys are used for the song, suggesting the underside of empire: the nostalgia and loss it entails of home and loved ones. It breaks off on the word *l'enfant*: the rocking child has been lulled to sleep, a respite from his sorrow.

In ancient myth, Hylas was the name of Heracles' beloved (the kidnapped son of the king of the Dryopes), seized for his beauty by the nymphs at Cios in Mysia during the Argonautic voyage, and never permitted to return home.[39] According to some versions Hylas drowned when the nymphs, attracted by his beauty, dragged him into their well. Some say he was given immortality.

This song about longing for a lost homeland we can almost say was a tragic cliché, at least in Euripides' plays. One need only think of the chorus in

Iphigenia in Tauris, longing for Greece (392–455), besides comparable complaints by the captive Greek attendants in Euripides' *Helen*. Silenus and the captive satyrs long for Dionysus and their familiar haunts in Greece in Euripides' *Cyclops*. This longing, if it is for a lost fatherland, can have revolutionary implications. Verdi's *Va, pensiero* (the song sung by the captive Hebrew slaves in *Nabucco*) aroused his audience and was sung during the *risorgimento* from 1848 to 1870, when Italy was being unified. *Nabucco* was performed in 1841 and *Les Troyens* in 1863, so Berlioz was probably familiar with this eloquent song about *Mia patria sì bella e perduta*.

The chieftains speak of leaving. Then we hear the common people, namely the sentries, who would rather stay. We have a glimpse of the lower classes. They talk about the pleasures in port as opposed to the hardships at sea. (This is the reverse of Purcell's sailors *agreeing* with their masters to leave; they were very glad to take a boozy, short leave of *their* women.) Berlioz's scene met with much criticism. Barzun said of the protests of the sentries at leaving Carthage, "As for the sentries' dialogue, its imputation that quartered troops enjoy idleness, women, and good food shocked the pure taste of Paris."[40] Carvalho took it out because it "seemed to him too familiar for the epic style."[41] He did not understand that Berlioz had humanized epic, giving consideration to the suffering of the weak and defeated while still maintaining the thrust of heroic destiny.

Énée sings a brilliant aria. He says that he must tell Didon once more of his love, and how fate drives him against his will. A chorus of shades (Priam, Chorèbe, and Cassandre) warns him, all the more effectively because they died with the one hope of a Troy reborn in Italy through the efforts of Énée. In their chants we hear the fate theme, with rhythmic repetitions of the same note beginning on the downbeat.

There are many Virgilian echoes of both plot and phrasing in Berlioz's opera, whereas in Purcell there is only a vague imitation. In Berlioz, as in Virgil, there are ghosts who have a role in shaping the future. Purcell instead gives us witches, which might reflect the taste of his time.

In the second act, the ghost of Énée's father urges him to leave, along with Hector, his sister Cassandre, and her lover (in the first act, the ghost of Hector had appeared alone). They yearn for a new empire, and claim what they think Énée owes them. *Pater* comes to ask for *patria*, and Cassandre presents the figure of a fatal love, the price that one must pay in the process of founding a new empire. Énée should take her courage as an example: she would not live with shame or dishonor. Énée cannot share empire, he must found his own and fulfill the fate that is owed to the Trojans: their *Italie*. The circle is complete and the debt has come due. Berlioz's own loyalty to his father and his family no doubt contributed to this particular choice. When Énée mentions his glory, the music is reminiscent of the Trojan anthem, which itself resembles the *Marseillaise*, or French national anthem, which Berlioz himself had reworked into a stirring setting.

Énée sees that he must leave immediately (unlike Purcell's courteous Aeneas), but he is intercepted by Didon. In Virgil, Aeneas is first visited by

Mercury as he is laying foundations for houses in Carthage. Virgil's Aeneas tries to leave unseen, but is intercepted by Dido. Finally, Virgil's Aeneas is awakened by Mercury as he sleeps on his ship and told to leave at once, which he does. Dido then cries out her passionate curses on his head.

The operatic Didon delivers more pleas than curses. She also wishes she had at least a child from Énée. We hear the Trojan March in the background. Énée says that although he still loves her he must leave and obey the gods. The Virgilian Aeneas is less gallant: he says he never promised marriage (*Aen.* 4. 339–340) and reminds Dido that his love is Italy: *hic amor, haec patria est* (*Aen.* 4. 347). In the opera, the next word after *je vous aime* is *Italie*, which Énée cries out with his soldiers. This close juxtaposition shows the conflict. The Trojan March is played in bitter triumph.

Didon asks her sister to entreat Énée to stay, but is told that he has sailed. She first orders the Trojans to follow with fire and sword, and curses him, saying she should have carved up Ascagne and served him to his father. She asks that a pyre be prepared with Énée's armor and gifts on it.

Didon foretells her death, and sings a farewell aria to the city. We have entered the world of grand opera. Berlioz, like Mozart, did not like the ariatic flourish for its own sake. Nevertheless, both of them are known for their spectacular arias (e.g., Mozart's *Fuor del mar* in *Idomeneo* and Berlioz's *Je vais mourir* here).

At first Didon, in a concluding recitative (no. 46), has her state of mind conveyed by shifting tonalities and wild orchestral motives. There are also constantly shifting tempi, and the main theme of *Nuit d'ivresse* is recalled. This variety reminds us of Monteverdi's approach towards a fluid musico-dramatic style, a fluidity that was soon to achieve its zenith in Wagner. The texture of the restless opening of *Symphonie Fantastique* resembles the texture of Didon's farewell here.

Her farewell uses primarily diatonic musical gestures as opposed to chromatic tonalities, and we see Didon growing calm amid her acceptance of death, expressed by the new harmonies. In Purcell, Dido's lament begins with an ascent and ends with a descent; Didon's aria begins with a descending melodic figure but ends with an ascending one, as if to affirm the nobility of death. As she takes part in the funeral ceremony and arranges Énée's arms (*D'un malheureux amour, funestes gages*), there are the same close intervals as in Hylas' song. The use of the clarinet recalls not only his song, but Andromache's first tragic appearance with her son. In fact, this lament is almost monotonal. We think of Berlioz doing fiery things coolly. We have seen that this scene moved him most, as did thoughts of his son (in the Hylas song) and the great separation he had to endure from his own beloved child. It is as if sorrow has forgotten how to soar, and is best expressed by the intensity of a few notes. It is Berlioz' musical genius to be able to feature the most complex and rich orchestral fabrics in alternation with the most simple and poignant. Didon's farewell is not as confident as Cassandre's. Didon saw defeat for her people, whereas Cassandre's vision was of a future glory. The music also conveys this.

Didon's farewell is like the leave that Sophocles' Philoctetes takes of his rocky retreat at Lemnos, which sheltered him for so many years (S. *Philoct.* 1452–1468). Didon bids farewell to her city and her people, as well as the skies of Africa, the stars, the nights—recalling a phrase from her aria with Énée. Philoctetes bids farewell to the land and its shelters, but Didon bids farewell to the civilization she founded. There are descending phrases in her farewell, reminding us that the descending tetrachord is still a sign of lament. A flat minor, a key of grief in this opera, is used by Cassandre to express her despair. Didon's main phrase is a descending arpeggiated octave, the reverse of the national anthems of both her country and the Trojans. There are more winds than strings, reminding us of the earlier peaceful septet welcoming night. .

A ritual follows with priests partaking in the ceremony. They pray for healing. We enjoy great religious music throughout the opera, from the hymns to Cybèle, to Ceres, and finally to the gods of the underworld in the concluding ritual that will end Didon's life. Cassandre's death is surrounded by ritual, and so is Didon's. We find chords, harmonies and choral ensembles reminiscent of Berlioz's great religious works. Berlioz was a fundamentally religious man and brought a singular passion and vision to religious music. Like Mozart, he remained faithful to many of his family's traditions throughout his life.

Anna and Narbal curse Énée. Didon says she feels peace returning. Didon climbs the pyre, and throws her veil along with Énée's toga upon it. Her *D'un malheureux amour, funestes gages* ("Fatal Mementos of an Unhappy Love") is peaceful, sung on the repeated note of C sharp, with the fate and death motif conveying her willing acceptance of both.

Didon takes up Énée's sword. She predicts Hannibal. She says her soul is full of pride, and so it is fitting that she descends to Hades with such a prediction on her lips. She stabs herself, and then sings on a repeated note of the fall of Carthage, the triumph of fate.

We see Didon identified with Carthage, a victim of empire. A pantomime unfolds of the Capitol of Rome, with legions passing in front and an emperor surrounded by poets and artists. We hear the Trojan march. Didon's last words are a cry, "Immortal Rome," on a rising arpeggio, a contrast to the all-too-mortal Didon, whose own farewell to her city (*Adieu, fière cité*) began in a descent. This may echo the earlier setting for Hector's prophecy, which would cause so much damage to Dido and her people. The Carthaginians join in a curse, calling for eternal hatred. The Punic cry is heard against the triumphal march. So the East yields to the West, descending into pain beneath the boot of the conqueror.

Berlioz balances actions: Cassandre and Didon share fatal loves and prophesy, and both take their lives in heroic action. Cassandre's death is a defiant gesture, depriving the Greeks of their triumph. Didon claims that she should die with the vision of Hannibal as her revenge, but her last words commemorate the downfall of Carthage. Didon's suicide is the more gratuitous. It would benefit her people if she could suppress her feelings and be the queen she was before the disastrous arrival of Énée. Albeit heroic in the way they address their misery, nevertheless Cassandre, the women of Troy, and Didon are all victims of men's violent foolishness.

Virgil did not vindicate Dido's heroism, but showed her more as a victim of her passion, joining in Hades other women lost in love and continuing there her futile hatred. In part she reminds us of the threat of the barbarian female, a Cleopatra. We remember that she was not barbarian at all, but a victim of Roman propaganda. Horace begins his ode celebrating her defeat with a summons to drink and dance. Cleopatra is called demented, drunk on hope, and finally not even a woman but a deadly monster (*fatale monstrum*, 1.37.21). Nevertheless, Horace offers her grudging respect for her bravery in killing herself. We can see how she resembles Dido. Dido is one of a series of victims of empire, and along with Turnus and his fate, forces serious questions to be asked. Berlioz arouses sympathy in us for Didon, but he also wants us to acknowledge the glory of empire to an even greater degree than did Virgil.

Berlioz adapts his source material to reach a clear artistic goal; in both parts of his opera a heroic woman is sacrificed to the inevitability of empire. Human suffering is given its tragic due, but the power and glory of conquest transcend individuals; male heroes mount their thrones across the bodies of women who die for love.

Énée is more romantic than in Virgil or Purcell. We believe his protestations of love, but we also believe his commitment to empire. Rather than wishing to have died at Troy (*Aen.* 1. 94–96), this Énée is brave. He speeds to fight Didon's enemies. Here also we have a mere suggestion in Virgil made explicit by Berlioz. Anna suggests that Aeneas might be a good ally for Dido in case of attack by Iarbas and other Africans (*Aen.* 4. 39–44). Berlioz stages an attack as Énée asks for a favorable alliance, and he steps forward boldly to offer his help to Didon; she accepts, and he goes to fight on her behalf and seek glory: "Tell our people glory summons us to a new undertaking" (p. 13). We do not see the final scene of the *Aeneid*, in which Aeneas kills Turnus in anger, violating his father's precept to spare the defeated. Énée is a hero worthy of the heroine Didon, and we see him only at his best.

Likewise Didon combines the qualities of a queen, devoted to her people, and the qualities of a woman because she feels the stirrings of love even before Énée appears: as she speaks of "a strange sadness," her sister predicts, "You WILL love, my sister." At the beginning of the opera, she appears rather like Euripides' Phaedra, about to embark on a fatal love. At the beginning of Virgil's epic Dido is wholly devoted to leading her people.

Virgil saw Dido as a threat to the future of Rome. A destructive love interferes with duty, *pietas,* and empire, *Italia.* Ominous mythological references appear in this opera as in Virgil's epic and as in Purcell's opera. One of the gifts that Ascagne offers is the veil of the faithless Helen (both in Virgil and Berlioz's opera), but now the one who will be unfaithful is the man. Virgil's attitude towards romantic love was typical of many in antiquity: *improbe Amor, quid non mortalia pectora cogis* (*Aen.* 4. 412), "Wicked love, to what ends do you not force mortal hearts!"[42] In Virgil we find Aeneas explicit about not offering marriage, and in claiming that his love was Italy (*hic amor, haec patria est*

[Italia], *Aen.* 4. 347, cf. *magno telluris amore, Aen.* 1. 171). This is a paraphrase of his fate: *per varios casus, per tot discrimina rerum / tendimus in Latium, sedes ubi fata quietas / ostendunt: illic fas regna resurgere Troiae (Aen.* 1. 204–206). Jove explicitly tells Venus of the empire that will be her son's: *imperium sine fine dedi (Aen.* 1. 279). Anchises exhorts his son Aeneas when he visits the underworld by showing him future heroes, all endorsements of the Roman empire. He claims others might excel in the intellectual and scientific arts, but the Romans were selected for empire:

> tu regere imperio populos, Romane, memento
> (hae tibi erunt artes) pacique imponere morem,
> parcere subiectis et debellare superbos. (*Aen.* 6. 851–853)

"You, Roman, remember (for these will be your special talents): to 'set the stamp of civilized usage upon peace,' spare the defeated, and defeat the proud."[43]

We have seen Aeneas nostalgic and longing for his own country, as he envies Dido's: *O fortunati, quorum iam moenia surgunt! (Aen.* 1. 47). Énée is not so blunt. He is more the Romantic, and pledges his love, not only at the beginning but also when he leaves. He says he is going to die, obedient to the gods and he loves Didon: Didon: "You are leaving me." Énée: "Only to die, obedient to the gods. I leave and I love you." We find neither the prediction of Énée's heroic death nor this expression of love in Virgil.

Berlioz's Didon, like Virgil's, is more vengeful than Purcell's, and she sees Hannibal in a vision that is comparable to Cassandre's. Didon is allowed to see her avenger and name him. Virgil's Dido can only tell her people to wage unending war, and to pray that an avenger will come from her bones: *aliquis nostris ex ossibus ultor (Aen.* 4. 625).

Berlioz's Didon is more powerful in her death: she can predict the future as Oedipus did when he was about to die in Sophocles' *Oedipus at Colonus.* Once again, *pace* Clément and McClary, we find in opera the active heroine. Didon's death becomes her victory. Like Cassandre and some of the other Trojan women, she chose to die when life became intolerable. In death she saved her honor. The overriding difference between Virgil's world and Berlioz's is the attitude towards empire. Virgil endorsed Augustus and his empire with reservations. Nevertheless, he realized that empire demands personal sacrifice. We are left with the picture of an abandoned Dido and a young Turnus cut down so that a new Troy can be founded.[44] We are equally aware of the price of empire along with its benefits. A case can be made that Augustus was influenced by the *Aeneid* in his subsequent moral and social legislation, but the acquisition of empire is never questioned.

We find some passages in Berlioz's *Mémoires* that elucidate his attitude. Berlioz says of his relation with his teacher Lesueur, "But there were some things about which we were both enthusiastic, and on which we were always certain to agree—Gluck, Virgil, and Napoleon."[45] Ferdinand Hiller says of Berlioz, "Below the surface he was an aristocrat and a conservative: he particularly disliked republicans and the mob."[46] Berlioz describes his travels thus: "When travelling in Austria, one must positively visit at least three of its capitals— Vienna, Pesth, and Prague. Certain wayward minds assert that Pesth is in Hungary, and Prague in Bohemia; but none the less do these two states form integral parts of the Austrian Empire, to which they are attached and devoted—soul, body and estate—much as Ireland is to England, Poland to Russia, Algeria to France; much as all conquered nations have always been to their conquerors."[47]

One might have hoped Berlioz to be more sensitive to the occupied, given that Harriet Smithson, his first wife and mother of his child, was born in Ireland. Far from it, Berlioz spoke of the Chartists being defeated in England to his great pleasure, saying to Harriet, "You know nearly as much about insurrections as the Italians do about writing symphonies. It's the same very probably with the Irish, and O'Connell was right in always saying: 'Agitate, Agitate! But do not budge!'"[48] Berlioz praised what he saw as the welcome incompetence of revolutionaries. Berlioz's contempt for "foreigners" was obvious, as he described the Irish in London, showing the signs of the poverty resulting from the British conquest: "London still slept; none of the Sarahs, Marys, Kates, who every morning wash the doorsteps were to be seen sponge in hand. A gin-sodden old Irishwoman smoked her pipe, huddled up alone at the corner of Manchester Square."[49] His contempt was not only for the Irish. Berlioz was early at a palace that housed an exhibition he was to judge, and he thought he was alone, "But there were three of us, a Chinaman, a sparrow and I. The *slits* of eyes of the Asiatic had opened before their time, or perhaps, like mine they had not closed at all." Berlioz says, "Good Morning" to him; "His only response was to get up, turn his back on me, open a cupboard and take out some sandwiches, with a rather contemptuous look on his face for such *barbarous* food. He evidently was thinking of soup made of swallows' nests, and those famous wood-louse jams for which Canton is famous. Faugh! The thought of such rude cookery makes me sick, and I slipped away."[50]

Virgil spoke of "monsters" in the *Aeneid*, such as Cacus in Book 8, slain by Hercules, and the human "demon" Mezentius in Book 10, slain by Aeneas. First Cacus and Mezentius are demonized so that their deaths are welcomed by "civilized" people. These then celebrate their culture heroes, like Heracles and Aeneas, whose own acts strangely resemble those of the "monsters" but are construed as heroic acts.

The culture hero subjects himself to the state, and this in itself can lead to a type of cruelty, as it does with *pius* Aeneas in his killing of Turnus. If you are right, and suffer, then you have no qualms about making your enemy—the threat of disorder—suffer.

Another thing that happens in the building of empire is that the new order defines itself by the elements it expels: the Spanish had to expel the Jews in the fifteenth century to define themselves as Spanish. The French in the mid-nineteenth century nostalgically see themselves as following up Napoleon's great conquest of Egypt fifty years (and fifteen governments) before. All the Roman generals from Pompey on had to make their mark on Egypt; Berlioz might be asking for a French conquest of North Africa in order to fit into that sequence, a new "Holy Roman Empire," now with a French accent. This then makes Dido not only like Cleopatra, but also the necessary sacrificial victim to the glory of greater France.

Wagner moved in the same direction in Germany, and we can see Berlioz contributing towards a formative stage in French nationalism. The sequence of unsuccessful monarchs might have given Berlioz the yearning for a strong, unifying leader, like Napoleon, just as the disastrous series of coups by Roman warlords gave Virgil a desire for Augustus.[51] And both artists had a healthy respect for power and possibly patronage.

Berlioz was duly impressed by Prince Metternich and regularly enjoyed being entertained by royalty. His political activity is reflected in his compositions: "Beale is going to publish it ["Apotheosis"] with the *Marseillaise*, the *Chant du Départ* and the genuine *Mourons pour la Patrie* of Rouget de Lisle, which I am likewise writing for him."[52] Berlioz found himself more comfortable in imperial England or Russia: "I can no longer think of any country for my musical career except England or Russia. I had long ago done with France; the last revolution has only made me more decided. I had to contend under the old government with the hatred aroused by my articles, the ineptitude of operatic managers and public indifference; there would now be besides, the crowd of great composers just hatched out by the Republic, popular, philanthropic, national and economic music. The arts in France are dead, and music in particular is already beginning to rot; bury it quickly! I can smell the fumes."[53]

Berlioz's comments about the Africans in his libretto show racism in addition to endorsing French imperialism. It was France's duty to impose civilization and law on the savages, like Virgil's Romans (*pacique imponere morem*). The final scene of the opera shows a splendid view of Rome, the fruit of conquest. The glorious "Trojan March" drowns out any objections by the Carthaginians, who will eventually be destroyed by Rome, as Didon herself points out in her final capitulation. Such is the dialectic between the conquerors and the conquered.[54]

B flat major concludes the opera, and the Trojan March has won, defeating even the final threats of the Carthaginians. As Robert Collet noted of *The Trojans* and the works of Rameau, Gluck, Lesueur, Méhul, and Meyerbeer, "If it can intelligibly be held that their works are undramatic (or perhaps the true word is untheatrical) in the sense that they would be quite unacceptable as ordinary stage works, they are truly operatic in a special sense, in that the music makes possible a kind of drama that humanly can be most deeply impressive, and that would otherwise be impossible on the stage."[55]

CONCLUSION

Berlioz achieves harmonically in the music the dramatic harmony he envisions on stage. There is a resolution of contrasts through the dominance of certain chords and rhythms: monotone over trill, and so forth. Virgil shows that human passion will always break through, but Berlioz wants complete resolution so that no discord survives, except in memory. Empire and harmony dominate at the end. The curses of the Carthaginians are resolved into a major key, and in our memory we still hear the triumphal march, and we see the capitol of the new empire with *Roma* written in blazing letters.

Berlioz's libretto has brought Virgil's shadowy poetic suggestions into the light. His text simplifies the allusive poetry, but reinstates the poetry through the music. The themes hauntingly recur to offer their own commentary, and massive choruses contribute to the majesty. They show how the fate of countries, not simply individuals, is at stake, but it is still the individuals who rivet our attention. Atmosphere is added by the music: battle scenes, peaceful nights, or the appearance of ghosts. Romantic love is created not only by the florid words, but by the lush music; this differs from the Virgilian original, which saw erotic love as unmitigated disaster for Aeneas. Nationalism and empire are new additions, perhaps hinted at in Virgil, but full-blown in Berlioz. Troy differs from Carthage; it is stark and masculine compared to the feminine sensuality of Carthage: two pictures painted by the music.

Berlioz has rearranged Virgilian events according to an emotional and musical logic. Characters are created that were only suggested in Virgil: Cassandra takes over Aeneas' major role during the fall of Troy. Women now equal men in their heroism. With great craft, Berlioz develops a precise structure for the two parts of his opera: both parts begin in celebration and light and end in tragedy and darkness; two women dominate in their heroic tragedies. They are victims to empire, equivalent to Turnus in the *Aeneid*. Berlioz's version of the fall of Troy owes a lot to Euripides' *Trojan Women* in that now instead of the glory of men in war, we come to appreciate the suffering of women from war. Berlioz goes one step further by juxtaposing glory and heroic suffering. Both parts end with fires illuminating the dark: one of Troy burning, and the other of Dido's pyre.

Clément bemoans the undoing of women at the hands of men: Cassandre and Didon are two such women, but they exercise choice in their circumscribed conditions and achieve tragic apotheosis. They both attain *jouissance* through their arias. Although they lose their lives, they gain applause that echoes down through the centuries. Sam Abel says, "What transforms Clément's view of operatic violence against women specifically into sexual violence are the intense musical climaxes that invariably accompany these acts, making them the most sexually charged moments in opera."[56] Berlioz speaks of Dido's expiration in what some could say were orgasmic terms: "But when I came to the despairing cries of the dying queen, 'Thrice rising on her elbow, thrice falling back,' and had to describe her wounds, and the anguish of her heart rent with its fatal passion; the cries of her distracted sister and nurse, and all the details of her death of torture, which moved even the gods to pity—my lips quivered, I could scarcely stammer out the words; and when I reached the line: *Quaesivit caelo lucem, ingemuitque reperta*, the sublime vision of Dido, 'seaking light from heaven, and moaning as she found it,' overwhelmed me, and I broke down utterly."[57]

Berlioz has allowed us a glimpse of the glories of empire. Nineteenth-century Romanticism colors his representations. We see the brilliant colors of a Delacroïx, Berlioz's contemporary, who also was enamored of the classics. He has shown us the glories of France interlaced with their classical precedents. Like Gros and David, Berlioz recounted the great deeds of empire.

We moderns may have more sympathy for Didon and less for empire, but Berlioz neatly seduces us into his world view. His alternation of light and dark, noble sentiments along with the comments of the people, add to the varied and persuasive texture. We admire the passion of the composer, although we may not share his ideals.

Berlioz's Didon and Énée are both heroic. In contrast to Purcell, who favored his Dido, the expressive music is equally divided. We admire Didon's heroic commitment to her passion and its consequences, and can say of her, as Horace did of Cleopatra, that she was "No lowly lady" (*non humilis mulier*, *Odes*, 1. 37. 31). Cassandre is a heroic counterpart to Didon. As the first part of the opera balances the second, we see that Cassandre counterbalances Didon. One can even argue a greater heroism for her, because conceivably Didon could still have helped her people. Cassandre sees that there is no escape for her or the other Trojan women unless they are willing to be slaves to the Greeks. These brave women refuse to lower their standards and choose like Sophocles' Ajax to die with honor: "The noble person must either live with honor or die with it," (479–480).

Berlioz's genius was great enough to express the heroism of both the women and the men. His orchestra is at its fullest splendor, and his love for his subject and text, coupled with his musical genius, has delivered us one of the greatest masterpieces in the history of music.

APPENDIX
OPERA AND MUSICAL THEATRE WORK ON AENEAS,
THE TROJAN WOMEN, AND CASSANDRA[58]

Johann Wolfgang Franck (1644–c.1710) (b. Unterschwaningen, Germany)
Aeneas der trojanischen Fürsten Ankunft in Italien (1680, not complete)

Gottfried Finger (c.1660–1730) (b. ?Olomouc, Moravia)
The Virgin Prophetess, or *The Fate of Troy* (1701)

Toussaint Bertin de la Doué (1680–1743) (b. Paris, France)
Cassandre (1706)

Francois Bouvard (1683–1760) (b. Lyons, France)
Cassandre (1706)

Pasquale Cafaro (1716–1787) (b. San Pietro in Galatina, Italy)
L'incendio di Troia (1757)

Michele Mortellari (c.1750–1807) (b. Palermo, Sicily)
Troia distrutta (1778)

Mykola Vitaliyovych Lysenko (1842–1912) (b. Hrynky, Ukraine)
Eneïda (1910)

Arthur Coquard (1846–1910) (b. Paris, France)
Cassandre (1881, *drame lyrique*, after Seneca)

Vittorio Gnecchi (1876–1954) (b. Milan, Italy)
Cassandra (1905)

Gian Francesco Malipiero (1882–1973) (b. Venice, Italy)
Vergilii Aeneis (1946)

Guido Guerrini (1890–1965) (b. Faenza, Italy)
Enea (1953)

Margaret Garwood (1927–) (b. Haddonfield, N.J., USA)
The Trojan Women (1967)

Theodore Antoniou (1935–) (b. Athens, Greece)
Cassandra (1969, music theatre work)

Joanna Bruzdowicz (1943–) (b. Warsaw, Poland)
Les Troyennes (1972)

Conrad Cummings (1948–) (b. San Francisco, CA, USA)
Cassandra (1984–1985: withdrawn, but developed as a dramatic scene)

Il Ritorno d'Ulisse in Patria by Monteverdi. Performed by Salzburger Festspiele, 1985.
Photos by Salzberger Festspiele/Weber.

Dido and Aeneas by Henry Purcell. Performed by the Mark Morris Dance Group. Photo by Cylla von Tiedemann.

Idomeneo, re di Creta by Mozart. Courtesy of the Los Angeles Opera, 1990. Photo by Robert Millard.

The Trojans by Hector Berlioz. Courtesy of the Los Angeles Opera. Photo by Robert Millard.

Elektra by Richard Strauss. San Diego Opera (1980). Sopranos Pauline Tinsley (left) as Elektra and Anne Evans as Chrysothemis. Conducted by Theo Alcantara. Directed by Regina Resnik. Photo by Ed Gohlich.

Oedipus Rex by Igor Stravinsky. Courtesy of the Canadian Opera Company, 1997. Dancer at the top of the photo: Jennie Ford. Photo by Michael Cooper.

Lee Breuer and Bob Telson's *The Gospel at Colonus*. Clarence Fountain (seated) and Martin Jacox. Goodman Theater Production. Photo by Liz Lauren.

Medea by Mikis Theodorakis. Das Meininger Theater, Spielzeit, 1994–1995.
Photos by Roland Reissig. Top photo: Aurelia Hajek as Koryphäe. Bottom photo:
Laurie Gibson as Medea, Zachos Terzakis as Jason.

Strauss's *Elektra:*
A Father's Daughter

INTRODUCTION AND BACKGROUND

Richard Strauss claimed, "Many now consider *Elektra* the acme of my work." Bryan Gilliam corroborates this and quotes Paul Bekker, the Berlin critic: "*Elektra*, with its originality, dramatic profundity and concentration, had not only surpassed any opera that Strauss had written thus far but all [operas] that other musicians of the present have attempted."[1] Stravinsky begged to differ: "My low esteem for Strauss's operas is somewhat compensated by my admiration for von Hofmannsthal."[2] Strauss, like most of the composers whose operas are here included, met with both extreme praise and violent criticism.

Strauss was always interested in the classics, and while he was in school at the Ludwigsgymnasium he set a chorus from Sophocles' *Electra* to music.[3] Later he composed much on other Greek themes and mythology, from the *Panathenäenzug* to *Ariadne auf Naxos* and *Die ägyptische Helena*, also written with his librettist for *Elektra*, Hugo von Hofmannsthal. His *Daphne* had a librettist (Joseph Gregor) vastly inferior to Hofmannsthal.

Electra was not popular in opera. She has no opera in the nineteenth century. Medea the child-slayer captured the imagination more than Electra the mother-slayer. Electra only helped Orestes, and there is no Jason as a love interest. Pylades is a poor substitute. Elektra is not punished, but she does commit suicide in an ecstatic way in Strauss's opera. This would satisfy nineteenth-century demands, but she is not the ideal heroine since she is fundamentally secondary to the main action of vengeance—although Strauss's music brings her center stage. He tapped into the neurotic picture that Jung had adumbrated as a possibility for a daughter who is over-attached to a father and who unconsciously incorporates the sexual into her actions. This brings our Elektra into the twenty-first century, along with Salome—good models for other sexually driven heroines like Berg's Maria in *Wozzeck* and his Lulu. In 1908 Freud and Jung attended the first international meeting of psychoanalysts in Salzburg. In 1909 we have the premiere of *Elektra*. Mahler, Strauss's close colleague, was psycho-analyzed by Freud at about this time. According to Freud, Elektra provides a perfect example of hysteria. One sees in this opera Schopenhauer's and Nietz-sche's philosophies of will coupled with Freud's sexual theories and death drive. The operas about Orestes and Electra in the twentieth century, with their themes of murder and vengeance, are particularly apt for this time with its devastating wars in which technology enables mass destruction to be carried out on a grand scale.

Critics show how the music enhances interpretation. Bryan Gilliam cites Strauss in his informative and sensitive study of Strauss's *Elektra:* "His musical setting both intensified the dramaturgy, especially through 'the force of its cli-maxes,' and structural unity."[4] As Strauss himself says, "The struggle between word and music has been the problem of my life right from the beginning, which *Capriccio* solves with a question mark." Perhaps *Elektra* solved it earlier.

Catherine Clément has described opera as systematically inscribing the un-doing of women and is consistent in her application of this theory to Strauss's *Elektra*. She narrowly interprets the character of Elektra as the instrument of two males: her father Agamemnon and her brother Orestes. According to Clément, Elektra, as her mother before her, simply carries out phallocratic dictates: "The dawn rising over Mycenae is the dawn of our repression." In addition she claims, "From crime to crime . . . the family history is perpetuated. It can come to an end later only though the intervention of men and the invention of law. . . . The women, the survivors, fight one another, each one the bearer of a man . . . the mother, dead. . . . With her the historic undoing and defeat of femininity begins. . . . The victorious woman, the one who defends the father's power, will, with her vengeance, have betrayed the cause of women."[5] Similar views were held earlier by Specht and Overhoff: "Elektra seems no more than a vessel to contain mourning, the mirror that reflects Agamemnon: he is the 'true hero' of the opera."[6] Clément would like to call Elektra's death madness, but I think this undercuts the heroism of her climactic dance.[7]

Since Foucault's studies, madness has been increasingly qualified by circ-umstance. Who defines what constitutes madness, and what are the underlying epistemological or political premises of the definition? Rhetoric often construes enemies or the "other" (one who does not conform) as mad.[8]

The time is ripe for feminist interpretations of predominantly male-domi-nated art forms, but a disservice is rendered to both artists and women when these interpretations contribute to a new restrictive code in which female charac-ters are not allowed the freedom of the males. It seems perverse that a man can die in glory or as a result of passion, as Ajax does—or Werther, Tristan, Romeo, Siegfried—while women are deprived of this defining and passionate gesture because of the dictates of a new political correctness. A comparable criticism applied to the male would say that all of these characters (except Ajax, who is quite explicit in rejecting female dominance, or even influence, from either

Athena or Tecmessa) died or committed suicide mainly as a result of being dominated by female characters. It is particularly appropriate to attempt a gender-blind reading of Electra, since Sophocles seems to have set as his tragic ideal a character—whether male or female—who refuses to yield to circumstance. Compare only his Antigone.

I would like to suggest a different reading of Strauss' Elektra, one that would empower her again with the autonomy and yearning for freedom that Sophocles originally gave her. I claim that Elektra acts in a complex way to achieve the goals of her particular passions; like Clément and Ewans, I shall use the modern opera to try to understand Sophocles' controversial heroine, whose significance for the present is epitomized in Heiner Müller's contention: "In the century of Orestes and Elektra that's rising, *Oedipus* will be a comedy."[9]

Sophocles' Electra is a valid heroine in her own right, dominated only by her own passionate choices. She kills in the service of revenge and freedom and, in Strauss's version, ecstatically dances herself to death at the climax of her life. In this opera she, like Achilles, prefers a short life with glory to a long life of no consequence. She escapes the agony of life, following her Sophoclean precedent: "I see the dead do not suffer" (*El.* 1170). Sophocles in his *Oedipus at Colonus* also has his chorus comment on the undesirability of an overlong life, quoting a maxim frequently used to illustrate Greek pessimism:

Never to have lived is best, ancient writers say;
Never to have drawn the breath of life,
Never to have looked into the eye of day;
The second best's a gay goodnight and quickly turn away.[10]

Sophocles' *Electra* has yielded perhaps the most controversial interpretations of any of the ancient Greek tragedies, except Euripides' *Bacchae*. The interpretations range from finding in Sophocles an endorsement of a Homeric type of vengeance for which the brother and sister are justified, to depicting them as a pair of monsters who commit the morally repugnant act of matricide.[11] Many modern interpretations see Electra as a character between these extremes: she represents both the civilized incentives leading to justice and the darker drive of human nature that actually delights in murder. This is also the "structuralist" position, which sets up and sometimes synthesizes polar opposites in an uneasy equilibrium.[12]

My own view of the action of Electra and Orestes presented by both Sophocles and Strauss in their dramas is more positive than negative. Strauss and Hofmannsthal make Elektra heroic, but like other Sophoclean heroes, she has alienating characteristics and commits antisocial acts; she nevertheless achieves the acme of passionate human fulfillment.[13] We may not like this version of the heroine, but we must admire her. She is a late romantic superwoman modeled on the heroic figures of Victor Hugo, Henrik Ibsen and Friedrich Nietzsche. At the time of his *Elektra*, and mainly because of it, Strauss was the leader of the avant-garde in Europe.

Elektra and her brother are sustained in their purpose by music and words that partake of the ritual and litany from the Catholic mass. We have seen that many European operas are firmly rooted in the Christian tradition, and many of the ancient gods and goddesses of myth put on Christian masks. *Elektra* may be a pagan and secular work, but it was still influenced by the ritual with which the Germanic Catholics were familiar.

This may be heroism, but the results are deadly, and the ritual may seem perverted to modern Christian people who claim they believe in a tradition that says that when struck one should "turn the other cheek." Homer and Sophocles, however, condoned vengeance and belonged to the tradition in which one helped one's friends and harmed one's enemies. Now a Catholic God sanctions vengeance.

ELEKTRA

Three of Aeschylus' seven surviving plays deal with the legend of Orestes; his *Oresteia* is named after the hero. In the second play, the *Choephoroi,* Aeschylus gives us a dutiful and religiously oriented Electra who carries out the will of Zeus, ratifying the values of the *polis* ("city"). Aeschylus' position assimilates the values of the old aristocracy to the new *polis,* while religion is used to shore up the traditional values of the old clans. The power of the Eumenides will reside in the Areopagus, and Orestes is seen to endorse the values of the old nobility by representing and serving the interests of the father. Through the establishment of a law court, vengeance in the future will be contained in the civilizing framework of the *polis.*[14] Aeschylus shows us the problematics of killing and sets out the conflicting rights involved. Clytemnestra, the victim of clan warfare, also has powerful arguments on her side.

Nine of Euripides' nineteen surviving plays deal with the family of Electra and Orestes. Euripides does not reflect the values of the clan, nor those of the city, but rather concentrates on the individual. Marginalizing the house and the *polis,* he enters into internal space; he shows us a psychologically unbalanced Electra, distraught that she is deprived of her inheritance (*El.* 1088–1090).[15] He presents a relatively sympathetic Clytemnestra and almost defensible Aegisthus, with more right on their side than the vicious and neurotic children who kill them.

Sophocles is the most dramatic of the three Greek tragedians, at least in creating an exciting plot, and he was the most successful at pleasing the Athenian public. He is the main source of Hofmannsthal's drama, and Strauss, when he saw Hofmannsthal's play (1906) was overwhelmed by its magic, kindled by the ancient model. A close inspection of opera generally, and of this musical masterpiece specifically, can help us understand the intent of the original master. In three of his surviving plays Sophocles mentions the family of Atreus (*Ajax, Philoctetes, Electra*), but only one speaks of the vengeance of Orestes and Electra.

Strauss's orchestration of his opera is monumental. One hundred and fifteen players were required, including heckelphone and basset horn, as well as the whole artillery of the Wagnerian orchestra to which Strauss became heir, which included Wagner's tubas, bass trumpet, and contrabass trombone. Strauss also divided the strings into first, second, and *third* violins, an experiment he never repeated. His idea was to give an even denser texture by multidivided strings as well as the enormous array of wind and brass.

Strauss uses repeated themes—particularly associated with Agamemnon and Orest—and sometimes the same theme for both of them, as if Orest were a type of avatar, or reincarnation. The music hints that at times Orest has become his father, or at least is inspired by him. In Sophocles' play, Electra greets Orestes as her father and explains that she sees her father in Orestes (*El.* 1361); Strauss conveys this same observation through the music alone, playing Agamemnon's theme when Orest sings. One might say that the music is to be perceived as another character, who adds further commentary to the text. When we hear Agamemnon's theme, even when there is no verbal allusion to him in the libretto, we are overwhelmed by his presence and the way he shapes the drama. He is both present and absent: we hear his trace in the music.

We also hear Freud and his followers in the music. The permeation of the Agamemnon motif is part of the obsession that feeds Elektra's hysteria. In her opening monologue, *Allein! Weh, ganz allein*, the orchestral accompaniment is riddled with Agamemnon motifs.

Strauss is programmatic in his music, using the music to represent not only the obvious, but the abstract. We hear the orchestra imitating dogs barking, horses neighing and galloping; and plucked strings can represent the brilliance of crystals.

As the opera begins, Elektra laments before the palace. We are soon introduced to Agamemnon's theme and Orest's theme. A group of women, some slaves and some overseers, voice their opinions. The one who defends Elektra is punished.

The underlying harmonic feature of Elektra's opening monologue is more than dissonance, it is bitonality. The chord (E flat major to D flat major) that opens the monologue has become famous as a herald of the murky tonality of late Romantic / early free atonal style.[16] Nevertheless, Elektra has passages of transparent diatonic music, but the swirling horns and chromatic passing notes that predominate in most of her music are revealing indicators of a troubled spirit. We find these major keys and diatonic progressions particularly in her interchange with her mother, as if to say musically and in clinical terms, "I may be sick, but you are sicker . . . and soon you will be dead."

In his *Electra*, Sophocles gives us a heroine who is concerned not so much about her inheritance (ll. 452, 457, 960) as she is about effecting her personal justice, including that of the *genos* ("race," "kin") and in this context, where tyrants rule, the exercise of clan justice frees not only the family, but the *polis*. From the working out of a family curse and the civilizing of blood feuds, we see a *polis* liberated by a hero and a heroine. Sophocles' Electra differs from her pious and rather ineffectual predecessor in Aeschylus. She is now a representative of the *genos*, fighting as Antigone did for the values of her family. But by freeing the *polis* from tyrants, a popular if anachronistic theme that Sophocles adopts, she is actively heroic. In this version Clytemnestra and Aegisthus are despicable in their abuses. Electra cites her noble birth and how it is outraged by the abuses done it both night and day (*El.* 257–260); Clytemnestra goes so far as to celebrate the murder of Agamemnon in a monthly ceremony (*El.* 277–281); she drove out her own children (*El.* 589–590); Aegisthus is called a tyrant (hardly a favorable title in Athenian ears, *El.* 661), and Clytemnestra resembles him as *tyrannos* (*El.* 664); she abuses her daughter (*El.* 1196); both Clytemnestra and Aegisthus are guilty of crimes, waste, and excess (*El.* 1289–1291).

Elektra continues her lament and talks of blood sacrifices to her murdered father: one hundred throats of horses and dogs are to be cut for sacrifice (we hear galloping and barking in the music). Elektra dances an ecstatic dance in triple rhythm, which anticipates her final dance.

Hofmannsthal's text changes much of the ancient text. Whereas Sophocles' Clytemnestra made a monthly sacrifice of sheep to celebrate the day she slew Agamemnon (*El.* 277–281), now Elektra claims as sacrifice the murderers themselves and then horses and dogs—domestic "pets"—in honor of her father and her successful vengeance. She is her mother's heir, but with a gruesome difference. She will replicate Achilles' brutal sacrifice of Trojan youths for Patroclus, or again Klytämnestra's own sacrifice of Agamemnon. Elektra has learned from her mother. Hofmannsthal describes in detail the orgy of blood that Klytämnestra performs to dispel her dreams. *Blut*, "blood," is repeated again and again, and with these repetitions it is as if Klytämnestra were hyperventilating, a symptom of hysteria. More savagery is added by Hofmannsthal to Sophocles' version.

Rain is linked with blood in the text and in the music. As Elektra cries to her father about her vengeance and the victorious rite to follow, in which blood will be shed to atone for the original bloody murder, she intones:

> *Von den Sternen*
> *stürzt alle Zeit herab, so wird das Blut*
> *aus hundert Kehlen stürzen auf dein Grab!*
> *So wie aus umgeworfnen Krügen wird's*
> *aus den gebundnen Mördern fliessen.*

> As all time rains down from the stars, so will
> the blood of a hundred throats rain down onto your
> grave. As from overturned pitchers, so will the blood
> flow from the bound murderers.

This can be Hofmannsthal and Strauss's echo of Aeschylus' Clytemnestra: after she has killed Agamemnon, she rejoices in Agamemnon's blood "as the earth rejoices in rain at the time when corn-ears ripen" (*Ag.* 1390–1392). Bryan Gilliam points out that blood in Elektra's opening scene "serves a threefold purpose—as a reference to Agamemnon's violent death, to the sacrificial blood that will avenge that death, and to the blood relation between Agamemnon and his children."[17] This blood is the blood of the *genos,* and its demands are Elektra's imperative.

We can also see some symbolism in the triplets mentioned earlier as suggesting water, or again in the pervasive triple time that characterizes Elektra's passionate dances. This tripartite musical imagery could allude to both the divine trinity and the human (Agamemnon/Elektra/Orest). As wine in the Catholic Mass is transubstantiated into the blood of Christ, so here the water that pervades the text is translated into the blood of the murderers, that which incarnates the vengeance of the children and their father.

This modern trope not only adds resonance to the past but is another endorsement of the rightness of the act of vengeance. There are bloody aspects to any mass or to any revolution, but at the moment of sacrifice there can be a magic space in which, as Seamus Heaney says, "The longed-for tidal wave / Of justice can rise up / And hope and history rhyme."[18]

Sophocles shows Electra as a noble heroine, devoted to her father and the *genos.* In Sophocles we find reference after reference to the father: "All night I mourn my father and lie alone on my bed" (*El.* 92–95). Electra claims she is the only one of the house to mourn (*El.* 100). She prays to various gods to watch over those who die unjustly and also punish those who violate the marriage bed. She cries out, "Avenge my father's murder." Marriage and murder are linked as they will be later (110–116). Electra, the "unwed," weeps all these years and longs for Orestes (164–172). She blames the murderers for despising the dead (234–235). She speaks of avenging justice, the blood justice owed one's kin (248).

Instance after instance can be listed to illustrate Electra's ties to her father. Clytemnestra scolds her for her devotion to her father (289–290). Electra calls her father "noble" (366), and Chrysothemis "base" (367): by betraying her father she has betrayed her kin (368). Electra refuses to use the name of mother for Clytemnestra, and calls her instead "mistress/master" (597).

Electra calls herself a noble woman who grieves over her violated father's home (257–258). She says she hates her mother because her mother forces her to live with her father's murderers (261–264). She sees Aegisthus sitting on her father's throne, wearing her father's robes, and lying with her father's wife.[19]

Chrysothemis tells Elektra that plans are being made for her imprisonment. Chrysothemis leaves with little mutual understanding reached. At least she has warned her sister.

Klytämnestra conducts a propitiatory sacrifice and decides to consult with Elektra in hopes of alleviating her nightmares. Elektra tells her mother that only one proper sacrifice is needed to banish her dreams. She plays with her mother mercilessly, spitting out at last that her mother herself is the required victim. Hofmannsthal deals with the undefinable, and the nightmare consists of a nameless horror:

Und doch kriecht zwischen Tag und Nacht,
wenn ich mit offnen Augen lieg', ein Etwas
hin uber mich. Es ist kein Wort, es ist
kein Schmerz, es drückt mich nicht, es würgt mich nicht.
Nichts ist es, nicht einmal ein Alp, und dennoch,
es ist so fürchterlich, dass meine Seele
sich wünscht, erhängt zu sein.

As I lie, between day and night, with open eyes,
a something crawls over me. It is not a word, it is not a pain; it
neither presses me, nor chokes me. It is nothing, not
even a nightmare, and yet it is so horrible that my
soul longs for death (literally, "to be hanged").

Dissonance conveys Klytämnestra's nightmare, but Elektra responds calmly in a C major phrase that anticipates the ending of the opera with a resolution in C major. Klytämnestra uses crystals to ward off her dreams. The gods are not on the side of the tyrants: superstition and nightmare prevail, so crystals are necessary for casting spells. Klytämnestra claims she is hung with stones, that they have special powers that can be harnessed if one knows how to use them. We hear the gems sparkle as the flutes play thirty-second note arpeggios, and the harp plays glissando chords with the strings playing a quarter-note pizzicato accompaniment, and all instruments play a descending melodic figure in harmonic unison. Not only does this suggest the brilliance of crystals, but also the magic they entail. The dissonance occurring off the beat and alternating with silence is disconcerting, and once again the music conveys the ineffable.

In this, dissonance shows Klytämnestra's complex emotional state of mingled terror and doubt, whereas major keys communicate Elektra's control of the situation and clear commitment to her goal. We hear Klytämnestra's restless soul, and Elektra's reply in C major suits her clear and guiltless response and is an anticipation of the final victorious chord in C major that concludes the opera.

Elektra and Orest carry out the will of the gods explicitly in Sophocles (35–50), implicitly in Strauss and Hofmannsthal, but Klytämnestra must resort to the pagan magic of crystals. Elektra and Orest enlist the Christian God instead of the pagan, through suggestive music and invocations that we have seen recall a sacred liturgy. The contrast of Elektra's harmonic sequences, as opposed to Klytämnestra's dissonance, lets the nonverbal replace the verbal and the music define the indefinable. Elektra triumphs in the music: the proper God and the proper keys are on her side.

As Elektra concludes her baiting of her mother, the maids enter and whisper something in Klytämnestra's ear. Klytämnestra leaves in good spirits, but tells nothing to Elektra.

Klytämnestra in Strauss and Hofmannsthal is irredeemably evil: she laughs when she is told of Orest's death. Sophocles' Clytemnestra has a moment where her motherly concern, albeit brief, appears. After the Paedagogus tells her that Orestes is dead, she says, "O Zeus, should I call this fortunate? It is horrible, yet for the best. How sad it is that I must save my life through things that pain me" (766–768). She may be a woman who wants to live, but she is still a mother mourning the loss of her child. Hofmannsthal will not grant us this softness in Klytämnestra.

Many have noted the irony and cruelty in the scene where Sophocles' Electra hears of her brother's death, and fondles the urn in which she thinks his ashes have been encased (a scene eliminated by Strauss and Hofmannsthal), although her brother stands before her. In Strauss, this dramatic irony and cruelty is transformed into Elektra's deceptive play with her mother, setting her up as the required victim to end her nightmares. Hofmannsthal concentrates more on the characterization of Klytämnestra here as an evil, haunted woman, and we are forced both textually and musically to enter into the world of nightmare.

Besides the urn scene, the Sophoclean debate between mother and daughter is also eliminated. A predominantly rational exchange has been transformed into an emotional one. The Sophoclean Electra concludes that she has learned crime from her mother the criminal (621). It is hard for us to see any crime, even a verbal one, in Hofmannsthal's Elektra, because the tyrants she eliminates are so obviously monsters. She is instrumental in killing her mother, but she does so in self-defense and to liberate the city.

Sophocles first has Chrysothemis tell Electra she thinks that Orestes has come back, just after Electra has been told that he is dead (871–925). Hofmannsthal, instead, has Chrysothemis say that messengers have come to tell of Orest's death. Sophocles gave us a ray of hope, but reverses it in a dramatic coup. Reversals are characteristic in Sophocles. Oedipus rejoiced at the news of his "father" Polybus' death, thinking he had escaped the curse of patricide, only to be plunged into the unremitting tragedy that followed his discovering his birth. Such reversals are dramatically satisfying, but they are not the *Sturm und Drang* of the Romantics, who sometimes prefer unadulterated evil and gloom.

Elektra tries to convince Chrysothemis to help her kill Klytämnestra and Aigisth. She refuses. Elektra addresses Chrysothemis as "the daughter of my mother, the daughter of Klytämnestra," a variation of the comment by Sophocles' Electra that it is frightful that she, the daughter of such a father, would forget him and concern herself only with her mother, called disparagingly "she who bore you" (342). Sophocles has used Chrysothemis to contrast with the more determined sister: the heroic and the noble as opposed to the one who "makes do." We appreciate Electra's defiance all the more by seeing Chrysothemis' compromises.

In the opera, Chrysothemis dreams of a life including marriage and children (in the play what Electra imputes to Chrysothemis, 947 ff., Hofmannsthal makes explicit). Chrysothemis in the play is endorsed by many later commentators as the "sane" character by comparison with Electra.[20] Electra sneers at what she considers ignoble concerns; her attitude, typical of the Sophoclean hero, can be alienating.

As Orest reveals himself to Elektra, the music is bleakly haunting, reminiscent of both the Agamemnon and Orest themes. These change into a romantic duet as Elektra and Orest sing of their love for each other, and Elektra makes him pledge not to leave her. The musical theme here is reminiscent of *Tod und Verklärung*, written nearly twenty years earlier. As the man described in this tone poem is transfigured by his death, so is Elektra by the arrival of Orest, who will also be the one to signal her death when she is fulfilled by vengeance. Both melodic phrases are built on the descent of a perfect interval. Both also are in D flat major, which is Strauss's key of "serenely elevated rapture."[21] Both the death in *Tod und Verklärung* and Elektra's death are marked by the ominous clang of the Chinese bass gong, and both indicate triumph by the final resolution in C major.

In both opera and play, Electra combines Homeric *arete* ("virtue") with concern for a *polis* that should be governed by qualified people. *Arete* in her case also represents the ideals of the *genos,* and she considers herself a true child of Agamemnon. According to Aeschylean and Aristotelian biology, Electra and Orestes' bloodline comes only from the father. Clytemnestra was merely the receptacle in which the seed was sown and then incubated.

Strauss and Hofmannsthal's opera presents a loyalty that reflects this genetic tie between the two children, and in fact reveals much that goes beyond loyalty and could be called incest. It is expressed here in aria, between Elektra and her brother when he reveals himself to her. This is unquestionably a love duet, and in its own way endorses the *genos.*

Sophocles' Electra loves her brother as she loved her father. She claims Orestes' death has been her death (*El.* 808), and she sees herself as deprived of both father and brother. She speaks of the noble and royal blood she shares with her brother, both sprung from a noble father (858–859). She asks Chrysothemis to join her in her noble deed of slaying their father's murderers, claiming that to live basely is a base thing for nobles (989), and that even without Orestes, she would have either lived nobly or died nobly (320–321). This is the ancient cry of the *genos,* that noble deeds and noble blood go together. Elektra says also that by such a brave act they would show piety and win good fame (973 ff., 984 ff.).

When Orestes reveals himself, Electra addresses him in terms of their race and blood (1232 ff.). She speaks to him as one would a lover or a god, and prays he will never be removed from her. Orestes goes into the palace, describing it as a place of ancient wealth (1393). Clytemnestra is heard asking for pity for herself, who bore him, but this only underlines the fact that the father was the one who generated him, and again the *genos* prevails (1410–1412): *Vater über alles.*

After the celebration of Orest's arrival, the gods are mentioned and invoked. The duet becomes a *makarismos*: "Blest is he." The ancient *makarismos* was generally a song of praise for the bride and bridegroom, or for the dead. Euripides often uses the *makarismos* in an ironic way in his plays, seemingly as praise for the living, but in fact directed towards someone who will be dead by the end of the play.[22] In Strauss's opera it is also used ironically, as part of a love duet between brother and sister, as the two prepare for murder. Earlier Elektra promised Chrysothemis marriage after the murder, and Elektra says she will be Chrysothemis' bridesmaid. The duet between brother and sister endorses their symbolic marriage, which will be achieved through the ritual of vengeance; Elektra sings this *makarismos,* which besides expressing her love, serves as a paean for victory:

Der ist selig, der seine Tat zu tun kommt,
selig der, der ihn ersehnt,
selig, der ihn erschaut.
Selig, wer ihn erkennt,
selig, wer ihn berührt.
Selig, wer ihm das Beil aus der Erde gräbt,
selig, wer ihm die Fackel hält,
selig, selig, wer ihm öffnet die Tür.

Blessed is he who comes to perform his deed,
blessed is the one who longs for him,
blessed who sees him,
blessed who recognizes him,
blessed who touches him.
Blessed who digs up the axe for him,
blessed the one who holds the torch for him,
blessed who opens the door for him.

This blasphemous yet evocative litany, which parodies the beatitudes from the Sermon on the Mount, is appropriately greeted by the Paidagogos, who asks if the two are mad, since a sound might give them away. This is also in Sophocles, and gives us a moment of *opera buffa* in a long *opera seria.*

The perverted litany that the children pray, "Blessed is he who does the deed. . . . Blessed is he who digs up the axe," is equivalent to the prayers uttered in Aeschylus' *Choephoroi* (e.g., 246 ff.), besides being reminiscent of litanies used in the Catholic Mass.[23] Here in Hofmannsthal's ritualistic text, Apollo, Zeus and Christ are conflated, and religion endorses the revolutionary coup.

The entire opera can be read along the lines of the mass, with Introit, Kyrie, Gloria, Credo, Benedictus, Sanctus, and Agnus Dei. Victims are offered to exorcise Klytämnestra's dreams. It is said that another victim will bring her nightmares to an end. She will be the victim, the *agnus* offered to the *deus.* The blood of the victims is turned into the wine of vengeance. After the sacrifice Elektra dances her *Alleluia,* and the ritual ends: *ite, missa est.* Elektra goes through her own death and transfiguration. This use of the religious in the secular was present from the first operas of Monteverdi. So also in Beethoven's *Fidelio,* Leonore offers bread to her husband (*Da nim das Brot*) as communion in a last supper rite before he will go off to his death. Needless to say, many of the masses written by opera composers share the characteristics of opera, particularly those of Mozart and Verdi.

Orest enters the house and Elektra is upset for a moment because she did not give him the ax that killed their father and that she has been hiding. He kills Klytämnestra to Elektra's cries, "Strike her again!" (Clytemnestra boasted about her three blows as she killed Agamemnon, *Ag.* 1347).

Elektra then meets Aegisth and leads the way to the palace with a torch. Aegisth comments on her good humor as she dances while she guides him. The dance suggests a sacred ritual with Elektra as a priestess leading her victim to the sacrifice. She is a priestess in the service of Dionysus and she leads Aegisth as a bacchante would, with a blazing torch and dance. When Aegisth realizes his danger and recognizes Orest, he screams out, "Is there no one to hear me?" Elektra answers from outside the palace, "Agamemnon does," and we hear a loud triumphant version of the Agamemnon theme as Aegisth pays for his crimes with his life.

Sophocles' Aegisthus and Orestes bandy grim words as Orestes orders him within the palace. In Hofmannsthal's version Elektra is solely responsible for delivering Aegisth to Orest waiting within. We do not have the ironic scene in Sophocles, where Aegisthus sees a body and thinks it is Orestes', but then finds it is Clytemnestra's, a grim reworking of the trick on Electra who had to hold her brother's "death urn." In Hofmannsthal's version there are no mistakes and little irony.

In a certain sense Electra, like other Sophoclean heroes, embodies Homeric values rather than those of the new democratic *polis*; the aristocratic *genos* counts for more. Like Achilles, she is a hero of deeds rather than words, and she is even impatient with the deceptions Orestes must practice for their own safety. She demands that Aegisthus' body be tossed to the animals. This is not an ordinary woman.

Sophocles' chorus cheers the children on for avenging wrongdoing (*El.* 1386–1388). The chorus says the children are blameless (1423), Aegisthus shows that he enforces his commands with violence (1461–1463), and Orestes concludes by saying that justice has been exacted from the lawless, and if this type of justice (capital punishment) were enacted more often there would be fewer crimes committed (1505–1507). No one refutes him, and the chorus praises newly won freedom. These words conclude the play (1508–1510).

There is no such moralizing from Orest in Hofmannsthal's text. Orest disappears into the house when he enters to slay his mother. He has no more to say. Nor do we have the chorus' affirmation of freedom (1508–1510). Instead, Hofmannsthal has given triumphant, poetic, and passionate words to Elektra. She dominates the stage. It is she who enacts her personal freedom, which coincides with that of the *polis*, in her final frenzied waltz. Once again the operatic heroine triumphs.

In Sophocles one can see the two children as heroic tyrannicides, and this had resonance for the Athenian audience, whose history featured the tyranny of Hipparchus who was killed by Harmodius and Aristogeiton, thereafter called "Tyrant Slayers."[24] Harmodius and Aristogeiton avenged what they thought was a slight to their *genos* rather than carrying out simple civic duty. Harmodius' sister had been slighted because she had been asked to be *a kanephoros* ("ritual basket carrier") and then rejected on the ground that she was not suitable (Thuc. *Peloponnesian War*, 6. 56–58; Arist. *Const. Athens* 18). Sophocles shows Aegisthus as a tyrant (*El.* 661). The children of Atreus were faithful to their *genos* and liberated the *polis* (984–85). We find some of this in Stauss/Hofmannsthal, but the focus is different, now on the heroine.

As Chrysothemis announces victory to the transfigured Elektra, the latter goes into a strange aria, claiming that she herself is the music of victory, and she knows that she must lead the dance, but the ocean weighs her down. She claims she enacts the will of the gods. She sowed the seeds of darkness and gathered in the harvest of joy. She was a corpse, but now is the fire of life, and her flame consumes the world's darkness. Her face is paler than the moon. (Earlier this pallor was Klytämnestra's, so Elektra has in a sense become a transfigured double of her mother.) If someone looks at her, he must know death, or be consumed with joy. Elektra asks Chrysothemis if she sees the light coming from her. She is the moon. Chrysothemis speaks of regained love, now that her brother is here. Elektra says love kills. For those who have such joy, she says, one can only be quiet and dance. Then she dances a deadly waltz and falls into a deathlike trance. Chrysothemis' last words are cries to Orest. Elektra, the *A-lektral*, "the bedless one," will not marry the living, but like Antigone, will go as a bride to the dead. She is married to death in her triumph and the whole opera has been her *makarismos.*[25]

Strauss and Hofmannsthal transfer devotion to the *genos* into the area of incest, and music contributes to the sensuality, besides underlining the heroic act. Aegisthus' own loyalty to his *genos* may have been intensified by the fact that he was conceived in the incestuous union between his father Thyestes and Thyestes' daughter Pelopeia (thus Aegisthus' sister and mother). Incest is suggested in this opera, and it is clear that vengeance is something due the beloved family member. Elektra dies for her brother and father, as Antigone died for her brother, in a type of mock marriage, or bridal *makarismos*, which Elektra celebrates in dance. The dance makes physical the love implied in the text. Love in her case will kill, as it killed in the past (*Liebe tötet* = Elektra's *Liebestod*). Strauss's Elektra claims that the light and music emanate from her: *Ob ich die Musik nicht höre? Sie kommt doch aus mir. . . . Seht ihr das Licht, dass von mir ausgeht?* Elektra is fulfilled by her vengeance and death, as Chrysothemis will be in marriage. Strauss's Elektra will remain intimately and symbolically endogamic. Segal anticipates Strauss and Hofmannsthal when he speaks of Sophocles' Electra: "Electra exemplifies interiority carried to its extreme," and further, "Electra's commitment to death over life is a condition not only of her soul but of her whole universe."[26]

Gilliam has an excellent analysis of the keys and themes that Strauss selected to suggest the complex concatenation of the characters' motives, feelings, and circumstance in this opera. Death for Elektra is every bit as fulfilling, transforming, and spontaneous as Isolde's in Wagner's earlier *Tristan und Isolde* (1865). The key of E major, the key of Elektra's dance, is typically used "to express Dionysian, passionate, or even erotic sensations in music, hence the use of E as tonal centre for *Don Juan.*"[27] Agamemnon's death is in C minor, as E flat minor conveys Elektra's death. It is most appropriate for Elektra's triumphal dance to be in a major variation of E, and for the entire opera to resolve in C major, the musical affirmation of Agamemnon's death avenged. Gilliam points out other uses Strauss made of C major to convey a type of triumph at the end of a work, namely "evoking the ultimate restoration of the soul in the coda of *Tod und Verklärung*; the perfection of nature in *Also Sprach Zarathustra*; the restoration of sexual harmony at the end of *Die Frau ohne Schatten*; and the final chorus of *Der Friedenstag*, where opposing armies are reconciled at the end of the Thirty Years War."[28] Since this final chord is a major version of the minor chord associated with Agamemnon's death, here is the ultimate victory of the *genos,* which Elektra joyously affirms in her bacchic dance. Ancient and modern religious associations, coupled with musical suggestions, show an Elektra transfigured in death and transsubstantiated into music. She is "the music / While the music lasts."[29]

Clément and McClary might say that to eliminate a female heroine in this way is hardly the politically correct thing to do. They juxtapose Elektra with Tosca, Mélisande, and the heroine of *Erwartung* singing her mad chromatics. Others simply see Elektra as neurotic.[30] I agree with Abbate who sees Elektra as more than this; she is a heroine triumphant in her song.[31]

Strauss and Hofmannsthal saw Elektra in broad terms. This heroine denies the role socially assigned her and commits herself to serving a larger purpose that both fulfills and destroys her. She is a model for all freedom-fighters. The opera shows us the richness of Sophocles' message, which is still blazingly effective. Many ancient tragedies *are* opera in their extravagance, endorsing the height of human achievement in realizing an ideal. The price paid is obvious. If one wills oneself to be Electra, one cannot be Chrysothemis.

The opera offers a reading of Sophocles that through alterations intensifies the core of the drama. It is a genuinely new creation, which also sheds light on the ancient work. The modern reworking creates and reflects new trends: this Elektra is Jung's wildest dream come true, the perfect model for the Electra complex. She has a single-minded loyalty to her father, and she invokes God the father to support her enterprise.

CONCLUSION

Sophocles and Strauss and Hofmannsthal give Electra an important victory. Certain abuses call for retaliation and killing the tyrants is essential for freedom, both Elektra's own and the city's. Even Elektra's death echoes the motif of freedom. Is life with Pylades to be preferred? Her identification with the aristocratic *genos* led to her adopting the noble heroic code we associate with Homer.

Elektra's defense of her blood relatives could be identified with the nationalism with which Strauss was familiar. In addition, some of the ideas that we find in Hofmannsthal have resonance not only in the psychology of the day, but also in Nietzschean philosophy. The whole myth of the house of Atreus is filled with murders and vengeance. The fascist *modus vivendi* found an ancient model in this myth. Hitler is waiting in the wings. Violence can have both negative and positive consequences, beneficial for Elektra, tragic for Germany.

Elektra is a tragic heroine, and yet one who fulfills herself. Her dance of death is a celebration at the peak of her life and power, her *aristeia* ("noble action"). She did not go gently, but danced into that good night, because her words and feet "had forked lightning."[32]

APPENDIX
OPERAS ABOUT ELECTRA (INCLUDING FILM MUSIC)

André-Ernest-Modeste Grétry (1741–1813) (b. Liège, Belgium)
Electre (1781–1782)

Jean-Baptiste Lemoyne (1751–1796) (b. Eymet, France)
Electre (1782)

Wolfgang Amadeus Mozart (1756–1791) (b. Salzburg, Austria)
Idomeneo, re di Creta (1781) [Electra is a secondary character]

Johann Christian Friedrich Haeffner (1759–1833) (b. Oberschönau, Thuringia)
Electra (1787)

Alberto Nepomuceno (1864–1920) (b. Fortaleza, Brazil)
Incidental music for *Electra* (no date)

Richard Strauss (1864–1949) (b. Munich, Germany)
Elektra (1909)

Mikis Theodorakis (1922–) (b. Smyrna, Turkey)
Elektra (1992)
Music and songs for Michael Cacoyannis' *Elektra* (1961)

Marvin David Levy (1932–) (b. Passaic, NJ, USA)
Mourning Becomes Electra (1967)

OPERAS ABOUT ORESTES

Carlo Francesco Pollarolo (c.1653–1723) (b. ?, Italy)
L'Oreste in Sparta (1697)

Giacomo Antonio Perti (1661–1756) (b. Bologna, Italy)
Oreste in Argo (1685)

George Frederick Handel (1685–1759) (b. Halle, Germany)
Oreste (1734)

Johann Friedrich Agricola (1720–1774) (b. Dobitschen, Saxe-Altenburg, Germany)
Oreste e Pilade (1772), rev. as *I greci in Tauride*

Carlo Monza (c.1735–1801) (b. Milan, Italy)
Oreste (1766)

Domenico Cimarosa (1749–1801) (b. Aversa, Italy)
Oreste (1783)

Giuseppe Moneta (1754–1806) (b. Florence, Italy)
Oreste (1798)

Vincenzo Federici (1764–1826) (b. Pesaro, Italy)
Oreste in Tauride (1804)

Conradin Kreutzer (1780–1849) (b. Messkirch, Baden, Germany)
Orestes (1818)

Sergey Ivanovich Taneyev (1856–1915) (b. Vladimir, Russia)
Oresteya (1895)

Paul Felix Weingartner (1863–1942) (b. Zara, Dalmatia)
Orestes: *Agamemnon, Das Totenopfer, Die Erinyen* (1902)

Darius Milhaud (1892–1974) (b. Aix-en-Provence, France)
Agamemnon, Les choéphores, and Les euménides (1913–1922)

Ernst Krenek (1900–1991) (b. Vienna, Austria)
Leben des Orest (1928–1929)

Henk Badings (1907–1987) (b. Bandung, Java)
Orestes (1954)

Flavio Testi (1923–) (b. Florence, Italy)
La furore di Oreste (1956)

Sir Harrison Birtwistle (1934–) (b. Accrington, England)
The Oresteia (1981)

Stravinsky's *Oedipus Rex:*
The King in a Trap

Sergei Prokofiev like many others, was dubious about this opera:

Stravinsky has been delivered of *Oedipus Rex*, a scenically static opera-oratorio in 2 acts.
. . . The librettist is a Frenchman, the text is Latin, the subject Greek, the music Anglo-
German (after Handel), it will be produced by a Monegasquan enterprise and on Ameri-
can money—the height of Internationalism.[1]

Prokofiev was a rival, so his criticism had a certain bite. Brecht said of the
Oedipus Rex, "One must simply copy that," and Benjamin Britten, "One of the
peaks of Stravinsky's output, this work [*Oedipus Rex*] shows his wonderful
sense of style and power of drawing inspiration from every age of music, and
leaving the whole a perfect shape, satisfying every aesthetic demand."[2]
Stravinsky represents a culmination of nineteenth-century musical tradition
and a challenging prologue for the twentieth. Just when we think we have neatly
slotted him in his historical place, he leaps out and defies classification. We try
to trap him by labeling the exceptional as "irony." Nevertheless, the irony is
often better applied to us: often the trap holds us, not him. He saw confinement
as liberating, form as facilitating. His genius is undeniable, and he laughs at his
interpreters (in all of his work, his sense of humor is mercurial). He is a composer who makes critics despair, or be seen as fools, or both. He has been regarded as a Zeitgeist, and Paul Horgan said, "It is my belief that the work of our
beloved Maestro [Stravinsky] will require the central decades of the twentieth
century to be known in cultural history as 'The Age of Stravinsky.'"[3]
Given the impossibility of "boxing Stravinsky," nevertheless Stravinsky is
known for three periods, Russian, neoclassical, and serial.[4] These are not clearly
defined, although dates have been proposed: The Russian period begins with his
first unpublished works in 1898 and lasts about fifteen years; it features, for

example, *Two Melodies of Gorodetzky* (1907/1908) and *Four Russian Songs* (1918/1919). The neoclassical period lasts about thirty years, from *Mavra* (1922) to *The Rake's Progress* (1948–1951). *Oedipus Rex* (1928) is in this neo-classical period.[5] Finally the serial period lasts about twenty years, from *Septet* (1952/1953) to his death in 1971. But there are obvious overlaps, or recapitula-tions, for instance *Canon on a Russian Popular Tune* (1965) and *Requiem Canticles* (1965–1966).

Stravinsky held citizenship first in his native Russia, then France, and finally the United States. He also lived for many years in Switzerland. His music reflects the national characteristics of the places where he lived: for instance, Russian folk music and religious music of various traditions, American jazz, and the twelve-tone system (as practiced by Schönberg). African music, with its contrapuntal rhythms, also influenced him. Among composers who influenced him were Rimsky-Korsakov, Mussorgsky, Tchaikovsky, Monteverdi, Pergolesi, Mozart, and Verdi (besides Italian opera in general).

Others have set this play to music, and the earliest I have located is the 1585 performance of *Oedipus Tyrannus* with choruses by Andrea Gabrieli. Henry Purcell added incidental music to the play in 1692. There are not many operas about Oedipus and, similar to the operas on Electra, none are in the nine-teenth century. This topic seems to appeal most to the twentieth century, and this may be because we live in the post-Freudian era. The theme of Oedipus is appropriate for modern *angst*. The Hutcheons speak of plays that echo Oedipus' theme, like Harry Kondoleon's *Zero Positive*.[6] In the latter play, plague is iden-tified with AIDS.

Catherine Clément also sees how Sophocles' Oedipus influenced several operas. She finds the riddle of the sphinx in Puccini's *Turandot*, and in Wagner's *Ring* sees Wotan as Oedipus and Antigone as Brünnhilde, who is there after men have perished.[7] She did not write about Jocasta, but if she can see triumph in Brünnhilde's death, then she should certainly find it here in Jocasta's, through the power of music.

Stravinsky said he was eager to realize "the idea which has pursued me for some time of composing an opera in Latin based on a universally known tragedy of the ancient world."[8] He was inspired with the idea on a trip to Italy in 1925. He said he stopped in Genoa and bought a life of St. Francis of Assisi. He was inspired to use Latin in his opera when he read about St. Francis using French as "the language of poetry, the language of religion, the language of his best mem-ories and most solemn hours, the language to which he had recourse when his heart was too full to express itself in his native Italian, which had become for him vulgarised and debased by daily use; French was essentially the language of his soul."[9] Stravinsky felt that Latin was equally rich. He enjoyed it not only for its formality, but its sacral and esoteric qualities.

Stravinsky was Russian Orthodox; nevertheless, instead of using Old Sla-vonic, the language of the liturgy with which he was familiar, he adopted the language of the Roman Catholic Church. Old Slavonic was barely intelligible to modern Slavs, and Latin shared this obscurity. There was also the additional consideration that the Orthodox rite forbade instruments, and Stravinsky could not imagine music sung without instruments. Stravinsky understood Latin with difficulty; it had a ritual and sanctified function for him: "an older, even an imperfectly remembered language must contain an incantatory element that could be exploited in music."[10] He explained, "The choice had the great advantage of giving me a medium not dead but turned to stone and so monumentalised as to have become immune from all risk of vulgarisation."[11] He turned to the monumental Greeks and what Aristotle considered the most monumental of plays: Sophocles' *Oidipous Tyrannos*. Stravinsky was looking for a universal plot. He said he wanted to distill the dramatic essence, and "to focus on a purely musical dramatisation." This opera would communicate through music and the sound of its words.

He consulted Cocteau, who he knew had abridged Sophocles' *Antigone* for performance, and asked him to collaborate on abridging *Oedipus Tyrannus*. At first Cocteau delivered a rather long and sophisticated version of the whole play, which Stravinsky slashed brutally. He told Cocteau to start again and make it simple. The final version was translated into Latin by the Abbé Jean Daniélou.[12] Cocteau then suggested they add spoken commentary in French, which would be useful for a French audience who might not understand the Latin.

Stravinsky became increasingly disillusioned with Cocteau's collaboration, and by the time of the performance had serious doubts about the necessity of any "explanatory" passages at all.[13] One of his nasty comments, which reveals a great deal about their relationship, came when he was told that Cocteau was dying, and he was asked to write a get-well note; he said, *Cocteau ne peut pas mourir sans faire réclame* ("Cocteau can't die without advertising himself").[14] He still remembered the first performance of *Oedipus*, in which Cocteau stole the dramatic thunder by his spirited deliveries in his role as speaker / commentator, an effect opposite to what Stravinsky intended.

Nevertheless, the speaker adds interesting counterpoint. Here are pure words that thrust us into a world without music. We remember that Greek tragedy alternated between speech and song, with dance accompanying the latter. The mass also has spoken and sung portions.

Oedipus Rex was composed after Stravinsky returned to the Russian Orthodox Church in April 1926. Stravinsky was "profoundly religious."[15] One can trace many influences in this opera, but indeed the religious is the most striking. Stravinsky himself says, speaking of the Latin:

As I had fully anticipated, the events and characters of the great tragedy came to life wonderfully in this language, and, thanks to it, assumed a statuesque plasticity and a stately bearing entirely in keeping with the majesty of the ancient legend. What a joy it is to compose music to a language of convention, almost of ritual, the very nature of which imposes a lofty dignity! One no longer feels dominated by the phrase, the literal meaning of the words. Cast in an immutable mold which adequately expresses their value, they do not require any further commentary. The text thus becomes purely phonetic material for the composer. He can dissect it at will and concentrate all his attention on its primary constituent element—that is to say, on the syllable. Was not this method of treating the text that of the old masters of austere style? This too, has for centuries been the Church's attitude towards music, and has prevented it from falling into sentimentalism, and consequently into individualism.[16]

This articulates the very core of modernism. These artists wanted to use the classics to transcend the individual and reach the universal, as did James Joyce in his *Ulysses* and T.S. Eliot in his *Wasteland* and *Four Quartets*.

Various sections of *Oedipus Rex* correspond to the mass, though there are also links with other forms of sacred music. Needless to say, this opera / oratorio projects a perverted ritual with its secular profanities. There is a distinct relationship between the *Kyrie* and the opening of the drama: the *Kyrie* asks the Lord to give mercy, and *Oedipus Rex* begins with a chorus of citizens approaching their lord and asking for mercy. The *Credo* and Gospel correspond to Creon's "deus dixit." There is a *Gloria,* which hails the arrival of Jocasta. This resembles the section in the liturgy dedicated to the Virgin Mary, the Mother of God. Here we have the queen, mother (and wife) of king Oedipus, greeted with a *Gloria!* One might discern the *Sanctus* and *Benedictus* in the gradual revelation of Oedipus' origin, in that he mistakes himself for the son of a god, and falsely exalts himself until the full truth is revealed. The confession before communion is paralleled by Oedipus' repetition of his wrongs (*nefastum est,* before *Lux facta est*). The *Agnus Dei* and sacrifice of Christ resemble the sacrifice of Oedipus for his people. In this text Oedipus leaves voluntarily. His departure will bring about the end of the plague, just as Christ's sacrifice expiated man's sins. Communion follows (the people expressing their gratitude for what Oedipus did for them positively). Oedipus leaves in a parallel to the *Dismissio.* Stravinsky saw music as facilitating communion when he said, "My epilogue will seek to determine the profound meaning of music and its essential aim, which is to promote a communion, a union of man with his fellow-man and with the Supreme Being."[17]

Stravinsky, like Nietzsche, saw music as approaching the ineffable. It is a means for seeing Plato's sun, when emerging from the cave, or intuiting it when inside. The resemblance to the Christian mass lends itself to this mystique. This is another extraordinary insight of modernism: the god of religion becomes the form of Truth and Beauty—or *da sein,* being itself.

The musical influences are Italian opera (especially in the parts of Oedipus and Jocasta), with direct quotations from Verdi, such as his *Otello,* jazz, with its syncopated rhythms (in Creon's report of Apollo's oracle); sacred music, from Gregorian chant to Monteverdi and Verdi (Creon and the chorus); folk music (the shepherd), and especially Russian, with many allusions to *Boris Godunov.* The chorus shouts *Gloria* like the peasants in the coronation scene of that opera.

The premiere of Stravinsky's *Oedipus* as an oratorio took place on May 30, 1927, in Paris. It was performed by the Russian ballet at a celebration of Diaghilev, on the twentieth anniversary of his company. Diaghilev commented that this was a strange contribution to his festivities (*un cadeau très macabre*).[18] It was performed in an austere manner, more so than Stravinsky desired. Resources were scarce, and he had only finished the music a few days earlier. It was performed first as an opera on February 23, 1928 in Vienna. A revised version from 1948 is what is mostly performed today.

For Stravinsky, classical was synonymous with the monumental. Stravinsky used austerity to achieve this effect. Likewise, Nijinsky in *L'Après-midi d'un faun* moved in silhouette to suggest a classical Greek frieze.

Stravinsky sought minimal movement on stage, and asked that the chorus members in *Oedipus Rex* sit in a row, with their heads hidden by cowls, and read their text from scrolls. The singers were to be lined up on platforms of varying height, with costumes and masks, only their arms and heads moving, so that they would resemble statues. Light would shine on them as they sang. Oedipus was lit throughout, except for one exit when he should sink "by means of a trapdoor, as in a fairy scene."[19] Creon and Jocasta were to be continually on stage (except for Oedipus' one exit, after which he would reenter wearing a mask indicating his blindness).

Ingmar Bergman, who successfully staged *The Rake's Progress* to Stravinsky's liking in Stockholm and was thinking of possibly filming *Oedipus Rex*, said he would stage it without masks: "A mask may be beautiful, and it can be a useful façade for all sorts of things, but the price, loss of contact, is too great."[20] We can see he has a different view from Stravinsky, who preferred classical distancing, or perhaps a *Verfremdungseffekt*, which would link him with Brecht. One reason Stravinsky gave for his "'wooden Indian staging concept of *Oedipus*" is, "The music is more important than the action, just as the words were more important than the action in Shakespeare."[21]

Stravinsky also defended the stylization in his notes for the *Poetics:* "Dialectics supposes that art is synonymous with free creation, but this is not so. Art is more free when it is more limited, more finished, canonical, dogmatic."[22] In his actual lecture he said, "The more art is controlled, limited, worked over, the more it is free."[23]

Cocteau, who made the first designs for the stage set, wanted his speaker to wear contemporary evening dress. The speaker in a sense acted like Sophocles' chorus. Stravinsky had additional notes for staging the oratorio as an opera, but its title, including the words "opera-oratorio," shows that he wanted to keep both in mind, thus making it available for concert performance. He seemed to want to retain the solemnity of a religious ritual. The social ritual was added by Cocteau.

OEDIPUS REX

There are obvious changes between the opera / oratorio that Stravinsky has created and the play that Sophocles delivered to Athens around 426 B.C. As with the other works thus far compared, the greatest differences are the additions provided by the music throughout. The language is changed from the flexible and rich poetic language of ancient Greek to a stilted and simplistic form of medieval Latin, whose closest tie is to the liturgy. Sophocles' long, flowing phrases, filled with imagery and word play, have been replaced with truncated lines, repetitions, rhymes, and insistent rhythms. The irony is still there—and some of the wit—but the poetic masterpiece has been transformed into a musical one: we search the Latin text in vain for Sophocles' genius. The text has also been reduced to its bare outlines, so some things are now scarcely intelligible.

The commentary professes to fill these gaps, but more often than not it is at war with the text; sometimes we simply are exposed to word-play amusing to the poet (Cocteau in one case, e.e. cummings in another). Stravinsky, as usual, blamed Cocteau for some of the initial failure. Cocteau, himself the first speaker, tried to deliver his lines in a dramatically expressive way at odds with the restrained delivery advocated by Stravinsky.

Stravinsky's opera / oratorio is more than a sum of its parts because it derives strength from its use of ancient tradition of the liturgy; there is also folk music, along with the other musical traditions mentioned earlier. This opera / oratorio transforms traditional elements into something unique and immediately identifiable as Stravinsky's creation, a cross between a sacred liturgy and the *Rite of Spring*. We have the same emphasis on rhythm that we find in all of Stravinsky's works, particularly a rhythm that goes against traditional accents; nevertheless, the rhythm is not as radical as we find in the *Rite* and other works, and the keys are treated harmonically to a greater extent than in that piece, or in even more radical ones like the *Octet*. We understand how this is neoclassic, not only with the choice of a classical theme, but through a more conventional use of rhythm and harmony (generally through the use of the tonic triad), although there are contrapuntal sections.[24] This aligns Stravinsky more with Handel than Bach. Stravinsky himself noted that the dotted rhythms he used in this opera and other works on classical themes (e.g., *Apollo, Orpheus,* and *Persephone*) were a reference to the eighteenth century:

My uses of them in these and other works of that period . . . are conscious stylistic references. I attempted to build a new music on eighteenth-century classicism using the constructive principles of that classicism . . . and even evoking it stylistically by such means as dotted rhythms.[25]

Since the voices are used as instruments, the words often simply add texture. Stravinsky also uses syllables as musical notes.[26] He often changes the usual accents of words, a technique that occurs also in Russian folk music.[27] Even the name Oedipus is accented differently in different places in this score: one time on the first syllable, another on the second. This increases the ritual quality, and we see that the individual is subjected to the ritual.

This music is more rhythmic and harmonically playful than polyphonic, although there are polyphonic devices such as fugal entries, particularly reminiscent of Handel. The rhythmic and harmonic variations add commentary to the text. Both tend to reinforce, as Cocteau suggests, the trap that closes on Oedipus. He cannot escape his fate, nor the music that will reduce him to a percussive monotone. Stravinsky, although he might deny it, by using repetitive figures adds additional information, as Wagner did with the *Leitmotif.* Note the use of E flat minor with the word "Thebes" (establishing a minor key for the city, which is ominous if we associate a minor key with something negative) and *eruam* ("I shall scour"), following the word "Thebes" appearing with a repeated note at a single pitch in a triplet figure, a ritualistic assertion in the midst of flourishes. The chorus uses the same repeated triplet for *trivium,* the fateful place where three roads meet, where Oedipus killed his father. The scouring will end with him, and the music suggests this in advance by linking the two words with the same musical figure.

To the influence of Italian and Russian opera, the English oratorio, Gregorian Chant, we must add Stravinsky's own recent ballets. The sacrifice in the *Rite of Spring* is an obvious parallel to the sacrifice of Oedipus, and there are many similarities in rhythm and dissonance between that work and Stravinsky's opera. In following Verdi, Stravinsky also followed Verdi's philosophy, which he quotes: "Let us return to old times, and that will be progress."[28] Stravinsky himself said, "A *renewal* is fruitful only when it goes hand in hand with *tradition.* Living dialectic wills that renewal and tradition will develop and abet each other in a simultaneous process."[29] He endorses tradition as T.S. Eliot does in "Tradition and the Individual Talent." Stravinsky's use here and elsewhere of "dialectic" suggests that he was seriously addressing with his musical innovations the political notion of dialectical materialism; one might compare Engels' application of Hegel's notion of history making its changes through a process of cancellation and recapitulation of previous moments at a higher level (*Aufhebung*). One might say, however, that Stravinsky was criticizing Communism for NOT following tradition.

The text is used as music, or rather percussion. The words are repeated in a percussive fashion, and various words such as *pestis* and *serva nos* are reiterated like drumbeats. They tattoo a pattern in our minds: the mesmerizing liturgy has begun. This shows another change from Sophocles, who engaged our mind as much as our ears. Words add an element to the ritual as we have noted, particularly Latin words that recall the liturgy, but repeated rhythms also increase the power of the ritual by an appeal to our emotional / sensual nature. Stravinsky endorses rhythm as a source of life: "Music exists if there is rhythm, as life exists if there is a pulse."[30] These rhythms, with their abrupt changes, "must have seemed to have more in common with African and Asian than with other European music."[31] Modern painting also shows the influence of Africa and Asia: for example, Gauguin, and Picasso's *Demoiselles d'Avignon* with their faces that resemble African masks.

The opera oratorio begins with a speaker, who originally spoke in French, but his speeches were later translated into the languages of the countries where the performance took place. The speaker claims he will function as the audience's memory, since the production has pared the original play to an abbreviated monumental form. Cocteau produced his own version of Sophocles' *Oidipous Tyrannos, La machine infernale* (1934), but this came later than the opera; the "infernal machine" is a trap that closes slowly on its victim. There are several allusions to this trap in his commentary on the opera. The prologue tells of a plague afflicting Thebes; the people invoke Oedipus to save them, since he had liberated them once before from the scourge of the Sphinx.

This is followed by a solemn lament by the chorus, and their voices combine with the orchestra so closely that it seems to be an additional instrument. Four chords dominate, and they will return at the end. The chords are faintly reminiscent of the four notes beginning the *Dies Irae* in the Gregorian liturgy. Leonard Bernstein traces it to the aria in Verdi's *Aida* in which Aida has just revealed her secret to Amneris and begs her for mercy; it begins *Pietà ti prenda*. Bernstein said when he remembered where these notes came from, "The whole metaphor of pity and power become clear; the pitiful Thebans supplicating before their powerful king, imploring deliverance from the plague . . . an Ethiopian slave girl at the feet of her mistress, Princess of Egypt."[32] The opening notes of *Oedipus Rex* also parallel the hymn to Phtah from *Aida:* here the people and priests are supplicating their god. Both are aptly prayers and thus comparable to the opening of the *Oidipous Tyrannos*, which begins with Oidipous addressing the people as his children. In the case of the hymn in *Aida*, the ritual aspect is even more apparent.

The chorus members beg Oedipus to save them. Now it is the chorus, rather than a priest, that invokes Oedipus at the beginning. Is this an emphasis on the collective rather than on the individual? One thinks of the gigantic choruses Stravinsky was used to hearing in Russia.

The parallel between the opening chorus with Stravinsky's own piano Serenade in A has been noted.[33] Stravinsky used a tonality without fifths, which allowed increased monotony, relieved only by the contrapuntal motion of the chorus.

The ritual choral prayer that opens the opera yields to Oedipus' florid assurances. He is like a priest, Christ incarnate, reassuring his people in the dulcet tones of an Italian tenor that he will find a solution. The florid line promises a rich solution. The chorus resumes its monotonous prayer, bringing us back to the reality of the plague. The timpani mark the chorus, whereas the oboe accompanies Oedipus' promise to find a solution, first through the dispatch of Creon, his wife's brother, to consult the oracle at Delphi. The timpani etch a pattern into our minds, a tattoo of fate and reality, in contrast to Oedipus' lyric assurances with oboe accompaniment. Pascal characterized man as *un roseau pensant*, "a thinking reed," and all of this same vulnerable fallibility is to be found in Oedipus, along with his intellectual prowess. The use of the woodwinds and the single human voice add to this commentary, so that the contrast with the inexorable chorus is emphasized: the individual in the face of tradition.

Oedipus promises to help, and tells the chorus he loves them. Love seems to be a motif and is expanded to include not only the love between a man and a woman, but a king and his people. Stravinsky objected to any mention of love, and regarded it as a sentimental addition by Cocteau.

The chorus members ask Oedipus what they should do. The parallels with the liturgy, from the initial invocation of God, and the begging for pity (*Miserere nostri, Domine, quia peccavimus tibi,* "Have pity on us lord, for we have offended you"), followed by the *Kyrie eleison* ("Lord have mercy") add to the religious quality. Oedipus is the lord made manifest, and Apollo delivers the word of God. The *Credo* leads to the Gospel section of the Mass. Tiresias comparably delivers the word of God.

Oedipus' first entrance returns us to the world of the individual hero, now in the form of an Italian tenor, or with the *melismata* of a Handelian *castrato*. Oedipus will learn to his dismay how much he is part of the general pattern: a cipher and a plaything of fate—this is expressed by the music. He will abandon his lyric flourishes and at the end he will be absorbed by the ritual and its rhythmic music. In his final chant he can only repeat his sins. He has adopted the universalizing music of the chorus in this confession.

Oedipus says that Creon has been to the oracle at Delphi, and he will tell them what is proper. Creon's arrival is greeted by the chorus, which cries *Vale*. The Latin here is not the Latin of a poet, and it reveals several embarrassing errors. *Vale* would work if it were the Greek *chaire,* which can be both greeting and farewell. In Latin the chorus seems to be saying "good-bye" to Creon as they welcome him. Also, the most important words in the text seem to me to be in Oedipus' admission of guilt (quoted above), which concludes with *lux facta est*. This passage contains the phrase *kekidi quem nefastum est*. Stravinsky chose the "k" because he favored the scholastic pronunciation to the one used in the church (and "k" lends itself more to his percussive techniques than the softer "c").[34] However, the musical accent changes the meaning: accented on the first syllable *kekidi* is the intransitive perfect form of *cado* and means "I fell down." But Daniélou would have us believe that Oedipus is saying "I killed." That would have entailed accenting *kekidi* on the second syllable for the transitive perfect of *caedo*, rather than *cado*. Stravinsky was often accused of having strange musical accentuation (on the less important syllables), particularly in his syllabification of a Latin text, because, as Gilbert Amy noted of his religious music, "The 'rhythmic theme' must impose its order on the Latin phrase even if this involves some mispronunciation."[35]

Stravinsky was notorious for his eccentric settings of language, preferring in most cases the sound of the music rather than the natural accentuation of the language he is using. An example is his idiosyncratic setting of the English in the "Lyke-Wake Dirge" of his *Mass*. There is something almost perverse about the way he enjoys accenting weak stresses.

Creon sings in a major key, in contrast to the minor keys we have been hearing. Creon begins by saying, "The god has spoken," and ends with a descending octave arpeggio to the words "Apollo has spoken," accompanied by solo trumpet. We find a parallel descent with a trombone doubling the voice in Mozart's *Tuba Mirum* from his *Requiem*. The killer of Laius, the former king, must be expelled from the city. Oedipus promises to find the killer, boasts about solving the riddle of the Sphinx, and promises to save the city again.

Creon makes his announcement with full orchestral accompaniment, including brass and timpani. His delivery of Apollo's message, *Apollo dixit deus*, corresponds to the *Dominus dixit* of the Mass, or the *Credo*. Handel, Vivaldi, and others have impressive settings of the *Dominus dixit*, and Stravinsky also uses this heritage, besides adding his own mélange of jazz and what he calls his *Folies Bergères* music. C major and the insouciance of the jazz convey well the self-confidence of Creon in the oracle. He is a man who knows his place, and according to him, if "God's in his heaven, all's right with the world." He is not cursed with the intellectual's questioning.

The chorus greets Tiresias, and he speaks to the accompaniment of music, which resembles the appearance of Pimen, the monk, in *Boris Godunov*, with the same instrumentation (bassoon, over a string accompaniment, although Mussorgsky adds a clarinet) and wandering scale line that suggests both contemplation and mysterious holiness.

Tiresias' lyric line is rich, allusive, and powerful in its authority. This meditative music reinforces Tiresias' plea to be left alone: *tacere fas* ("it is right that I remain silent"). The *fas* in this phrase includes the idea of religious right, and this connotation does not exist in the Greek.

The stage instructions call for Tiresias to come out of a grotto, to which, after his aria, he returns. When Tiresias makes his fateful pronouncement, he does it in D Major (which key accompanies Oedipus' final words *Lux facta est*); major keys seem to indicate divine authority. We find the same device in Richard Strauss's *Salome*. Jokanaan (John the Baptist) always delivers his warnings in major keys, which contrast with the roving chromatics and dissonance of the others.

We miss Tiresias' inspired language from the original Greek, replete with ambiguity. Simplicity replaces ambiguity, unless it is unintentionally added from ignorance, as seems the case when Jocasta addresses her brother and Oedipus as *reges*, "kings" (although this word may indicate generic royalty, probably like Homeric heroes being called *basilees*, which can mean both "kings" and "royalty"). But this still makes Tiresias' statement that "the murderer of the king is a king" ambiguous since *rex* is used in both cases, by him and by Jocasta. Thus either Creon or Oedipus could have been the king that Tiresias said killed the king. The ambiguity is increased since one does not hear Tiresias bluntly saying that Oidipous is the killer (*OT* 362: "I say you are the murderer of the man whom you seek"). The now elliptical phrase ("the murderer of the king is a king") is repeated rhythmically by the speaker, who in this case enters the music and becomes himself another instrument.

When the king realizes that he is a suspect, he plaintively claims that envy hates the fortunate; the plaintive note is augmented by the transition to a minor key for his entry, after an assertive major. Significant musical commentary is provided by the pitiful response of Oedipus to Tiresias. Using Tiresias' final note of D as a pivot, he jerks the line into another key, E flat. Tiresias used the tonic of D major, and Oedipus raises the key one semi-tone, using D to suggest a 7th, leading to the new tonic in E flat. It was as if he diminished the importance of what Tiresias was saying, and musically we are presented with another way of looking at the situation, namely that Tiresias and Creon are plotting against Oedipus, rather than Oedipus being in fact culpable. D major will be the key in which he states *Lux facta est.* Oedipus will end up trapped in the key that Tiresias selected. There is also a parallel with the theme accompanying the shepherd, who reveals the truth like Tiresias: both have bassoon accompaniment. This instrument suggests a rustic horn, such as one used in the mountains, and also a type of purity is possibly gained by this type of isolation.

The speaker says that Oedipus questions "the fountain of truth," the seer Tiresias. Because of the seer's reticence, Oedipus accuses him of being the killer. Angered, Tiresias responds with the accusation that the killer of the king is a king.

The entire quarrel between Creon and Oidipous is omitted, and the debate between Tiresias and Oidipous is reduced to its barest outline. This opera resembles a statue by Giacometti with its spare skeletal outline in comparison with the fully fleshed-out poetry of the original play. So we miss the glorious line where Oidipous uses jolting metonomy: *tuphlos ta t'ota, ton te noun, ta t'ommat' ei,* "You are blind in your ears, your mind and your eyes," (*OT* 371). The repetition of the "T's" in the original Greek convey anger and the spitting that accompanies it, as Oidipous accuses Tiresias of the blindness that at this point can more aptly describe Oidipous' own state of knowledge. This is marvelous irony: Oidipous is blind in his mind and ears (at this point he will neither listen nor learn) and he will be blind in his eyes by the end of the play, but then he can see with his soul.

In the opera, we are not shown in a developed way how Oedipus' anger makes him blind, since, instead of understanding or seeing, he simply accuses. Oedipus' knowledge will come when he "sees the truth," but by then the pain is too strong, and he blinds himself so he does not have to see the world in which he caused and suffered so much pain.

The speaker intervenes, saying that Jocasta will calm the princes and shame them to leave off their quarreling, but the entire scene in which Oedipus threatens Creon with death for his part in the conspiracy with Tiresias is eliminated. Without this scene, Jocasta's aria, "Princes, aren't you ashamed?" does not make as much sense. When Oedipus is at his most fierce, we understand how he could have killed his father in anger. This might then constitute what Aristotle calls *hamartia,* the complex term that is often reduced to "tragic flaw" in English.

Jocasta's entrance is signaled by a stirring march in C major. The chorus hails her with the word *Gloria,* corresponding to another portion of the mass, the salutations to the divine queen, the Virgin Mary, the mother of God. One recalls Monteverdi's Penelope. Jocasta resembles Penelope in that, as the man is buffeted about by fortune and is seen as weak and ineffective, the woman is a rock. The role of Jocasta in the opera has definitely changed from that in Sophocles. She is a diva in every sense of the word; not only is she the operatic sovereign, but in the Gloria there are suggestions of her literal divinity.

This music is reminiscent, as others also have remarked, of the scene when the Tsar first appears in *Boris Godunov.*[36] In both operas the people are greeting their ruler with a word that means "glory": *gloria* in Latin and *slava* in Russian, both repeated percussively. There is irony here, in that it is Jocasta who is hailed formally, not Oedipus. Does the mother have most of the power? This passage has its religious associations and in many ways—such as its florid orchestration with brass and timpani—resembles the *Gloria* from Beethoven's *Missa Solemnis*, a mass, that like Mozart's *Requiem,* is significantly in D minor, the key of Jocasta's main aria.

Jocasta delivers a typical Verdian aria, complete with ABA form and *Caballeta*, and asks the "kings" (*reges*) if they are not ashamed of their quarreling. Oedipus joins in, and also shares the florid style of Italian opera. A duet follows in which Jocasta continues to assert that oracles are liars, and Oedipus to insist that he is afraid. This resembles Mozart's ensembles, where the characters sing their contradictory truths. Not much communication here. The ritual continues.

Jocasta's aria with Oedipus establishes her as his lover, and parallels many love duets from other operas. It is the outstanding duet of the opera, and taps into lyrical love in the Italian tradition. Jocasta's suicide, too, is a dramatic gesture that gains in importance in the way the messenger recounts it. Thus she joins other divas in affirming herself in what is usually seen as a negation (suicide). In Sophocles Oedipus was strong, but in Stravinsky he seems a weak boy, and in every instance, Jocasta as mother and wife has a strength that he lacks.

Minor keys used by the chorus and in the main arias of Oedipus and Jocasta predominate in this opera. Oedipus and Jocasta also indulge in chromatic runs and abrupt key changes. Their complex, tragic life is reflected in their music. This contrasts with the representatives of the gods, who use major keys.

Both Oedipus and Jocasta use the flowery notes of Italian opera. They often sing in minor keys rather than in the major that seem to characterize the sacred. Creon is sober and restrained in his lyric lines, retaining something of the liturgical element: he delivers his messages confidently in C major. The *Gloria* hailing Jocasta is also in this optimistic major key, a key that seems to endorse the status quo. Oedipus brings it into C minor with his first doubting questions when Jocasta appears.

Jocasta's brilliant aria completes the *Gloria*. It has an introduction, with harp and flutes announcing her, then a standard ABA form, with a wind accompaniment dominated by the oboe and clarinet. These mingle with her voice as she counters the "gospel" by denying the truth of oracles. The piccolo joins the oboe and clarinet in her "windy" declaration. The harp and flutes, suggesting "angelic" insight, lead into the more sensuous winds. The A portion of this aria is snake-like, sinuous, and insidious, the snake seducing Eve, and she seducing Adam now in the form of Oedipus. With the snake suggestion, Jocasta becomes the Pythia (Apollo's oracle, and named after the python that Apollo slew when he took over the oracle at Delphi) and Gê, the earth goddess, to whom the python answered.

Stephen Walsh has noted the resemblance between Jocasta's frenetic vocal line and the Queen of the Night's in Mozart's *Magic Flute*.[37] She, like the Queen of the Night, is dedicated to the service of untruth, and her vocal line is as florid as her lie is elaborate. This contrasts with Sarastro's simple and sober music, which embodies "moral truth."

One wonders about the Abbé's command of Latin. In addition to the *Vale* for *Ave* above ("Good-bye" for "Hello") *Mentiantur* is used incorrectly for *mentiuntur* in this aria. Both verbs mean "lie," but the "a" instead of "u" is wrong. The strange form *Miki* occurs rather than *mihi* (when Oedipus speaks to the chorus after Creon's aria) and this may reflect the medieval spelling of *michi* for *mihi*.

We miss Sophocles' most famous lines. For instance, Jocasta puts Oidipous' fears to rest about having sexual intercourse with his mother, as the oracle said he would, by saying, "Many men have had intercourse with their mothers in dreams" (*OT* 981–982). This follows the hubristic comment that it is better to live as one would (*OT* 979), since one cannot foresee anything (she claims oracles lie).

Jocasta mentions that Laius was killed at a crossroads (*trivium*). Oedipus remembers killing a man at a crossroads. He is afraid.

The chorus takes up the chant of *trivium*, a simple repetition in comparison with Jocasta's florid delivery. Oedipus starts to roam around the keys, as he says he is frightened. For a moment his vocal line becomes as spare as the chorus', recited on a single pitch. With no accompaniment, he says he killed an old man at a crossroads. Jocasta simply repeats what she said before, as if she does not hear him, or is trying to drown him out. She uses the word *cave*, "beware," raising the image of fear, and Oedipus repeats that he is frightened (*pavesco*). Their duet builds to a climax with full orchestra, now including timpani. Oedipus says he will seek out the one witness because *he* will know the truth. The word *trivium* has already been linked in the music with the *oracle*, and the music has corroborated what Tiresias has said: the oracle and Oedipus' murder are one; the king has been killed by a king, Laius by Oedipus. The music itself is the oracle, which we should believe.

Oedipus' role in the opera has been reduced from the role Sophocles gave Oidipous. He is no longer at the center of his own drama, but in some cases rather a helpless spectator. In turning the *Oidipous Tyrannos* into a ritual, Stravinsky has sacrificed Oedipus in more ways than one.

Does this diminution of Oidipous reflect a new Russian attitude towards the masses, giving them more power than the individual? Is the individual sacrificed for the benefit of the whole of society, as we see in the fertility ritual enacted in Stravinsky's *Rite of Spring,* or as Christ in the liturgy? Tragedy no doubt had a religious origin, and the major dramatic festivals were linked to the worship of Dionysus. Nevertheless they celebrated the human hero.[38] Elliot Carter has claimed that *Oedipus Rex* is the humanistic rite of spring. We see the link with Idomeneo, two kings who brought disaster on their people.

We have lost the multifaceted, difficult hero Sophocles gave us. We are not impressed here by Oedipus' dogged pursuit of the truth, as we are in the ancient play; instead we note the stupidity of this rather vain boy.

In Greece, and in Sophocles' plays in particular, there is still the emphasis on the hero, rather than on society at large; at least there is a counterpoint between the two.[39] Oedipus, overwhelmed by fate, by his mother and by Italian opera, appears as a cipher in this opera / oratorio by Stravinsky, Cocteau, and the Abbé Daniélou. He is simply the victim, whose tenor voice against the inexorable basses and baritones of all the other male singers reveals his youth and vulnerability. He whines like a child, after Tiresias reveals that a king is the murderer of the king.

Jocasta has gained in centrality. In Sophocles, when she enters to quiet the dispute between Oidipous and Kreon, she is overwhelmingly maternal. Here she retains that trait with an added regality that enhances her power. She rises above the petty wrangling of the men. When she kills herself, it is because the world has betrayed her. She has been tricked by fate into committing an act that violates her true nature (like Ajax being driven mad and killing the animals in Sophocles).

In some versions the *Gloria* is repeated at the beginning of the second act, and Stravinsky endorsed the reprise in the score; otherwise it simply ends the first act, as it often did in performance. This contributes towards the general somber aspect of this second act. Stravinsky has undoubtedly returned Sophocles' tragedy to its ritual origins: the individuality of the hero is lost, and instead we focus on the communal experience of the sacrifice. The sober choruses express the vital concerns of the masses in contrast to the more egotistic and individual concerns of the "stars," Oedipus and Jocasta.

Stravinsky says that the first act should be "bathed in sunshine, in blue colour decorated with white draperies."[40] The second act is to be more somber, and, "The new background is black."[41] This is in preparation for the final ritual: a requiem.

The messenger arrives from Corinth and delivers his message about Polybus' death, and his tale wanders over the keys as he elaborates his story that Polybus was not Oedipus' father. He is accompanied by a contrabassoon, adding "weight" to his text. There are also suggestions of folk music, reminding one of Stravinsky's earlier works in this area. There are accentual and rhythmical shifts, and this parallels the excited meters of Greek tragedy, such as dochmiacs (featuring a foot of five syllables, often with the first and fourth short, and the others long) used at moments of crisis. The messenger uses refrains rather than the *da capo* aria of the major figures, and this also characterizes folk music in contrast to Italian opera.[42]

In his final oration about Jocasta's death, the messenger uses the octotonic scale, something that Stravinsky introduced into his religious music, such as the *Symphony of Psalms* (1930).[43] The messenger is a type of priest to whom the chorus (congregation) responds.

Much of Stravinsky's religious music was written after he returned to the Russian Orthodox Church in 1926 and also after Oedipus Rex (1928). He wrote a Credo (1932), an Ave Maria (1934), a Kyrie and Gloria (1944), and then a Mass (1948). Stravinsky said he wrote for the mass "very cold music, absolutely cold, that will appeal directly to the spirit."[44] The same could be said of the majority of the music for the *Oedipus Rex*. Other religious music followed and all shared common characteristics with this opera.

The shepherd appears, announced by pastoral music, including the 3/4 rhythm we are familiar with from the time of Monteverdi, and indeed the entrance of Eumaeus, the rustic shepherd in *Il ritorno d'Ulisse*. This melody resembles a *berceuse*, or lullaby, appropriate for this discussion of a baby. The key of D dominates, and this was the key used by Tiresias when he made his fateful revelation, and is that used by Oedipus when he admits *Lux facta est*.

Oedipus resumes his blind optimism, signaled by the major key in reaction to this announcement. He is excited about learning his origin. He launches into an ABA aria complete with flourishes. This reproduces the temporary optimism we find in Sophocles' version, which increased the height from which Oedipus will fall. As Oedipus sings the elaborate *ego exul exsulto* ("I an exile exult"), the line resembles Mozart's *Exsultate jubilate*. The music brilliantly reinforces Oedipus' delusion.

Jocasta leaves. Oedipus says she is ashamed of what he will hear, but he says he looks forward to learning about his origin. Oedipus is still intellectually blind, but the next words identify him as the son of Laius and Jocasta, the murderer of Laius, and the husband of Jocasta his mother. The darkness of his acts is brought to light.

The messenger and the shepherd deliver the truth in a duet, appropriately again in triple time. The chorus repeats the truth in a percussive monotone.

The shepherd is seen to resemble Tiresias. His *ranz de vaches* is accompanied by two bassoons. Both the monk and shepherd have a commonsensical simplicity and scorn the usual social and city settings. The rustic-sounding bassoons link the shepherd (*omniskius*: "all-knowing") with Tiresias ("the fountain of truth"). The choice of similar instruments also suggests we shall hear comparable truth from both.

We hear notes that demand resolution (a seventh chord), as the chorus sings the words *falsus pater*, but resolution does not follow. (Earlier Jocasta's main aria featured several diminished sevenths, e.g., on *clamare* and *ululare*—ominous words, since the cries and lamentations will directly relate to the *falsus pater* being discovered).[45] The diminished seventh is a common theatrical device in Verdi's operas. Stravinsky also noted the play between music and text by commenting on the positive significance of major keys and the negative significance of minor ones: "I have used such images myself, for example in the 'false relation' of the tritone at *falsus pater* in *Oedipus Rex*."[46]

The speaker tells us that the witness of the murder "emerges from the shadow (*sort de l'ombre*)," in addition to a messenger who will tell Oedipus that Polybus has died, but that Polybus was only his adoptive father. Jocasta suddenly realizes the truth and tries to stop Oedipus from further inquiry. Then she flees. Oedipus is still uncomprehending.

In the original *Oidipous*, on hearing the news that Polybus is dead, says he is relieved that he has not killed his father, but that now he is worried about marrying his mother. This makes sense of the messenger saying that Polybus is not Oedipus' father. In the opera there is no reason for the messenger volunteering information about Oedipus' paternal origin at this point.

The arrival of the shepherd who knows all is announced by the chorus:

> Adest omniskius pastor
> et nuntius horribilis.

We usually think of Christ as the pastor of men, and also omniscient as God. But instead of the good news of the *New Testament*, another messenger delivers horrible news, and our perverted ritual continues. The messenger speaks in telegraphic form and by the third line of his message has revealed that Polybus is not Oedipus' real father (*Mortuus est Polybus . . . non genitor Oedipodis*). This Latin resembles the medieval Latin of the liturgy that includes short lines, assonance, and occasional rhyme (as in the *Carmina Burana*, set to music by Carl Orff), more than classical Latin. With significant chromatics and dissonance, the chorus repeats that Polybus is not the real father; the *falsus pater* is announced by the diminished seventh, which demands resolution. As the harmonic progression calls for another chord, so we wait to hear the next announcement. After the messenger says he took the baby he found on the mountain from a shepherd, the shepherd begins to sing his story. Rustic music accompanies him, with a rhythm suitable for rocking a baby, a lullaby in 3/4 time.

In the messenger's story about the shepherd we find another mistake, if not in the Latin, then in the logic: *Reppereram in monte, attuleram pastori*, "I had found him in the mountain and had taken him to the shepherd." In the play by Sophocles the messenger was given the baby *by* the shepherd and the messenger then took the baby to Polybus, the king of Corinth. There is a moment of confusion in both the libretto (just cited) and the original play (1026) about whether the baby was found by or given to the messenger. Sophocles' Oidipous clears this up by asking the shepherd if he gave the baby to the messenger, but this libretto simply has the shepherd repeat that the baby was found in the mountain.

The shepherd says that he had best be quiet (his key is the same as Jocasta's, G minor, linking the two: both tell the truth as they know it, but do not know where this truth may lead). Oedipus sings a joyous aria based, as others have noted, on one of the Lanner waltzes in *Petrouchka*, although Stravinsky said it was influenced by Beckmesser's lute song in Act 2 of Wagner's *Die Meistersinger*.[47] This song is in a confident F major. Does this suggest that Oedipus is like Petrouchka, a "real" puppet struggling against the inevitable? Or, as Stephen Walsh suggests (but immediately rejects on the ground of Oedipus' sincerity), does he resemble the self-aggrandizing Beckmesser?[48]

The shepherd finally identifies Oedipus: "He is the son of Laius and Jocasta, the slayer of Laius, his parent, the husband of Jocasta, his parent," with no explanation of how the baby got there, or how Jocasta gave him the child for disposal, except for the statement that he was "abandoned by his mother." One might even speculate that she left the baby on the mountain herself. Another change shows us the shepherd of the opera speaking without the coercion exerted on him in the original (when Oidipous threatens him with torture, *OT* 1152).

Oedipus' last words are particularly moving, as is his music, which has now achieved the austerity of plainchant. No longer does the lyricism of Italian opera convey Oedipus' boasts and exultation. He now realizes he is the victim, the lamb of God proceeding to the slaughter. We hear now an *Agnus Dei, qui tollit peccata mundi* as Oedipus confesses:

Natus sum quo nefastum est,
concubui cui nefastum est,
kekidi quem nefastum est.
Lux facta est.

With the coming of light (from D minor to D major), the sins are perhaps absolved, and the prayer for peace, *dona nobis pacem*, is parallel to the end of the opera: *tibi valedico*.

The theme of fate and truth is reiterated as a dominant recurring theme in the opera. When Tiresias reveals the truth, the key words are heralded by a *forte* in the winds, just as Mozart would underline key passages (such as the Commendatore's curse in *Don Giovanni*). The word *peremptor* ("murderer") is marked with rhythmic emphasis and descends an octave, comparable to the phrase *Apollo dixit.* This emphasis shows musically that Apollo told the truth. The haunting rhythm and descent are echoed at the end, when Oedipus says *Lux facta est*, and the rhythm at the end is even slower (whole notes rather than half notes). Oedipus' final lines now are simple against a simple orchestral accompaniment. *Lux facta est* descends an octave, as did *Apollo dixit* earlier, and also Tiresias' pronouncement. The Christian God and Apollo, the sun god, have been conflated. Both bring the truth to light. Now that Oedipus can see the truth, he will be in darkness forever.

Gone are the resplendent choruses of *Oidipous Tyrannos*, including the one that considers human happiness an illusion, just after Oidipous has discovered his identity (1186–1222). The generations of man are seen as nothing. There is a word play on numerical quantities, combining the suggestion that these generations have not even lived, besides their happiness being equivalent to zero (1187–1188). Numbers figure prominently in the imagery of the play. Even the discovery of Oidipous' identity itself hinged on numbers: if the murderers had been "many," he, acting alone, would be guiltless.

The ancient chorus continues, after its observation that man is nothing, to say that human happiness is simply a "seeming" (1191), and then fades even from that. The instructive example is Oidipous' *daimon* ("fate/inner god," 1194) itself. So the chorus calls no man truly happy (an anticipation of the conclusion, that no one should be thought to be happy until his final day). These philosophical and poetic observations do not appear in the new text.

The speaker intervenes to tell us that Jocasta is dead, "La tête divine de Jocaste est morte." These words have a tragic resonance, and the head (*la tête*) represents the person, a type of synecdoche that implies respect; that it is called divine also confirms that Jocasta is regarded as a type of divinity.[49] She is the *monstre sacré*, a perverted holy mother, who is revered, as Oidipous himself is in Sophocles' *Oedipus at Colonus.*

The speaker tells us that the queen has hung herself and Oedipus has put out his eyes with her dress ornament. At times the commentator seems hardly needed and adds nothing to what we see. At other times we are misinformed, such as here when the speaker says, "You will now hear the famous monologue, 'The Divine Jocasta is Dead,' a monologue in which the messenger describes the death of Jocasta." The messenger, in fact, simply repeats that the divine Jocasta is dead, and the chorus in turn repeats that she has hung herself. The famous monologue from the Sophoclean original has disappeared.

Cocteau reminds us of the trap again, "*Le roi est pris.*" With an allusion to a hunt, *On le chasse*, Oedipus is compared to a beast that will be driven out. It is said, however, that he was loved (*on t'aimait*). The speaker's monologue is punctuated by trumpet fanfares. This again adds to the suggestion of ritual. It is like the bells ringing in the mass to signal the presence of Christ, or that the mass is ended.

The messenger and chorus conclude the opera with the account of Jocasta hanging herself, and Oedipus putting out his eyes. The music brilliantly returns to the beginning (with the main four-note theme and a percussive bass in a minor third) as the king Oedipus saves his people by exiling himself from Thebes, a conclusion that fulfills the omens of the beginning. The ring composition is complete. This choral ending resembles those of Handel's oratorios besides the conclusions of the ancient Greek drama. The personal is universalized. This is not the first time that Stravinsky has made a Greek myth Christian in its emphasis. He did the same, for instance, with the myth of *Persephone*.

The opera omits the final meeting with Creon, who puts Oidipous in his place by saying that he no longer has power, and should not continue to want to rule in all things (*OT* 1522–1523). We do not see the blind Oidipous mourning with his children, who are also his siblings, as he does at the end of the play. The pathos of the final scene in the Sophoclean play is replaced by ritual. In a way this makes the opera / oratorio more optimistic. The scapegoat has been found, and driven out. God is sacrificed for man. There is hope for the citizens, who derive benefits from the sacrifice of the exalted individual. Sophocles' bleak ending will only allow Oidipous to be redeemed in the later *Oedipus at Colonus*. No words of love or pity end the Sophoclean play, but Oidipous' fate is simply offered as a warning for others. The tragedy of the Greek original is complete, whereas in the opera / oratorio there is hope. That hope is not for Oedipus, but in the redemption offered by the Christian ritual and the sacrificed scapegoat.

In this opera / oratorio the chorus is confined to prayers, greetings, and sometimes banal commentary, usually simply echoing what it has just heard. Its climactic moment seems to be when they are given a chance to describe Jocasta's suicide and Oedipus' self-blinding, usurping the role of messenger in the original play. We realize more and more how this opera / oratorio is a masterpiece by virtue of the music and little else. We search vainly for the marriage of words and music found in virtually all the other operas investigated thus far. The words are there simply to give nuances to the human voice, and the strange ritual quality of the Latin adds to this effect. At times it sounds like an incantation, at others a litany, and it is also the language of prayer. The Greek text has been reduced to Latin shorthand; it is not the meaning of the words that comes across, but only the association of Latin with Christian ritual.

Oedipus emerges from the shadows wearing a mask that depicts blood dripping from his eye sockets. He is mute as a beast, one that has been hunted. The words of man fail him; no operatic flourishes, nor even plainchant, but silence as well as blindness accompanies our *monstre sacré*. There is a return to the opening chant, which becomes softer as the chorus bids Oedipus farewell and reiterates its love for him:

Vale, Oedipus,
miser Oedipus noster,
te amabam, Oedipus.
Tibi valedico, Oedipus,
tibi valedico.

The messenger and chorus function as the priest and the congregation. Communion is over. The victim has been sacrificed. When the essential sacrifice has taken place in the liturgy, the congregation are told they may depart because the ritual has finished: *Ite: missa est* ("Go: it is accomplished"). Oedipus is sent out of the city as the congregation is usually sent out at the end of the mass. These communicants have been relieved of their sins, but Oedipus himself, as sinner and redeemer, must live with the constant memory of his sins.

At the beginning of the opera, Oedipus says he loves his subjects, but now at the end of the play his subjects say that they loved him (*on t'aimait, te amabam*), and they drive him out of the city, very gently, as Cocteau says. The past tense is significant: this shows a reversal of love, as it is a reversal of Oedipus' circumstance. The words take up a theme (love) sounded at the beginning of the play, just as the music at the end repeats the opening music, with what could be a reminder of the Requiem theme. Both words and music construct an organic whole. The first theme described the misery of the plague, and the last reprise tells of Jocasta's death, with all its implications for Oedipus. The general misery has been traced to its source, and the music's riddle is solved, along with Oedipus': the end is the beginning.

The Chorus also says that it pities Oedipus (*te miseror, / Miser Oedipus*). This fits not only the *Agnus Dei* from the standard liturgy, but it is also a type of prayer that concludes the Requiem mass. *Dona eis pacem* ("give them peace") seems to be contained in the final words to Oedipus: *tibi valedico* ("I wish you farewell").

The last words are like a litany from the liturgy. The chorus / congregation verbalizes its pity for Oedipus as Christ for his sacrifice, as it concludes this opera / oratorio / mass. The chorus speaks of its love. *Pax* may now descend, because the lamb of God is sacrificed.

We miss the famous saying by the chorus to conclude the play: "Call no man happy, until he has seen his final day." Variations of this splendid saying are found in the plays of the three major playwrights of fifth-century Athens, and its meaning is discussed by Aristotle.[50]

The rich imagery and word play of Sophocles is missing from the modern libretto; there are, nevertheless, some inspired moments in the text. Oedipus' final admission of his sins, with the concluding *lux facta est*, has its own brilliance. The Christian heritage is added to the Greek heritage. *Lux facta est*, we recall, occurred in the Latin translation of the bible describing the creation of the earth ("let there be light, and there was light," *Genesis* 1). In the *New Testament*, John uses the image of Christ as the light of the world, bringing light to mankind (12.1). Here Oedipus is first created as himself, with the knowledge of who he is. Tiresias says in the Sophoclean text: "This day will give birth to you, and destroy you" (438). It is the day that will bring Oedipus into the light and first let him be seen as the individual he truly is. This invokes the Platonic notion that seeming may be identical to being, but until one can provide reasons for it, it is mere opinion. In Greek the verb that means "I know" is in the perfect tense but has a present meaning, from a stem that means "I see." Oedipus sees and knows through the light of knowledge: *lux facta est.* So also the phrase *omniskius pastor* is derived from the Christian tradition, and Christ is the all-knowing pastor of his disciples. *Omniskius* is not classical Latin, but a word that enters the language after the death of Boethius in the sixth century A.D. This medieval quality also locates the language more in the church than in classical Rome.

Although the outline of the myth was known to the ancient Greek audience, the audience was nevertheless eager to see how an ancient playwright would develop the theme. Sophocles added suspense, as clue after clue is dropped, and yet Oidipous misses them. Sophocles postpones the climax to the very point where the shepherd is threatened with torture to reveal the truth. Yet there is little suspense in this opera / oratorio. This brings us closer to the mass: a known ritual eliminates suspense.

One might say that, in Stravinsky's version, Oedipus is simply a victim of fate.[51] This reduces Sophocles' complex thought. This opera / oratorio shows us a victim, and we have little of the dogged determination of Sophocles' Oidipous, who would not give up his search, no matter what the cost to him; his virtue is intellectual curiosity. In the opera he is trapped in the ritual as much as by fate.

The gospel may be said to continue as Oedipus' origin is made clear. The consecration and eucharist portion of the Mass follow. Oedipus will suffer so that his people can thrive: *hoc est enim corpus meum quod pro vobis tradetur*, "This is my body which will be given up for you." We have an additional death, Jocasta's. In the opera Oedipus goes into exile for his people. *Agnus dei, qui tollis peccata mundi: miserere nobis*, "Lamb of God, who takes away the sins of the world, have pity on us." Oedipus is the sacrificial lamb, carrying his own sins on his back as he leaves the city. He has solved the latest riddle and leaves;

the city is redeemed. *Ite: missa est*. The Mass is ended. It is over and Oedipus is dismissed. The ancient play does not end with Oedipus leaving the city. Word still has to come from Delphi; we do not even have the consolation of knowing what will happen: we are left "Waiting for Apollo."

Oedipus Rex is truly a monumental creation, as Stravinsky intended. The music comes from a tradition, and it creates a tradition of neoclassicism with many imitators, like Carl Orff. The theme repeated at the end refutes, in a way, the ending of Greek tragedy. There the singularity of the tragedy shows barren destruction as the fate of the protagonist. In this opera / oratorio, with the entire work illustrating the classic ABA form (theme, variation, reprise), one has an idea of circularity not present in Greek tragedy. The Mass is something celebrated again and again, and the death depicted is a renewal of life for man. In Sophocles' *Oidipous Tyrannos*, it is the destruction of the particular man. The liturgy delivers truth and salvation to the masses; Greek tragedy shows how a heroic, essentially good individual can come to complete destruction through various concatenations of fate and free will. The ancient Greek play is a warning, whereas the Christian Mass is a consolation. Stravinsky tries, it seems, to combine the two, but at times the joints creak.

The quiet ending with repeated single pitches seems to show that all the flourishes have been absorbed into this parable of fate, of man's inexorable journey towards death: from Oedipus' C major opening to a G minor choral conclusion, Oedipus is separate from, yet joined to, the mass of mankind. He is a redeemer, and yet condemned. The Christian liturgy, through words and music, makes Christ the ultimate redeemer.

CONCLUSION

By conflating the Mass with ancient tragedy, perhaps Stravinsky reveals his own pessimism, yet at the same time his hope for some type of redemption. As this opera shows his genius in the music, it also represents a quietism in its ritual optimism. The emphasis is on collective renewal and rebirth rather than the death or destruction of the individual. The gentle farewell the chorus delivers mediates the horror and shock revealed by the chorus in Sophocles' play. That play's final words, "Call no man happy until he has seen his final day," can imply that death will be the only possible release from this world's pain.

In this opera / oratorio Oedipus is a Christ figure, although culpable in a way that Christ was not. The city is saved. The king is dead spiritually, physically "fled." With the ritual of the Mass underlying so much, the new king is God, and all mankind, as represented by the people of Thebes, can hope for redemption. This work is not simply addressed to a human audience: God is supposed to listen. Stravinsky has revived the ancient work in a way that keeps its original sacred character, now translated to modern Christianity.

The Greek and Christian expectations of the afterlife differ radically, and this is reflected in the changes that occur between the ancient play and the opera. For the ancient Greek, death is "no longer to look upon the light of the sun," to enter the underworld where the shades of the dead are blown about like dry leaves. Thus death is also intimately connected with a cessation of light, and Oedipus' spiritual death is symbolized by his putting out his eyes. Images of light therefore are particularly rich in the ancient text of this play. On the other hand, for the Christian, death is a transition, a liberation, a transfiguration into something wondrous, which approaches, is even absorbed into, its source in God. For the Greek, to contemplate death is to face nothingness, along with the cessation of light. Stravinsky thus contradicts not only Sophocles' focus on the individual, but also the hero's choice to negate (choosing blindness over sight in *Oidipous Tyrannos*, or death in *Oedipus at Colonus*). Musically, Oedipus is absorbed into the chorus: philosophically he is denied not only his particularity, but also the definition that his own particular death would give him.

Stravinsky was eclectic and conservative, surviving as best he could, in as comfortable circumstances as he could manage. He was himself as rigid as some of his rhythms. His modernistic machine-like rhythms reflect the reproduction of cold technology in both painting and sculpture that was taking place at this time: cubism, the repetitive machine-like abstractions of Mondrian, Duchamp, and Léger. We find this repetition in the arrangement of the windows in the buildings of Louis Sullivan, or Walter Gropius, Mies van der Rohe and Le Corbusier's *machines à habiter*. Stravinsky gave us machines to hear, as indeed we might say of the music of Stravinsky's contemporary Edgard Varese. Stravinsky sweeps us into modernity and gives us an aural abstraction of the concrete. At times the assault on our ears replicates that of our overcrowded, noisy world with its repetitious sounds. As Adorno says, "Like jazz, Stravinsky's imitation of the compulsion to repeat has its origins in the mechanization of the labour process."[52] He goes on, "His [Stravinsky's] imprisonment within eternal sameness is also an imprisonment within culture. This chains him to affirmation and establishes a sinister alliance between his music and the gruesome abominations it documents. . . . Repetition is a characteristic of what has been reduced to the animal plane."[53] In my opinion, Adorno's overvaluation of Schoenberg's originality by comparison with Stravinsky's "sameness" sometimes allows him to appreciate neither the latter's genius nor the former's shortcomings. Stravinsky was too great an artist to allow his music to be considered as rigid as just described. He is too grounded in the folk tradition of Russia, which is sensuous and earthy, and from which his predilection for metrically irregular music comes, to be labeled simply cold or machine-like. *The Rite of Spring* has is "mechanistic" moments, which are probably more properly called "ritualistic," but at the same time it is an extremely sensual work, and not at all cold. *The Rake's Progress* is passionate and lyrical, not at all rigid (but that was his Mozartian renaissance). He has constantly dared to find new horizons.

Our twentieth-century operas have religious overtones (*Elektra*, *Medea*) and two of them follow the liturgy closely (*Oedipus*, *Gospel at Colonus*). The eighteenth- and nineteenth-century operas were free of this close link. Thus opera seems to have come full circle and to have returned to some of the religious suggestions that Monteverdi first made, and even more so in the case of those who use the entire ritual as a model. Stravinsky's use of rite is not only distancing but universalizing. This is different from Elektra and Medea, who harness ritual to achieve vengeance. They particularize it, adapting it to a particular and bloody end. On the other hand, both *Oedipus Rex* and the *Gospel at Colonus* try to show man as a victim who can obtain a type of redemption through religion, ritual, and music. This is a general and more merciful end.

Monteverdi adapted epic in his *Il ritorno* and Stravinsky Greek tragedy, but Monteverdi and Stravinsky were not fully able to reconcile the philosophical contours of the original to their Christian purposes. Though Monteverdi prided himself on highlighting the text and Stravinsky unashamedly subverted it, yet both use the power of music to universalize: we lose the focus of the Greek original on the suffering unto death of the heroic individual, which is precisely the development that tragedy took as it emerged from ritual.

The role of the diva also reinforces Jocasta, and she grows in presence and strength even as Oedipus is weakened. She is the heroic, tragic individual in this opera, and must die. Her music, as a coloratura mezzo-soprano, enhances her as a queen. Her vocal line lends her a majesty and dignity that makes us understand that she is not only Oedipus' queen, but also his mother. The regal music that announces her also shows us who is actually in power. Oedipus' music is whining by comparison.

The mezzo diva dominates, and both Poizat and Koestenbaum recognize her power. Poizat says that the voices considered most erotic are the transsexual ones, such as a deep voice in a woman.[54] As Koestenbaum says, "The diva's will to power culminates in a scene of vindication," and he goes on to quote Nellie Melba: "In thirty seconds, I knew that I had won."[55] Jocasta may die, but she wins, both in her florid arias and in the way she knows the truth earlier than Oedipus. Whereas the original Oidipous had a moral strength in his endurance and choice to live, here Jocasta seems to have taken the hero's way out. Oedipus walks off into obscurity. His weakness is completed by the music. He is Christ complete with sin, and not having redeemed his people. Christ chose to die to redeem mankind. Oedipus chooses to live and is exiled.

It is obvious that some of the drama is lost when the ancient dramatic text is abbreviated and then translated by a priest whose mastery of Latin is questionable. Stravinsky did not want rivals, and in this sense, he chose his librettist well. Stravinsky is seductively modern, and we might say postmodern with his eclectic pastiche of past and present. His spell is cast, and we are under its influence; however, we might wish to escape. We are as much prisoners of Stravinsky's music as Oedipus is of fate, because Stravinsky's music is a translation of the world we live in. At times one longs to return to the simpler and yet more profound messages of the ancient text, and a world where language is not simply noise but still has meaning.

APPENDIX
OPERAS ABOUT *OEDIPUS TYRANNUS*[56]

Pietro Torri (c.1650–1737) (b. Peschiera, Italy)
Edippo (1729)

Henry Purcell (?1659–1695) (b. London, England)
Incidental Music for Plays:
Oedipus (1692)

Thomas Augustine Arne (1710–1778) (b. London, England)
Oedipus, King of Thebes (1740)

Marc-Antoine Désaugiers (1742–1793) (b. Fréjus, France)
Le petit Oedipe (1779)

Nicolas-Jean Le Froid de Méreaux (1745–1797) (b. Paris, France)
Oedipe et Jocaste (1791)

Joseph Martin Kraus (1756–1792) (b. Miltenberg am Main, Germany)
Oedip (1785 [lost])

Ruggero Leoncavallo (1857–1919) (b. Naples, Italy)
Edipo re (1920)

George Enescu (1881–1955) (b. Liveni-Virnav, Roumania)
Oedipe (Tragédie Lyrique) (1936)

Igor Stravinsky (1882–1971) (b. Oranienbaum [Lomonosov], Russia)
Oedipus Rex (1927)

Carl Orff (1895–1985) (b. Munich, Germany)
Oedipus der Tyrann (1959) (Ein Trauerspiel des Sophocles von Hölderlin)

Harry Partch (1901–1974) (b. Oakland, CA, USA)
King Oedipus (Music Dance Drama, after W.B. Yeats, 1952)

Helmut Eder (1916–) (b. Linz, Austria)
Oedipus (1960)

Josep Soler Sardà (1935–) (b. Vilafranca del Penedès, Spain)
Edipo y Yocasta (1972)

Peter Schickele [P.D.Q. Bach] (1935–) (b. Ames, IA, USA)
Oedipus Tex (1988)

Wolfgang Rihm (1953–) (b. Karlsruhe, Germany)
Oedipus (1987)

Mark-Anthony Turnage (1960–) (b. Grays, England)
Greek (1988)

Charles Chaynes (1925–)
Jocaste (1993?)

The Gospel at Colonus:
Black Pearls and Greek Diamonds

INTRODUCTION

Up to this point, the operas I have investigated from the sixteenth century to the twentieth were created by major composers of Europe. Now we go to the new world, and the first opera performed there was on a classical theme: *La Partenope*, with music by Manuel de Zumaya (c.1678–1756) was performed in Mexico in 1711 for the Duke of Linares, the viceroy who loved Italian opera (Silvio Stampiglia composed the libretto and Handel had originally set it to music in 1708).

The opera for this chapter is from a different background. *The Gospel at Colonus* is a creation from the United States that grew out of the African-American musical tradition. Dvorak earlier took his themes for the New World Symphony from both the African-American and Native American music, not only because he thought this was America's best music, but because it was the most nationalistically representative. George Gershwin and Aaron Copland paid homage to African-American jazz, as did other American and European composers. For instance, England's Michael Tippett incorporated blues into his opera, *The Ice Break* (1977).

Ben Halley, Jr., and Fourteen Karat Soul toured a version of *Sophocles' Oedipus at Colonus* in the 1980s around America and Europe. Lee Breuer and Bob Telson, the director and the composer, expanded this earlier version, and their first performance was part of the Brooklyn Academy of Music's Next Wave festival in 1983. It immediately made its mark as a union of classical drama and the Oedipus myth with traditional gospel music, an opera profoundly representative of the African-American musical heritage.

This is not the first time that we have seen Oedipus cast in the figure of Christ: Stravinsky's *Oedipus Rex* in many ways is modeled on a Christian ritual, as is Breuer's opera. Many other operas also transform ancient heroes and heroines into Christian figures, and borrow music from the Christian rite. Theodorakis' *Medea* has music that derives from the Greek Orthodox Church. Monteverdi's Penelope and Stravinsky's Jocasta are equated with the Virgin Mary, and Strauss's Elektra and Orestes offer perverted prayers reminiscent of the Catholic mass as they set out to exact their vengeance. The influence of the Catholic ritual is also apparent in Mozart's *Idomeneo*.

The movement from secular to religious performance is not simply one-way. Both Verdi's and Mozart's masses resemble their operas and *vice versa*. The sacred and the secular crisscrossed in Monteverdi. Sometimes the marriages seem natural; at others divorce might be preferable. Nevertheless, opera has its own traditions and can gain from ritual reinforcement. The *Gospel at Colonus* uses the black gospel tradition and in spite of jarring differences—such as between Oedipus and Christ—the mixture is provocative, rewarding, and enriching.

There are few operas on the subject of *Oedipus at Colonus*; I have only located two from the eighteenth century, in addition to this one in the twentieth. It is less popular than *Oedipus Tyrannus* (which also appealed mostly to the eighteenth and twentieth centuries), but both probably are regarded as too intellectual or philosophical in content. Intellectual debate suited the eighteenth century, so that might explain its presence there. One can also see a modern appeal for a post-Freudian generation. The *Oedipus at Colonus* is particularly appealing for a Gospel tradition. Here we have a figure who can be identified with Christ and at the same time with man, a sinner whose sins can be redeemed. Christ gave his life for just such human sinners.

The gospel song evolved around 1850 in an urban setting where temporary tents were erected for traveling ministers.[1] It combined music of African origin with Christian music in much the same way that the *macumba* ceremony in the Caribbean and South America combined African and Christian ritual and was performed in Christian churches.[2] It is possible that the African tradition from which gospel music drew is even older than Greek tragedy. In any case there is equal mystery about the beginnings of both the African ritual and Greek tragedy. An African dictum tells us, "The spirit will not descend without song," and there was a lot of singing in the early African-American churches. LeRoi Jones expands on this:

Because the African came from an intensely religious culture, a society where religion was a daily, minute-to-minute concern, and not something relegated to a specious once-a-week reaffirmation, he had to find other methods of worshipping gods when his white *captors* declared that he could no longer worship in the old ways. . . . The Negro church, whether Christian or "heathen," has always been a "church of emotion." In Africa, ritual dances and songs were integral parts of African religious observances, and the emotional frenzies that were usually concomitant with any African religious practice have been pretty well documented, though, I would suppose, rarely understood. This heritage of emotional religion was one of the strongest contributions that the African culture made to the Afro-American. And, of course, the tedious, repressive yoke of slavery must well have served to give the black slave a huge reservoir of emotional energy which could be used up in his religion.[3]

With emancipation in 1863 the secular tradition grew.[4] W.E.B. Du Bois tells us, "The negro church antedates the negro home." Sidran says that "'devil music' becomes early blues; and the black musician begins to take on the social functions of black preacher."[5] A Patriarch of the Holiness church has claimed, "The devil should not be allowed to keep all this good rhythm."

There was a strong black minstrel tradition in the South. Soon it found its way into organized churches: Baptist, Methodist, and later Pentecostal. If they were black and included gospel music, they were given the generic name "folk churches." In 1921, 165 songs were published with the title *Gospel Pearls*. Besides traditional hymns, many new "revival" songs were included.

Gospel music has certain characteristics: "hand clapping, foot stomping, call-and-response performance, rhythmic complexities, persistent beat, melodic improvisation, heterophonic textures, percussive accompaniments, and ring shouts. . . . The quality of the singing was distinctive for its shrill, hard, full-throated, strained, raspy, and/or nasal tones, with frequent exploitation of falsetto, growling and moaning."[6] The instruments are mainly guitars, banjos, piano, harmonicas, and later organ, tambourines, drums, saxophone, and trombone. Singers would join and leave at will, adding descant or polyphony as the mood struck them; they could improvise harmony, melody, or words. Dancing is an integral part, and people do this *ad lib*. There are two main styles: the male gospel quartet, which often sings *a capella* (snapping their fingers and slapping their thighs), and the gospel chorus, which is made up of women dressed in choir robes. The latter are often accompanied by a piano and also clap their hands. If the music was fast, rhythm predominated; if slow, the melody was embellished. Both the instruments and this style are incorporated into *Gospel at Colonus*.

Quincy Troupe's poetry well describes the ecstatic state that occurs in the gospel context:

> within an avalanche of glory hallelujah skybreaks
> spraying syllables on the run, spreading
> sheets, waving holy sounds, solos sluicing african bound
> transformed here in america from voodoo into hoodoo
> inside tonguing blues, snaking horns, where juju grounds down sacred up in chords,
>   up in the gritty foofoo
> magical, where fleet rounds of cadences whirlpool as in rivers . . .
> as in the pulpit, when a preacher becomes his words
> his rhythms those of a sacred bluesman, dead outside his door
> his gospel intersecting with antiphonal guitars, a congregation of amens
> as in the slurred riffs blues strings run back echoing themselves
> answering the call, the voice cracked open like an egg, the yolk running out
> the lungs imitating collapsed drums & he
> is the rainbowing confluence of sacred tongues, the griot

the devotion of rivers all up in his hands, all up in his fingers
his call both invocation & quaking sermon
running true & holy as drumming cadences
brewed in black church choirs, glory hallelujah vowels
spreading from their mouths like wolfman's mojo
all up in mahalia jackson's lungs
howling vowels rolled off hoodoo consonants, brewing
magic all up in the preacher's run, of muddy water
strung all up in the form drenched with coltrane
riffin' all up in miles of lightning hopkins mojo songs
blues yeasting lungs of bird
when music is raised up as prayer & lives
healing as june's sun quilted into black babies
tongues, sewn deep in their lungs as power
& blueprinted here in the breath of rappers.[7]

Many of the characteristics of the blues are also used in *Gospel at Colonus*: "the call-and-response, rhythmic vitality, musical density, predilection for duple meters, improvisation and "bent note" scale."[8] Scalar bent tones borrowed dominant and diminished seventh chords from keys unrelated to the diatonic key. The blues also include some of the earliest hymns, for example, Blind Willie Johnson's "God Don't Never Change":

Praise God
God don't never change
Oh
Always will be God.

Spoke to the mountain
Said, How great I Am
Want you to get up this morning
Skip around like a lamb . . .

God in the pulpit
God way down at the door
It's God in the Amen corner
God's all over the floor.

Well it's God
God don't never change
Ohhhh-ahh
Always will be God.[9]

Some of the blues religious songs are more evidently complaints, or ways to explain abuses, like Blind Willie Johnson's "Jesus is Coming Soon":

Well I thought
I got some warning
Jesus coming soon . . .

Read the Book of Zacharias
Bible plainly says
Said the people in the cities dying
'Counta their wicked ways.[10]

Bible stories are often told in blues, such as one about Samson called "If I Had my Way," also by Blind Willie Johnson. In *Gospel at Colonus* another tradition is adopted; Greek tragedy is used in place of the Bible: the preacher begins, "I take as my text this evening the *Book of Oedipus*."[11] Like Greek tragedy, the Pentecostal service attempts to provide *katharsis* and relief from suffering and misery; human pain is elevated into a formal creation of beauty, which affords pleasure. Christian dogma also offers salvation, or an escape from evil and death.[12]

In the gospel canon of hymns, certain names predominate: Homer A. Rodeheaver, Charles A. Tindley, and Thomas Andrew Dorsey. In this last case, his own hymns and his type of hymn were called "Dorseys." Lucie Campbell, "Sister" Rosetta Tharpe, Bessie Griffin, Sallie Martin, Kenneth Morris (who worked with her), and W. Herbert Brewster, Sr., were other notable gospel composers. Brewster made the use of triplets popular, besides florid melismatic cadenzas and tempo changes. Hymns attributed to Dr. Watts generally had a slow tempo. Roberta Martin was known for integrating the choirs and featuring men and women singing together. Mahalia Jackson and the "Clara Ward Singers," both taught by Dorsey, charged fees for their appearances, as did the "Fisk Jubilee Singers." Many of the singers made a reputation for themselves and were in demand for traveling to various congregations.

Major cities that featured gospel music were Chicago, Philadelphia, and Memphis. Many of the writers of Gospel also wrote blues, and this showed strongly in the music of Dorsey, who based himself in Chicago.[13] "Holy rollers" is a term that white people applied to this type of music.

Black music recapitulates the black historical experience and can be an assertion of identity.[14] The spiritual merged with "soul" music in the mid-1950s. As Sidran claims, in the soul movement there is a new cultural self-definition and "a new sense of community in black culture becomes evident."[15]

Black music is the quintessential American music.[16] The blues, however, have now been appropriated by the white culture. Maurice Chittenden, speaking of the blues revival, quotes an entrepreneur Isaac Tigrett, who plans to open a House of Blues in London's Soho district: "The blues community is now 90% white. . . . The blacks turned their backs on it during the civil rights movement. They saw it as poor self-image: the rag-tag man singing on the porch."[17] So traditional music can also be *rejected* as constituting identity after it becomes part of the main-stream culture. Now African-American political protest has found its way into rap.[18]

Perhaps this explains why Bob Telson and Lee Breuer are the white masterminds of *Gospel at Colonus*. For the most part, black traditional music has become an American product. Nevertheless, black gospel music is still going strong in black churches, and *Black Nativity,* a play that provides a gospel context for the Christmas story, is performed yearly.[19]

John Shepherd urges that critical analysis be joined to sociological analysis.[20] In the case of the Gospel tradition, the culture of the oppressed provided tools for escape and the preservation of sanity, besides an illusion of freedom. This phenomenon has been noted in other cultures, such as the Irish, and Seamus Deane says:

Official jargon represents something more and something worse than moral obtuseness. It also represents power, the one element lacking in the world of the victims where the language is so much more vivid and spontaneous. . . . The voice of power tells one kind of fiction—the lie. It has the purpose of preserving its own interests. The voice of powerlessness tells another kind of fiction—the illusion. It has the purpose of pretending that its own interests have been preserved.[21]

In original black gospel culture, the voice of powerlessness sang and gained power that is still growing.

GOSPEL AT COLONUS

No two performances of the *Gospel at Colonus* are alike, and the congregation choir interacts constantly with the other actors and singers. This is an interactive creation and much is unpredictable; spontaneous emotions add to every performance.

The very form that most of the hymns take, the return to the first theme, or the beginning ABA, is suggestive of man's coming from and returning to God. There is a divine cycle, and man expresses it musically as well as verbally. This form comes more from opera than from gospel hymns.

The texts are also significant, and have the form of prayers. The musical expression involves total commitment, not only pursuing the limits of the human voice, but dancing to exhaustion. One does not leave a performance without hearing, seeing, and feeling God, and particularly God in man.

It is clear that Breuer is giving us the highlights from Sophocles' *Oedipus Tyrannus* (*circa* 426 B.C.) and *Antigone* (*circa* 442 B.C.), as well as *Oedipus at Colonus* (*circa* 405 B.C.). These three plays range over the entire period of the extant plays. In the mythic cycle, the chronological sequence is *Oedipus Tyrannus, Oedipus at Colonus,* followed by *Antigone.* It is incorrect to call them a trilogy. All they have in common are the names of some characters and a common derivation from myths about Oedipus and his family. The myth, however, varies from play to play. The main concentration of the *Gospel* is on *Oedipus at Colonus,* shortened as is usual for opera, but the most famous lines and speeches from the earlier plays are included.

The cast is larger than in the original play, which had three, maybe four, actors, and a chorus of fifteen. The simplification and shortening of the original text means more emphasis on the emotional than the intellectual sphere.

Oedipus and Antigone each have spoken and sung parts performed by singers, on the one hand, and on the other a speaking actor and actress, respectively. The spoken parts carry the names Preacher for Oedipus and Evangelist for Antigone. There is also a preacher *per se* and a pastor, and they take other parts. The former is one who has a more rhetorical mode, a typical story-teller; the latter is more lyrical, with spiritual messages. Theseus is also played by the pastor, with only a spoken part. A deacon plays Creon, and he also only speaks, as indeed does Testifier Polyneices. Ismene only sings.

This device of having two performers for one role has something cinematic about it. Hans Jurgen Syberberg did this in his film *Parsifal* (1982). He had singers record the score; the actors mimed it. Breuer fulfills the need for a singing voice and a speaking voice.

In addition there is a Choragos [*sic*: for Chorêgos], Balladeer, choir and soloists. Besides this there are various other musical groups, such as the Five Blind Boys of Alabama. The main instruments are organ, piano, guitar, African finger cymbals, tambourine, drums, trombone, saxophone, and clarinet.[22]

The action takes place in a Pentecostal church. Detailed directions for the set are given in the libretto.[23] There is a pulpit and seats for the deacons and choir. A giant backdrop is explicitly described: "From floor to flies, serving as a cyclorama is a great painting of the Last Judgment, a Judgment more Rousseau than Renaissance, more Africa than Europe, in which all the planets, plants, insects, animals and human beings rise toward us from a panorama so far below as to show the curvature of the earth—part Eden, part Colonus' sacred grove."[24] Costumes are bright, typical of the African-American gospel tradition. The sections correspond to sections of a traditional Christian service with *Introit, Credo, Gospel, Confession* before *Communion, Gloria, Consecration, Sanctus, Agnus Dei, Requiem,* and finally a Hallelujah chorus, then a closing hymn. The names of parts of the Protestant gospel service are given throughout: *Welcome; Invocation; Rite; Prayer; Jubilee; Lament; Teachings; Mourning; Doxology: The Paean; Closing hymn;* and *Benediction.* Titled parts of the original Greek play appear too, such as Choral Odes from *Oedipus at Colonus* and *Antigone.*

Organ music with typical church progressions, such as the IV-I plagal cadence, accompanies the congregation's entrance. The Preacher begins with words from the end of the *Oedipus Tyrannus* (1522–1523): "Think no longer that you are in command here, / But rather think how, when you were, / You served your own destruction." He welcomes his congregation and announces to them that the text for the day is taken from the *Book of Oedipus.* He goes on to tell of Oedipus' murder of his father and incest with his mother, and his self-blinding: "and the blood burst from his ruined sockets like red hail." Throughout this the congregation voices responses. The Preacher goes on to quote from *Oedipus* (lines 275–279), but claims it is *Exodus,* thus calling a Greek play by a biblical name, and perhaps it is apt: Exodus describes the Israelites in exile, and comparably Oedipus is forced to leave his city and become a wanderer. The first song, "Live where you can," follows, sung by a female soloist (the singer Antigone) and choir accompanied by a band playing in unison. It is the Invocation (comparable to the Introit). The passage is based on texts from *Oedipus Tyrannus* that contain Oedipus' advice to his children to live where they can, and also the more general advice, that every man should consider his last day. This is a "quotable quote" taken from *Oedipus Tyrannus* for dramatic advantage. The bleak ending of that play, with man seen in his lowest state, is where this *Gospel* begins, thus enhancing the final transformation.

Sometimes the ancient words of the play are twisted to suit the new Christian context. When the Preacher begins with the words "Think no longer that you are in command here," the implication of the Sophoclean words in the new context is that God is in command, and the sooner man learns that, the better. So also the words "Let every man in mankind's frailty / Consider his last day; and let none / Presume on his good fortune until he find / Life at his death, a memory without pain," are followed by "Amen" and the idea is not to exalt oneself as a human being, because in the human condition one's fortune will change. Pride precedes a fall, but if one trusts in God, then eternal happiness, something afforded no one in this world, will be the reward. In a sense the Gospel is the antidote to Greek tragedy, smoothing the harsh edges of the latter and indulging those who long for an afterlife. Many practicing Christians share this belief, as indeed many ancient Greeks believed in their pantheon of gods. But the Greek Hades, even with its Elysian Fields, was not a Christian paradise. The Greeks had no great expectation of life after death, at least not until Plato. The Elysian fields are not paradise. The gospel service can be akin to the Eleusinian mysteries, or other initiation rites seeking to ensure a better afterlife, some offering, so to speak, a map to Hades. In these religious rites, one loses oneself to gain a new being beyond in the afterlife: modern Christians and the ancient Greeks share in this mystery.

To the thought of considering one's last day are added the ideas of redemption for the lost and songs to please God, a fitting beginning for this folk opera. The first hymn shows programmatic touches. The rhythm is slow as the chorus advocates, "Stay, don't go away," but quickens when they speak of a fleeting life such as the youthful pleasures that fade quickly. It becomes more active and melismatic to accompany the words "Be happy as you can." A soloist executes decorated contrapuntal figures against a choral background, rather like a descant, "the high florid part added above the melody of a hymn."[25] The form of this section is ABCBA showing the ring form typical of most of the hymns in this opera, with a beginning, variation, and return to the beginning, sometimes more elaborate than the first appearance.

Then the gospel begins. Antigone tells how Oedipus rose to power by solving the riddle, and then fell from that power. She quotes from *Oedipus Tyrannus* as mentioned above. Then other words from the same text are varied in the Pastor's vocal line above the Hammond organ: "Alas for the seed of men. / What measure shall I give these generations / That breathe on the void and are void / And exist and do not exist" (*OT* 1186–1188). Oedipus' story is generalized as a moral lesson.

Blindness is a theme in this modern work, as well as in Sophocles' play.

When he had sight, Oedipus could not see the truth; when blind, he finally sees. His own blindness is augmented here by a blind chorus (in every production so far, although not so specified in the libretto), which adds an other-worldly quality because of its isolation from the world due to the blindness of its members. In the context of this drama, they sing symbolically like angels.

The figure of the blind black male singer is well-established; for example, one thinks of Ray Charles and Stevie Wonder. A handicap becomes an asset. Their bodies sway as if controlled by the music. One also thinks of Homer and Tiresias, the blind poet and the blind prophet.

Oedipus asks Antigone where they are. She tells him, Colonus. Both the last of the Theban plays written by Sophocles, *Oedipus at Colonus*, and the service, have clearly begun. A singer sings in falsetto without accompaniment excerpts from the choral "Ode to Colonus" (*OC* 668–719). The congregation shout encouragement, typical of a revival service, and the singer adds embellishments in the second repetition of the first verse.

When Oedipus asks where he is, the entire chorus responds as against a single voice in the Greek tragedy. A person sings the solo, "Fair Colonus," a beautiful lyric study. The solo uses the pentatonic scale with an ABA form for three verses. Since it is unaccompanied we might draw an analogy with Gregorian Chant, and the high voice of the falsetto reminds us of the then popular *castrato* (a mutilation that the early music-loving church allowed for the sake of art). A high voice (*castrato*, tenor, or soprano) can be equated with closeness to God and Beauty.[26] In this Ode, the falsetto voice comes close to imitating the nightingale it describes. Not only is the range programmatic, but there is an elaborate lyric turn on the word "nightingale" as if its very song were being reproduced.

Another programmatic touch is on the final word of the Ode, "long." It is protracted in a long, complex figure created by the singer. There are many other programmatic passages that illustrate the words musically, in a manner familiar in opera; this type of "literal" music was also prominent in Monteverdi.

The Ode resembles "A Voice Foretold," which comes later and also speaks of Colonus. Both are simple, slow, and unaccompanied, but the latter features the quintet with the soloist. "Fair Colonus" describes the locale in terms of ideal beauty. The unaccompanied chant adds to the religious quality. We feel this land is truly God's creation.

The congregation responds to the solo singer of the ode, and this song, "Stop! Do Not Go On!" contrasts with it. Instead of a solo we have two choruses. This song features the triple meter "Gospel Shuffle," with a soft-shoe rhythm in the percussion accompaniment, and a swinging melody in the pitched instruments; these move in unison during the last measure of each phrase. This makes the melody typical of jazz or swing in featuring a "stop rhythm" (it literally stops after one note for two rests), which makes it apt for the words that say "Stop! Do not go on!" There is a bluesy progression in the key of C major, and we have the suggestion of a slow march, also compatible with the theme—one wanting to progress and the other to halt that progress.

Perhaps the contrast between this song and the last ode is the same as that between divine and secular. One might even say that whereas the former illustrates a creation of God, the latter suggests the error of man: Oedipus should not be stopped, and Theseus will have to educate his people accordingly.

"Do Not Go On" is in the ABA form typical for this Gospel. The B section is sung by Oedipus asking for sanctuary; appeal alternates with the rejection. Counterpoint of affirmation and denial come from both choruses. The last section is a variation of the first verse, and as the chorus says, "Do not go on!" Oedipus answers, "Do it, Do it," and howls in a climactic expression of his yearning and disappointment. In every version I have seen he is hoisted by a member of the citizen chorus at the end of the song and physically carried to the place where he started.

We hear Oedipus' sung plea (the second section of the "Stop" song), "Here I stand a wanderer / On life's journey / At the close of the day / Hungry and tired / Beaten by the rain / Won't you give me shelter / All I need is a resting place / Promised so long ago." This not only excites pity, but falls into the biblical notion of a promised land and also the tradition of sheltering the stranger (it was also Greek to respect the *xenos*, "stranger"). In the Christian tradition, this stranger could be Christ, and in the ancient Greek tradition it might be a god in disguise: it was better to play it safe by welcoming the guest from afar.

The Choragos starts to question Oedipus about his origin, and Oedipus responds. When the chorus interrogates Oedipus in *Oedipus at Colonus*, it does it with much less sympathy than this choral leader, who acts in the manner of a preacher hearing a confession.

At this point Ismene appears and sings with two men and a woman (the Ismene quartet) "How Shall I See You Through My Tears?"[27] This is also typical of the jazz tradition. Ismene sings this in the bright key of G major. The accompaniment, sung by the chorus in an ascending two-part counterpoint on the words "Father, Sister," shows a typical expression of joy (the rising figure) used throughout the opera. These tears are tears of happiness at the reunion of daughter with father and sister. This part is varied both vocally and rhythmically; contrapuntal melodic figures emphasize rhythmic variations. The voices, rhythm, and accompaniment align themselves with the words "Destiny brings you back to me," so the music itself suggests a controlling destiny, besides varying the texture of the piece. This lyrical section features a duet / dialogue between Oedipus and Ismene, who alternate measures as in a be-bop alternation of solos between members of the ensemble. The Evangelist recites the B section in an ABA form, so that lyric section alternates with spoken section. The father and daughter can only soar in music, whereas the Evangelist gives a nonlyrical account of the strife between the brothers.

The Evangelist, speaking as it were for Ismene, gives a quasi-spoken rhythmic history of Oedipus' two sons, and how they strove for power instead of sharing it. Now the younger one is bringing an Argive army against Thebes to regain rule. Oedipus curses them, "Let them kill each other." The music plays in the background and then takes up the reprise, "How shall I see you through my tears?" We might say that tears are a unifying symbol in Oedipus' history, although for a moment these tears are tears of joy.[28]

The Choragos returns to his questioning and we find ourselves witnessing a confession. Oedipus admits his crimes, but claims innocence because he killed his father in self-defense and married his mother in ignorance. We could almost say this is the absolution part of the confession.

Oedipus sings with his quintet "A Voice Foretold," which tells of his dying at a grove sacred to the Eumenides. Now, he says, he has found this grove here at Colonus. This is again in ABA form, with a quasi-spoken part by Oedipus praying to the "Ladies whose eyes are terrible." The singer and chorus end with the concluding part of the first verse: "Where pain unending / Ends for me / Where I shall find / Sanctuary." This music is more lyrical and sacred. In this it resembles "Fair Colonus" (without the falsetto, but now the voice of an old man) and in fact is describing the same sacred place. The quintet seems to corroborate Oedipus, as if it was the incarnate voice of God, and it ends in harmony on the word Sanctuary. Oedipus prays to the "ladies whose eyes are terrible" in a half-spoken section. He recounts the prophecy that he will bring benefits to the place, but he reiterates that this is his prayer, that here he be given rest.

It seems as if Oedipus' prayers are answered when Theseus appears (he is played by the Pastor). Breuer and Telson wanted to alternate slow lyric sections with faster ones, and also main songs with secondary ones, so they rearranged the order of the text in some cases, as when they have Ismene appear earlier and Theseus later than in the play. In the play Theseus does not appear as if in response to a prayer, but his spontaneous appearance is a dramatically effective move in the *Gospel*.

The Gospel's Theseus delivers a "sermon" above an accompanying organ. This corresponds to the play (*OC* 551 ff.), but words are added to remind us that we are in a new type of religious setting. For instance, Theseus is made to say, "He has asked for grace!" Fitzgerald translates Sophocles, "What grace (*charis*) is this you bring to us." *Charis* here translated as "grace," in Greek usually means a "boon" or "favor." Christian grace is something different, a mysterious gift from God to produce in man a "state of grace." Sometimes the modern simply does not match the ancient.

Theseus tells Oedipus he has heard of him, and he will not refuse him sanctuary. This section may be equivalent to the *Gloria* and is a jubilant gospel chorus, "We will never drive you away from peace in this land." This begins slowly and then is followed by fast rhythm in a gospel two-step in which clapping accompanies dancing. There is again an ABA form with the chorus providing the two A sections, and the B section performed by Oedipus and his quintet (he is the fifth, so the quartet is background): Oedipus, in the B portion, speaks and sings in a declamatory voice, of being a wanderer who is now coming to rest. This section also fits the fast rhythm.

The quintet with the Choragos, "We Will Never Drive You Away" has a slow hymn-like beginning, featuring a rising figure of triadic chords in the bright key of G flat major, with a four-part harmonic texture accompanying a freely improvised solo voice, which echoes each section of the text. This is music for a procession, as Oedipus is led to a white piano that appears, a lyrical equivalent of the holy grove: music here is a type of god, and instruments are its altar. Then begins a fast gospel two-step with dancing.

The dance sequence resembles the dances featured at *Carnaval* in Brazil, with the congregation on its feet and taking part. Oedipus recites / sings an account of his suffering, and now he has reached a sacred resting place. This section punctuates the ABA form, his section being B. This fast-moving chorus contrasts with his plaintive and earnest narration. In the 1985 version, the Choragos screams at the reiteration of the promise that Oedipus will not be driven away. Oedipus' significant howling when he appealed for sanctuary now becomes a scream celebrating the fulfillment of his prayer.

Creon enters, played by an elderly deacon. All fall silent. He says that he has come to bring Oedipus home, and he appeals to Oedipus. Oedipus refuses, saying he would not be welcomed into the city. Creon tells Oedipus that he has seized his daughters, to force him to return. Oedipus curses Creon: "May God, watcher of all the world, / Confer on you such days as I have had / And such age as mine." An organ accompanies this curse as if to make it sacred and guarantee its fulfillment, organ music being closely associated with Christian worship of God. The curse echoes the earlier curse on his children: Oedipus is still harming his enemies. In an elaborate section, based on an A minor seventh chord, both the solo Oedipus and the quintet scold Creon. The choir repeats Oedipus' complaint and alternates with him in a way that adds rhetorical force to the refusal.

In the original play Theseus drives out Creon and says that he will recover Oedipus' daughters. Here Creon leaves spontaneously, and the Pastor is suddenly transformed into Theseus, who promises that he will retrieve the daughters. Some changes are made to ease the incorporation of these texts from Sophocles' other plays. The Preacher who comments on Creon's seizing of the children says, "In taking his daughters he has effectively / Taken his eyes and left him helpless, / As if standing in the wind of death." This last phrase is taken from the ode from the *Antigone*, "Numberless are the World's Wonders" (*Ant.* 332–364): "From every wind / He has made himself secure—from all but one: / In the late wind of death he cannot stand." We are still aware of artifice replacing logic. Mixing Sophoclean plays and ancient with modern religion does not always work.

This musical rendition puts us in the "holy" mode. The melody is lyrical and slow, with figures that illustrate the various words, such as a melismatic flourish on the words for wind and rain, which are smoothed out in the phrase "in the late wind of death." The entire piece gets more florid towards the end, as do all the pieces in this work. Each verse repeats the words, "Numberless are the world's wonders / But none more wonderful than man," and the music becomes more elaborate with each recurrence. We hear a contrast with the accompaniment for the text describing the "late wind of death": one note underlies the words, suggesting the inexorability of death in contrast to the *numberless* wonders of man, whose accompaniment features varied note-filled rhapsodic passages. Matching the more somber theme, the key is C minor. It is also homo-rhythmic, with triadic harmonies in the chorus. In the first stanza the lyric line of the male solo resembles Gregorian chant. We saw this before in the *Ode to Colonus*, which had few melismatic figures. The second stanza features a solo female voice, an octave higher. The final verse rises on the last words and re-solves itself in E flat major, adding to this otherwise somber piece a note of opti-mism. The piece is considered so important that it has to be conveyed simply by dramatic speech, and then sung. No word is missed, but it has to be made divine by the music, as Oedipus himself is transformed at the end. The harmonic tex-ture moves from minor to major in the coda to confirm this salvation. Music alters the bleaker message of the classical play.

A musical rendering of the words from the choral ode by the quartet with the choir accompanying a solo voice followed the spoken recitation. The act concludes with a general view of man, setting the tone of the *Gospel* as a moral tale, illustrating both man's virtues and limitations, to be overcome through the grace of God.

The ending of the first act of *Gospel* takes the specific facts of Oedipus' plight and universalizes them in its description of man's aptitudes and limita-tions. He can do so much, but cannot overcome death. In this new setting, the need for God is obvious. With God's help man may overcome death. The ancient context is bleaker, simply stressing man's impotence against death. Man is warned to be virtuous and pious, but there is no redemption. It takes Christ and the Gospel to introduce this notion. Christ dies and is resurrected. This happened to ancient gods, like Dionysos, and the occasional hero, like Heracles, but in Christianity all men can do as Jesus did: die and be resurrected.

The second act begins with a lament by Oedipus, "Lift me up," mourning the disappearance of his daughters. This is sung over an ostinato line of guitars and drums, suggestive of blues. The chorus in the original play supports Theseus in his recovery of Oedipus' daughters and recites the words "I . . . wish the wind would lift me like a dove" to view the fray. In the *Gospel*, Oedipus, rather than the chorus, says, "I wish the wind would lift me / So I could look with the eyes of the angels / for the child that I love . . . . I wish the Lord would hide me in a cloud . . . . / I'd fall like a rain of fire / And I'd lie like a shroud." Was "shroud" selected simply because it rhymed with "cloud"? It is an inept line to follow "I'd fall like a rain of fire." But these additions bring us again into the Christian tra-dition. Instead of the Greek chorus lofted like a dove to see and gloat over a vic-tory, Oedipus wants to be able to find his children. Mention of the angels and the Lord shows us the new context. The wings of the dove take on a new signifi-cance, with intimations of the Holy Ghost, innocence, and peace.

This section ("Lift me Up") is a lamentation, which has its programmatic touches. An eight-bar introduction by the solo guitar leads to a two-measure ostinato figure that is repeated throughout the aria. The solo melodic line is a four-note scale derived from an A minor blues scale and is sixteen measures long. The Oedipus quartet/quintet adds emphasis with sustaining chords at the word "dove" in "I wish the wind would lift me like a dove." They also occasionally join the solo voice at the words, "I wish the wind would lift me." A slow, dragging triple-meter indicates Oedipus' hopelessness. On the third iteration of the phrase "I wish the wind" there is an ascending leap to a lowered seventh scale degree, whose unresolved character might indicate his frustration.

Another child appears: Polyneices. He speaks over the music, which conveys what the balladeer calls him, "Evil." We remember that early name for the blues, "devil music." Polyneices admits he has been evil, disloyal to his father. This is another type of confession: testifier Polyneices speaks, and the Balladeer sings ritualistically in a repetitive form. Polyneices shouts at his father: he begs for a response and forgiveness.

The sisters return and greet their father. Theseus has rescued them. In the original the daughters are returned before Polyneices appears. In the *Gospel* their appearance interrupts Polyneices' plea. It makes little sense this way and, in Sophocles, it is effective to hear Polyneices speak without interruption. With the return of the daughters we have an intrusion of joy, which also is jarring against the blues music. Polyneices asks his sisters to intervene for him.

The Balladeer anticipates Oedipus by calling Polyneices evil, and insults him in a way that is hardly what we find in the original. First he says "You're so evil!" Then, "He's so slick." Vernacular is interspersed with Fitzgerald's rounded phrases. This musical section accompanying Polyneices is a *basso continuo* for guitar and drum revolving around two notes. The repetitive quality suggests that the speaker Polyneices is merely repeating a well-rehearsed tale that is, in fact, false. The Preacher/Oedipus calls Polyneices "Liar" (another addition, although it summarizes some of what Oedipus says) and accuses him of disloyalty. The singer Oedipus curses Polyneices, saying that he will fall, along with his brother, in mutual murder. Oedipus' curse is sung, whereas Polyneices' appeal is only spoken. It is as if the music reaffirms the divine power behind the curse.

Antigone's pleas on behalf of her brother are omitted. In most performances Polyneices' military allies do not appear, as they do in the libretto. They seem gratuitous and are in fact often eliminated in performance of the opera. We have a perverted *Agnus Dei*: a scapegoat has been found, and in this confession absolution has been refused.

The evangelist Antigone recites the verses from Sophocles' *Antigone*: "Love, unconquerable waster of men, / Surely you swerve upon ruin here. .... / And mortal man, in his one day's dusk, / Trembles before your glory" (*Antigone* 781–790). This is an extraordinary insertion here. This ode, which begins "Love Unconquerable," is quite appropriate in the *Antigone*, but inappropriate here, because it says, "You have made bright anger strike between father and son," namely Creon, who has ordered the execution of his son Haemon's beloved bride Antigone. What has love to do with the rupture between Oedipus and Polyneices? This division is based on a drive for power, hatred, and pride. Oedipus felt he was spurned by his sons and driven out of Thebes. Hence the hatred for his sons (note "sons," not "son" as in the above ode), whose only love is power and their own self-aggrandizement. He curses them accordingly. Whereas the ode beginning "Numberless are the world's wonders" from the *Antigone* could probably fit any Greek tragedy, the ode "Love Unconquerable" is suited to the original context rather than the modern work, where it seems to have been gratuitously added.

There is a difference between God's love in the Christian tradition and Oedipus' in Greek tragedy. If a person asks for forgiveness and resolves to do better, God forgives. Not Oedipus. Thus the ancient play is inevitably the deeper tragedy. This work conflates ancient Greek culture, and Catholic, Protestant, Pentecostal, and African traditions. Sometimes this works well, sometimes not.

The Preacher Oedipus now delivers the famous chorus on old age from *Oedipus at Colonus* (1211–1248), with the choir and organist accompanying it with background and responses. This adds to the sacred quality, as did the "Ode to Man" from the *Antigone*. Sometimes the singer adds his or her own commentary; for instance, in all the productions I have seen, Oedipus screams on the word "death" in this ode to old age, and earlier he howled on the words "Stop" and "Sanctuary," which refer to Colonus, the place where he will meet death and be transfigured. Is his shriek the "cry of the angel," a signal that he is prepared to meet death? It is both his agony and his triumph.

Lightning strikes, and the choir comments, "God's lightning opens up the ground." The libretto calls for a repetition of the lightning, and in the 1985 production a column is split and lightning has scorched the piano.[29] There is a strange light now, akin to a solar eclipse with predominant reds and purples.

When Oedipus hears the thunder and sees the lightning, he knows his time has come; the chorus sings "O Sunlight of No Light," actually bidding farewell to the light. This is in a slow duple meter, which suggests a funeral march, and is in the key of G minor, which modulates to B flat major, signifying Oedipus' own transition to paradise. Ascending figures accompany the words "this is the last my flesh will feel," once more suggesting transfiguration. The organ chords suggest the music heard in Christian funeral homes, signifying respect for the dead. As if angels' horns announced paradise, trumpets provide background to the secrets Oedipus tells Theseus (cf. *Tuba Mirum* in the Requiem Mass). We might view this section as the consecration with secret prayers.

Theseus affirms to Oedipus that his hour has come. Oedipus says, "My soul sinks in the scale," recalling an image from the *Iliad*, which also occurs in Sophocles' *Oedipus at Colonus* (1508). A balladeer and the Choragos quintet, standing in for Oedipus, sing farewell to the sun, "O sunlight of no light" (1549).

In a passage reminiscent of the secrets spoken by the priest or minister at the time of consecration, we are told that Oedipus' burial place must be kept secret, and then all the land and people will be blessed. Oedipus' last words are spoken by the preacher, and he gives a blessing, "Remember me. Be mindful of my death. / And be fortunate for all the time to come."[30] Thus helping his friends, he departs.

Oedipus, in the 1985 production, sinks down, along with his quintet, all resting their heads on the piano, which is their bier. They then disappear into an open grave (in fact the open pit in the stage, which hides the piano).

A *Requiescat* passage follows: "Let not our friend go down in grief and weariness. . . . / O eternal sleep / Let him sleep well." Now we also have found the true *Agnus Dei* (in contrast to the false scapegoat of Polyneices), one whose death will benefit others; the *Agnus Dei* from the Requiem mass concludes with the words *Dona eis requiem sempiternam*, "Give them [the dead] eternal rest." The Choragos Quintet led by the soloist sing their wishes for peace, and since their song begins with no instrumental background, it resembles plainchant. Towards the end the full orchestra enters and describes Oedipus' descent. The piano disappears. The Sophoclean chorus also prays to the gods and says: "I call on you [death] who are eternal sleep," (1578), so we see the similarity between ancient and modern prayers.[31] The implication is that Oedipus be granted eternal sleep.

The libretto tells us that the "singers of the role of Oedipus descend on their white piano—their bier—into the underworld. A violet light appears as from a volcanic cleft." Mourning begins, and Antigone laments in E minor with despairing words. As she cries, her vocal line descends the interval of a sixth or an octave. It is a wail of suffering. This is a particularly moving passage for everyone who has lost someone beloved. The chorus gives her a brief call and response. This is also the first time that Antigone the speaker has a lyrical passage. Suffering has taught her to sing.

Theseus tells Antigone not to mourn. The Doxology, otherwise called the paean, "Lift Him Up," begins slowly, as do most sacred songs, and then there follows a type of Hallelujah chorus with spirited dancing in a gospel two-step rhythm. This is a typical gospel chorus, owing very little to *Oedipus at Colonus*. This is a celebration and the resurrection in music and dance, beginning slowly with an organ and a soloist like the other "sacred" pieces, but then developing into an orchestral celebration with full choir. The choir is used as a rhythmic and harmonic ostinato, like a vocal "riff" produced by a jazz band when accompanying the solo trumpet or trombone or saxophone. The soloist freely improvises around the same text. As the notes rise, and go higher, the text reaffirms this ("Lift him higher"), and the soloist has several peak notes, held for a length of time that requires special virtuosity.

This might be considered the communion section of the mass, which includes the whole community in union with God, and with both the living and the dead, since at this point we see Oedipus and his quintet rise with their piano to join the living: "The white grand piano ascends. The singers of Oedipus also emerge, clapping from the grave."[32]

We have Christian dogma enacted before our eyes. Oedipus is truly immortal. We have seen him die and now he is resurrected. This is very different from Sophocles' intent. Not everyone is deified as is the protective hero Oedipus. Nor do we see him return. The mourning of Antigone will last.

Although we see his piano rise and Oedipus clapping on the stage, we are probably meant to see his return as symbolic. Otherwise the messenger speech, which describes his death, is nonsense. In most performances we see Creon also joining the celebration. The tempo is fast, with the whole congregation dancing.

These additions are jarring, though the music and performance tend to elide the discrepancies and contradictions with the original text.

The Preacher's speech follows. He tells of Oedipus speaking to his daughters as they helped him bathe and change his clothes in preparation for death. He tells them that they will no longer need to care for him: "I know it was hard, my children, and yet one word / Frees us of all the weight and pain of life. / That word is love. Never shall you have more / From any man than you have had from me" (1615–1618). "Love" is, of course, resonant in the Christian tradition (and in opera): Oedipus loves his daughters in the way God loves mankind. "A voice cried out and he left. No one knows his end, but it was wonderful: he died of no painful disease and without mourning" (1663–1665).

There are several problems in making Oedipus suit a Christ image, as indeed we have seen in Stravinsky's opera. Perhaps Oedipus is simply "Everyman," a sinner, set against the gospel's claim that there are no men born who are not sinners, and no sinner who cannot potentially be saved. Yet it is hard to see Oedipus' particular sins as Everyman's—in spite of Freud's insistence on the complex—and what has been prophesied in the play is hardly something consonant with Christian doctrine. Oedipus loves his friends and hates his enemies, an old Greek maxim. Christ preached universal love (*agape*, as opposed to *eros*, or *philia*), endorsing a policy of "turning the other cheek" and loving one's neighbor as oneself.

Oedipus curses his own sons, condemning them to death at each other's hands: not only does Oedipus kill his father, but he kills the offspring of his incestuous union with his mother. As a sacred hero, he will be a protecting divinity for Athens, guarding them against their enemies, fighting, for instance, against the Thebans if they attack, as they did during the Peloponnesian War. *Oedipus at Colonus* was written during that war, and the political implications of what Oedipus would mean for Athens as a protector was vivid in Sophocles' mind. Oedipus' actions hardly accord with Christian doctrine. Oedipus joined the ranks of other "sinners" who became heroes in the technical sense that they protect the territory where they were buried (in this case Athens). The mythical Oedipus was comparable to Ajax, whose ghost was seen fighting on the side of Athens against the Persians at Salamis.

In Oedipus' prayer to the "Ladies [the Eumenides] whose eyes are terrible," he reiterates his role in bringing protection to the place, "Conferring benefits on those who received me, / A curse on those who have driven me away." Here the prayer echoes the Greek maxim "to help one's friends and harm one's enemies." The section is a literal rendering of *OC* 84–110, and in this it jars somewhat with the Christian sentiments in the rest of the opera.

The ancient play, Christian ritual, and a modern performance make a strange mixture. For instance, an intermission is hardly true either to the ancient play or to the modern revival service. The different parts combine in different ways. Nevertheless, there are interesting results. For example, the religious quality of ancient drama reappears.

The closing hymn is "Let the Weeping Cease." This is a slow, passionate hymn expressing faith and calling for an end to lamentation. It is based on the choral words that end Sophocles' play, "Cease from lamentation, for all these things are right" (1777–1779). The last words become the final words spoken by the Preacher: "These things are in the hands of God."[33] The text is considered as holy as the music, so the conclusion is spoken above a musical accompaniment.

This final hymn begins slowly with an organ accompaniment and is a type of theme and variation. The key of G major and a simple sixteen-bar melody structured on the major triad is repeated four times, first with solo, then joined by quartet, then joined by the entire chorus and orchestral accompaniment, finally with hand claps and spoken text above the melody. This is a clear climax to conclude this gospel opera, and the resolution is in a major key and on a high note. The music throughout confirms the Christian doctrine of redemption with its celebration of immortality in a continued life with God. They have sung a holy song unto the Lord.

CONCLUSION

Gospel at Colonus features not only brilliant and inspiring music from the African-American tradition, but merges it with one of the greatest classical texts of antiquity. Sometimes the fit is uncomfortable, but as Christianity accepts all comers, so this opera / service takes the classical text as affirming God and man's salvation. Past merges with present and promises a bright future, with all believers glory-bound to paradise. Not just one single Oedipus is the hero now; all mankind shares in the divine promise.

We have also come full circle, and this opera resembles the earliest opera Women are once again elevated in opera. We have a female chorus in addition to and equal to the male choruses. Ismene is strikingly lyrical and has a greater role than in the original. Antigone's part is also expanded, and additions from the play about her are freely incorporated. This *Gospel* in a sense becomes the tragedy of Antigone, since we see how deeply she feels Oedipus's death, and this is conveyed by the music. Like Electra, Antigone is strongly attached to her family: her father and her brother. She dies because she buries Polyneices, executed by Creon whose orders she violated. Her loyalty to her brother naturally follows her loyalty to her father; her whole life centers around caring for those to whom she is related. In the original *Oedipus at Colonus*, she was the one who suffered the loss of Oedipus most. In the *Gospel*, she is comforted by the Christian solace offered her, but it is difficult not to share her pain when we hear her moving lament and see her tears. Here is true operatic pathos, and the diva breaks our hearts.

We have also come full circle, and this opera resembles the earliest opera not only in taking over mythical and religious themes, but in the form and characteristics of the music. *Gospel at Colonus* is closer to Monteverdi and Mozart than to Strauss. It goes back even earlier in the way it is faithful to the original Greek tragedy; the text is a translation of the play rather than a free invention by a librettist on themes suggested by the myths.

It is interesting that this opera, the most modern considered here, has also returned to the earliest music: the Gregorian Chant and the melismatic music is typical of Monteverdi and Mozart. The use of the organ as a *basso continuo* also accords with Mozart's operas and allows freedom to the recitative delivered above it. We also see a similarity in performance practice between the figured bass of the Baroque with the chord chart of the jazz or blues musician. No two performances of *Gospel at Colonus* can be the same because there are too many variables that are part of the service, and the cast depends on individual inspiration in the form of improvisation (which takes us back to prenineteenth-century practices). The active use of improvisation was another very distinctive quality in performances rarely employed in classical music after the 1850s. It certainly distinguishes this score, and indeed for many years there was no score at all. This is what living music should be.

This is a fitting production for America, "the melting pot of the world," which likes to contrast its democratic ideals with the more aristocratic ethos of Europe. And where did democracy come from? Historians trace the birth of democracy to Athens and the Cleisthenic reforms in 507 B.C., but others argue that democracy began in 462 B.C. with the radical democratic reforms of Ephialtes.[34] In any case, the origin remains Greek. For many years democracy in America, like democracy in ancient Athens, was confined to male citizens. Many African-Americans were slaves to begin with. Blues and jazz grew out of this experience and so did the black gospel tradition. Here one could obtain freedom in a limited form, and the church talked of a salvation available to everyone (as democracy was not, and never has been). Like Monteverdi, who found freedom from the Gonzagas in the church and his music, so did the African-Americans in *their* church and *their* music. My book traces the intermittent rise and fall of freedom, but this black gospel opera nostalgically revives the freedom possible through music. It is also a freedom based on a profound awareness of the contribution of women.

Oedipus is seen leaving a place that he knows would deprive him of his freedom, seeking sanctuary in a place of his choice. This is the story of the African-Americans who not only were enslaved and given a legalistic and technical freedom, but who now have to fight daily to find a sanctuary, a place of their choice that accepts them not only as equals, but accords them the honor that is their due. This cry is not simply like Moses' "Let my people go," but "Let them rest where they will" and "Let them work and enjoy the fruits of their labors with equality." Oedipus provides a particularly apt myth, and Breuer and Telson provide the musical realization of a dream. This is a celebration of liberation theology.

APPENDIX
OPERAS ABOUT *OEDIPUS AT COLONUS*[35]

Antonio Sacchini (1730–1786) (b. Florence, Italy)
Oedipe à Colonne (1786)

André-Ernest-Modeste Grétry (1741–1813) (b. Liège, Belgium)
Oedipe à Colonne (unperf.)

Niccolò Antonio Zingarelli (1752–1837) (b. Naples, Italy)
Edipo a Colono (1802)

Lee Breuer (1937–) / Bob Telson
Gospel at Colonus (1982)

Theodorakis and Euripides' *Medea:* The Wife and Mother from Hell

Medea haunts our imagination. Made famous in antiquity by Euripides, Apollonius Rhodius, Seneca, Ovid, and others, she is firmly installed in the modern psyche.[1] She is the philanderer's nightmare: the former wife who drives a dragon-drawn chariot; the child-slayer who escapes punishment. Medea is the woman who kills her husband's lover, who murders her own children. She is the folk archetype: we read about her in the news, see her in plays, on the screen—and we hear her sing. Medea is always around with her pain, her vengeance, and her eternal fury.

Medea is admirable, strange, and horrifying; her story shocks in every century. She is particularly suitable for opera with its grand gestures; a dangerous barbarian princess is bound to pack in the audiences.

Mikis Theodorakis uses the energy of this now universal symbol and creates a musical metamorphosis of her passion, her sufferings, and her triumph. She stands for the Greek nation itself: the people who were victimized and took their vengeance. He says of his work, "For the first time there was a reconciliation, an *eros*, a deep spiritual bond between my work and our entire people. It appears that this great euphoria I was experiencing was the source of such an endless pouring out of melodies and ideas. The triumph of my music was helping to tear into pieces all barriers, all political and artistic establishments that had besieged me; leaders, violence and ugliness that had besieged me from all political sides: the right, the left, the center, that is to say the totality of political power structures in Greece; the East and the West, that is to say, the totality of the political ideologies that I had found frightening. As early as the 1950s I had begun to see clearly that behind the facade of the political parties was hidden the unattractive face of the authoritarian elites and all the negatives that were oppressing me and which had forced me to isolate myself inside the 'caves' of my house in Paris with symphonic music as my companion." Music restores him to the values of the Greek people, and not merely the elite. He continues in this vein when he says, "Let us appease the angry gods and banish the wicked high priests and pharisees. Let's restore the position that Greece had in the hearts of simple men in all the world when the litany of sound and sights/visions were important."

BACKGROUND

I have located sixty-four operas based on or including the myth of Medea (besides one modern musical): thirteen come from the seventeenth century, twenty-six from the eighteenth, eight from the nineteenth, and seventeen—plus many revivals—from the twentieth.[2] The ages of absolutism (seventeenth century) and imperialism (nineteenth century) seem less prepared to sanction a rebellious Medea. The eighteenth and twentieth centuries have been more faithful to the original Euripidean text, with its powerful Medea, who, after she achieves her vengeance, gloats from her dragon chariot with impunity at Jason's impotence. She is most popular in the twentieth century; operas like Rolf Liebermann's *Freispruch für Medea* (1995), Michael John LaChiusa's *Marie Christine* (1999), and books like Christa Wolf's *Medea Stimmen* (1998) show her as an appealing heroine for our time and represent her faithfully in her complex passionate totality. This is what Theodorakis does.

When women's rights are taken seriously (eighteenth and twentieth centuries), Medea is a tragic and powerful heroine who achieves a successful vengeance and escapes with impunity: even the titles celebrate her bloody victory, for example, Giuseppe Moneta's *La vendetta di Medea* (1787). When women's rights are not an issue or not taken seriously (seventeenth and nineteenth centuries), operas about Medea are fewer; in them she is usually either weak and submissive and commits no crime or is punished for her violent acts. This is not to say that there are no exceptions to such claims; I only propose that the majority of the evidence points in this direction. Medea in opera is a barometer of sexual politics.

The eighteenth century produced treatises like Jean Jacques Rousseau's *Discours sur l'origine et les fondements de l'inégalité parmi les hommes* (1755); this debate was over universal equality. David Hume (1711–1776) in his *A Treatise of Human Nature* and *Essays Moral, Political and Literary* wrote about how women are undervalued. Beaumarchais wrote subversively in *Le mariage de Figaro* (1784), which includes the victories of the valet over his master, and women over men. Mozart and Da Ponte's opera (1786) was faithful to this. Napoleon said that this work was the first stone flung in the French Revolution.[3] Nevertheless, it is only in the twentieth century that women finally gained the vote: 1920 in the United States and 1945 in France. Fifth-century Athens, eighteenth-century France, and twentieth-century Greece have been cultures where democracy was either practiced—although with limitations that excluded women and minorities—or discussed as an ideal to be achieved.[4]

In the seventeenth century art pursued the bizarre and exceptional; music also showed freedom in its use of modes and dissonance without the regularized adherence to major and minor keys that would take place in the eighteenth century.[5] In the nineteenth century romantic independence was stressed. One might think that Medea would be popular in these centuries, but the emphasis on individualism did not extend to females as independent, unconventional, and successful in crime as she was, and the statistics of operas written about her support this. The eighteenth and twentieth centuries were periods large enough in their universalizing concepts to contain even Medea.

Not only does Medea herself change throughout the ages, so does her adversary Jason. He is courtly and romantic in the seventeenth century; reasonable and rather idealistic in the eighteenth century; torn by self-doubt and lingering romantic attachment to Medea in the nineteenth; in the twentieth he comes full circle back to the calculating, cruel sophist that Euripides first showed us.[6]

Many operas on Medea follow Seneca's interpretation of Medea as the "Wicked Witch of the East." Turning Medea into a witch is a way of showing her evil, and underlining the necessity for control and justification for denying women rights. One also wonders if many of these librettists know only Seneca but not Euripides.

Tragedies about Medea with only incidental music were performed at the beginning of the seventeenth century: Pierre Corneille's *Médée* in 1635, and *La conquête de la toison d'or* in 1661. Although opera began as a revival of ancient Greek drama, a little earlier around 1600, it was not until 1648 and Francesco Cavalli's *Giasone* that Medea appeared in a full-scale opera. The first time Medea's name is in the title of an opera is in Antonio Giannettini's *Medea in Atene* in 1675: this opera concentrates on her career in Athens following the devastation she left behind her in Corinth.

Francesco Cavalli's *Giasone* (1648), based on the *Argonautica* of Apollonius of Rhodes, was the most popular opera of the seventeenth century, and shows a benign Medea helping Hypsipyle to wed Jason and live happily ever after. This opera is more a comedy than a tragedy, although there are tragic scenes and impressive laments. For the most part, the story line resembles plots by Menander and Greek new comedy (also the Greek novel), with its adventure, romance, and mistaken identities. It is typical of the seventeenth century, which was the age of the happy ending. There are two ways of limiting Medea: either to show her as weak and acquiescing, as she is here, or to punish her, as was frequent in operas of the nineteenth century.

Marc-Antoine's Charpentier's *Médée* in 1693 was composed to a libretto by Thomas Corneille, who adapted his brother Pierre's work. She kills her children and celebrates her successful vengeance. Since Charpentier's opera is on the cusp of the eighteenth century, I think it represents the taste of that time more than the seventeenth. Other operas in the eighteenth century also show Medea in all her glory. For instance, Joseph-François Salomon wrote a *Médée et Jason* to a text by Simon-Joseph Pellegrin after Ovid's *Metamorphoses*, which was performed in 1713. Medea achieves a bloody vengeance and triumphantly escapes; orchestral interludes link the scenes and acts with dramatic commentary.

Georg Benda composed his *Medea* (1775) with a libretto by Friedrich Wilhelm Gotter. Gotter's text shows us a humanized Medea who is barely able to carry out her murderous plans, but finally her anger prevails. She escapes in a cloud chariot and flaunts her victory over Jason, who commits suicide by falling on his sword.

Luigi Cherubini's *Médée* was written in 1797, and it shows many features of nineteenth-century romanticism. Médée here is more wicked than in Charpentier's or Benda's opera. Hell will receive her rather than Athens. The Eumenides drag her off, rather like Don Giovanni at the end of Mozart's opera. We focus on an evil woman taking her frightful revenge. The idealism of the French revolution has turned into the aftermath: bloodshed and violent reprisals. Médée now must be punished. Likewise, in Giovanni Pacini's *Medea* in 1843, we find the romantic Medea, one who does frightful things and must be punished, but who inflicts that punishment on herself by suicide.

Medea is a potent symbol for the twentieth century and represents a woman successfully fighting back, albeit with tragic results for herself—Robert Wilson has produced various versions of *Medea* in plays and film, including *Deafman Glance* in 1970, a prologue (1980), and an overture (1982). Gavin Bryars collaborated with Robert Wilson on an opera, *Medea*, in 1984, and like Theodorakis, returned to Euripides' text. Darius Milhaud wrote a *Médée* (1940) just before France fell to the Nazis. Tony Harrison wrote a libretto for *Medea: A Sex War Opera* (1985), commissioned by the Met, but never performed because Jacob Druckman did not complete the score.[7] He makes the point that not only women kill their children. Men are indicted as much as women for filicide. La Chiusa's *Marie-Christine* (2000), a Broadway hit, puts Medea into the context of the American South and shows us a woman of color fighting back against a man who discards her for a white bride who, he thinks, will make him more upwardly mobile.

Mikis Theodorakis' opera based on Euripides' *Medea* is a splendid example of how a modern work can elucidate an ancient text. He has said of his own work, "In the beginning was the word. This truth colours all my work—to the point where no one needs to do more than place the piece of poetry in the foreground, in order to explain my music." He passionately respected Euripides and this story of an abused woman who exacts her vengeance.

At the same time as elucidating the text, his opera incorporates song and dance and elicits a total response from the audience. This response is perhaps part of what Aristotle meant by *katharsis,* achieved by means of a ritual that engages the body along with the mind. While it may not resolve all the controversies over her character, Theodorakis' *Medea* allows us to appreciate the complexities of this powerful heroine.

One interpretation of Theodorakis' work could construe the myth as a paradigm for Greek history: Greece's occupation and exploitation, its revenge, and the stabbing of its own best-beloved, as it did during the civil war. Instead of concentrating on Medea's hate, Theodorakis depicts the sufferings of both sides. His Medea is all the richer for it. Women realize that their suffering can be political in origin, so they want political solutions. Theodorakis shows us that women often have political purposes that clash with their personal lives. He is also more sympathetic to Jason, besides expressing the theme of universal suffering.

Theodorakis' biography, with its account of the intermittent persecutions and celebrations of his work, reads like a history of Greece.[8] He was one of the leaders of the resistance to the Greek Junta, the military dictatorship that held power from 1967 to 1974. He was imprisoned and tortured for his beliefs, but never gave up.

From 1940 to 1960 Theodorakis wrote symphonic works and a ballet called *Antigone*, which was performed at Covent Garden in London in 1959. From 1960 to 1980 he composed melodies to accompany both Greek and foreign poetry, including many productions of ancient classics such as Minotis' production of the *Phoenissae* (Euripides); Mouzenidis' *Ajax* (Sophocles) and *Troades* (Euripides); Evangelatos' *Suppliants* and *Trilogy* (Aeschylus); Koun's *Knights* (Aristophanes); and Solomos' *Hecuba* (Euripides); among others. In 1987, his fourth Symphony was performed and it consisted of two parts: Aeschylus' *Eumenides* and Euripides' *Phoenissae.* In the same year, his ballet based on *Zorba* was performed in Verona's opera house, along with Verdi's *Aida* and Puccini's *Turandot.*

He mastered melody and felt he was able to meet Euripides on his own terms, as an equal. He made the *logos* lyrical as he translated Euripides himself from ancient into modern Greek and set his own words to music. He admired melodies from many sources: "A genuine and truthful composer is one who gives birth to genuine and true melodies, as has been the case with Monteverdi, Bach, Mozart, Beethoven, Stravinsky, Prokofiev, Weber, Shostakovich, Gershwin, Tsitsanis, Hadjidakis, and Dylan." Classics continue to influence him. In a letter he said that he felt inspired to compose a *Medea* in honor of Verdi, an *Elektra* in honor of Puccini, and a *Hecuba* in honor of Bellini.[9] His first opera actually was in honor of the brave poet who died tragically, *Kostas Kariotaki,,or The Metamorphoses of Dionysos*, and was performed at the Lyriki Skene in 1987. His *Medea* was performed in 1991, and he finished an *Elektra* in 1992, and in 1996, an *Antigone*. They comprise a trilogy of operas based on Greek tragedy.

Theodorakis says Euripides saw man as more autonomous and responsible for his own choices, in contrast to Aeschylus, who saw man more as a plaything of the gods.[10] Modern man faces the existential question of his own identity and has to come to terms with Sartre's insight: *"L'Enfer, c'est les Autres"* (*Huis Clos*, sc. V). Tragedy helps with the ultimate confrontation: self-knowledge. Theodorakis couples music with words to make our experience of the modern opera as intellectually and emotively cathartic as the experience of ancient tragedy.

Theodorakis had at his disposal the palette of minimalism and other forms of modern music, but instead he chose to keep many of the traditional elements that we have come to appreciate in Italian opera of the nineteenth and early twentieth centuries. Like the Italian masters, he is highly original in using and combining traditional European symphonic music with folk music; *Rembetika*, the augmented second, the pentatonic scale, and the ancient modes all suggest the "oriental," and even at times Orthodox liturgical music. His *melos* also has elements from the music of Crete, demotic and laic melodies, Arabic and Turkish themes, jazz, symphonic music, and the general classical heritage of Europe. His simplified approach to vocal counterpoint asserts the primacy of the verbal text. At times the orchestration adds a colorful dance motif, often derived from the Greek and Arabic dances with which he is familiar. Theodorakis calls his music "metasymphonic," because it consists of a synthesis of Western music with these Eastern elements.[11]

MEDEA

This is the only opera in this study whose libretto is a direct translation of the original. This work contrasts with most operas based on preexisting literary texts, which are usually reduced to allow room for the added music and repetitions and keep the performance within manageable limits. Most literary texts are reduced by half for opera.[12]

Because of the length of Theodorakis' *Medea*, which incorporates the entire text, various sections are usually omitted in actual performance, although Theodorakis prefers no cuts. At Bilbao the performance (with cuts) was about three hours, in contrast to less than two hours for the play. Perhaps Theodorakis' *Medea* as written would be over six hours in performance. The music is fundamental for interpreting the comparisons and contrasts between Euripides' and Theodorakis' works. In his fidelity, Theodorakis follows Euripides in his tragic, nonmelodramatic grandeur by showing us a Medea who suffers, but is heroic and escapes.

This merging of modern with ancient genius, Theodorakis with Euripides, tempers Euripidean irony, but emphasizes the tragic. Theodorakis' Medea is a woman, not a witch, and in this I believe he is true to Euripides.

Theodorakis has a background in working with choruses, yet here many of the choral passages are delivered by the choral leader. The scoring often shows an antiphonal and responsorial vocal setting that allows for greater understanding of the text. At the same time the use of beautifully lush nineteenth-century harmonies and polyphonic textures in the orchestra vividly contrast with the plainsong/Gregorian chant recitatives that form part of the composer's material for the chorus.

Jason is a tenor and Creon and Aegeus are basses. This adds to the authority of the latter two, and, since most tenors have the romantic leads in opera, this suggests Jason's love for Medea. Medea is a *soprano dramatico* and the nurse is a mezzo. Medea's being a soprano emphasizes her femininity and perhaps her motherliness and purity. Many have noted that opera mezzos by contrast are often *femme fatales* (e.g., Carmen), or *soubrettes*, that is, "clever and experienced females" (e.g., Despina in *Cosi Fan Tutte*, or Eunice in Previn's *A Streetcar Named Desire*).

The opera begins with a theme for the clarinet in the key of A minor, outlining the A-diminished scale, which suggests Medea, vengeance, death, fate, and passion. It is similar to the theme that Theodorakis used years before in his prologue to Cacoyannis' *Elektra* (1961), but there it was accompanied by other woodwinds in addition to the clarinet, with percussion and a more obviously Middle Eastern rhythm. The theme in the *Medea* will recur just before she kills her children. In this thematic reminiscence we see a parallel between Electra's and Orestes' just vengeance against Aegisthus and Medea's against Jason. The nurse, a mezzo-soprano, gives us the celebrated prologue that begins Euripides' play. A modal "Byzantine" theme is introduced that accompanies the words telling of Medea's flight from Colchis after helping Jason steal the Golden Fleece by murdering her brother. Medea is the foreigner and is thus associated with a "foreign" theme. Forgetting Procne and others of her ilk, Jason will accuse Medea of committing acts no civilized Greek woman would commit. The music goes along with her being characterized as foreign, and for a Greek this would mean "barbaric."

There are other programmatic touches, where the music reproduces what it describes, such as a theme that seems to suggest waves or a storm. This can be interpreted either literally (rolling of waves during Medea's voyage to Corinth) or figuratively (her rage), among other possibilities.

The tutor emerges with the children; he is a bass and sings of the new disaster Medea must face: exile. We hear more of the storm and the oriental motif. A march-like theme illuminates the nurse's comment that Medea will not rest until someone is hurt, whether friend or foe (*Med.* 94–95). This is a clear allusion to what we know is the central theme of *Medea*: she kills her children for vengeance against Jason.

This march-like theme tells us that Medea is as powerful as any soldier. Theodorakis' martial suggestion shows Medea as not only a Sophoclean but a Homeric hero. There is the assertion that recurs various times throughout the play: Medea does not want her enemies to laugh at her (e.g., *Med.* 383 and 404). Her honor is all-important, and this is the primary concern of the Greek hero in Homer.[13] Medea says that she does not want to be considered weak or powerless, but by being a bane to her enemies and a boon to her friends hers is a life of fair fame (807–810). Even when Medea makes her famous claim that she would rather stand in the front of the battle line three times than bear a child once (251), she illustrates by her actions that she does not fear standing in battle. It is this that the music emphasizes.

We hear Medea cry within the house, and the chorus prays to the gods to hear this pitiful woman crying for death. A chorale theme mixes with discords rendered by the brass. Traditional religious music is violated by cries in the music that replicate the cries of the woman: human events contradict the divine scheme, which urges order and harmony.

Medea addresses the women of Corinth. A tuba predominates as Medea speaks of the abuse of women by men. The aria reaches a climactic high note with Medea's comment that women are best suited for bloody vengeance. This follows a type of repetitive song, with its rocking motion suggesting a lullaby and childlike innocence. We hear this lullaby against her words of vengeance, so the music prophetically suggests that the children be a weapon for this vengeance, as sleep will merge into death.

Brass predominates at the entry of Creon and his interchange with Medea. The brass of power overcomes the complaints of strings. The Medea motif, with its Byzantine modes and harsh gongs and exotic finger cymbals, appears here again in the major key. It is as if Medea were presenting her best public picture, and a major key symbolizes this public stance better than a minor one.

A male chorus accompanies Creon, Jason, and Aegeus. In this opera, Theodorakis shows us many uses of the mixed choir, with men and women confronting each other as they support conflicting claims.

The female chorus sings a type of barcarole on a modal scale that accompanies words. It suggests liturgical music and the laments from Asia Minor.

When Jason appears the theme is once again predominantly brass, as with Creon's. There is a strong descending theme rather like the theme that signifies Wotan's power and decline in *The Ring*. The descending theme will occur to end the play, but the power will now be in Medea's hands. Her dragon-drawn chariot will carry her off to safety.

The exchange between Medea and Jason is expressed in another theme, nervous and jagged, which conveys conflict. Interrupted lines of music convey their argument in clipped phrases.

Jason's and Creon's words indicate that Medea is angry because of her sexual loss (*Med.* 284 and 527 ff). The music, however, shows us that it is a conflict between warriors, Medea and Jason, and that the basis is honor.

Aegeus' meeting with Medea is characterized by the brass, as was Creon's. The meeting in this case is between equals, whereas with Creon, Medea was the victim and suppliant. This act ends with a swearing of oaths. This is an interesting use of modern religious music, which blends with the mention of the Greek gods. Medea and Creon swear before a statue of Zeus. The music is reminiscent of Greek Orthodox services, and the religious quality is obvious. There is a formality in this use of the chorus: one is aware of collective will and prayer rather than an individual's desire. Theodorakis has endorsed Medea's plea, with the sanction of modern gods as well as ancient ones.

The second act begins with morose strings in a rising theme of three notes. The chorus sings about Athens as Medea stands and meditates. When the chorus reaches the subject of her children, the music becomes more agitated.

Jason enters and Medea persuades him to plead that the children may stay. She gives the children gifts of a tiara and veil for the princess against a theme that suggests magic. It is announced by a tuba against tympani, with wide atonal intervals and an F minor arpeggio (F-A flat-C-E flat).

The chorus meditates morosely on the unfolding events. A tutor enters with the children, and their mother plays with them. We hear the second children's theme, which suggests walking, rather like the theme from Prokofiev's *Peter and the Wolf.* It occurs in both Acts 1 and 2. The words and gestures are sadder than the music. The brass offers spirited commentary. As Medea herself becomes overwhelmed with sadness, she contemplates changing her plans. But then Medea remembers her faithless husband with the princess; there is discord in the lyrical line, and trumpet joins with drums in affirming her vengeance. The magic theme returns against wave-like broken chords in the strings. As her love for the children is expressed in words, the earlier, softer theme returns. But she thrusts the children away and begins an ecstatic dance in tragic celebration of her anger's triumph. The way Medea changes her mind in an emotionally tortuous situation is well conveyed by all three media: words, music, and dance.

The chorus follows with a march-like motif, which then yields to an anguished weaving of the melodic line, predominantly in the strings. The messenger enters, and when Medea asks him to recount what happened, we hear a dance motif with castanets, in triple meter.

The fate/death/Medea theme that opened the opera in its minor key is now followed by the ominous tam tam, or gong, which can symbolize death, time, and the inexorable. The key is wrenched into A major, and Medea sings an emotive aria in 3/4 rhythm: this is the only section of the score marked with a key signature. This aria shows Medea as resigned, yet passionately glorying in her tragic decision. She says that she will kill her children, and now she must go forward. In the recurrence of Medea's clarinet theme besides the theme of the children, we see the most powerful elements of this opera: Medea herself, her passion, and the children as the most apt agents for her vengeance. The triple meter and triplet ornamentation add graceful dance-like rhythms to the text. These rhythms are also most often associated with Medea, whereas march-like rhythms characterize both Creon and Jason. The 2/4 or 4/8 rhythm of the *Chassipiko,* the more masculine "butcher's dance" in the folk tradition, is suitable for Jason, the butcher of Medea's dreams. The *Rembetika* free rhythms and the triplets of *Zembekiko* remind one of the music that the exiles used as their own *katharsis* following the catastrophe in 1921–1923, when Greeks were forced out of Asia Minor. These Ionian Greeks resettled in Greece proper and were thus foreigners in their own land; their plight resembles Medea's exile to a new homeland where she is treated as a stranger even when things are going well. Greece itself is culturally and geographically located between East and West; thus Medea can become a metaphor for Greek history.

The climactic moment of Medea's decision to kill her children is enhanced by the music. The major key and the waltz-like rhythm are at odds with the tragic text. The music well represents the ambiguity of a woman's triumph along with her sorrow. Aristotle's famous statement that Euripides was the most tragic of the tragedians is illustrated by Medea calling herself the unhappiest of women. This display of bravura adds another dimension to the text and brilliantly colors Medea's tragic heroism. She is driven to the limit of human emotion, and defines herself by her act. The dance rhythm at the climax of her decision links Medea with Elektra and Salome. She is fulfilled and defined by her gruesome act. She is as heroic as Elektra, and as Salome she gets what she wants and a part of her dies in that fulfillment.

Theodorakis has set Medea's lament in a soaring major key. He used this same jarring juxtaposition before when he wrote songs to commemorate Antonio Torres Heredia's arrest and death. As Gail Holst says of that setting, "The actual murder is described in a deceptively gay passage which slows to a climax in a cadence mirroring the opening phrase. It is a heroic death."[14] Here Theodorakis brilliantly underscores the tragic dilemma of Medea's decision: she will kill her beloved children to achieve her heroic vengeance, something signified by the transition from a minor key to a deceptively gay major key.

Medea's theme recurs and builds to a climax, and we hear the children's cries. There is a crash in the orchestra; both the rhythm and atonality in this scene could have come from the *Rite of Spring*.

The choral leader begins a lamentation as Jason appears. At first the music conveys the violence of the confrontation between Medea and Jason. But Jason then sings a lament with a theme that resembles one (Theodorakis' *Asma Asmaton*, based on the biblical *Song of Songs*) from *The Ballad of Mauthausen* song cycle (1965). Gail Holst spoke of the emotional symbolism: "Soon after the dictatorship began in 1967, she [Maria Farandouri] moved to London and began performing Theodorakis' songs in concerts there. It was in those traumatic days that I first heard her perform *Mauthausen* [a song cycle by Theodorakis to texts of Iakovos Kambanellis, who was a surviving prisoner from that concentration camp]. It was an unforgettable experience. Here was a young woman with a voice as rich and powerful as any I have ever heard, performing songs of almost unbearable beauty. The composer of the songs was in jail, his music banished in his own country. The audience wept as they listened and sang softly along with the singer. . . . Now I understood that I was hearing something that western music had lost, something that combined the mass appeal of popular music with the sophistication and sensitivity of the best of classical music."

The final plainchant lamentation by Jason has nothing dance-like in it. Dance rhythms are associated with Medea's final victory. Hers are the triple-metered arias, which suggest a type of freedom, whereas Jason is trapped by four-square duple meters: the tools he uses for domination, force, and power, end up dominating and destroying him. Gail Holst claims of the *Axion Esti*, the great composition by Theodorakis based on the poem of the Nobel Prize poet Odysseus Elytis, "It was closely guided by the structure of the poem in which the sacred and pagan symbolism of the number three plays an important part."[15] The number three, associated with the trinity, may symbolize an additional divine endorsement of Medea, since, as we noted, most of her music is in triple time. She herself certainly shows the characteristics of a goddess, but Euripides' genius shows that she is equally human. Theodorakis ties the myth into Euripides' interpretive genius through music by way of symbolic associations.

Medea has for accompaniment long and soaring melodies in the strings, the woodwinds, and gentle chimes, while Jason and Creon are backed by aggressive marches in the lower brass, with crashing percussion. This reverses at the end, where Medea has aggressive music in the brass and percussion, but Jason's final lament incorporates chimes and is a true dirge, resembling *moirologia*, the lament that women sing at funerals.

A powerful chorale follows as the chorus prays to the gods to bring light and scatter the shadows. Religion adds its touch and transforms Euripides' formulaic ending into a prayer for peace, and a plea to the gods to bring light and scatter the shadows. Medea joins in.

A descending arpeggio (diminished seventh on A) by the tuba ends the opera as Medea arises in her dragon-drawn chariot carrying the bodies of the children. Medea has a power theme in the brass, and it ends the opera in dissonance that tentatively resolves in a chord on A. For a moment we see and hear the resolution of tragedy, which we know can never be fully resolved.

At the end of the play Euripides shows us a Medea who goes too far. By killing the children, she causes a shift in our sympathy, just as in the *Bacchae* we see that Dionysus goes too far in his vengeance; in both cases vengeance involves infanticide: he or she who gives life can take it away. The power of music shifts our sympathy.

Some of the "oriental" musical themes associated with Medea also influence our perception of her. She switches between Asiatic and Greek themes so that the music makes us see her both as strange and familiar, the barbarian but also a part of ourselves.

The pervasive use of the tuba implied power when it appeared before, and now it becomes Medea's power theme in the brass. By showing this power shift, Theodorakis musically illustrates how Medea has adopted Jason's weapons. It is with difficulty that their dissonance is harmonized at the end. Only the chorale of the gods began and ended in a major key. Jason and Medea's dissonance will remain in our mind every bit as much as their harmony.

The final confrontation between Medea and Jason appears vividly in the music, but we have an addition that makes us understand Euripides' text in a new way. Not only does Medea take over Jason's dominant role, but Jason takes over Medea's role of lamentation. The music shows the reversal, and what characterized one at the beginning now characterizes the other at the end. In the touching lament for Jason, we are allowed to appreciate his loss more than the words can say. Theodorakis' lament for Jason shows him in the same light that Seneca did in his sympathetic modification of Euripides. We hear how Jason cared for the children.[16]

Jason's lament—intermingled with a noble chorale—undercuts the bitter exchange between Jason and Medea that Euripides used to end his play. Euripides employed a vigorous *Verfremdungseffekt* not only by Medea's killing the children, which alienates her from the audience's sympathy, but also by exchanged insults in the furious debate between her and Jason, which serve to alienate the audience from both of them. Euripides' culminating *agon* ("verbal debate or contest") might validate some of Nietzsche's criticisms: poetry is lost when debate takes over. Theodorakis makes the poetry soar once again, now on the wings of music.

CONCLUSION

The Medeas of Euripides, Charpentier, and Theodorakis are successful in their vengeance: these Medeas escape to lead new lives. Cavalli shows her innocent. On the other hand, Cherubini and Pacini have Medea punished or suicidal.[17] Her character and fate differ with the way women are viewed; she illustrates alternately women as tame and docile; or awesome in their passion, and demanding respect; or demonic, inviting punishment and control. This reflects the psychological and political needs of different periods.

Medea as *Zeitgeist* triumphs in the twentieth century. Theodorakis emphasizes loss by both the male and by the female. Medea triumphs, but the price she has paid is dear, and Jason's anguish is translated into heart-rending song. Greece understands lamentation, from the early times when women conducted a ritual of cries and tears for the departed. Theodorakis shows us conflict and its aftermath, with an emphasis on tears.

Aristotle and Nietzsche would be pleased with Theodorakis' rendering, because he effectively incorporates some of the Aeschylean and Sophoclean genius into the Euripidean text. In Theodorakis' opera we find the religiosity and mystery of Aeschylus coupled with the nobility Sophocles gave to his heroes and heroines. In the *Medea*, Euripides questioned both religion and heroism by undermining their ethical basis. Through Theodorakis' musical transformations, *katharsis*, "purification," and *anagnorisis*, "recognition," are perhaps better effected, since both seem augmented by the audience's identification with the characters. Intense villainy in a character tends to destroy the audience's will to identify with that character, and may be a dramatic failure, as Aristotle claimed, using Menelaus in the *Orestes* to illustrate his point (*Poetics* 1454a).

We see that Aristotle's ideas of *katharsis* and *anagnorisis*, types of particular inner experience each spectator undergoes, are merged in Theodorakis' opera. Theodorakis' *Medea* is a new Hermes, leading us into the inner world, and we emerge with new insights. We perceive the universal, and through this art we learn "all we shall know for truth, / Before we grow old and die."[18] Theodorakis has brought Euripides into modern times and into a modern nation. In his own way, he is true to Euripides and aims at the heart.

APPENDIX
SOME OPERAS ABOUT OR INCLUDING MEDEA

Francesco Cavalli (1602–1676) (b. Crema, Lombardy, Italy)
Giasone (1648)

Giovanni Faustini (1615–1651) (b. Venice, Italy)
Medea placata (libretto, composer unknown, 1662)

Wolfgang Carl Briegel (1626–1712) (b. Königsberg, Germany)
L'enchantement de Medée (1688)

Domenico Freschi (c.1630–1710) (b. Bassano del Grappa, Italy)
Teseo trà le rivali (1685)

Jean-Baptiste Lully (1632–1687) (Giovanni Battista Lulli, b. Rome, Italy)
Thésée (1675)

Antonio Draghi (c.1634–1700)
La conquista del vello d'oro (1678)

Marc-Antoine Charpentier (1634–1704) (b. Paris, France)
Médée (1693)

Johann Löhner (1645–1705) (b. Nüremberg, Germany)
Theseus (1688)

Bernardo Sabadini (?–1718) (b. ?Venice, Italy)
Teseo in Atene (1688)

Antonio Giannettini (1648–1721) (b. Fano, Italy)
Medea in Atene (1675)

Pascal Collasse (1649–1709) (b. Reims, France)
Jason, ou La toison d'or (1696)

Joseph-François Salomon (1649–1732) (b. Toulon, France)
Médée et Jason (1713)

Johann Sigismund Kusser, aka Cousser (1660–1727) (b. Pressburg, Germany)
Jason (1692)

Georg Caspar Schürmann (1672/3–1751) (b. Idensen, Germany)
Giasone (1707)

Antonio Maria Bononcini (1677–1726) (b. Modena, Italy)
La conquista del vello d'oro (1717)

Johann Christian Schieferdecker (1679–1732) (b. Teuchern, Germany)
Medea (1700)

Francois Bouvard (1683–1760) (b. Lyons, France)
Médus, roi des Medes (1702)

George Frederick Handel (1685–1759) (b. Halle, Germany)
Teseo (1712)

Nicola Porpora (1686–1768) (b. Naples, Italy)
Giasone (1742)

Giovanni Francesco Brusa (?1700–after 1768) (b. Venice)
Medea e Giasone (1726)

Giovanni Battista Pescetti (?1704–1766) (b. Venice, Italy)
La conquista del velo d'oro (1740)

Georg Gebel (b. 1709–1755) (b. Brieg, Germany)
Medea (1752) Lost

David Perez (1711–1778) (b. Naples, Italy)
Medea (1744)

Jean-Joseph Cassanéa de Mondonville (1711–1772) (b. Narbonne, France)
Thésée (1765)

John Christopher Smith (1712–1795) (b. Ansbach, England)
Medea (1760–61)

Giuseppe Scolari (?1720–after 1774) (b. ?Lisbon, Portugal)
Il vello d'oro (1748–1749)

Georg Anton Benda (1722–1795) (b. Staré Benátky, Prussia)
Medea (1775)

François-Joseph Gossec (1734–1829) (b. Vergnies, France)
Thésée (1782)

Francesco Piticchio (fl.1760–1800) (b. ?Palermo, Sicily)
La vendetta di Medea (1798)

Johann Gottlieb Naumann (1741–1801) (b. Blasewitz, Germany)
Medea in Colchide (1788)

Giuseppe Gazzaniga (1743–1818) (b. Verona, Italy)
Gli Argonauti in Colco (1790)

Peter Winter (1754–1825) (b. Mannheim, Germany)
Medea und Jason (1789)

Giuseppe Moneta (1754–1806) (b. Florence, Italy)
La vendetta di Medea (1787)

Gaetano Marinelli (1754–1820) (b. Naples, Italy)
La vendetta di Medea (1792)

Gaetano Andreozzi (1755–1826) (b. Aversa, Italy)
Giasone e Medea (1785)

Johann Christoph Vogel (1756–1788) (b. Nuremberg, Germany)
La toison d'or (1786 revived as *Médée de Colchos*, 1788)

Maria Luigi Carlo Zanobi Salvator Cherubini (1760–1842) (b. Florence, Italy)
Médée (1797)

Gaspare Spontini (1774–1851) (b. Maiolati near Lesi, Italy)
Il Teseo riconosciuto (1798)

Simon Mayr (1763–1845) (b. Mendorf, Germany)
Medea in Corinto (1813)

Stefano Pavesi (1779–1850) (b. Casaletto Vaprio, Italy)
La vedetta di Medea (1804)

Carlo Coccia (1782–1873) (b. Naples, Italy)
Teseo e Medea (1815)

Saverio Mercadante (1795–1870) (b. Altamura, Italy)
Medea (1851)

Giovanni Pacini (1796–1867) (b. Catania, Sicily)
Medea (1845)

Zdenek Fibich (1850–1900) (b. Vseborice, Bohemia)
Medea (1863 Lost)

Vincenzo Tommasini (1878–1950) (b. Rome, Italy)
Medea (1902–4)

Darius Milhaud (1892–1974) (b. Aix-en-Provence, France)
Médée (1939)

Pietro Canonica (1869–1959) (b. Turin, Italy)
Medea (1953)

Edward Staempfli (1908–) (b. Bern, Switzerland)
Medea (1954)

Granpiero Tintoni (b. ?)
Medeae Senecae Fragmina (1961)

Rolf Liebermann (1910–) (b. Zürich, Switzerland)
Freispruch für Medea (1995)

Mikis Theodorakis (1925–) (b. Smyrna, Turkey)
Medea (1991)

Felix Werder (1922–) (b. Berlin, Germany)
Medea (1985)

Jonathan Elkus (1931–) (b. San Francisco, Calif., USA)
Medea (1970)

Alva Henderson (1940–) (b. San Luis Obispo, Calif., USA)
Medea (1972)

Gavin Bryars (1943–) (b. Goole, England)
Medea (1984)

Adriano Guarnieri (1947–) (b. Sustinente, near Mantua, Italy)
Medea (1991)

Pascal Dusapin (1955–) (b. Paris, France)
Medeamateriel (1992)

Gordon Kerry (1961–) (b. Melbourne, Australia)
Medea (1992)

Michael John LaChiusa (1961–) (b. Chappaqua, N.Y., USA)
Marie Christine (1999)

John Fisher (1963–) (b. San Francisco, California)
Medea, The Musical (1995)

Further attested by *The Oxford Dictionary of Opera* are Johann Casper Kerll's opera on
Medea (they do not give the name of the opera, but only the date 1662); Fontelle (1813);
Selli (1839); and Bastide (1911).[19]

Coda

There is change in the ways classics are used in opera throughout the centuries. At the beginning, in the seventeenth century, since opera was considered a revival of Greek tragedy, it was natural that most operas were based on classical themes. The most popular subjects were epic, historical, and mythical. Ancient heroes could embody the values of absolutist regimes. This was the age of the happy ending, and gods and nobles figured in lavish prologues. In the eighteenth century we have five times as many operas on classical themes as in the seventeenth century, and the most in any century. In this age, the classics were used to convey some of the ideals of the Enlightenment. The nineteenth century had the fewest operas based on the classics, which could be regarded as elitist, or affirming the values of the upper classes. In this century opera expressed nationalistic, revolutionary, or romantic aspirations, and ordinary people could assume mythic stature. For example, Daniel-François-Esprit Auber's *La Muette de Portici* (1828) had a plot based on the revolution at Naples in 1647, a performance of which led to a revolution in Belgium. Large choruses perhaps reflected the new importance of the masses. Magical themes, ghosts, and deals with the devil also reflected some of the escapist preferences, cf. Weber's *Der Freischütz* (1821), Berlioz's *La Damnation de Faust* (1846), Wagner's *Der fliegende Holländer* (1843), Massenet's *La fiancée du diable* (1854), *Rubenstein's Demon* (1871), and many operas on the subject of *Der Vampyr*.

In the twentieth century there are fewer operas written in general, but more are on classical themes than in the seventeenth or nineteenth centuries (twice as many as in the nineteenth century), and there are many revivals. This is also the century that particularly prized the authenticity of the original classics, and there are versions in the twentieth century that are based on literal translations. The ancient myths are vehicles for conveying modern concerns. We see a return to the fifth-century tragic subjects and texts: they speak to people who have known

Auschwitz and Hiroshima. In this century we know the horror of mass murder, and how many human beings can die in an instant because of "advanced" technology. Many operas reflect a taste for realism. Now there are antiwar operas, like Benjamin Britten's *Owen Wingrave* (1974) or Hans Werner Henze's *We Come to the River* (1976).

There is a ritualistic aspect to some of the recent operas; fears and hopes are expressed, and music embodies prayer. Philip Glass's *Satyagraha* (1981) is both antiwar and religious, ending with Gandhi's blessing his thirty comrades in a musical incantation repeated thirty times. Now there are more Asian themes in operas than in any other century, reflecting the opening up of the world, for example, Isidore De Lara's *le réveil de Bouddha* (1904). Operas based on Greek tragedy show the influence of religion while intoning the message, *memento mori*: "Remember your Mortality." This awareness of death can enhance life.

In modern times the most frequently performed operas on classical themes are usually from the eighteenth or twentieth century: Monteverdi's *Orfeo*, *Il ritorno d'Ulisse in Patria*, and *L'Incoronazione di Poppea*; Charpentier's *Médée*; Cherubini's *Medea*; Gluck's *Orfeo ed Euridice*; Purcell's *Dido and Aeneas*; Handel's *Agrippina, Giulio Cesare, Semele, Xerxes* (*Serse*), and others by him; Rameau's *Castor et Pollux*; Mozart's *Idomeneo: Rè di Creta* and *La Clemenza di Tito*; Richard Strauss's *Elektra* and *Ariade auf Naxos* (1909); Stravinsky's *Oedipus Rex* (1927); Poulenc's *Les Mamelles de Tirésias* (1947); Michael Tippett's *King Priam* (1962); and many more. Even comedies are based on the original classical models, particularly on Aristophanes' *Lysistrata*: Paul Kont's *Lysistrate* (1961), Arghyris Kounadis' *Lysistrate* (1983), and Karel Kupka's *Lysistrata* (1958). The antiwar theme is obvious. There are many reworkings of Euripides' *Bacchae*, such as Szymanowski's *Król Roger* (1926) and Partch's *Revelation in the Courthouse Park* (1961); John Buller not only composed the music, but wrote his libretto in Greek in his *Bakhai* (1992). These may reflect the modern fear of a charismatic and powerful leader who goes too far, or the dictator. There are many also on *Prometheus*, perhaps on the other type of leader, a strong revolutionary one who serves the people: for instance, Carl Orff's *Prometheus* (1967) or Luigi Nono's *Prometeo* (1984). The many Antigones also corroborate this thrust for human rights, for example Carl Orff's *Antigonae* (1949) and William Russo's *Antigone* (1967), to say nothing of the various operas on Medea, which may reflect an interest in women's rights (see the chapter on Theodorakis' *Medea*).

Many historical developments are reflected in these operas. Music is truly political, as Plato observed, and in this tour through the centuries of opera I have attempted to show how these works were not only products of their times, but also part of their propaganda. Christian ideas figure prominently in the operas written during the time the church held power. Monteverdi not only has pagan gods and goddesses, but he shows us the Virgin Mary in the guise of Penelope, and Ulisse is a sinner redeemed by grace at the end (Nettuno must forgive him, and *Giove amoroso* extends his mercy, yielding to Giunone's persuasions). Penelope in her mercy will also forgive Ulisse for his absence and accept him again as her husband, but only after he has proved himself worthy of her. Love has a redemptive role both here and in Mozart's *Idomeneo*. In *Il ritorno*, the greatest heroism is shown by the woman who is faithful, withstanding the blandishments of the suitors for years.

Il ritorno d'Ulisse reflects the politics of the times and the struggles of the gods (like nobles, from strong families such as the Gonzagas) that affect the human beings (Ulisse, paralleling the long-suffering Monteverdi, entered the church, in part to escape the unreliability of the Gonzagas, and this church also colors his mythology).

Purcell's *Dido and Aeneas* lays out morals for young girls and warns them against overstepping their bounds. There are always witches to abet evil and young men ready to seduce. In a way it is a Restoration *Pilgrim's Progress*, and the main message urges young girls to say no to seducers and temptation. Since Nahum Tate, the librettist, could rewrite Shakespeare, he was hardly averse to rewriting Virgil's passionate chronicle and transforming Dido into a cultivated, controlled, although errant queen. Her soaring music and clear vision make her the superior of Aeneas, who has no aria and who wavers in his decisions. She sings what has been called the greatest lament in the history of opera, "When I am laid in earth."

The supernatural element is provided by the witches, and they represent a phenomenon that was taken seriously at the time. The emphasis is on civilizing the untamed, and the British were willing to fill this role in their long history of conquest and colonization. The civilized art of Purcell represents these ideals.

Mozart brings us back to the gods, but now they are ethical. We have a Poseidon very different from the pettily angry god of *Il ritorno*. This Poseidon is won over by love and a sense of justice. There are humanitarian and egalitarian concerns, which surface for the first time and presage *The Marriage of Figaro*, Beaumarchais' subversive farce. Enlightenment humanism colors the text, and Mozart's music makes the values soar. The heroism, as in Euripides, is now that of women, or the young. Ilia is the true heroine who is willing to sacrifice herself for her beloved. In this she contrasts with the king Idomeneo who, to save himself, has put his son in jeopardy. Opera is the perfect medium to celebrate the new heroism and attract the patronage of rulers like Joseph II, who, at least for a while, had progressive ideas.

Berlioz shows his nationalistic loyalty in his endorsement of empire in *Les Troyens*. Here is a passionate Dido fiercely opposing Aeneas, as she does in the *Aeneid*, but not in the tamed version of Purcell. One is meant to feel the inevitability of her defeat as one hears the final triumphant hymn to Rome, with Troy rebuilt and restored in Italy. For a while Aeneas and Dido teach the African natives civilization as they overrun their land. Later Aeneas teaches Dido also. We think of the defeat of the Carthaginians by Rome and Cato's bloodthirsty demand, *Carthago delenda est*. The French *mission civilatrice* is also apparent, the opera coinciding with the growth of the French empire in Africa.

In spite of her defeat, Dido's majesty is affirmed by her music. At the same time that empire is endorsed by Berlioz, we are aware of the terrible destruction it entails when a queen like Dido must be sacrificed. She does not go quietly, but accompanied by eloquent curses and moving lamentation. Here the true grandeur is Dido's, not Rome's.

Richard Strauss followed in Wagner's footsteps, and his *Elektra* parallels Nietzsche and Wagner in the depiction of unbridled passion and confidence in the race, which leads to a fiery violence fanned by a will to power. Strauss's music shows the triumph of passion over reason, and the notes escape the control of stable keys. Religion is used as an ally. He and Berlioz show a type of Nietzschean heroism and a thrust for independence and freedom at the same time as they delineate controlling regimes. Elektra defies her fate by dancing herself to death at the peak of her triumph. She crystallizes her victory for all time.

Igor Stravinsky's *Oedipus Rex* creates a ritual from obsessive rhythms and shows how text should be a handmaiden to the music; words now serve a ritualistic rather than semantic function. Words become music. One can lament that both text and the music are not equal in their strength. Jocasta however is an impressive queen mother in every sense of the word. She totally dominates Oedipus. She is hailed in semireligious terms and shares this allusive divinity with Penelope. Her music makes her Oedipus' superior; he wanders from key to key until the final revelation, when he sees he must go into exile. His musical wandering replicates what will become his actual wandering, since he is forced to leave his kingdom. Jocasta's lush coloratura evocations will be resurrected in the audience's memory after her death.

Lee Breuer's *Gospel at Colonus* uses African religion and the rhythms of blues and jazz to recreate the demise of a sinner redeemed by Christ: Everyman. It also shows the tragedy of Antigone, not only by giving her moving arias, but by adding the text from Sophocles' play about her to this opera. We see her as the anchor of the family: a universal woman who cares for and mourns the men who are lost through their own folly.

This work reflects that great creation of African-Americans, the product of their sufferings when they first reached America, and which continue into the present. They found an escape through religion and music, or in Marx's words, "the sigh of the oppressed creature, the soul of a soulless world." It is music that speaks to everyone who has suffered and longs for salvation of one kind or another. It is not only soul music, it is music for the heart, the mind, and the body. It is also the most authentic, beautiful, and creative American music.

The note of freedom is sounded again by Mikis Theodorakis in his *Medea*, which replicates the sufferings of the Greek nation in both victories and defeats. It is a solemn meditation on the aftermath of vengeance. Theodorakis realizes how no one wins when victory entails killing one's own best beloved, whether one's ideals, or one's own children.

Medea in opera is a *Zeitgeist* and symbol of how women are regarded throughout the centuries. She flourishes most in the twentieth century. These operas, including the one by Theodorakis, show her in all her power: she exacts a vengeance for her wrongs and escapes with impunity. She suffers, but she triumphs.

Seeing how words have been valued has been an interesting part of my excursion through the centuries. They are stressed by Monteverdi and Purcell. Mozart said he favors the music over the text, but he was fortunate to have several good librettists, and, in spite of what he says, he never slights the meaning of the words. Berlioz and Strauss value the word enormously, but the music goes further and tries to express the unspoken emotions behind the words. Music had done this, and will always do this, but Berlioz and Strauss (like Wagner) try to go further and express complex psychological states through their music and librettos.

For Stravinsky it is the music that counted most; he uses the sound of language as another instrument. Breuer is closer to Stravinsky, and the music dominates. He uses words for drumbeats. Both Breuer and Stravinsky have their incoherent moments. This may signify a decline in appreciation for words in the twentieth century. The new shift is to the visual and aural. Words become ritualistic and at times function as prayers or incantations.

Theodorakis does not follow this trend, and in his opera we find a perfect marriage of words and music. Theodorakis returns to Monteverdi and prizes words. Suffering comes through in both the music and the treasured ancient text, painstakingly translated by Theodorakis into modern Greek.

The musical translation of the text takes many forms. It can be programmatic and echo what is described, or it can contradict what is being said and thus provide additional commentary: music can reveal secrets. Music can translate emotion and allow the audience to share in the same experience as the characters. The music varies with each composer: it can reflect the fashion of the period (or rebellion against it), history, and personal choices. The choice of classic is often shaped by an historical mood in addition to the personal desire of the composer. By going to an old master whose genius has been proven by time, the opera is sure of a good text, as long as the librettists do a decent job, as they have in most of the examples presented here.

Another interesting shift is from the professional librettist (*Il ritorno, Idomeneo*) to the composer himself (*Troyens*) to the established playwright (*Elektra*) and back to the original text (via Latin in Stravinsky, a close translation into English in Breuer/Telson, Greek in Theodorakis). The professional librettist adapted himself to the music and the age. The composer expressed ideas important to him, including the readings with which he was familiar (Berlioz added Shakespeare to Virgil), a poet or playwright added to the drama, and finally one appreciates the ancient geniuses on whose works these operas are based. The ancient works tell us about our own times. In our century, we prize these timeless tragedies, which speak eloquently to us through music.

One may also ask why some adaptations work better than others. Penelope and Dido in opera gain in stature by comparison with the original epic. One cannot say that the opera is better than the epic, but perhaps the opera reflects a change in the way that women were regarded. In these cases the adaptation is interesting, informative, and exciting. Strauss' Elektra is transformed, but also faithful to the original: this is another successful adaptation in which the nineteenth century meets ancient tragedy and joins the twentieth century in each revival. Stravinsky's libretto is secondary to his music, and the weakness of Oedipus is a falling-away from the power of the original. His Jocasta gains from Oedipus' loss, as Purcell's Dido does from Aeneas'. Medea's original majesty is resurrected by Theodorakis, and she is a symbol of women's increased rights in the twentieth century. In all these instances, the ancient classics are enriched by the additional layer of meaning and symbolic value given them by the operas. The operas also shed new light on interpreting the originals.

Clément's fundamental work has been expanded by McClary and others like Poizat, Koestenbaum, and Abel, who realize that what a woman may lose in dying she gains in her aria. I have tried to show how a woman, thought to be a victim, becomes a heroine through her suffering and her song, and achieves a type of victory. Death in opera is often transfiguration, as the Hutcheons have illustrated.

History is as important as gender relations in shaping these operas, and sometimes is at the basis of gender relations, as we have seen in the different treatments of Medea. The early composers were dependent on kings or aristocrats, and the later ones on their public. All struggled against misunderstanding and longed for acceptance and security. There is a progression from the earliest opera to the latest in attitudes toward class. The latest operas are the most democratic and secular. Instead of individual aristocrats, the emphasis is now on humanity, and Oedipus is a paradigm for "Everyman" as sinner. Even the music in *Gospel at Colonus* owes something to early opera with its programmatic effects and its formality. Just as Monteverdi, a "slave" in the court of the Gonzagas, escaped in his music, so did the African-Americans in their own music when they were slaves in America. Theodorakis also returns to traditional forms, using music from the Greek Orthodox church and folk songs, particularly the laments from the disaster in Asia Minor in 1922, when so many Greeks were killed or forced by the Turks to leave their homes. The heroic violence in the music and themes of Berlioz and Stravinsky is now seen not as the glory envisioned by the nineteenth-century nationalists. Total destruction is a twentieth-century experience, and it gives us second thoughts about the heroism of the victor.

As Euripides' antiwar and antiheroic messages prevail in modern times over those of Aeschylus and Sophocles, we find a comparable development in a new opera of despair, for instance, Alban Berg's *Lulu* and *Wozzeck* and Bernd Alois Zimmermann's *Die Soldaten*. At times this despair is countered by a new religiosity and by the security offered by the use of older musical forms and allusions to ancient texts in our latest operas based on the classics. Each of the operas I have investigated also shows heroism in the face of suffering, writ large and sung passionately. These operas, like Greek tragedy and ancient epics, are creative acts of defiance in a chaotic world. The operas we have looked at here reflect the currents of the times. They transfer the heroism of classical epic and tragedy into the heroism of opera. Women, now demigoddesses as divas, have large roles and in many cases eclipse the men.

People need to sing their sorrow and joy; sometimes they use the classics, which eloquently tell their tales. These operas celebrate the passionate memory of the human race.

Notes

PRELUDE

1. Michael Ewans, *Wagner and Aeschylus: The Ring and the Oresteia* (London: Faber and Faber, 1982) and P.E. Easterling, *Cambridge Opera Handbook,* Derrick Puffett, ed. (Cambridge: University Press, 1989), pp. 10–16.

2. See M.S. Silk and J.P. Stern, *Nietzsche on Tragedy* (1981; rpt. Cambridge: University Press, 1990). There is an interesting discussion of this work and its relation to opera in Herbert Lindenberger, *Opera: The Extravagant Art* (1984; rpt. Ithaca, N.Y.: Cornell University Press, 1985).

3. Susan McClary: *Feminine Endings: Music, Gender and Sexuality* (Minneapolis: Minnesota University Press, 1991), p. 4. See also Ruth A. Solie, ed., *Musicology and Difference: Gender and Sexuality in Music Scholarship* (Berkeley and Los Angeles: University of California Press, 1993).

4. These claims are in Donald Jay Grout, with Hermine Weigel, *A Short History of Opera*, Williams, 3rd ed. (New York: Columbia University Press, 1988), pp. 11 and 13.

5. Peter Burian has a brief section in *The Cambridge Companion to Greek Tragedy*, ed. P.E. Easterling (Cambridge: Cambridge University Press, 1997), pp. 261–271. He gives Jacopo Peri's *Euridice* as the first surviving opera, p. 262. He does not mention Giulio Caccini's version of *Euridice*, also in 1600, and that the version by Jacopo Peri in 1600 performed at the Pitti Palace in Florence contained additions by Caccini. Burian does not mention the earlier opera by Peri, with parts by Jacopo Corsi, *Dafne* (1598), which Grout calls the first opera, but whose music does not survive, *Short History of Opera*, p. 43.

6. Roland Barthes, *S/Z: An Essay*, Richard Miller, trans., 1974; rpt. (New York: Hill and Wang, 1986).

7. Linda and Michael Hutcheon, *Opera: Desire, Disease and Death* (Lincoln: University of Nebraska Press, 1996).

8. Wayne Koestenbaum, *The Queen's Throat: Opera, Homosexuality, and the Mystery of Desire* (New York: Poseidon Press, 1993).

9. Michel Poizat, *The Angel's Cry: Beyond the Pleasure Principle in Opera*, Arthur Denner, trans. (Ithaca, N.Y.: Cornell University Press, 1992).

10. Philip Brett, Elizabeth Wood, and Gary C. Thomas, eds., *Queering the Pitch: The New Gay and Lesbian Musicology* (New York: Routledge, 1994).

11. Corrine E. Blackmer and Patricia Juliana Smith, eds., *En Travesti: Women, Gender, Subversion, Opera* (New York: Columbia University Press, 1995).

12. Mary Ann Smart's edition of *Siren Songs: Representations of Gender and Sexuality in Opera* (Princeton, N.J.: Princeton University Press, 2000).

13. Theodor Adorno, "Bourgeois Opera" in *Opera Through Other Eyes*, David Levin, ed. (Stanford, Calif.: Stanford University Press, 1994), p. 36.

14. My disagreements will become clear in my chapter on *Les Troyens*.

15. Edward Said, *Culture and Imperialism* (New York: Knopf, 1993).

16. Paul Robinson *Opera and Ideas: From Mozart to Strauss* (1985; rpt. Ithaca, N.Y.: Cornell University Press, 1987); Jane Fulcher, *The Nation's Image: French Grand Opera as Politics and Politicized Art* (Cambridge: Cambridge University Press, 1987); Anthony Arblaster, *Viva la libertà: Politics in Opera* (London: Verso, 1992); Herbert Lindenberger, *Opera: The Extravagant Art* (Stanford, Calif.: Stanford University Press, 1998; *The Urbanization of Opera: Music Theater in Paris in the Nineteenth Century*, Mary Whittall Gerhard, trans. (Chicago: University of Chicago Press, 1998).

17. Hans Robert Jauss, *Toward an Aesthetic of Reception*, Timothy Bahti, trans. *Theory and History of Literature*, Vol. 2, (Minneapolis: University of Minnesota Press, 1982).

18. Joseph Kerman, *Opera as Drama* (1956; rpt. and rev. Berkeley: University of California Press, 1988); Herbert Lindenberger, *Opera The Extravagant Art* (Ithaca, N.Y.: Cornell University Press, 1984); Peter Conrad, *A Song of Love and Death: The Meaning of Opera* (London: Chatto and Windus, 1987); Gary Schmidgall, *Shakespeare and Opera* (Oxford: Oxford University Press, 1990); Robert Donington, *Opera and its Symbols: The Unity of Words, Music and Staging* (New Haven, Conn.: Yale University Press, 1990).

19. See Wye Jamison Allanbrook's *Rhythmic Gesture in Mozart: Le Nozze di Figaro and Don Giovanni* (Chicago: University of Chicago Press, 1983).

20. See useful studies like *The Work of Opera: Genre, Nationhood, and Sexual Difference*, eds. Richard Dellamora and Daniel Fischlin (New York: Columbia University Press, 1997).

21. See Edward Said, *Musical Elaborations*, pp. 94–105: "Obviously I'm *not* saying that classical forms like the sonata are neurotically un-beautiful. . . . But I am proposing that one can think about musical elaboration as something to be returned to for reasons other than its finished perfection, that the essence of the elaboration can be transformative and reflective" (p. 102). He goes on to say of Richard Strauss's music that it is "radically, beautifully elaborative, music whose pleasures and discoveries are premised upon letting go, upon not asserting a central authorizing identity, upon enlarging the community of hearers and players beyond the time taken" (p. 105).

22. Peter Sellars, from a lecture at La Jolla, in 1992.

23. Said, *Musical Elaborations* (New York: Columbia University Press, 1991), xviii.

24. Brigid Brophy, *Mozart the Dramatist: The Value of his Operas to Him, to His Age and to Us* (New York: Da Capo, 1988).

25. Catherine Clément, *Opera, or the Undoing of Women*, Betsy Wing, trans. (Minneapolis: University of Minnesota Press, 1988). Many of Clément's ideas are echoed,

varied, and sometimes more subtly defined by Susan McClary, who also wrote the introduction to Clément's book.

26. Sam Abel, *Opera in the Flesh: Sexuality in Operatic Performance* (Boulder, Colo.: Westview Press, 1996), p. 64.

27. "*Piangi, piangi, o misera*, Putting the Words into Women's Mouths: Ruth Padel on the Female Role in Opera," *London Review of Books* 19.2 (23 Jan. 1997): 12–17.

28. One thinks of Carolyn Abbate's *Unsung Voices: Opera and Musical Narrative in the Nineteenth Century* (Princeton, N.J.: Princeton University Press, 1991); Koestenbaum's *The Queen's Throat*; and the collection of essays in *Reading Opera*, Arthur Groos and Roger Parker, eds. (Princeton, N.J.: Princeton University Press, 1988).

29. It would be nice to have a website that would list operas based on classics and be continually updated.

30. See Ewans, cited in note one; Bernard Fenik, *Homer and the Nibelungenlied: Comparative Studies in Epic Style* (Cambridge, Mass.: Harvard University Press, 1986); and "Wagner," in H. Lloyd-Jones, *Blood for the Ghosts: Classical Influences in the Nineteenth and Twentieth Centuries* (Baltimore, Md.: Johns Hopkins University Press, 1982), pp. 126–142. Lloyd-Jones questions the influence of Aeschylus' *Oresteia* on Wagner's *Ring.* He sees more influence from Aeschylus' *Prometheus Bound.*

31. Conrad, *A Song of Love and Death*, p. 324.

32. Quoted by Igor Stravinsky, *Poetics of Music in the Form of Six Lessons*, Arthur Knodel and Ingolf Dahl, trans. (1942; rpt. Cambridge, Mass.: Harvard University Press, 1970), p. 43.

THE BIRTH OF OPERA AND THE USE OF CLASSICS

1. See H.F.W. Sternfeld, *The Birth of Opera* (1993; rpt. Oxford: Clarendon Press, 1994); and Sutherland Edwards, *History of the Opera, from Monteverdi to Donizetti*, 1 (1862; 2nd ed., New York: Da Capo Press, 1977).

2. Edwards, *History of the Opera*, p. 3.

3. See for instance *The Definitive Kobbé's Opera Book*, ed., rev. and updated by The Earl of Harewood (1919; New York: G.P. Putnam, 1987). "At the end of the sixteenth century a small group of aristocratic intelligentsia [had] the avowed intention to reproduce as far as possible the combination of words and music which together made up Greek theatre," p. 3.

4. Joseph Kerman, *Opera as Drama* (1956; new and rev. ed., Berkeley: University of California Press, 1988), p. 19.

5. See the elucidating comments by F.W. Sternfeld, *The Birth of Opera, passim.* He starts by saying, "In the beginning was the myth, and the myth was that of Orpheus," p. 1.

6. Kerman, *Opera as Drama*, p. 19.

7. For the theory of innovation, see Leo Schrade, *Monteverdi: Creator of Modern Music* (New York: Da Capo Press, 1979). For the view of Monteverdi as building on what existed in a new creative way, see Silke Leopold, *Monteverdi: Music in Transition*, Anne Smith, trans. (Oxford: Clarendon Press, 1991). The titles of their books suggest their respective views. Monteverdi's development of *parlar cantando*, or "speaking while singing," allowed him to be construed as either the "progenitor of the great bravura aria or as the point of reference for such composers as Gluck and Wagner, who sought to reaffirm the primacy of drama," Poizat, *The Angel's Cry*, p. 52.

8. Ficino founded the Platonic Academy in 1462.

9. Donington, *Opera and its Symbols*, p. 4, 43, *et passim*.

10. Pierre de Ronsard, *Oeuvres complètes*, H. Vaganay, ed. Vol. 4 (Paris, 1924), p. 159, cited in Donington, *Opera and Its Symbols*, p. 23.

11. For a comprehensive presentation of all that is now known about ancient Greek music see Andrew Barker, *Greek Musical Writings:* 1. *The Musician and His Art* (1984; rpt. Cambridge: University Press, 1989), and 2. *Harmonic and Acoustic Theory* (Cambridge: University Press, 1989); M.L. West, *Ancient Greek Music* (Oxford: Clarendon Press, 1992). Also useful are: Giovanni Comotti, *Music in Greek and Roman Culture,* Rosaria V. Munson, trans. (Baltimore: Johns Hopkins University Press, 1989); Martha Maas and Jane McIntosh Snyder, *Stringed Instruments of Ancient Greece* (New Haven: Yale University Press, 1989); and Warren D. Anderson, *Ethos and Education in Greek Music: The Evidence of Poetry and Philosophy* (Cambridge, Mass.: Harvard University Press, 1968) and *Music and Musicians in Ancient Greece* (Ithaca, N.Y.: Cornell University Press, 1994). All these have useful bibliographies. On the *aulos*, see the excellent exposition by M.L. West, *Ancient Greek Music*, pp. 81–107.

12. See E.R. Dodd's *The Greeks and the Irrational* (Berkeley: University of California Press, 1951); Bruno Snell, *The Discovery of the Mind*, Thomas Rosenmeyer, trans. (Oxford: University Press, 1953), and Thomas MacCary, *Childlike Achilles* (New York: Columbia University Press, 1982).

13. Quoted by Frantisek Deak in *Symbolist Theatre: The Formation of an Avant-Garde* (Baltimore: Johns Hopkins University Press, 1993), p. 131.

14. Conrad, *A Song of Love and Death*, p. 185.

15. Walter Benjamin, *The Origin of German Tragic Drama,* John Osborne, trans. (London: Verso, 1977).

16. For a discussion of Monteverdi's *seconda prattica* and the debate over it, see Leopold, *Monteverdi*, pp. 42–52.

17. See "Empirical reception theory: actual responses to texts," in Robert C. Holub, *Reception Theory: A Critical Introduction* (London: Methuen, 1984), pp. 134–146.

18. See Roland Barthes, "Structural Analysis of Narratives," in *Image Music Text,* Stephen Heath, trans. (London: Fontana Press, 1977), p. 121. Barthes elaborates on the "pheno-song" (performative communication) and the "geno-song" (volume and space . . . the diction of language), two types that he derives from Julia Kristeva's classifications, p. 182. Breath is *pneuma*: "soul," " breath of life." Barthes adds the concept of "grain," or the physical rather than communicative aspects of music, which he claims could lead to a "different history of music," p. 189. Carolyn Abbate, in her *Unsung Voices*, adds this theoretical dimension to her assessment of opera and questions traditional interpretations.

19. D. Mace, "Pietro Bembo and the Literary Origins of the Italian Madrigal," *Musical Quarterly* (1969): 65 ff.

20. For the symbolism involved see K.P. Aerke, *Gods of Play: Baroque Festive Performances as Rhetorical Discourse* (Albany, NY: SUNY Press, 1994), *passim*.

21. Conrad, *A Song of Love and Death*, p. 195.

22. See Jane Fulcher's *The Nation's Image*, and Gary Tomlinson's *Monteverdi and the End of the Renaissance* (1987; rpt. Berkeley: University of California Press, 1990) for a good description of some of these changes.

23. This thesis was developed by Jon Solomon, in "The Neoplatonic Apotheosis in Monteverdi's *Orfeo*," delivered at a Monteverdi panel for the American Philological Association organized by the present author with Robert Ketterer, held in Washington, D.C., December 1993. He points out how Ficino and Matteo Palmieri may very well have influenced the version with the revised ending of *Orfeo* by Alessandro Striggio, Monte-

verdi's librettist. Stanley Cavell, in *A Pitch of Philosophy: Autobiographical Exercises* (Cambridge, Mass. and London, England: Harvard University Press, 1994), p. 134, sees Monteverdi as the source of the happy ending. Cavell also gives a philosophical interpretation of the myth, quoting a sixteenth-century Italian translator of Ovid's *Metamorphoses*, who interprets Orpheus' myth as "man's loss of the soul whenever he abandons reason and turns back: that is, to pursue blameworthy and earthly concerns." Cavell goes on, "This moralism is particularly striking in view of the ease with which the moral can be seen to be about skepticism, about the loss of the world through an impossible effort to certify its existence by means of the senses, especially through looking," p. 140. Perhaps music gives us a more reliable account of the world.

24. Brian Behan, *Mother of All the Behans: The Story of Kathleen Behan as Told to Brian Behan* (London: Hutchinson, 1984), p. 115.

25. See Herbert Lindenberger, *Opera: The Extravagant Art.*

26. Jacques Attali, *Noise: The Political Economy of Music,* Brian Massumi, trans. (Minneapolis: University of Minnesota Press, 1985), p. 4.

27. *Ibid.*, p. 19. Of course, some music can be subversive, and sometimes it is successful; at other times, it is banned, like "The Wearing of the Green" in certain places in occupied Ireland, or "*Deutschland, Deutschland, Über Alles*" (music from Haydn) in postwar Germany.

28. F.W.J. Schelling's disparaging remarks in his *Philosophie der Kunst* are cited by Lindenberger, *Opera in History*, p. 282.

MONTEVERDI'S *IL RITORNO D'ULISSE IN PATRIA*

1. For the early date (1640 vs. 1641) of *Il ritorno* I follow Wolfgang Osthoff, "Zur bologneser Aufführung von Monteverdis 'Ritorno d' Ulisse' im Jahre 1640," *Anzeiger der Philosophisch-historischen Klasse der Österreichischen Akademie der Wissenschaften* 8 (1958): 155–160.

2. Ellen Rosand, "Iro and the Interpretation of *Il ritorno d'Ulisse in patria*," *Journal of Musicology* 7 (1989): 64.

3. Don Michael Randel's comment on Monteverdi, *Harvard Concise Dictionary of Music* (Cambridge, Mass.: Belknap Press, 1978), p. 290.

4. McClary, *Feminine Endings*, p. 36.

5. *Ibid.*, p. 39.

6. *Ibid.*, p. 49.

7. Clément, *Opera, or the Undoing of Women*, p. 91.

8. Gary Tomlinson finds that Petrarchan and Marinist [Giambattista Marino] ideals clash in Monteverdi's last operas, with the latter winning. The late operas "reveal Monteverdi's fascination with the trappings of style and structure, at times almost to the exclusion of the emotions and meaning such elements were made to convey in his earlier works. They threaten to substitute surface structure and ornament for deeper expression, virtuosity for introspection. They bear, in short, many of the earmarks of Marinist poetics." *Monteverdi,* p. 218. I agree that Monteverdi has brilliant form, but I think that through that form emotions can be even better expressed. Stravinsky expressed this power well when he said, "The more art is controlled, limited, worked over, the more it is free." *Poetics of Music*, p. 63.

9. For the full text see Rosand, "Iro," pp. 160–161.

10. Thomas Walker's entry on Badoaro in *The New Grove Dictionary of Opera*, Stanley Sadie, ed., Vol. 1 (New York: R.R. Donnelley, 1992), p. 277.

11. Tomlinson, *Monteverdi*, p. 215, n.1. See also Wolfgang Osthoff, "Zu den Quellen von Monteverdis 'Ritorno di Ulisse in patria,'" *Studien zur Musikwissenschaft* 23 (1956): 67–78.

12. Quoted in Tomlinson, *Monteverdi*, p. 24.

13. See *Il ritorno d'Ulisse in patria: Drama in musica di Claudio Monteverdi* (Rome: Universal Edition, 1930). A libretto is *Il ritorno d'Ulisse in patria* in *The Operas of Monteverdi* (London: Calder Publications, 1992), pp. 87–128. All translations are my own.

14. This conflation of Christian with pagan was frequent in the period. See also Luis Vaz de Camões who wrote *Os Lusiades* (*The Lusiads*) in Macao (published in 1572). This is the Portuguese national epic about the voyage of Vasco da Gama to India, in which Christian saints and particularly the Virgin Mary cooperate with pagan gods (particularly Venus).

15. See Sappho, 104a in *Sappho et Alcaeus*, Eva-Maria Voigt, ed. (Amsterdam: Polak & Van Gennep, 1971), pp. 117–118.

16. *Penelope's Renown: Meaning and Indeterminacy in the Odyssey* (Princeton, N.J.: Princeton University Press, 1991), p. 191. Nancy Felson-Rubin has a chapter on Penelope as a heroine in *Regarding Penelope: From Character to Poetics* (Princeton, N.J.: Princeton University Press, 1994), pp. 93–107. See also Helene P. Foley, "Penelope as Moral Agent" in *The Distaff Side: Representing the Female in Homer's Odyssey*, Beth Cohen, ed. (Oxford: Oxford University Press, 1995): "Because Penelope shares Odysseus' values and is both constrained and willing in a situation of hopeless uncertainty to sacrifice her own needs for the benefit of others, her female difference contributes to rather than undermines the social order." It is this positive quality which Monteverdi and Badoaro emphasize. See also Lillian Eileen Doherty, *Siren Songs: Gender, Audiences and Narrators in the Odyssey* (Ann Arbor: University of Michigan Press, 1995), who sees a more controlled Penelope: "The *Odyssey*'s female characters are contained within a framework of meaning whose terms are set chiefly by males," p. 177. In the opera Penelope gains respect and power.

17. Thomas MacCary, "When God Became Woman." Unpublished monograph of the same name.

18. See "Wert, Tasso, and the Heroic Style," the two chapters on "Marinism and the Madrigal," and "The meeting of Petrarchan and Marinist Ideals" in Tomlinson's *Monteverdi and the End of the Renaissance*, pp. 58–72 and 165–239.

19. Claudio Monteverdi, "After reflecting that according to all the best philosophers the fast pyrrhic measure was used for lively and warlike dances, and the slow spondaic measure for their opposites, I considered the semibreve, and proposed that a single semibreve should correspond to one spondaic beat; when this was reduced to sixteen semiquavers, struck one after the other, and combined with words expressing anger and disdain, I recognized in this brief sample a resemblance to the passion which I sought, although the words did not follow metrically the rapidity of the instrument." Foreword to *Madrigali guerrieri ed amorosi*, in the original edition (Venice, 1638), published in Vol. 8 of Malipiero's edition of the collected works, and cited in *Source Readings*, p. 413.

20. Giovanni Maria Artusi, quoted in *The Operas of Monteverdi*. Nicholas John, ed. (New York: Riverrun, 1992), p. 2.

21. Leo Schrade, *Monteverdi: Creator of Modern Music* (New York: Da Capo Press, 1979), p. 244.

22. Theoclymenus also said that Telemachus' rule was affirmed by the appearance of a hawk holding a dove (*Od.* 15. 525–534).

23. Monteverdi, quoted in *Source Readings in Music History: From Classical Antiquity Through the Romantic Era,* Oliver Strunk, ed. (New York: Norton, 1950), p. 413. Monteverdi mistakenly cites *Rhetoric,* rather than *Republic* by Plato. (*Rhetoric* is by Aristotle, not Plato.)

24. Gregory Nagy emphasizes craft, with the implication of deceit, as a characteristic of both Odysseus and Penelope, in contrast to the heroic noble virtues of Achilles and Ajax in the *Iliad,* who both prize strength over cunning. *The Best of the Achaeans: Concepts of the Hero in Archaic Greek Poetry* (Baltimore: Johns Hopkins University Press, 1979), p. 45.

25. The widow of Don Ferrante Gonzaga di Bozzolo, by whom she had eight children, had made a scandalous (in Ferdinando's eyes) and clandestine marriage with Vincenzo II Gonzaga. Ferdinando accused her of treason and witchcraft, finding this a convenient way of getting rid of her. Following the custom of the time, her servants were tortured to deliver their testimony: *The Letters of Claudio Monteverdi,* Denis Stevens, trans. and intro. (Cambridge: Cambridge University Press, 1980) p. 270. Isabella won her case, and sued for damages. Vincenzo tried to have Isabella assassinated, but he failed.

26. We get a feeling for the times in *The Letters of Claudio Monteverdi,* just cited. A good account of magic in the period and its influence on music is Gary Tomlinson, *Music in Renaissance Magic: Toward a Historiography of Others* (Chicago: University of Chicago Press, 1993).

27. This is my translation.

28. See fr. 6 in the section on Archilochus, *Euterpe: An Anthology of Early Greek Lyric, Elegiac, and Iambic Poetry,* Douglas E. Gerber, ed. (Amsterdam: Hakkert, 1970).

29. Rosand, "Iro" (see note 2).

30. I am grateful to Elaine Fantham, who observed that Giove was addressed as *amoroso* by the chorus in her commenting on our papers at the panel on "Monteverdi and the Classics" at the American Philological Association (1993) mentioned above.

HENRY PURCELL'S *DIDO AND AENEAS*

1. Gustav Holst, quoted in Ellen T. Harris, *Henry Purcell's Dido and Aeneas* (1987; rpt. Oxford: Clarendon, 1989), p. 154.

2. William H. Cummings, *The Great Musicians: Purcell,* Francis Hueffer, ed. (London: Sampson Low, Marston & Company, 1903), p. 33.

3. Robert Etheridge Moore (*Henry Purcell & the Restoration Theatre,* foreword by Sir Jack Westrup, 1961; rpt. Westport, Conn.: Greenwood Press, 1974) gives *King Arthur, The Fairy Queen, Dioclesian, Bonduca, The Indian Queen* and *The Tempest.* Ellen Harris does not include *The Tempest* in her list, but instead *Timon of Athens.* Few scholars now attribute *The Tempest* to Purcell.

4. The German *Singspiel* is another example of sung portions alternating with spoken dialogue (e.g., Mozart's *Die Zauberflöte*). As Harris observed (see note 1), such was the English aversion to a full evening's entertainment of musically continuous opera that even the first Italian opera to be performed in eighteenth-century London, *Arsinoe* of 1705, was cut, translated into English, and "introduced" by a one-act spoken play.

5. Busenello and Franceschi both opted for a happy ending by having Dido marry Iarbas. In Graupner/Hinsch Anna takes over the rule and marries Juba, the Prince of Tyre. Metastasio adds a love interest: Selene, Dido's sister, declares her love for Aeneas (she is

rejected). A villain Osmide also plots to gain Dido's throne. Desmarets and Gillot give us more insight into and sympathy for Aeneas and are more balanced in this way than Purcell and Tate.

6. This date is controversial and has been debated in the pages of *Early Music* for much of this decade. One of the more significant articles is by Andrew R. Walkling, "Political Allegory in Purcell's Dido and Aeneas," *Music & Letters* 76.4 (November, 1995): 540–571. He reviews the controversy and opts for 1687.

7. See the vocal score of *Dido and Aeneas*, Edward J. Dent and Ellen Harris, eds. (1987; rpt. with corr. Oxford: University Press, 1989). Translations of the Virgil are my own. My textual citations are from *Dido and Aeneas, An Opera by Henry Purcell*, ed. Edward J. Dent (Oxford: Oxford University Press, 1925).

8. For this theory see John Buttrey, "Dating Purcell's *Dido and Aeneas*," *Proceedings of the Royal Music Association* CIV (1967–1968): 51–62.

9. Curtis Price's entry on *Dido and Aeneas* in *The New Grove Dictionary of Opera*, 1:1169. He articulated this theory earlier in *Henry Purcell and the London Stage* (Cambridge: Cambridge University Press, 1984). It is interesting that the Irish identified with Dido and the Carthaginians. The ending of Brian Friel's *Translations* refers to Carthage, and identifies its overthrow by Rome with the British invasion of Ireland in *Selected Plays* (1984; rpt. London and Boston: Faber and Faber, 1990), pp. 171–246. This ending includes a speech about empire by Hugh: "*Urbs antiqua fuit*—there was an ancient city which, 'tis said, Juno loved above all the lands. And it was the goddess's aim and cherished hope that here should be the capital of all nations—should the fates perchance allow that. Yet in truth she discovered that a race was springing from Trojan blood to overthrow some day these Tyrian towers—a people *late regem belloque superbum*— kings of broad realms and proud in war who would come forth for Lybia's [sic] downfall," Friel, *Selected Plays*, pp. 446–447. The lines just quoted are a paraphrase of Virgil's *Aeneid*, 1.12–22. "Libya's downfall" here is obviously also Ireland's. Another Irish play, Frank McGuinness's *The Carthaginians* (1988), is a protest against Bloody Sunday, which took place in Derry (the Irish name for Londonderry) on January 30, 1972, when British paratroopers opened fire on unarmed Irish civil rights marchers, killing thirteen of them. The play has a sympathetic character named Dido (a gay queen) who comforts those mourning their losses. The play concludes with a litany of the names of the victims. Compare Berlioz's *Les Troyens* where France is identified with Aeneas/ Rome, in condescending and hostile relations with North Africa: civilize the natives or let them burn. Curtis Price also cites Thomas Shadwell's *The Lancashire Witches* (1681) as a source: "The leader, Mother Demdike, is a model for the Sorceress in *Dido*, especially in her unmotivated evil-doing," *Henry Purcell and the London Stage*, p. 232.

10. Walkling, "Political Allegory," p. 553.

11. Price's article on *Dido and Aeneas* in *The New Grove Dictionary of Opera*, 1: 1169.

12. Arthur Keith Holland, *Henry Purcell: The English Musical Tradition* (1932; rpt. Freeport, New York: Books for Libraries, 1970), p. 181.

13. From early times the church persecuted witches: see the *Malleus Maleficarum*, by Henry Kramer and James Sprenger, who were commissioned by a Papal Bull of 1484 to investigate witchcraft. James I wrote a book called *Demonology*. Bridgid Brophy mentions a "diatribe against women, who, thanks to their greater carnality, are held primarily responsible for witchcraft," *Mozart, The Dramatist: The Value of his Operas to Him, to his Age, and to Us* (1964; rev. ed. with Preface, New York, Da Capo Paperback, 1988), p. 116.

14. Emma Wilkins, *London Times* (Friday, June 21, 1996), 6. She discusses witch-craft under the Stuarts as shown in *A Discourse of Witchcraft as It Was Acted in the Family of Mr Edward Fairfax of Fuystone in the County of Yorke in the year 1621*. Wil-kins records that it was not until 1736 that the law allowing execution for witchcraft was repealed.

15. Witches are still alive and well in England today, according to T.M. Luhrmann, *Persuasions of the Witch's Craft: Ritual Magic in Contemporary England* (Cambridge, Mass.: Harvard University Press, 1989).

16. *Grove Dictionary*, p. 1170. Banquo says of the witches, "You should be women, / And yet your beards forbid me to interpret / That you are so," Shakespeare, *Macbeth* I. iii. 45–47.

17. This baroque quality is what Brooks Otis calls the "subjective style," in *Virgil, A Study in Civilized Poetry* (Oxford: University Press, 1963).

18. From the introduction to *The Prophetess, or the History of Dioclesian* (1691), quoted in Moore, *Henry Purcell & the Restoration Theatre*, p. 2.

19. From the time of Monteverdi the descending tetrachord was the most popular figure for expressing grief.

20. Harris, *Henry Purcell's Dido and Aeneas*, pp. 94–95.

21. *Ibid.*, p. 96.

22. The quality of this key was noted by Moore, *Henry Purcell*, p. 86.

23. That opera shows a conflict between an evil scheming woman (the Queen of the Night) and a man who represents virtue (Sarastro). Mozart and his librettist were both in-fluenced by the Masons, who excluded women from their organization.

24. See the article by Bernard Knox on this imagery in the *Aeneid*, "The Serpent and the Flame," *American Journal of Philology* 71 (1950): 379–400.

25. In Ovid's *Heroides* VII, Dido complains to Aeneas that she burns with passion like torches or incense (23–24). See also note 24 above.

26. See my "Terms for Life in Homer: An Examination of Early Concepts in Psychology," *Transactions & Studies of the College of Physicians of Philadelphia* 4.1 (March, 1982): 26–58.

27. John Sullivan, "Dido and the Representation of Women in Vergil's *Aeneid*," in *The Two Worlds of the Poet: New Perspectives on Vergil*, Robert M. Wilhelm and Howard Jones, eds. (Detroit: Wayne State University Press, 1992), p. 64.

28. Her delicate use of rhetoric by comparison with the Virgilian Dido may link her with the Ovidian version (*Heroides* 7). In Ovid she also accuses Aeneas of being a liar, and claims that she has not been the first to be deceived by him (81–82).

29. Thomas D'Urfey, quoted in Dent and Harris, eds., *Dido and Aeneas*, p. 33.

30. Mark Goldie, "The Earliest Notice of Purcell's *Dido and Aeneas*," *Early Music* XX (1992): 392–400.

31. Robert Etheridge Moore, in speaking about the sacrificial scene in *Circe*, says, "It is thoroughly characteristic of the Restoration's employment of music, the turbulence of the emotional imbroglio followed abruptly by the ceremonious calm of the incantation. This is a frame of mind which permeates Restoration heroic drama, a bizarre world in which the baroque taste for bringing together violent disparates under the regulation of a grandiose decorum found its last expression in English civilization," Robert Etheridge Moore, *Henry Purcell & the Restoration Theatre*, p. 14.

32. Paul Robinson says that Aeneas "may well be the weakest protagonist in any important opera," *Opera and Ideas: From Mozart to Strauss* (1985; rpt. Ithaca, N.Y.: Cornell University Press, 1987), p. 152. I do not agree. I find his rejecting his destiny

charming, and this gives him strength in his display of *noblesse oblige* to a woman. See also Wilfrid Mellers, "The Tragic Heroine and the Un-hero" in *Purcell: Dido and Aeneas, an Opera*, Curtis Price, ed., Norton Critical Scores (New York & London: W.W. Norton, 1986).

MOZART'S *IDOMENEO, RE DI CRETA*

1. Karl Barth, cited by Wolfgang Hildesheimer, *Mozart*, Marion Faber, trans. (1977; rpt. London: Dent & Sons, 1982), p. 15.

2. See Donald J. Grout, *A Short History of Opera*, 2nd ed. (New York: Columbia University Press, 1965), pp. 208–218.

3. Nicholas Till said, "Joseph II, whose passionate belief in the moral power of the theatre led him to promote the Viennese theatre as one of the cornerstones of his reforming programme, was as keen on opera as on spoken drama (and much keener on *opera buffa* than *opera seria*, of which there were no new examples in Vienna during his reign)," *Mozart and the Enlightenment: Truth, Virtue and Beauty in Mozart's Operas* (New York and London: W.W. Norton, 1992), pp. 46–47.

4. Christian Gottfried Körner, quoted in Daniel Heartz, *Mozart's Operas*, Thomas Bauman, ed. with contributing essays (Berkeley, Los Angeles, Oxford: University of California Press, 1990), p. 37.

5. William Mann claimed that *Idomeneo* "is patently the greatest *opera seria* ever written," *The Operas of Mozart* (London: Cassell, 1977), p. 256. More significant perhaps is Mozart's own claim, as related by Alfred Einstein: "It is said that he valued and loved *Idomeneo* most among all his works, and this any true musician can easily understand." *Mozart, His Character, His Work* (1945; rpt. New York, Oxford: Oxford University Press, 1962).

6. Strauss reworked Mozart's *Idomeneo* "to rescue it and bring it up to date, so that it would be an acceptable repertoire piece for the Modern German stage," Norman Del Mar, *Richard Strauss: A Critical Commentary on His Life and Works*, 2 (1969; rpt. Ithaca, N.Y.: Cornell University Press, 1986), p. 376. For an account of the changes see Del Mar, pp. 381–384.

7. James Diggle has said to me in personal correspondence, "The ending we have is demonstrably post-classical; and its versification shows it could not have been composed before early Byzantine times."

8. See the fragment quoted by Aelian cited in James Diggle's edition, *Euripidis Fabulae*, 3 (Oxford: Clarendon Press, 1994), p. 422.

9. The Enlightenment's obsession with reconciliation is also seen in Mozart's *Entführung aus dem Serail*, which follows the lines of *Iphigenia among the Taurians*: A young European woman (Constanze) is held in bondage by a Turkish sultan, and her European lover comes to release her. At the moment of freedom, however, they are caught and must face the sultan's wrath. Then it is revealed that the sultan was once treated unfairly by the young man's father; nevertheless, the sultan releases the young people and the opera ends on a sublime note of transcendental humanism. This reflects the orientalist predilections of the period, which show the oriental as more civilized than his European counterpart—as Montesquieu did in his *Lettres Persanes*. Religion and politics count for far less than man's innate love for justice and mercy. We compare also the Countess' forgiveness of the Count—for the third time that day—at the end of *Figaro*.

10. Quoted in Till, *Mozart and the Enlightenment*, p. 264.

11. Joseph II for all his enlightened views was not spared the occasional *gaucherie*: he told Mozart that his *Entführung aus dem Serail* had "too many notes." But Mozart replied, "Exactly the right number, your majesty." Emperor Ferdinand of Austria continued these critical *faux pas* by saying that *The Marriage of Figaro* was "far too noisy."

12. "In the final pages of *Opera*, Clément delivers an invocation for all the women victims of the operatic stage," McClary's foreword to *Opera*, xvii.

13. See the excellent biography, persuasive in its psychological detail, by Maynard Solomon, *Mozart: A Life* (New York: HarperCollins, 1995).

14. See Till's chapter on *Idomeneo* in *Mozart and the Enlightenment*, pp. 60–82.

15. Mozart: *The Man and the Artist Revealed in His Own Words*, Friedrich Kerst, compiled and annotated, Henry Krehbiel, trans. and ed. (1926; rpt. New York: Dover, 1965), pp. 16–17.

16. The expected aria that ended a scene could impede the drama. Metastasio's librettos were formally predictable and often undramatic. Mozart was more sensitive to dramatic flow.

17. Wolfgang Amadeus Mozart, quoted in Giorgio Pestelli, *The Age of Mozart and Beethoven*, Eric Cross, trans. (1979; rpt. Cambridge: Cambridge University Press, 1990), pp. 280–281.

18. See Wolfgang Amadeus Mozart, *Idomeneo: An Opera in Three Acts for Soli, Chorus and Orchestra with Italian and German Text*. Vocal Score, K 06504 (Miami: Belwin/Kalmus), and Wolfgang Amadeus Mozart, *Idomeneo* (New York: Metropolitan Opera Guild, 1988). All translations are my own.

19. We can associate storms with love, as Virgil did in *Aeneid* Book 4 with the storm caused by Juno to bring the lovers, Dido and Aeneas, together.

20. W. Mozart, *The Letters of Mozart and his Family*, 3rd ed., Emily Anderson, trans. (London, 1985), p. 26:10.81.

21. Brophy, *Mozart, The Dramatist*, p. 239.

22. Wolfgang A. Mozart quoted in Rudolph Angermüller, *Mozart's Operas*, Stewart Spencer, trans. (New York: Rizzoli, 1988), p. 82.

23. Here we are reminded of Racine's heroines Phèdre and Attalie. They also seem to prefer the unattainable.

24. Mann, *The Operas of Mozart*, p. 276.

25. Nicholas Till claims, "Surely he must have identified the operatic situation with his own revolt against the overbearing, sacrificial demands of his father, and with the fact that to obtain his freedom he had had to leave Salzburg (his home town, however much he hated it) for Vienna," *Mozart and the Enlightenment*, p. 82. Even if such considerations influenced Mozart, I am sure that among his personal associations he was remembering the loss of his mother, and that *all* his experience of suffering was expressed through these poignant notes.

26. Quoted in Angermüller, *Mozart's Operas*, p. 82.

27. Baron Grimm, quoted in *Autonomy & Mercy, Reflections on Mozart's Operas*, Marion Faber and Ivan Nagel, trans. (Cambridge, Mass.: Harvard University Press, 1991), p. 12.

28. Walter Burkert, *Greek Religion*, John Raffan, trans. (Cambridge, Mass.: Harvard University Press, 1985), p. 248.

29. Thomas Hobbes, *Leviathan* (1651; rpt. London: Harmondsworth, 1968), p. 197, quoted in Till, *Mozart and the Enlightenment*, p. 69.

30. See *Ibid.*, p. 63.

31. Lessing, quoted in *Ibid.*, p. 118.

32. Voltaire, quoted in *Ibid.*, p. 63.

33. See Heartz, *Mozart's Operas*, p. 9, and also Till, *Mozart and the Enlightenment*, pp. 63–71.

34. Johann Pezzl, quoted in Angermüller's *Mozart's Operas*, p. 79.

35. Von Grimm, quoted in Heartz, *Mozart's Operas*, p. 9.

36. Euripides, Fr. 292, August Nauck, *Tragicorum Graecorum Fragmenta, Supplementum adiecit Bruno Snell* (Hildesheim: Georg Olms, 1964), p. 447.

37. My translation of a fragment of Protagoras' "On the Gods," Hermann Diels/Walther Kranz, *Die Fragmente der Vorsokratiker* II (1907; rpt. Dublin, Zurich: Weidmann, 1970), p. 265.

38. See Marianne McDonald, "Iphigenia's *Philia*: Motivation in Euripides' *Iphigenia at Aulis*," *Quaderni Urbinati di Cultura Classica* N.S. 34.1 (1990): 69–84.

39. Racine's *Iphigénie en Aulide* was turned into an opera, *Ifigenia in Aulide* by Carl Heinrich Graun, with a libretto by Villati and Frederick the Great, and staged in 1748.

40. See Marianne McDonald, "Cacoyannis's and Euripides' *Iphigenia*: The Power of the Powerless," *Pozorište* 56.10 (1989): 54–58; see also my "Cacoyannis's and Euripides' *Iphigenia*: The Dialectic of Power," in *Classics and Cinema*, Martin M. Winkler, ed. (Lewisburg, Pa.: Bucknell University Press, 1991), pp. 127–141.

41. Cited by Heartz, *Mozart's Operas*, p. 9.

42. Mozart said of this, "Odd that everyone should hurry off stage just so that Madame Elettra can be alone," Heartz, *Mozart's Operas*, p. 30.

43. Quoted in Hildesheimer, *Mozart*, pp. 234–235.

44. See the paintings by Boucher and Fragonard, which so often depict both gods and humans in amorous adventures. The all-pervasive theme is love.

45. Till, *Mozart and the Enlightenment*, p. 74.

46. Julian Rushton says that this tonal descent from D major to C minor is "a symbol of Elettra's descent to the depths, to Hades, the world to which she most naturally belongs." He points out that her "address to Idamante and her love aria are both in major and are related as tonic (C) and dominant (G)," Julian Rushton, *W.A. Mozart, Idomeneo*, *Cambridge Opera Handbook* (Cambridge: Cambridge University Press, 1993), p. 142.

47. Noted by Pestelli, *The Age of Mozart and Beethoven*, p. 90.

48. See the interesting commentary on this by Anthony Arblaster, in his chapter on "Mozart: Class Conflict and Enlightenment," in *Viva la Libertà: Politics in Opera* (London, New York: Verso, 1992), p. 17.

49. Pestelli, *The Age of Mozart and Beethoven*, p. 176.

BERLIOZ'S *LES TROYENS*

1. Jacques Barzun, *Berlioz and His Century: An Introduction to the Age of Romanticism* (1956; rpt. Chicago: University of Chicago Press, 1982), p. 118.

2. Cited in Robert Craft, *Stravinsky: Glimpses of a Life* (New York: St. Martin's Press, 1992), p. 252.

3. Igor Stravinsky & Robert Craft, *Conversations with Igor Stravinsky* (1958; rpt. Berkeley/Los Angeles: University of California Press, 1980), p. 29.

4. Robinson, *Opera and Ideas*, p. 59.

5. Jacques Barzun, "*Les Troyens* at the Met," *The New Criterion* 2.7 (March 1984): 44.

6. David Cairns, "Berlioz and Virgil: A Consideration of *Les Troyens* as a Virgilian Opera," *Proceedings of the Royal Musical Association* [*RMA*] 95 (1969): 109.

7. Barzun, *Berlioz and his Century*, p. 413, n. 2.

8. When I speak of the characters in the opera, I shall use the French names, but when I speak about the classical characters, I shall use the Latin versions: e.g., Cassandre in the opera, and Cassandra in Virgil's epic.

9. See the review article by Edward Said on *Les Troyens* in *The Nation* (June 27, 1994): 916–920. He is sensitive to Berlioz's imperialist overtones, with this proviso: "I do not want to suggest that Berlioz was an imperialist in a reductive sense, any more than I want to argue that *Les Troyens* is a crudely ideological opera. Nevertheless, I believe that it is incomprehensible as a great work of art without some account of the heady grandeur it shares both with Virgil as the poet of empire and with the imperial France in and for which it was written." Paul Robinson expands this idea: "*The Trojans* is a musical embodiment of the Hegelian idea of history," *Opera and Ideas,* p. 109. Many works now recognize the influence of imperialism on opera, like Herbert Lindenberger's *Opera in History*, with a chapter on "Opera/Orientalism/Otherness," pp. 160–190; see also Todd Porterfield's *The Allure of Empire: Art in the Service of French Imperialism 1798–1836* (Princeton, N.J.: Princeton University Press, 1998). The English used the classics in a comparable way: See Victoria Tietze Larson, "Classics and the Acquisition and Validation of Power in Britain's 'Imperial Century' (1815–1914)," in *International Journal of the Classical Tradition* 6.2 (Fall, 1999): 185–225.

10. Quoted in Steven Huebner's entry in *The New Grove Dictionary of Opera*, 3: 368.

11. Berlioz, "Première représentation de *La perle du Brésil*," *Journal des débats* (Nov. 27 1851); "Première représentation d'*Herculanum*," *Journal des débats* (March 12, 1859); "Prémiere représentation de *Lalla Roukh*," *Journal des débats* (May 23, 1862).

12. See *Memoirs of Hector Berlioz: From 1803 to 1865 Comprising his Travels in Germany, Italy, Russia, and England.* Rachel and Eleanor Holmes, trans., Ernest Newman, ed. and rev. (New York: Dover, 1960), p. 502.

13. Lindenberger, *Opera in History*, p. 184.

14. Berlioz calls Iarbas a Numidian rather than a Gaetulian.

15. See the libretto of G. Schirmer's Collection of Opera Librettos in the series by the Metropolitan Opera, Hector Berlioz, *Les Troyens: Opera in Five Acts,* in French, David Cairns, trans. (Wisconsin: Hal Leonard, 1973), and for orchestral score: *Hector Berlioz: New Edition of the Complete Works, The Complete Works: Les Troyens,* Hugh Macdonald, ed., Vols. 2, a-b (Basel: Bärenreiter Kassel, 1969). All the translations are mine.

16. Christa Wolf wrote her novels *Kassandra Erzählung* in 1983 and *Medea Stimmen* in 1998; both Cassandra and Medea are popular in opera and both are presented sympathetically by Wolf as particularly apt for the twentieth century as universal symbols of women.

17. Barzun, *Berlioz and His Century*, p. 330.

18. See my "*Sunt Lacrimae Rerum*," *Classical Journal* 68 (1972–1973): 180–181.

19. Berlioz, *Memoirs*, p. 201.

20. There are other sources for Berlioz, although Virgil was certainly Berlioz's main inspiration. Purcell/Tate seem to have been more influenced by Ovid's Dido. Ovid expands Virgilian images: for example, Virgil's Dido says that Aeneas is born of the Caucasus rocks and Hyrcanian tigresses nursed him (*Aen.* 4. 366–367), whereas Ovid's Dido says that rocks, oaks, savage beasts and the wild sea bore him (*Heroides* 7. 37–40).

Berlioz's Didon claims that some hideous wolf of the forest bore and nursed Énée, no doubt mixing in a bit of Livy's legend of Romulus and Remus. Nevertheless Berlioz follows Ovid in emphasizing the drama of love to a greater degree than did Virgil.

21. Quoted by Hugh MacDonald in *Hector Berlioz: Les Troyens,* Ian Kemp, ed., *Cambridge Opera Handbook* (Cambridge, New York, New Rochelle, Melbourne, Sydney: Cambridge University Press, 1988), pp. 50–51.

22. Ian Kemp, "The Unity of *Les Troyens,*" in his handbook, *Les Troyens,* p. 117.

23. Julian Rushton, "The Musical Structure," in Kemp's handbook on *Les Troyens,* pp. 132–133.

24. Conrad, *A Song of Love and Death,* p. 135.

25. I omit the mention of the "daughter of Tyndareus" (i.e., Helen) in the interpolated passage (2. 567–588) that is now generally conceded to be from Servius in the *Vita Vergilii.* It is even more negative toward Helen than the genuine references in Virgil's *Aeneid.*

26. See Rushton, "The Musical Structure," in Kemp's *Les Troyens,* p. 133.

27. Rushton, *Ibid.,* p. 132.

28. Ian Kemp, ed., "The Unity of *Les Troyens,*" *Cambridge Opera Handbook,* p. 115.

29. See Cairns, "Berlioz and Virgil" in Kemp's handbook on *Les Troyens,* p. 84.

30. See Cairns, "Berlioz and Virgil," pp. 101–102. See also Jean Aujean, "Virgile et l'Enéide" in Berlioz, *Les Troyens, L'avant scène opéra* 128/9 (1990): 6–9.

31. We recall also Hector's prayer for Astyanax, that he be distinguished among the Trojans, and like his father great in bravery, that he rule with strength, that one day people may say he is better than his father, and that he bear the bloody spoils of his defeated enemies, and gladden his mother's heart, *Il.* 6. 476–480. Virgil characteristically stresses socially oriented *labor* over personal love: see my "Aeneas and Turnus: *Labor vs. Amor,*" *Pacific Coast Philology* VII (1972): 43–48. Specifically, Virgil and Berlioz differ from Homer but follow Sophocles in seeing the culture hero as sacrificing himself to save the state.

32. This is comparable to Euripides' orientalizing the Phrygian in his *Orestes* (1369–1526). Here the slave sings in an exotic and barbaric style. The Greeks called people who did not speak Greek "barbarians" because they seemed to be saying "Bar-Bar," like sheep.

33. "In the orchestra there is a big gong, a little gong, a pair of cymbals, a kind of wooden box or bowl placed on a tripod which is struck with two sticks, a wind instrument rather like a coco-nut, this is just blown into and makes a howling sound—Ho! Ho!; and lastly a Chinese violin . . . the two strings are discordant, and the sound which results is awful. . . . [The player] does not observe any division relative to tones, semitones or any interval at all. This produces a continuous series of scratchings and feeble mewings and gives the idea of the pulings of a new-born infant or a ghoul or vampire. . . . I shall not try to describe the jackal cries, the death rattles, the turkey gobblings, in the midst of which in spite of close attention I could only discover four perceptible notes (d, e, b, g). . . . [The dancers] looked like a troupe of devils twisting, grimacing, jumping, to the hissing of all the reptiles, the roaring of all the monsters, the metallic din of all the tridents and all the cauldrons of hell. . . . It will be difficult to convince me that the Chinese people are not mad." Berlioz, from an article describing a performance of Chinese music for the *Débats,* cited in A.W. Ganz, *Berlioz in London* (New York: Da Capo Press, 1981), p. 116.

34. See Cairns, "Berlioz and Virgil," p. 109.

35. Compare Verdi's "La donna è mobile" from *Rigoletto* (1851), another opera close in date to *Les Troyens* (1863).

36. Note the ominous allusion to the faithless Cresside. Likewise, Purcell compared Dido and Aeneas to Venus and Adonis, another fatal love. We remember also Virgil's description of Aeneas' "marriage," with the nymphs making dirge-like sounds implying disaster.

37. See Michel Foucault, *The History of Sexuality*: Vol. 1: *An Introduction*, Robert Hurley, trans. (1978; rpt. New York: Vintage, 1980); Vol. 2: *The Use of Pleasure*, Robert Hurley, trans. (New York: Pantheon, 1985); Vol. 3: *The Care of the Self*, Robert Hurley, trans. (New York: Pentheon, 1986).

38. Barzun, *Berlioz and his Century*, p. 431.

39. Hylas' story can be found in Apollonius Rhodius' *Argonautica* and Valerius Flaccus' *Argonautica*; also in works by Theocritus, Apollodorus, Propertius, Hyginus and Ovid. According to Apollonius Rhodius, Hylas was the victim of a nymph who was the guardian of a well in Mysia. Hylas leaned over the water to drink, and the nymph was so taken by his good looks that she made him her husband (*Arg.* I. 1221–1239, 1325).

40. Barzun, *Berlioz and his Century*, p. 385.

41. Berlioz, *Memoirs*, p. 501.

42. Cf. Medea's "Oh, what a great evil is love for mortals!" E. *Med.* 330.

43. I have translated this quotation except for the phrase beginning "set the stamp" which I owe to R.G. Austin's commentary, *P. Vergili Maronis Aeneidos Liber Sextus* (Oxford: Clarendon Press, 1977), p. 263.

44. See also the symbolic implications of Aeneas exiting Hades through the gate of ivory, whence arise false dreams, whereas from the gate of horn true ones issue (*Aen.* 6. 893–896). Many claim Aeneas takes this exit route because he is a false shade, that is, he is a living human being. Is empire itself, represented by Aeneas, a false dream if it entails the destruction of so many innocent people?

45. Berlioz, *Memoirs*, p. 16.

46. *Ibid.*, p. 103.

47. *Ibid.*, p. 381. He reveals the same complacency in his categories as Aristotle, who claims that slaves are by nature slaves, and rightly subordinate to their masters, as women, inferior to men, are rightly subjected to their superiors. Man is by nature the head of the household: "The person who by nature is subject to another is by nature a slave." . . . "Some are necessarily born either to rule or to be ruled." . . . "As between male and female, by nature the male is superior and the female inferior; so also by nature one is the leader and the other the led" (*Politics*, 1254 a-b).

48. Ganz, *Berlioz in London*, p. 59.

49. *Ibid.*, p. 102.

50. *Ibid.*, p. 103. These memoirs are interesting in that Berlioz shows the Chinese man's contempt for Western food. Both cultures see the other as barbaric.

51. Flaubert, a little younger than Berlioz, had a complicated desire to marry new bourgeois energy to old aristocratic values. He spent time in Africa and tacitly endorsed the French acquisitions. See Fredric Jameson, *The Political Unconscious: Narrative as a Socially Symbolic Act* (London: Methuen, 1981).

52. Letter to Morel, 1848, *Berlioz in London*, p. 48.

53. Letter to d'Ortigue, 1848, *Berlioz in London*, p. 51.

54. See Edward Said's *Orientalism* (New York, Vintage Books, 1979) and *Culture and Imperialism*. See also the Field Day Pamphlets, Seamus Deane, ed. (Belfast: Dorman & Sons), including his *Civilians and Barbarians* (1983) and *Heroic Styles: The Tradition*

of an Idea (1984); the first six pamphlets were collected and published as *Ireland's Field Day* (London: Hutchinson, 1985; University of Notre Dame Press, 1986) and Series 5 as *Nationalism, Colonialism and Literature,* introduction by Seamus Deane (Minneapolis: University of Minnesota Press, 1989); see also his important *The French Revolution and Enlightenment in England, 1789–1832* (Cambridge, Mass.: Harvard University Press, 1988), which has great bearing on the context of this opera. See also his edition of *The Field Day Anthology of Irish Writing* (Derry: Field Day, dist. Norton, 1991), in three volumes (soon to be four) with the splendid commentary on the use of texts as imperialist propaganda.

55. Meyerbeer, quoted by Louise Goldberg in "Performance History and Critical Opinion," in Ian Kemp's handbook on *Les Troyens,* p. 193.

56. Abel, *Opera in the Flesh,* p. 100.

57. Berlioz, quoted in *Memoirs of Hector Berlioz,* Ernest Newman, trans., p. 7.

58. For operas on Dido see appendix to Purcell's opera.

STRAUSS'S *ELEKTRA*

1. Cited by Bryan Gilliam, *Richard Strauss's Elektra* (Oxford: Clarendon Press, 1991), p. 14.

2. Igor Stravinsky and Robert Craft, *Conversations with Igor Stravinsky,* p. 75.

3. I shall refer to the Sophoclean heroine as Electra, and in Strauss's opera as Elektra, and comparably for the other characters, distinguishing the ancient figure from the operatic one, as in the other chapters. An earlier version of this chapter appeared as "Electra's *Kleos Aphthiton:* Sophocles into Opera" in *Modern Critical Theory and Classical Literature,* Irene J.F. de Jong and J.P. Sullivan, eds. (Leiden/New York/Köln: Brill, 1994), pp. 103–26. The scores used are *Richard Strauss's Elektra: An Opera in One Act,* conductor's score (Miami, Fla.: Kalmus, 1908), *Richard Strauss's Elektra,* piano and vocal score by Carl Besl (1908; rpt. London: Boosey & Hawkes, 1943). The text of Sophocles' *Electra* that I use is in *Sophoclis Fabulae,* H. Lloyd-Jones and N.G. Wilson, eds. (Oxford: Clarendon Press, 1990). All translations are mine. My citations of the German are from the Metropolitan Opera Libretto for *Elektra* (New York: Rullman, 1909).

4. Gilliam, *Richard Strauss's Elektra,* pp. 104–105, quoting R. Schuh, ed., *Richard Strauss, Recollections and Reflections,* L.J. Lawrence, trans. (London: Greenwood, 1953), p. 154. Gilliam is also essential reading for those who wish to know the etiology of Strauss's composition of *Elektra.* His bibliography is to be recommended for those interested in the latest works (up to 1991) and also some of the older and most important works on Strauss's *Elektra.*

5. Catherine Clément, *Opera, or The Undoing of Women,* pp. 76–77.

6. Richard Specht, *Richard Strauss und sein Werk,* Vols. 1 and 2 (Leipzig: E.P. Tal, 1921). See also Carolyn Abbate, "Music and Language in Strauss's Opera," in *Richard Strauss: Elektra, Cambridge Opera Handbook,* D. Puffett, ed., p. 111. She cites elucidating statements by K. Overhoff, *Die Elektra-Partitur von Richard Strauss: Ein Lehrbuch für die Technik der dramatischen Komposition* (Salzburg: Pustet, 1978), and Specht.

7. "The chromatic excess of the madwoman became even more intense with Elektra," McClary, *Feminine Endings,* p. 101.

8. See Michel Foucault, particularly *Histoire de la folie* (Paris: Librairie Plon, 1961), and *Madness and Civilization: A History of Insanity in the Age of Reason,* Richard Howard, trans. (New York: Random House, 1965).

9. *Hamletmachine and Other Texts for the Stage*, C. Weber, ed. (New York: Performing Arts Journal Publications, 1984), p. 29.

10. Translation by W.B. Yeats, *The Collected Poems of W.B. Yeats* (1903; rpt. New York: Macmillan Co., 1940), p. 223.

11. For the "Homeric," fundamentally positive interpretation of Sophocles' *Electra*, see, e.g., Cedric H. Whitman, *Sophocles: A Study of Heroic Humanism* (Cambridge, Mass.: Harvard University Press, 1951); S.M. Adams, *Sophocles the Playwright, Phoenix*, supp. 3 (1957). M. Linforth, "Electra's Day in the Tragedy of Sophocles," *University of California Publications in Classical Philology* 19.2 (1963): 89–126; A.J.A. Waldock, *Sophocles the Dramatist* (1951; rpt. Cambridge: Cambridge University Press, 1966). For the negative interpretation see J.H. Kells, who says, "The play is a continuous exercise in dramatic irony," and, "Electra [is] herself a Fury . . . straining to catch her mother's dying cries, hissing in her venom (1410 f), gloating in hideous triumph," *Sophocles: Electra* (Cambridge: Cambridge University Press, 1973), p. 11, and Michael Ewans, "Dominence and Submission, Rhetoric and Sincerity: Insights from a Production of Sophocles' *Electra*," *Helios* 27.2 (Fall 2000): 123–136. See also J.T. Sheppard, "The Tragedy of *Electra*, According to Sophocles," *Classical Quarterly* 12 (1918): 80–88. "*Electra*: A Defense of Sophocles," *Classical Review* 41 (1927): 2–9; "*Electra* Again," *Classical Review* 41 (1927): 163–165. G. Murray expresses the view that this drama shows a "combination of matricide and good spirits," introduction to *Electra, The Plays of Euripides* (London: George Allen & Co., 1914). II. vi. According to James Diggle, Denys Page in his lectures used to call this play "Matricide without Tears" (referring to Ratigan's *French without Tears*). For a general bibliography on the varying positions see Charles Segal, *Tragedy and Civilization: An Interpretation of Sophocles* (Cambridge: Cambridge University Press, 1981), p. 461, n. 3. David Grene says, "The *Electra* is perhaps the best-constructed and most unpleasant play that Sophocles wrote," ed. with R. Lattimore, *The Complete Greek Tragedies* 2 (1942; rpt. Chicago: Chicago University Press, 1992) p. 336.

12. See Segal, *Tragedy and Civilization*, pp. 249–291, for a persuasive exposition of the structuralist position. For a variation of this interpretation see also M. Blundell, *Helping Friends and Harming Enemies: A Study in Sophocles and Greek Ethics* (Cambridge: Cambridge University Press, 1989), p. 183, and the interesting chapter by R.P. Winnington-Ingram, *Sophocles: An Interpretation* (Cambridge: Cambridge University Press, 1980), pp. 217–247.

13. This is the hero so well described by Bernard Knox: "The thing that distinguishes nearly all of them [Sophoclean heroes/heroines] is their irreconcilable temper: the greatness of their passion brought them into conflict with men and even with the gods, and rather than accept the slightest diminution of that high esteem their pride demanded, they were ready to kill and die," *The Heroic Temper: Studies in Sophoclean Tragedy* (Berkeley: University of California Press, 1966), p. 56.

14. For a good account of the *Oresteia*'s relation to the Areopagus, see Robert W. Wallace, *The Areopagos Council, to 307 B.C.* (1985; rpt. Baltimore: Johns Hopkins University Press, 1989), pp. 87–93.

15. Cacoyannis found Euripides' Electra so unappealing that in his film (1961), which he says is based on Euripides' play, he portrayed an essentially Sophoclean Electra; see M. McDonald, *Euripides in Cinema*, p. 283. See also Patricia Easterling, "Elektra's Story," in Puffett, *Richard Strauss, Elektra, Cambridge Opera Handbook*, pp. 10–16: I am surprised that Easterling, in giving background for this opera, hardly indicates that the three representations by Aeschylus, Sophocles and Euripides show us three different heroines. From Easterling's title and exposition a person might be led to believe

that there *was* one consistent story. The dissonance among the three versions might be interpreted as cacophony by some, or a strange harmony by others, but at least they should be acknowledged.

16. Richard Blackford kindly provided this example.

17. Gilliam, *Richard Strauss's Elektra*, p. 27.

18. Seamus Heaney, *The Cure at Troy: A Version of Sophocles' Philoctetes* (Derry: Field Day, 1990), p. 77.

19. Gilliam's *Richard Strauss's Elektra* is an invaluable book, but he occasionally seems wrong about Greek tragedy. For example, he says that Sophocles "makes it clear that Clytemnestra's greatest transgression in Electra's eyes, was the fact that she now shared Agamemnon's bed with the accomplice," p. 29. This was *Euripides'* emphasis, not *Sophocles'*, and Hofmannsthal took it over into his play. Gilliam was in this case misled by Hofmannsthal. Sophocles' Electra is quite clear that the *murder of her father by her mother*, NOT her sharing Aegisthus' bed, is the greatest reason for her hating her mother: Electra begins her *agon* (a verbal debate common in tragedy) by saying, "You say you killed my father. What admission could be more vile?" (559). So also Gilliam claims, "Sophocles' Clytemnestra is a character not tormented by dreams of Orestes," p. 30. This ignores Clytemnestra's unsettling dream (called a "fear that comes at night," 410), whose threat she urgently seeks to counteract by sending Chrysothemis to offer libations at her father's grave. In this dream Agamemnon took his staff from Aegisthus and planted it next to the hearth; a huge, fruitful branch grew and shadowed all the land of Mycenae. Electra immediately realizes that Orestes was behind this dream (*El.* 459–460). Not only is Gilliam wrong about Sophocles' Clytemnestra, who is troubled by her dreams and the return of Orestes, but in Hofmannsthal this nightmare is said to derive from some nameless horror. So what Gilliam says of Sophocles' Clytemnestra could be better applied to Hofmannsthal's. Gilliam is much better on the music than on Sophocles.

20. "Sophoclean scholars have concluded that Chrysothemis, though weak, is fundamentally right," Whitman, *Sophocles*, p. 156. Whitman's comment may be exaggerated but has a certain truth to it if one condemns murder or vengeance on principle.

21. David Murray's entry under Strauss, Richard in *The New Grove Dictionary of Opera*, 4: 570.

22. For the general use of the *makarismos* and also its ironic use in the plays of Euripides, see M. McDonald, *Terms for Happiness in Euripides* (Göttingen: Vandenhoeck und Ruprecht, 1978), pp. 171–174.

23. Thomas Murphy in his *Sanctuary Lamp* also used words from the Catholic ritual along with the *Oresteia* to color his own theme of vengeance and resolution, "Thomas Murphy's *The Sanctuary Lamp*: The Light at the End of the Night," M. McDonald, *Ancient Sun Modern Light*, pp. 171–185.

24. See Diane M. Juffras, "Sophocles' *Electra* 973–985 and Tyrannicide," *TAPA* 121 (1991) 99–108. Her conclusion is, "In lines 973–985, as Electra takes on Orestes' role, she imagines not only the public favor due any heroic act, but an honor that an Athenian audience might recognize as that bestowed on its tyrannicides," p. 108. Electra says, "Everyone will say such things about us two that both in life and death our fame will not fade" (984–985).

25. Electra possibly derives her name from alpha privative and *lektron*, "bed." J.D. Denniston, *Euripides' Elektra* (1939; rpt. Oxford: Clarendon Press, 1968), p. x. See note 22 on the *makarismos*.

26. Segal, *Tragedy and Civilization*, pp. 257 and 249.

27. Gilliam, *Elektra*, p. 68.

28. *Ibid.*, p. 227.

29. T.S. Eliot, *Four Quartets*, "The Dry Salvages," *The Complete Poems and Plays: 1909–1950* (1950; rpt. New York: Harcourt Brace Jovanovich, 1980), p. 136.

30. See, for instance, C. Wintle, "Elektra and the 'Elektra Complex'" in *Richard Strauss: Salome/Elektra*, English National Opera and The Royal Opera Guide Series, N. John, ed. (London: John Calder, 1988).

31. Abbate says, "Clément neglected their [tragic operatic heroines'] triumph: the sound of their singing voices. . . . I start with this image of woman undone by plot yet triumphant in voice in order to underline a position taken in my own book, which explores the idea of voice. . . . What I mean by 'voice' is, of course, not literally vocal performance, but rather a sense of certain isolated and rare gestures in music, whether vocal or nonvocal, that may be perceived as modes of subjects' enunciations," *Unsung Voices*, Preface, ix. See Puffett, "The protean Elektra of this reading is a far cry from the empty vessel, the woman without access to deed or action, envisaged by some critics (those, it must be said, who are deaf to the opera's voices, reading words alone)," *Cambridge Opera Handbook*, p. 127. K. Segal sees this heroine's final dance in Nietzschean terms: "Elektra is both regaining the true self that she has had taken from her and is re-entering the ground of Being, a state in which she feels a heavy but visionary joy." "Hofmannsthal's *Elektra*: From Drama to Libretto" in *Richard Strauss: Salome/Elektra*," N. John, ed. p. 58.

32. Variation of, "Because their words had forked no lightning they / Do not go gentle into that good night," Dylan Thomas, *The Poems of Dylan Thomas*, Daniel Jones, ed. (1937; rpt. New York: New Directions, 1971), p. 208.

STRAVINSKY'S *OEDIPUS REX*

1. Prokofiev, quoted by Malcolm Hamrick Brown, "Stravinsky and Prokofiev: Sizing Up the Competition," in *Confronting Stravinsky, Man, Musician, and Modernist*, Jann Pasler, ed. (Berkeley: University of California Press, 1986), pp. 47–48.

2. See Britten's enthusiastic review, *Tempo*, 120 (March 1977): 10–12.

3. Paul Horgan, *Encounters with Stravinsky: A Personal Record* (1972; rev. Middletown, Conn.: Wesleyan University Press, 1989), pp. 156–157.

4. See Pasler, introduction to *Confronting Stravinsky*, xiii. See also Mikhail Druskin, *Igor Stravinsky: His Personality, Works and Views*, Martin Cooper, trans. (1979; rpt. in English, Cambridge: Cambridge University Press, 1983), pp. 23–28.

5. When I refer to the opera I shall use *Oedipus Rex* as the title, and Oedipus for the character. When I refer to Sophocles' play, I shall use *Oidipous Tyrannos* and Oidipous. The other characters will remain the same in both.

6. Linda Hutcheon and Michael Hutcheon, *Opera, Desire, Disease, Death* (Lincoln, Neb.: University of Nebraska Press, 1996). pp. 203–204.

7. Clément, *Opera, or the Undoing of Women*, pp. 161–162.

8. This is from a letter cited by Stephen Walsh in *Stravinsky: Oedipus Rex, Cambridge Music Handbooks* (Cambridge: Cambridge University Press, 1993), p. 6.

9. Eric Walter White, *Stravinsky: The Composer and His Work*, 2nd ed. (Berkeley: University of California Press, 1984), p. 327.

10. Druskin, *Igor Stravinsky*, p. 153.

11. White, *Stravinsky*, p. 328.

12. An English version of Cocteau's French text was produced by e.e. cummings.

13. One good account that reveals the strain in the relationship is given by Paul Horgan, about a London production of the *Oedipus Rex* in 1929: Cocteau hogged the limelight, missed his cues, stubbornly refused to cooperate with the orchestra, and bowed prematurely so the audience drowned out Stravinsky's conclusion with their applause. *Encounters with Stravinsky: A Personal Record*, pp. 114–117.

14. Robert Craft, *Stravinsky: Chronicle of a Friendship* (1963; rev. and expanded, Nashville, Tenn.: Vanderbilt University Press, 1994), p. 353.

15. Craft, *Stravinsky: Glimpses of a Life*, p. 288.

16. Igor Stravinsky, *An Autobiography* (1936; rpt. New York: W.W. Norton & Company, 1962), p. 128.

17. Igor Stravinsky, *Poetics of Music*, p. 18. Craft shows a more elaborate version in Stravinsky's notes for the *Poetics*: "The true meaning of music. Like all the creative faculties of man, music is a quest for unity, communion, union with fellow beings and with Being [illegible word], Monism, the Creator." Quoted in Craft, *Stravinsky*, p. 98.

18. White, *Stravinsky*, pp. 337–338.

19. I have used two librettos and scores for this opera. The orchestral one is *Oedipus Rex: Opéra-oratorio en deux actes d'après Sophocle, par* Igor Stravinsky *et* Jean Cocteau (1927; rpt. and rev. London: Boosey & Hawkes, 1948). The other score I use is Igor Stravinsky, *Oedipus Rex: Réduction pour chant et piano* (1927; rpt. and rev. London: Boosey & Hawkes, 1948).

20. Craft, *Chronicle of a Friendship*, p. 248.

21. *Ibid.*, p. 452.

22. Craft, *Stravinsky: Glimpses of a Life*, p. 96.

23. Stravinsky, *Poetics*, p. 63.

24. See Roger Sessions, "On *Oedipus Rex*," in *Stravinsky in Modern Music (1924–1946)*, compiled and intro., Carol J. Oja, foreword, Aaron Copland (New York: Da Capo Press, 1982), pp. 9–16.

25. Igor Stravinsky and Robert Craft, *Conversations with Igor Stravinsky*, p. 21.

26. As Richard Taruskin says, "The accents of spoken language were merely there to be manipulated like any other musical parameter, for the sake of musical enjoyment. . . . In this . . . he [Stravinsky] sought in the aesthetic stance of folk arts the seeds and the validation of an authentic modernism. Though it may bother us that he saw fit to set the poetry of Auden or of Gide as if it were a Russian limerick, that is what he did, and seriously." *Stravinsky Retrospectives*, Ethan Haimo and Paul Johnson, eds. (Lincoln, Neb.: University of Nebraska Press, 1987), p. 196. Mikhail Druskin has said, "During his [Stravinsky's] Russian period it was the play of speech-accents in folksong that had helped him to elaborate his method of motivic variation," *Igor Stravinsky*, p. 146.

27. For Stravinsky and his misplaced accents replicating a live tradition in Russian folk music, see Taruskin, "Stravinsky's 'Rejoicing Discovery' and What it Meant: in Defense of his Notorious Text Setting," in *Stravinsky Retrospectives*, pp. 162–199. Also useful is Boris Vladimirovich Asaf'yev, who noted that Stravinsky's musical devices with rhythm and use of keys was "comparable to the enjambment, dislocated syntax, and so forth of the Russian poets of the time," quoted in Craft, *Stravinsky*, p. 261.

28. Stravinsky, *Poetics*, p. 43.

29. *Ibid.*, p. 117.

30. Quoted in Craft, *Stravinsky*, p. 215.

31. Craft, *Stravinsky*, p. 216.

32. Quoted by Craft, *Stravinsky*, p. 382. Its four notes resemble the great four-note themes in various works, from Monteverdian laments to Wagner's *Liebestod* in *Tristan*

and Isolde. Stephen Walsh sees this scene as reminiscent of the opening of Verdi's *Otello*: a crowd come to their savior with their pleas, a savior who is soon to meet his downfall. He goes on to say of the various reminiscences of this orchestral theme and the choral one, "But the more subliminal source of both figures is surely Gregorian chant (perhaps even the 'Dies irae'), and it is an important similarity that both openings make repeated melodic reference to plainsong, and through it to the idea of the crowd as supplicants before a priest or before God himself," *Stravinsky,* p. 35. Walsh claims, "[Verdi's *Otello*] is a significant parallel, since Otello's fall is by far the most classical in Verdi's tragedies," *The Music of Stravinsky* (Oxford: Clarendon Press, 1988), p. 139.

33. Walsh, *Stravinsky,* pp. 32 and 40.

34. Paul Griffiths, *The Master Musicians: Stravinsky* (New York: Schirmer/Macmillan, 1992), p. 88.

35. Gilbert Amy, "Aspects of the Religious Music of Igor Stravinsky," in Pasler, *Confronting Stravinsky,* pp. 198–199.

36. In a personal communication, Richard Blackford mentions that he read somewhere that Stravinsky remarked wryly and half apologetically that the brass writing in the *Gloria* was straight out of a Hollywood movie. It would be typical of Stravinsky to combine Mussorgsky with Hollywood.

37. Walsh, *Stravinsky,* p. 51.

38. See Arthur Pickard-Cambridge, *The Dramatic Festivals of Athens,* 2nd ed., rev. by John Gould and D.M. Lewis (1968; rep. with supp. and corr., Oxford: Clarendon Press, 1991), pp. 57–63 and *passim.*

39. See Cedric H. Whitman's *Sophocles: A Study of Heroic Humanism* (Cambridge, Mass.: Harvard University Press, 1951) and Bernard Knox's *The Heroic Temper: Studies in Sophoclean Tragedy.*

40. *Score,* iv.

41. *Ibid.*

42. This was noted by Walsh in *Stravinsky,* p. 58.

43. *Ibid.,* p. 65.

44. Program/libretto for Sony's recording of *Igor Stravinsky, Sacred Works: Cantata, Mass, Canticum Sacrum, Threni,* etc., p. 11.

45. See a discussion of the diminished seventh as a dramatic device (often denoting suspense, besides functioning as a modulating pivot) in Louis Andriessen and Elmer Schönberger, *The Apollonian Clockwork: On Stravinsky,* Jeff Hamburg, trans. (Oxford: Oxford University Press, 1989), pp. 72–73.

46. Igor Stravinsky and Robert Craft, *Expositions and Developments* (1959; rpt. in paperback, Berkeley: University of California Press, 1981), p. 108.

47. Walsh, *Stravinsky,* p. 54.

48. *Ibid.*

49. Cf. the beginning of Sophocles' *Antigone, Ismenes kara,* literally "head of Ismene," which can be translated "O my very own sister."

50. We find this phrase ("count ye no man happy until he die") and a pertinent discussion of it in the confrontation of Croesus and Solon in Herodotus, *Histories* I. 32; it is attributed to Solon, but is probably an even older folk maxim. It appears in Aeschylus' *Agamemnon,* 928–929, Sophocles' *Tyndareus* (frg. 588, Nauck), *Trachinians* 1–3, and *Oidipous Tyrannos* 1528–1530, Euripides' *Heracleidae* 865–866, *Andromache* 100–103, *Trojan Women* 509–510; and *Iphigenia at Aulis,* 160–162. Aristotle discusses the philosophical implications in the *Nicomachean Ethics,* 1. x. See Richard Jebb's discussion of this in his edition of *Sophocles: The Plays and Fragments, The Oedipus Tyrannus,* 1

(1883; rpt. Cambridge: Cambridge University Press, 1902), pp. 199–200, note on line 1529.

51. That this is not Sophocles' conception is argued by E.R. Dodds, "On Misunderstanding the *Oedipus Rex,*" *Greece and Rome,* n.s. 13 (1966): 39–49; rpt. in E. Segal, ed., *Oxford Readings in Greek Tragedy* (Oxford: Oxford University Press, 1983), pp. 177–188. See also Bernard Knox, *Oedipus at Thebes: Sophocles' Tragic Hero and His Time* (New York: Norton, 1975): "Oedipus represents man's greatness . . . self-discovery as heroic action," pp. 51–52.

52. Theodor Adorno, *Quasi una fantasia: Essays on Modern Music,* Rodney Livingstone, trans. (1963; rpt. London, Verso, 1992), p. 158.

53. *Ibid.,* pp. 174–75.

54. *The Angel's Cry,* p. 105.

55. *The Queen's Throat,* p. 91.

56. See next chapter for operas on *Oedipus at Colonus.*

THE GOSPEL AT COLONUS

1. Eileen Southern, *The Music of Black Americans: A History* (1971; rpt. 2nd ed. New York: Norton, 1983), p. 444.

2. "Most importantly, 'spirit possession' was renovated from its African form. This use of music to create a fusion of spirit and flesh is perhaps more important than the fact of the survival of overt Africanisms. . . . Black music became, ultimately, a kind of popular religion in and of itself, retaining the important socio-religious properties that had been developed during the earliest neo-Christian rituals," Ben Sidran, *Black Talk* (1971; rpt. New York: Da Capo, 1983), p. 17.

3. LeRoi Jones, *Blues People: The Negro Experience in White America and the Music that Developed from It* (New York: Morrow Quill, 1963), pp. 34–41.

4. See the useful history given in Ben Sidran, *Black Talk* (1971; rpt. with a new preface by Archie Shepp, New York: Da Capo Press, 1981), pp. 183–185. Also useful is Frank Tirro, *Jazz, A History* (1977; 2nd ed., New York: W.W. Norton, 1993).

5. Sidran, *Black Talk,* p. 183.

6. Southern, *The Music of Black Americans,* pp. 446–447.

7. Quincy Troupe, *Poems by Quincy Troupe: Avalanche* (Minneapolis: Coffee House Press, 1996), pp. 54–55.

8. Southern, *The Music of Black Americans,* p. 449.

9. *The Blues Line: A Collection of Blues Lyrics from Leadbelly to Muddy Waters,* complied by Eric Sackheim (Hopewell, N.J.: The Echo Press, 1993), pp. 98–99.

10. *Ibid.,* p. 105.

11. Lee Breuer claims, "As was the classic Greek performance, the Pentecostal service is a communal catharsis which forges religious, cultural and political bonds," *The Gospel at Colonus: An Adaptation by Lee Breuer* (1985; rpt. New York: Theatre Communications Group, 1989), p. 4. Most of this text is a paraphrase of the translation by Robert Fitzgerald and Dudley Fitts, *Sophocles: The Oedipus Cycle* (1939; rpt. New York: Harcourt Brace Jovanovich, 1977).

12. Lee Breuer, *Gospel,* acknowledgements, p. ix.

13. The sacred and secular interpenetrate in Gospel music, and this has occurred throughout the ages. For instance, in the sixteenth century we find John Taverner's Mass based on the "Western Wynde," a popular song.

14. "We must take account of the work of those within the expressive culture of the Black Atlantic who have tried to use its music as an aesthetic, political, or philosophical marker in the production of what might loosely be called their critical social theories," Paul Gilroy, *The Black Atlantic: Modernity and Double Consciousness* (Cambridge, Mass.: Harvard University Press, 1993), p. 79.

15. Sidran, *Black Talk*, p. 185.

16. "It may not be readily conceded now that the song of the Negro is America's folk song; but if the spirituals are what we think them to be, a classic folk expression, then this is their ultimate destiny," Alain Locke, quoted in Gilroy, *The Black Atlantic*, p. 91.

17. Isaac Tigrett, quoted in Maurice Chittenden, "Return of Blues Velvet," *London Sunday Times* (28 July 1996): 9. It is interesting that "Disney owns 10% of his [Tigrett's] company and Harvard university has a $32m investment."

18. As Tricia Rose says of rap, in speaking of how black music has evolved in America, "African-American music and culture, inextricably tied to concrete historical and technological developments, have found yet another way to unnerve and simultaneously revitalize American culture." *Black Noise: Rap Music and Black Culture in Contemporary America* (Hanover, N.H., and London: University Press of New England, 1994), p. 185.

19. "Gospel music was still performing its social function, conveying good news in bad times," Anthony Heilbut, *The Gospel Sound: Good News and Bad Times* (1971; rpt. with corr. and new preface and postscript, New York: Limelight Editions, 1985), p. 332. This includes a useful discography.

20. John Shepherd, *Music as Social Text* (Cambridge: Polity Press, 1991). See in particular his Part 3, "Musical Sociality and Musicology," pp. 189–223.

21. Seamus Deane, introduction to *Selected Plays of Brian Friel* (London: Faber and Faber, 1984), p. 18.

22. In fifth-century Athens the *chorêgos* could either be the chorus leader or the man who sponsored the chorus. I shall follow Breuer's spelling and usage.

23. *Gospel at Colonus: An Adaptation by Lee Breuer.* I shall refer to this book as *Libretto* in future notes.

24. Breuer, *Libretto*, pp. 3–4.

25. Stanley Sadie, ed., *The Norton/Grove Concise Encyclopedia of Music* (New York: W.W. Norton & Company, 1988), p. 205.

26. See Poizat, *The Angel's Cry: Beyond the Pleasure Principle in Opera*, p. 41.

27. Tears in the Christian tradition are often considered an indicator of closeness to God: one weeps for the pain in this world and also for the joy of salvation in the next. Cf. *lacrimae Christi*, the imprint of His tears on the miraculous Veronica's veil.

28. In Sophocles Ismene says that she cannot look on Oedipus or Antigone because of her sorrow (*OC 326*) at seeing their misery, but this has been transformed by Fitzgerald's translation and the music into tears of joy.

29. Breuer, *Libretto*, p. 44.

30. Oedipus varies Dido's last words, which are "Remember me, but ah, forget my fate" (Purcell's *Dido and Aeneas*). Oedipus identifies himself with his fate, which finally has fulfilled him.

31. This is Hugh Lloyd-Jones' translation, *Sophocles: Antigone, The Women of Trachis, Philoctetes, Oedipus at Colonus*, Loeb Series, 2 (Cambridge, Mass.: Harvard University Press, 1994), pp. 576–577.

32. Breuer, *Libretto*, p. 52.

33. Breuer, *Libretto*, p. 56. "The role of the black Preacher became that of performer as well as that of black truth-teller," Sidran, *Black Talk*, pp. 20–21.

34. See Mogens Herman Hansen, *The Athenian Democracy in the Age of Demosthenes: Structure, Principles and Ideology*, J.A. Crook, trans. (1991; rpt. Oxford: Blackwell, 1993), pp. 27–37 and James L. O'Neil, *The Origins and Development of Ancient Greek Democracy* (Lanham, Md.: Rowman & Littlefield, 1995).

35. For other operas about Oedipus see appendix in last chapter.

THEODORAKIS AND EURIPIDES' *MEDEA*

1. Some of the material from this chapter appeared in my "Ancient *Katharsis* into Modern Opera: Theodorakis' *Medea*," *The Journal of Modern Greek Arts* 1 (Spring 1994): 37–44, and "Medea as Politician and Diva: Riding the Dragon into the Future," in *Medea: Essays on Medea in Myth, Literature, Philosophy and Art*, James J. Clauss and Sarah Iles Johnston, eds. (Princeton, N.J.: Princeton University Press, 1997) and *"Medea è mobile*: The Many Faces of Medea in Opera," in *Medea in Performance: 1500–2000*, Edith Hall, Fiona MacIntosh, and Oliver Taplin, eds. (Oxford, Legenda, 2000), pp. 100–118.

2. My major source for these figures is *The New Grove Dictionary of Opera*, Stanley Sadie, ed., in four volumes. See appendix for four additional operas from *The Oxford Dictionary of Opera*, John Warrack and Ewan West, eds. (Oxford/New York: Oxford University Press, 1992), entry under *Medea*, p. 455.

3. Quoted in Till, *Mozart and the Enlightenment*, p. 145.

4. There are those like Richard Leppert, in "Music, Domestic Life and Cultural Chauvinism: Images of British Subjects at Home in India," who see elements in the eighteenth century as reaffirming hierarchy and thus sanctioning control of others, for example, the woman in a family, or a native people in imperialism; and of course he is correct. My point, however, is that in this century ideas of equality were also being disseminated, as evidenced by so many performances of operas about an assertive *Medea* in *Music and Society: The Politics of Composition, Performance and Reception*, Richard Leppert and Susan McClary, eds. (1987 rpt. Cambridge: Cambridge University Press, 1992).

5. See Susan McClary, "The Politics of Silence and Sound," Afterword to Jacques Attali, *Noise: The Political Economy of Music*, pp. 154–156.

6. See my *Ancient Sun, Modern Light: Greek Drama on the Modern Stage*; Hellmut Flashar, *Inszenierung der Antike: Das griechische Drama auf der Bühne der Neuzeit* (München: C.H. Beck, 1991); *Medea: Essays on Medea in Myth, Literature, Philosophy and Art*, Clauss and Johnston, eds. (See also note 4).

7. See McDonald, *Ancient Sun, Modern Light*, pp. 115–125.

8. Two useful books in English that give us background are: George Giannaris, *Mikis Theodorakis: Music and Social Change* (New York: Praeger, 1972) and Gail Holst, *Theodorakis: Myth & Politics in Modern Greek Music* (Amsterdam: Hakkert, 1980). There is hardly a mention of Theodorakis that does not involve social context.

9. Unpublished letter from Theodorakis to the author, April, 1992.

10. *Ibid.*

11. Introduction by Mikis Theodorakis in Giannaris, *Mikis Theodorakis*, p. x. Holst further classifies Theodorakis' music into "seven categories, all based on song," and the music from the score to *Elektra* is classified as "metasymphonic," *Mikis Theodorakis*, pp. 62–63.

12. An example is Strauss's *Salome*. Strauss was enthralled by the production of Oscar Wilde's play in a translation by Hedwig Lachmann, produced by Max Reinhardt's company in Berlin in 1903. His libretto for the opera reduced this translation by half.

13. Bruno Snell claims, "With Homer shame (*aidos*) regulates the attitude of man to his fellow man. Each individual considers whether or not his reputation, his authority, or his honor has been injured. In later times, however, behavior is determined by a consciousness of guilt," *Poetry and Society: The Role of Poetry in Ancient Greece* (1961; rpt. Freeport, N.Y.: Books for Libraries, 1971), p. 73. Medea prizes honor, and it is the slights to her honor that impel her to commit her dreadful act of vengeance. There is thus the suggestion of an archaic, even primitive, cast to her character.

14. Holst, *Theodorakis*, p. 125.

15. *Ibid.*, p. 84.

16. Martha Nussbaum has noted: "By stressing that his motive was sincere love for his children and fear for their safety, not greed or callousness, Seneca gives him a new humanity and dignity," *Medea,* Clauss and Johnston, eds., p. 230.

17. Charpentier and Cherubini are both on the cusps of their periods, and I see them as more indicative of the subsequent centuries, Charpentier of the eighteenth, and Cherubini of the nineteenth.

18. William Butler Yeats, "A Drinking Song," *The Collected Poems of W.B. Yeats*, 2nd ed. (1950; rpt. New York: Macmillan, 1961), p. 92.

19. John Warrack and Ewan West's entry in *The Oxford Dictionary of Opera* under *Medea*, p. 455. They spell Kerll as Kerl and Collasse as Colasse. They list an opera by Robert Wilson in 1982, but he only designed the set that year for Charpentier's *Médée.*

Selected Bibliography

MONTEVERDI

Arnold, Denis. *Monteverdi: The Master Musicians Series.* 1963; rpt. London: J.M. Dent and Sons, 1990.

—— and Nigel Fortune, eds. *The New Monteverdi Companion.* London: Faber and Faber, 1985.

Bukofzer, Manfred F. *Music in the Baroque Era: From Monteverdi to Bach.* New York: Norton, 1910.

Chafe, Eric T. *Monteverdi's Tonal Language.* New York: Schirmer Books, 1992.

Fabbri, Paolo. *L'incoronazione di Poppea: Coronation of Poppea.* Trans. Geoffrey Dunn. London: Gaber Music, 1977.

——. *Monteverdi.* Trans. Tim Carter. New York: Cambridge University Press, 1994.

Gardiner, John Eliot. *Monteverdi, L'Orfeo.* Ed. David Butchart. London: J & W Chester, 1987.

Harnoncourt, Nikolaus. *Baroque Music Today: Music As Speech: Ways to a New Understanding of Music.* Trans. Mary O'Neill. Ed. Reinhard G. Pauly. Portland: Amadeus, 1982.

——. *The Musical Dialogue: Thoughts on Monteverdi, Bach and Mozart.* Trans. Mary O'Neill. Ed. Reinhard G. Pauly. Portland: Amadeus, 1989.

John, Nicholas, ed. *The Operas of Monteverdi.* New York: Riverrun, 1992.

Leopold, Silke. *Monteverdi: Music in Transition.* Trans. Anne Smith. Oxford: Oxford University Press, 1991.

McClary, Susan. *The Transition From Modal to Tonal Organization in the Works of Monteverdi.* Ann Arbor: University Microfilms International, 1976.

Monteverdi, Claudio, and Hans Werner Henze. *Il ritorno d'Ulisse in patria: Die Heimkehr des Odysseus in sein Vaterland.* Libretto by Giacomo Badoaro. Piano Reduction by Matthias Buch, Martin Focke. New York: Schott, 1982.

——. *Il ritorno d'Ulisse in patria.* Ed. Paul Daniel. Trans. Anne Ridler. London: English National Opera, 1989.

Prunieres, Henry. *Monteverdi: His Life and Work.* Trans. Marie D. Mackie. 1926; rpt. Westport, Conn.: Greenwood Press, 1974.

Rosand, Ellen. *Opera in Seventeenth-Century Venice: The Creation of a Genre.* Berkeley: University of California Press, 1991.

Schrade, Leo. *Monteverdi: Creator of Modern Music.* New York: Da Capo Press, 1979.

Stevens, Denis. *Monteverdi: Sacred, Secular, and Occasional Music.* London: Associated University Press, 1978.

——, ed. *Monteverdi, Claudio. L'Orfeo: Favola in musica. For Soloist, Chorus and Orchestra.* Sevenoaks, England: Novello, 1967.

——. *The Letters of Claudio Monteverdi.* Trans. Denis Stevens. New York: Cambridge University Press, 1980.

Tomlinson, Gary. *Rinuccini, Peri, Monteverdi, and the Humanist Heritage of Opera.* Ann Arbor, Mich.: University Microfilms International, 1979.

——. *Monteverdi and the End of the Renaissance.* Berkeley: University of California Press, 1987.

Whenham, John, ed. *Claudio Monteverdi: Orfeo.* Cambridge: Cambridge University Press, 1986.

PURCELL

Bianconi, Lorenzo. *Music in the Seventeenth Century.* Trans. David Bryant. Cambridge: Cambridge University Press, 1982.

Blow, John. *Venus and Adonis: A Masque.* Ed. G.E.P. Arkwright. New York: Broude Brothers, 1968.

Craven, Robert Russell, ed. *A Critical Old-Spelling Edition of Nahum Tate's Brutus of Alba.* New York: Garland, 1987.

Cummings, William H. *The Great Musicians: Purcell.* Ed. Francis Hueffer. London: Sampson Low, Marston & Company, 1903.

Dent, Edward J. *Foundations of English Opera: A Study of Musical Drama in England During the Seventeenth Century.* Ed. and intro. Michael M. Winesanker. 1928; rpt. New York: Da Capo Press, 1965.

——, and Ellen Harris, eds. *Henry Purcell: Dido and Aeneas*: Vocal Score. 1925 Dent; rpt. with rev. Oxford: Oxford University Press, 1989.

Dryden, John. *All for Love.* Ed. N.J. Andrew. 1975; rpt. London: A. and C. Black, 1993.

Harris, Ellen T. *Henry Purcell's Dido and Aeneas.* Oxford: Clarendon Press, 1987.

Holland, Arthur Keith. *Henry Purcell: The English Musical Tradition.* 1932, rpt. Freeport, N.Y.: Books for Libraries, 1970.

Holst, Imogen. *The Great Masters, Henry Purcell, The Story of His Life & Work.* London: Hawkes and Son, 1961.

Keates, Jonathan. *Purcell.* London: Chatto & Windus, 1995.

King, Robert. *Henry Purcell.* London: Thames and Hudson, 1994.

Mainifold, J.S. *The Music in English Drama: From Shakespeare to Purcell.* London: Rockliff, 1956.

Marlowe, Christopher. *The Complete Plays.* Ed. and Intro. J.B. Steane. 1969. New York: Penguin, 1986.

Middleton, Thomas. *The Witch.* Ed. Vivian Ridler. 1948; rpt. Oxford: Oxford University Press, 1963.

Moore, Robert Etheridge. *Henry Purcell & the Restoration Theatre.* 1961; rpt. Westport, Conn.: Greenwood Press, 1984.

Muller, Julia. *Words and Music in Henry Purcell's First Semi-Opera, Dioclesian: An Approach to Early Music Through Early Theatre.* Vol. 28. New York: Edwin Mellen Press, 1990.

Playford, John. *An Introduction to the Skill of Musick.* 12th ed. Corr. and Am. by Henry Purcell, with Selected Chapters from the Thirteenth and Fourteenth Editions, New Int. Glossary, and Index by Franklin B. Zimmerman. New York: Da Capo Press, 1972.

Price, Curtis. *Henry Purcell and the London Theatre.* Cambridge: Cambridge University Press, 1984.

——, ed. *Henry Purcell, Dido and Aeneas, An Opera.* New York & London: W.W. Norton, 1986.

Westrup, J.A. *The Master Musicians: Purcell.* New York: Pellegrini and Cudaby, 1949.

MOZART

Angermüller, Rudolph. *Mozart's Operas.* Trans. Stewart Spencer. New York: Rizzoli, 1988.

Baker, Richard. *Mozart.* London: Macdonald, 1991.

Barth, Karl. *Wolfgang Amadeus Mozart.* Trans. Clarence K. Pott. Grand Rapids, Mich.: William B. Eerdmans, 1986.

Bauman, Thomas. *W.A. Mozart: Die Entführung aus dem Serail.* 1987. Cambridge: Cambridge University Press, 1991.

Beaumarchais, Pierre-Augustin Caron. *The Barber of Seville and The Marriage of Figaro.* Intro. and Trans. John Wood. New York: Penguin, 1964.

——. *Le Barbier de Seville, Le Mariage de Figaro, La Mere coupable.* Ed. René Pomeau. Paris: Garnier-Flammarion, 1965.

Berlioz, Hector. *Mozart, Weber and Wagner: With Various Essays on Musical Subjects.* Trans. Edwin Evans. London: W.M. Reeves, 1969.

Brophy, Brigid. *Mozart the Dramatist: The Value of his Operas to Him, to His Age and to Us.* New York: Da Capo, 1988.

Carter, Tim. *W.A. Mozart: Le Nozze di Figaro.* New York: Cambridge University Press, 1987.

Clive, Peter. *Mozart and His Circle: A Biographical Dictionary.* New Haven: Yale University Press, 1993.

Dent, Edward J. *Mozart's Operas: A Critical Study,* 2nd ed. Oxford: Clarendon; New York: Oxford University Press, 1991.

Donington, Robert. *Baroque Music: Style and Performance, A Handbook.* New York: Norton, 1982.

Einstein, Alfred. *Mozart: His Character, His Work.* Trans. Arthur Mendel and Nathan Broder. New York: Oxford University Press, 1945.

Eisen, Cliff. *Mozart Studies.* New York: Oxford University Press, 1991.

Elias, Norbert. *Mozart: Portrait of a Genius.* Ed. Michael Schröter. Trans. Edmund Jephcott. Berkeley: University of California Press, 1993.

Gay, Peter. *The Enlightenment: An Interpretation / The Rise of Modern Paganism.* New York: Norton, 1966.

——. *The Enlightenment: An Interpretation / The Science of Freedom.* New York: Norton, 1969.

Gutman, Robert W. *Mozart: A Cultural Biography.* New York: Harcourt Brace, 1999.

Heartz, Daniel. *Mozart's Operas.* Ed. Thomas Bauman. Berkeley: University of California Press, 1990.

Hildesheimer, Wolfgang. *Mozart.* Trans. Marion Faber. 1977; rpt. London: J.M. Dent and Sons, 1982.

Hodges, Sheila. *Lorenzo Da Ponte: The Life and Times of Mozart's Librettist.* New York: Universe Books, 1985.

Hughes, Spike. *Famous Mozart Operas: An Analytical Guide for the Opera-Goer and Armchair Listener,* 2nd ed. New York: Donover, 1972.

Landon, H.C. Robbins. *The Mozart Essays.* New York: Thames and Hudson, 1995.

Mann, William. *The Operas of Mozart.* London: Cassell, 1977.

Marchall, Robert L. ed., *Mozart Speaks: Views on Music, Musicians, and the World.* New York: Schirmer Books-Maxwell MacMillan International, 1991.

Maunder, Richard. *Mozart's Requiem: On Preparing a New Edition.* Oxford: Clarendon Press, 1988.

Mozart, Wolfgang Amadeus: *Idomeneo.* An Opera in Three Acts for Soli Chorus and Orchestra with Italian and German Text. Vocal Score. K06504. Miami, Fla.: Belwin: Kalmus, n.d.

——. *Idomeneo: A Serious Opera in Three Acts.* Orchestral Score. K 366. New York: Kalmus, n.d.

——. *Requiem,* in Full Score. New York: Dover Publications, n.d.

Nagel, Ivan. *Autonomy and Mercy: Reflections on Mozart's Operas.* Trans. Marion Faber and Ivan Nagel. Cambridge, Mass.: Harvard University Press, 1991.

Osborne, Charles. *The Complete Operas of Mozart.* New York: Da Capo Press, 1978.

Pestelli, Giorgio. *The Age of Mozart and Beethoven.* Trans. Eric Cross. Cambridge: Cambridge University Press, 1984.

Robbins-Landon, H.C. and Donald Mitchell, eds. *The Mozart Companion.* 1956; rpt. Boston: Faber and Faber, 1990.

Robinson, Paul. *Opera & Ideas: From Mozart to Strauss.* Ithaca: Cornell University Press, 1985.

Rushton, Julian. *W.A. Mozart: Don Giovanni.* Cambridge: Cambridge University Press, 1981.

——. *W.A. Mozart: Idomeneo.* Cambridge: Cambridge University Press, 1993.

Sadie, Julie Ann, comp. and ed. *Companion to Baroque Music.* New York: Schirmer Books–Maxwell Macmillan International, 1990.

Solomon, Maynard. *Mozart: A Life.* New York: HarperCollins, 1995.

Stafford, William. *The Mozart Myths: A Critical Reassessment.* Stanford, Calif.: Stanford University Press, 1991.

Steptoe, Andrew. *The Mozart—Da Ponte Operas, The Cultural and Musical Background to Le nozze di Figaro, Don Giovanni, and Cosi fan tutte.* New York: Oxford University Press, 1988.

Till, Nicholas. *Mozart and the Enlightenment: Truth, Virtue and Beauty in Mozart's Operas.* London: Faber and Faber, 1992.

Wyzewa, T. de, and G. de Saint-Foix. *Wolfgang Amadeus Mozart: 1756–1777 L'enfant prodige et le jeune maître.* Paris: Robert Laffont, 1936.

BERLIOZ

Barzun, Jacques. *Berlioz and His Century: An Introduction to the Age of Romanticism.* 1956; rpt. Chicago: University of Chicago Press, 1982.

Berlioz, Hector. *Memoirs of Hector Berlioz: From 1803 to 1865 Comprising his Travels in Germany, Italy, Russia, and England.* Rachel and Eleanor Holmes, Trans. Ernest Newman, Ed. and Rev. New York: Dover, 1960.

——. *Mémoires.* Paris: Gregg International, 1969.

——. *Symphonie Fantastique.* Orchestral Score. New York: Kalmus, n.d.

——. *Les Troyens.* Hugh Macdonald, ed. *New Edition of the Complete Works. Les Troyens.* Vols. 2a-b. Orchestral Score. Kassel: Bärenreiter, 1969.

——. *The Art of the Conductor: The Theory of his Art.* Trans. John Broadhouse. St. Clair Shores: Scholarly Press, 1970.

——. *Gluck and His Operas: With an Account of Their Relation to Musical Art.* Trans. Edwin Evans. 1915, rpt. London: William Reeves, 1972.

——. *La Prise de Troie (The Conquest of Troy).* Orchestral Score. New York: Kalmus, n.d.

——. *La Prise de Troie: Poème lyrique en trois actes et cinq tableaux. Partition Chant et Piano. Réduction de L. Narici.* New York: Classical Vocal Reprints, n.d.

——. *Les Troyens: An Opera in Five Acts for Soli, Chorus and Orchestra with French Text: Vocal Score.* New York: Kalmus, 06106, n.d.

——. *Les Troyens à Carthage.* Orchestral Score. New York: Kalmus, n.d.

——. *Les Troyens: Opera in Five Acts.* Trans. David Cairns. Metropolitan Opera Libretto. Milwaukee, Wis.: Hal Leonard (G. Schirmer), 1973.

Brook, Donald. *Five Great French Composers: Berlioz, César Frank, Saint-Saëns, Debussy, Ravel: Their Lives and Works.* 1946, rpt. Plainview: Books for Libraries, 1971.

Cairns, David. *Berlioz.* Vol. 1: *The Making of an Artist* (1803–1832). Berkeley: University of California Press, 2000.

——. Vol. 2: *Servitude and Greatness* (1832–1869). Berkeley: University of California Press, 2000.

Fulcher, Jane. *The Nation's Image: French Grand Opera as Politics and Politicized Art.* Cambridge: Cambridge University Press, 1987.

——. *French Cultural Politics & Music: From the Dreyfus Affair to the First World War* New York/Oxford: Oxford University Press, 1999.

Ganz, A.W. *Berlioz in London.* 1950, rpt. New York: Da Capo Press, 1981.

Kemp, Ian, ed. *Hector Berlioz: Les Troyens. Cambridge Opera Handbook.* Cambridge: Cambridge University Press, 1988.

Köhler, Karl-Heinz, Hugh Macdonald, and John Warrack. *Early Romantic Masters 2: Weber, Berlioz, Mendelssohn.* 1980; rpt. New York: Norton, 1985.

Ravel, Maurice. *L'enfant et les sortilèges. Poème de Colette.* Trans. K. Wolff. *Partition, Chant et Piano.* Paris: Durand, n.d.

Rushton, Julian. *The Musical Language of Berlioz.* Cambridge: Cambridge University Press, 1983.

STRAUSS

Birkin, Kenneth. *Richard Strauss: Arabella.* New York: Cambridge University Press, 1989.

Del Mar, Norman. *Richard Strauss, A Critical Commentary on His Life and Works.* 3 vols. 1978; rpt. Ithaca, N.Y.: Cornell University Press, 1986.

Gilliam, Bryan. *Richard Strauss's Elektra.* New York: Oxford University Press, 1991.

——, ed. *Richard Strauss and his World*. Princeton, N.J.: Princeton University Press, 1992.

John, Nicholas, ed. *Richard Strauss: Salome and Elektra*. Opera Guides. London: John Calder, 1988.

Metropolitan Opera Libretto: Elektra. New York: Rullman, 1909.

Newman, Ernest. *Richard Strauss*. 1908; rpt. Freeport: Books for Libraries, 1969.

Puffett, Derrick, ed. *Richard Strauss: Salome*. New York: Cambridge University Press, 1989.

Schuh, Willi, ed. *Richard Strauss: Recollections and Reflections*. Trans. L.J. Lawrence. 1953; rpt. Westport, Conn.: Greenwood Press, 1974.

Strauss, Richard. *Salome / Elektra*. Ed. Nicholas John. London: John Calder; New York: Riverrun, 1988.

——. *Elektra: An Opera in One Act, Op. 58: Conductor's Score*. Miami, Florida: Edwin F. Kalmus, n.d.

——. *Elektra in Full Score*. New York: Dover Publications, 1990.

——. *Elektra*. Piano and Vocal Score by Carl Besl. Trans. Alfred Kalisch. New York: Boosey & Hawkes, 1943.

——. *Elektra: Tragödie in einem Aufzuge von Hugo von Hofmannsthal*. Trans. Alfred Kalisch. New York: Boosey and Hawkes, n.d.

STRAVINSKY

Andriessen, Louis, and Elmer Schönberger. *The Apollonian Clockwork on Stravinsky*. Trans. Jeff Hamburg. New York: Oxford University Press, 1989.

Auden, W.H. *The Dyer's Hand and Other Essays*. Selected by Edward Mendelson. 1948; rpt. New York: Vintage Books/Random House, 1989.

Blumenthal, Eileen, and Julie Taymor. *Julie Taymor: Playing with Fire*. New York: Harry N. Abrams, 1995.

Craft, Robert. *Stravinsky: Glimpses of a Life*. New York: St. Martin's Press, 1992.

——. *Stravinsky: Chronicle of a Friendship*. Nashville, Tenn.: Vanderbilt University Press, 1994.

Druskin, Mikhail. *Igor Stravinsky: His Personality, Works and Views*. Trans. Martin Cooper. New York: Cambridge University Press, 1983.

Griffiths, Paul. *Igor Stravinsky: The Rake's Progress*. New York: Cambridge University Press, 1982.

——. *The Master Musicians: Stravinsky*. New York: Schirmer Books, Maxwell Macmillan, 1992.

Haimo, Ethan, and Paul Johnson, eds. *Stravinsky Retrospectives*. Lincoln, Neb.: University of Nebraska Press, 1987.

Horgan, Paul. *Encounters with Stravinsky: A Personal Record*. 1972; rev. Middletown, Conn.: Wesleyan University Press, 1989.

Lampert, Vera, László Somfai, Eric Walter White, Jeremy Noble, and Ian Kemp. *The New Grove Modern Masters: Bartok, Stravinsky, Hindemith*. New York: Norton, 1984.

Mussorgsky, Modest Petrovich. *Boris Godunov: Popular Musical Drama in Four Acts with a Prologue after Pushkin and Karamzin*; Ed. and Instrumented by N.A. Rimski-Korsakov with the Scene at Vasily Blazhenny Cathedral Added. Instrumentation of the Scene by M.M. Ippolitov-Ivanov. 2 Vols. New York: Kalmus, n.d.

Nicholas, John, *Mussorgsky–Boris Godunov*. First published in Great Britain, 1982, by John Calder, Ltd., London. First published in the USA, 1982 by Riverrun, New York, N.Y. Copyright English National Opera and The Royal Opera, 1982.

Oja, Carol. J., comp. *Stravinsky in Modern Music (1924–1946)*. Foreword by Aaron Copland. New York: Da Capo, 1982.

Pasler, Jann, ed. *Confronting Stravinsky: Man, Musician, and Modernist*. Berkeley: University of California Press, 1986.

Stravinsky, Igor, and Jean Cocteau. *Oedipus Rex*. Trans. e.e. Cummings. *Réduction pour chant et piano*. 1927; rpt. and rev. New York: Boosey & Hawkes, 1949.

Stravinsky, Igor. *Igor Stravinsky: An Autobiography*. 1936; rpt. New York: Norton, 1962.

———. *Poetics of Music in the Form of Six Lessons*. 1942; rpt. Cambridge, Mass.: Harvard University Press, 1970.

———. *Oedipus Rex: Opera-Oratorio en deux actes d'après Sophocle*, Orchestral Score. Rev. London: Boosey & Hawkes, 1948.

Stravinsky, Igor, and Robert Craft. *Conversations with Igor Stravinsky*. 1958; rpt. paperback, Berkeley: University of California Press, 1980.

———. *Expositions and Developments*. 1959; rpt. paperback, Berkeley: University of California Press, 1981.

———. *Memories and Commentaries*. 1959; rpt. paperback, Berkeley: University of California Press, 1981.

———. *Oedipus Rex, The Rake's Progress*. Ed. Nicholas John. New York: Riverrun, 1991.

Verdi, Giuseppe. *Aïda*: Opera in Four Acts. Libretto by Antonio Ghislanzoni. Trans. Walter Ducloux. Milwaukee, Wis.: Hal Leonard, G. Schirmer, 1963.

Walsh, Stephen. *The Music of Stravinsky*. 1988; rpt. Oxford: Clarendon Press, 1993.

———. *Stravinsky: Oedipus Rex*. Cambridge: Cambridge University Press, 1993.

White, Eric Walter. *Stravinsky: The Composer and His Works*, 2nd ed. 1966. Berkeley: University of California Press, 1979.

GOSPEL AT COLONUS

Breuer, Lee. *The Gospel at Colonus*. New York: Theatre Communications Group, 1989.

Dizikes, John. *Opera in America: A Cultural History*. New Haven: Yale University Press, 1993.

Gilroy, Paul. *The Black Atlantic: Modernity and Double Consciousness*. Cambridge, Mass.: Harvard University Press, 1993.

Harris, James F. *Philosophy at 33 1/3 rpm: Themes of Classic Rock Music*. Chicago: Open Court, 1993.

Heilbut, Anthony. *The Gospel Sound: Good Times*. New York: Limelight Editions, 1985.

Jones, LeRoi. *Blues People: The Negro Experience in White America and the Music that Developed from It*. New York: Morrow Quill, 1963.

Rose, Tricia. *Black Noise: Rap Music and Black Culture in Contemporary America*. Hanover, N.H.: Wesleyan University Press, 1994.

Sackheim, Eric, ed. *The Blues Line: A Collection of Blues Lyrics from Leadbelly to Muddy Waters*. Hopewell, N.J.: Ecco, 1993.

Sidran, Ben. *Black Talk*. New foreword by Archie Shepp. 1971; rpt. New York: Da Capo, 1981.

Southern, Eileen. *The Music of Black Americans: A History*, 2nd ed. 1971; rpt. New York: Norton, 1983.

Tirro, Frank. *Jazz: A History*, 2nd ed. 1977; rpt. New York: Norton, 1993.

THEODORAKIS

Giannaris, George. *Mikis Theodorakis: Music and Social Change.* New York: Praeger, 1972.

Hall, Edith, Fiona MacIntosh, and Oliver Taplin, eds. *Medea in Performance: 1500–2000.* Oxford: Legenda, 2000.

Holst, Gail. *Theodorakis: Myth and Politics in Modern Greek Music.* Amsterdam: Adolf M. Hakkert, 1979.

MISCELLANEOUS

Abbate, Carolyn. *Unsung Voices: Opera and Musical Narrative in the Nineteenth Century.* Princeton, N.J.: Princeton University Press, 1991.

Abraham, Gerald. *The Concise Oxford History of Music.* New York: Oxford University Press, 1985.

Adorno, Theodor W. *Quasi una Fantasia: Essays on Modern Music.* Trans. Rodney Livingstone. 1963; rpt. New York: Verso, 1992.

Aerke, K.P. *Gods of Play: Baroque Festive Performances as Rhetorical Discourse.* Albany, N.Y.: SUNY Press, 1994.

Anderson, Warren D. *Ethos and Education in Greek Music: The Evidence of Poetry and Philosophy.* Cambridge, Mass.: Harvard University Press, 1966.

——. *Music and Musicians in Ancient Greece.* Ithaca, N.Y.: Cornell University Press, 1994.

Arblaster, Anthony. *Viva la Libertà!: Politics in Opera.* New York: Verso, 1992.

Arnold, Denis, ed. *The New Oxford Companion to Music.* Two Vol. 1983; rpt. with corr. Oxford: Oxford University Press, 1995.

Arnold, Denis, and Anthony Newcomb, eds. *The New Grove Italian Baroque Masters.* New York: Norton, 1984.

Attali, Jacques. *Noise: The Political Economy of Music.* Trans. Brian Massumi. Minneapolis: University of Minnesota Press, 1985.

Barker, Andrew, ed. *Greek Musical Writings: I–The Musician and His Art.* Cambridge: Cambridge University Press, 1989.

——, ed. *Greek Musical Writings: II–Harmonic and Acoustic Theory.* Cambridge: Cambridge University Press, 1989.

Barry, Kevin. *Language Music and the Sign: A Study in Aesthetics, Poetics and Poetic Practice from Collins to Coleridge.* 1987; rpt. Cambridge: Cambridge University Press, 1989.

Barzun, Jacques. *Critical Questions: On Music and Letters Culture and Biography 1940–1980.* Ed. and Intro. Bea Friedland. Chicago: University of Chicago Press, 1982.

Beaussant, Philippe. *Lully ou Le musicien du Soleil.* Florence: Gallimard, 1992.

Berry, Wallace. *Musical Structure and Performance.* New Haven, Conn.: Yale University Press, 1989.

Blackmer, Corrine E., and Patricia Juliana Smith, eds. *En Travesti: Women, Gender, Subversion, Opera.* New York: Columbia University Press, 1995.

Brett, Philip, Elizabeth Wood, Gary C. Thomas, eds. *Queering the Pitch: The New Gay and Lesbian Musicology.* New York: Routledge, 1994.

Brown, Calvin S. *Music and Literature: A Comparison of the Arts.* London: University Press of New England, 1987.

Burmeister, Joachim. *Musical Poetics.* Trans. and Intro. Benito V. Rivera. New Haven, Conn.: Yale University Press, 1993.

Carter, Tim. *Music in Late Renaissance & Early Baroque Italy.* Portland, Ore.: Amadeus, 1992.

Cassirer, Ernst. *The Philosophy of the Enlightenment.* Trans. Fritz C. Koelln and James P. Pettegrove. Princeton, N.J.: Princeton University Press, 1979.

Cavell, Stanley. *A Pitch of Philosophy: Autobiographical Exercises.* Cambridge, Mass.: Harvard University Press, 1994.

Citron, Marcia J. *Gender and the Musical Canon.* Cambridge: Cambridge University Press, 1993.

Cixous, Hélène, and Catherine Clément. *The Newly Born Woman.* Trans. Betsy Wing, Intro. Sandra M. Gilbert, *Theory and History of Literature,* Vol. 24. 1986; rpt. Minneapolis, London: University of Minnesota Press, 1993.

Clément, Catherine. *Opera, or the Undoing of Women.* Trans. Betsy Wing. Minneapolis: University of Minnesota Press, 1988.

Comotti, Giovanni. *Music in Greek and Roman Culture.* Trans. Rosaria V. Munson. Baltimore: Johns Hopkins University Press, 1989.

Conrad, Peter. *A Song of Love & Death: The Meaning of Opera.* London: Chatto and Windus, 1987.

Cook, Nicholas. *Music, Imagination and Culture.* Oxford: Clarendon, 1990.

Cooke, Deryck. *Vindications: Essays on Romantic Music.* Cambridge: Cambridge University Press, 1982.

——. *The Language of Music.* 1959; rpt. Oxford: Oxford University Press, 1990.

Copland, Aaron. *What to Listen for in Music.* Intro. William Schuman. New York: McGraw-Hill Book Company, 1985.

Dahlhaus, Carl. *The Idea of Absolute Music.* Trans. Roger Lustig. Chicago: University of Chicago Press, 1989.

Dean, Winton. *Essays on Opera.* Oxford: Clarendon Press, 1990.

Dellamora, Richard, and Daniel Fischlin, eds. *The Work of Opera: Genre, Nationhood, and Sexual Difference.* New York: Columbia University Press, 1997.

Donington, Robert. *The Opera.* New York: Harcourt Brace Jovanovich, 1978.

——. *Baroque Music: Style and Performance, A Handbook.* New York: Norton, 1982.

——. *The Interpretation of Early Music.* New York: Norton, 1989.

——. *Opera and its Symbols: The Unity of Words, Music, and Staging.* New Haven: Yale University Press, 1990.

Dorian, Frederick. *The History of Music in Performance: The Art of Musical Interpretation from the Renaissance to Our Day.* New York: Norton, 1942.

Downs, Philip G., ed. *Anthology of Classical Music.* New York: Norton, 1992.

Dunn, Leslie C., and Nancy A. Jones, eds. *Embodied Voices: Representing Female Vocality in Western Culture.* Cambridge: Cambridge University Press, 1994.

Edwards, Sutherland H. *History of the Opera From Monteverdi to Donizetti,* 2nd ed. 1862. Vols. 1 and 2. New York: Da Capo Press, 1977.

Ewans, Michael. *Wagner and Aeschylus: The Ring and the Oresteia.* London: Faber and Faber, 1982.

Fenik, Bernard. *Homer and the Niebelungenlied.* Cambridge, Mass.: Harvard University Press, 1986.

Gaffurio, Franchino. *The Theory of Music.* Trans. Walter Kurt Kreyszig. Ed. Claude V. Palisca. New Haven: Yale University Press, 1993.

Gerhard, Anselm. *The Urbanization of Opera: Music Theater in Paris in the Nineteenth Century*. Trans. Mary Whittall. Chicago: University of Chicago Press, 1998.

Gilbert, Sandra M. *Theory and History of Literature*, Vol. 24. 1986; rpt. Minneapolis: University of Minnesota Press, 1993.

Goehr, Lydia. *The Imaginary Museum of Musical Works: An Essay in the Philosophy of Music*. Oxford: Clarendon, 1992.

Groos, Arthur, and Roger Parker, eds. *Reading Opera*. Princeton, N.J.: Princeton University Press, 1988.

Grout, Donald J. *A Short History of Opera*, 2nd ed. New York: Columbia University Press, 1965.

——, with Claude V. Palisca. *A History of Western Music*, 3rd ed. 1960; rpt. New York: W.W. Norton, 1980.

——, and Hermine Weigel Williams. *A Short History of Opera*, 3rd ed. New York: Columbia University Press, 1988.

Hammond, Frederick. *Music and Spectacle in Baroque Rome*. New Haven, Conn.: Yale University Press, 1994.

Harewood, The Earl of, ed. and rev. *The Definitive Kobbé's Opera Book*. 1919; rpt. with rev. New York: G.P. Putnam's Sons, 1987.

Headington, Christopher, Roy Westbrook, and Terry Barfoot. *Opera—A History*. London: Arrow Books, 1987.

Hermand, Jost, and Michael Gilbert, eds. *German Essays on Music: Theodor W. Adorno, Ernst Bloch, Thomas Mann, and Others*. New York: Continuum, 1994.

Hindley, Geoffrey, ed. *Larousse Encyclopedia of Music*. Intro. Antony Hopkins. New York: Crescent Books, 1971.

Hollander, John. *The Untuning of the Sky: Ideas of Music in English Poetry 1500–1700*. 1961; rpt. Hamden, Conn.: Archon Book—Shoe String Press, 1993.

Howard, Patricia, ed. *C.W. von Gluck: Orfeo*. New York: Cambridge University Press, 1981.

Hutcheon, Linda, and Michael Hutcheon. *Opera: Desires, Disease, Death*. Lincoln, Neb.: University of Nebraska Press, 1996.

Jahn, Otto. *Gesammelte Aufsätze Über Musik*. 1866; rpt. Westmead, England: Gregg International Publishers, 1969.

Jauss, Hans Robert. *Toward an Aesthetic of Reception*. Timothy Bahti, Trans. *Theory and History of Literature*, Vol. 2. Minneapolis: University of Minnesota Press, 1982.

Kamien, Roger, ed. *The Norton Scores: An Anthology for Listening*. 4th ed. Vol. 1. New York: Norton, 1984.

Kennedy, Michael. *The Concise Oxford Dictionary of Music*, 3rd ed. New York: Oxford University Press, 1980.

Kerman, Joseph. *Contemplating Music: Challenges to Musicology*. Cambridge: Harvard University Press, 1985.

——. *Opera as Drama*. 1956; New and Rev. ed. Berkeley: University of California Press, 1988.

Knapp, J. Merril. *The Magic of Opera*. New York: Da Capo Press, 1984.

Koestenbaum, Wayne. *The Queen's Throat: Opera, Homosexuality, and the Mystery of Desire*. New York: Poseidon Press, 1993.

Kramer, Lawrence. *Music as Cultural Practice, 1800–1900*. Berkeley: University of California Press, 1990.

Krausz, Michael, ed. and int. *The Interpretation of Music: Philosophical Essays*. Oxford: Oxford University Press, 1993.

Krehbiel, Henry Edward. *Chapters of Opera: Being Historical & Critical Observations & Records Concerning the Lyric Drama in New York from its Earliest Days Down to the Present Time.* New York: Henry Holt and Company, 1908.

Lee, M. Owen. *First Intermissions: Twenty-one Great Operas Explored, Explained and Brought to Life from the Met.* New York: Oxford University Press, 1995.

Leppert, Richard, and Susan McClary, eds. *Music and Society: The Politics of Composition, Performance and Reception.* 1987; rpt. Cambridge: Cambridge University Press, 1992.

Levin, David J., ed. *Opera Through Other Eyes.* Stanford, Calif.: Stanford University Press, 1994.

Levine, Robert, and Elizabeth Lutyens. *Opera Small Talk.* Concord, Mass.: Cherubino Press, 1993.

Lindenberger, Herbert. *Opera: The Extravagant Art.* Ithaca, N.Y.: Cornell University Press, 1984.

——. *Opera in History: From Monteverdi to Cage.* Stanford, Calif.: Stanford University Press, 1998.

Maas, Martha, and Jane McIntosh Snyder. *Stringed Intruments of Ancient Greece.* New Haven: Yale University Press, 1989.

McClary, Susan. *Feminine Endings: Music, Gender, and Sexuality.* Minneapolis: University of Minnesota Press, 1991.

Martens, Frederick H. *A Thousand and One Nights of Opera.* New York: D. Appleton and Company, 1926.

Marvall, José Antonio. *La Cultura del Barroco.* 1975. Rpt. *Culture of the Baroque, Analysis of a Historical Structure.* Trans. Terry Cochran. Vol. 25. *Theory and History of Literature.* Minneapolis: University of Minnesota Press, 1986.

Mondadori, Arnoldo, ed. *The Simon and Schuster Book of the Opera: A Complete Reference Guide: 1597 to the Present.* 1977; rpt. New York: Fireside Book, 1985.

Mordden, Ethan. *Opera Anecdotes.* New York: Oxford University Press, 1985.

Newman, Ernest. *Gluck and the Opera: A Study in Musical History.* 1895; rpt. New York: AMS Press, 1978.

——. *Musical Studies.* 1905; rpt. New York: Haskell House, 1969.

O'Grady, Deirdre. *The Last Troubadours: Poetic Drama in Italian Opera 1597–1887.* New York: Routledge, 1991.

Orgell, Stephen. *The Jonsonian Masque.* New York: Columbia University Press, 1981.

Palisca, Claude V. *Baroque Music,* 3rd ed. 1968; rpt. Englewood Cliffs, N.J.: Prentice-Hall, 1991.

——. *Humanism in Italian Renaissance Musical Thought.* New Haven, Conn.: Yale University Press, 1985.

Picerno, Vincent J. *Dictionary of Musical Terms.* Brooklyn: Haskell House Publishers, 1976.

Plaut, Erica A. *Grand Opera: Mirror of the Western Mind.* Chicago: Ivan R. Dee, 1993.

Playford, John. *An Introduction to the Skill of Musick.* Ed. Henry Purcell. Intro. Franklin B. Zimmerman. 12th ed. New York: Da Capo, 1972.

Pleasants, Henry. *Opera in Crisis: Tradition, Present, Future.* London: Thames and Hudson, 1989.

Poizat, Michel. *The Angel's Cry: Beyond the Pleasure Principle in Opera.* Ithaca, N.Y.: Cornell University Press, 1992.

Prout, Ebenezer. *Double Counterpoint and Canon.* New York: Haskell House Publishers, 1963.

Quint, David, Margaret Ferguson, and G.W. Pigman III, eds. *Creative Imitation: New Essays on Renaissance Literature in Honor of Thomas M. Greene.* Vol. 95. Binghamton, N.Y.: Medieval and Renaissance Texts and Studies, 1992.

Rahn, John. ed. *Perspectives on Musical Aesthetics.* New York: Norton, 1994.

Remnant, Mary. *Musical Instruments: An Illustrated History from Antiquity to the Present.* Portland: Amadeus Press, 1989.

Robinson, Paul. *Opera & Ideas: From Mozart to Strauss.* 1985; rpt. Ithaca, N.Y.: Cornell University Press, 1987.

Rosen, Charles. *The Classical Style: Haydn, Mozart, Beethoven.* 1971; rpt. New York: W.W. Norton, 1972.

Rosenthal, Harold, and John Warrack. *The Concise Oxford Dictionary of Opera*, 2nd ed. New York: Oxford University Press, 1990.

Rowell, Lewis. *Thinking About Music: An Introduction to the Philosophy of Music.* Amherst: University of Massachusetts Press, 1983.

Rushton, Julian. *Classical Music: A Concise History from Gluck to Beethoven.* New York: Thames and Hudson, 1986.

Sadie, Stanley, ed. *History of Opera.* New York: Norton, 1990.

——, ed. *The New Grove Dictionary of Opera.* 4 Volumes. New York: R.R. Donnelley & Co., 1992.

Sadie, Stanley, and Alison Latham. eds. *The Norton/Grove Concise Encyclopedia of Music.* New York: Norton, 1988.

Said, Edward W. *Orientalism.* 1978; rpt. New York: Vintage, 1979.

——. *Musical Elaborations.* New York: Columbia University Press, 1991.

Schmidgall, Gary. *Shakespeare and Opera.* New York: Oxford University Press, 1990.

Schonberg, Harold C. *The Lives of the Great Composers.* New York: Norton, 1981.

Shepherd, John. *Music as Social Text.* Cambridge: Polity, 1991.

Simon, Henry W. *100 Great Operas and Their Stories.* New York: Doubleday, 1960.

Smart, Mary Ann. *Siren Songs: Representations of Gender and Sexuality in Opera.* Princeton, N.J.: Princeton University Press, 2000.

Solie, Ruth A., ed. *Musicology and Difference: Gender and Sexuality in Music Scholarship.* Los Angeles: University of California Press, 1993.

Sontag, Susan. *Illness as Metaphor.* New York: Farrar, Straus and Giroux, 1978.

——. *AIDS and Its Metaphors.* New York: Farrar, Straus and Giroux, 1988.

Sternfeld, F.W. *The Birth of Opera.* 1993; rpt. Oxford: Clarendon Press, 1994.

Stockdale, F.M., and M.R. Dreyer. *The International Opera Guide.* North Pomfret: Trafalgar Square Publishing, 1990.

Stroff, Stephen M. *Opera: An Informal Guide.* Chicago: A Cappella Books, 1992.

Strunk, Oliver, ed. *Source Readings in Music History: From Classical Antiquity Through the Romantic Era.* New York: Norton, 1950.

Subotnik, Rose Rosengard. *Developing Variations: Style and Ideology in Western Music.* Minneapolis: University of Minnesota Press, 1991.

Sypher, Wylie. *Four States of Renaissance Style: Transformations in Art and Literature 1400–1700.* 1955; rpt. Gloucester: Doubleday, 1978.

Tomlinson, Gary. *Music in Renaissance Magic: Toward a Historiography of Others.* Chicago: University of Chicago Press, 1993.

Wallace, Robert W., and Bonnie MacLachlan, eds. *Harmonia Mundi: Musica e filosofia nell' antichità.* Rome: Edizioni dell'Ateneo, 1991.

Warrack, John, and Ewan West. *The Oxford Dictionary of Opera.* London, New York: Oxford University Press, 1992.

Weaver, WIlliam. *The Golden Century of Italian Opera from Rossini to Puccini.* New York: Thames and Hudson, 1980.

West, M.L. *Ancient Greek Music.* Oxford: Clarendon Press, 1992.

Wölfflin, Heinrich. *Principles of Art History: The Problem of the Development of Style in Later Art.* Trans. M.D. Hottinger. New York: Dover, 1950.

——. *Renaissance and Baroque.* Trans. Kathrin Simon. Intro. Peter Murray. 1966; rpt.; Ithaca, N.Y.: Cornell University Press, 1990.

Zietz, Karyl L. *Opera! The Guide to Western Europe's Great Houses.* Santa Fe, N.M.: John Muir Publications, 1991.

Partial List of Operas
and Demi-Operas Based on Classics,
Including Historical Topics

Giulio Caccini (1551–1618) (b. Rome or ?Tivoli, Italy)
Il rapimento di Cefalo (1601–1602)
Euridice (1600–1601)

Jacopo Peri (1561–1633) (b. Rome or Florence, Italy)
Dafne (1597–1598)
Euridice (1600)
Le nozze di Peleo e Tetide (unperf.)
Adone (unperf.)
Iole ed Ercole (unperf.)

Claudio Monteverdi (1567–1643) (b. Cremona, Italy)
Orfeo (1607)
Arianna (1608: lost except for lament)
La nozze di Tetide (1617: lost)
Andromeda (1620: lost)
Mercurio e Marte (1630: lost)
Proserpina rapita: anatopismo (1630: lost except for one trio)
Lamento della Ninfa (1638)
Il ritorno d'Ulisse in patria (1640)
La nozze d'Enea con Lavinia (1641) (lost)
L'incoronazione di Poppea (1642)

Agostino Agazzari (?1579–1642) (b. Siena, Italy)
Eumelio (1606)

Marco da Gagliano (1582–1643) (b. Florence, Italy)
La Dafne (1608)

Heinrich Schütz (1585–1672) (b. Kostritz, Germany)
Dafne (1627)
Zwo Comoedien (1935: two musical dramas, one about Orithyia and the other about the harpies and Phineus)
Orpheo und Euridice (1638)

Stefano Landi (bap. 1587–1639) (b. Rome, Italy)
La morte d'Orfeo (1619)

Domenico Mazzocchi (1592–1665) (b. Civita Castellana, Italy)
La catena d'Adone (1626)

Francesca Manelli (c.1595–1667) (b. Tivoli, Italy)
Andromeda (1637)
La Delia, o sia la sera sposa del sole (1639)
L'Adone (1639)
Il ratto d'Europa (1653)
La Filo, overo Giunone repacificata con Ercole (1660)

Luigi Rossi (?1597–1653) (b. Torrenaggiore, Italy)
Orfeo (1647)

Giovanni Felice Sances (c.1600–1679) (b. Rome, Italy)
Ermiona (1636)
Mercurio esploratore (1662)
Apollo deluso (1669)
Aristomene Messenio (1670)

Francesco Cavalli (1602–1676) (b. Crema, Italy)
Le nozze di Teti e di Peleo (1639)
Gli amori d'Apollo e di Dafne (1640)
Didone (1641)
Egisto (1643)
Doriclea (1645)
Titone (1645)
Giasone (1648)
Euripo (1649)
Oristeo (1651)
Calisto (1651)
Orione (1653)
Ciro (1653)
Xerse (1654)
Statira principessa di Persia (1655)
Erismena (1655)
Artemisia (1656)
Hipermestra (1658)
Antioco (1658)
Elena (1659)
Ercole amante (1662)
Scipione affricano (1664)
Mutio Scevola (1665)

Pompeo magno (1666)
Eliogabolo (1668)
Coriolano (1669)
Narciso et Ecco immortalati (1642)
Deidamia (1644)
Il Romolo e l'Remo (1645)
La prosperità di Giulio Cesare Dittatore (1656)
Helena rapita da Theseo (1653)
La pazzia in trono, overo Caligola delirante (1660)

Benedetto Ferrari (1603/4–1681) (b. Reggio Emilia, Italy)
Il pastor regio (1939)
La ninfa avara (1641)
Egisto (1651)
Enone abbandonata (1651)
Gli amori di Alessandro Magno, e di Rossane (1656)

Antonio Bertali (1605–1669) (b. Verona, Italy)
Theti (1656)
Gli amori d'Apollo con Clizia (1661)
Il Ciro crescente (1661)

Francesco Sacrati (1605–1660) (b. Parma, Italy)
La Finta pazza (1641)
Il Bellerophonte (1642)
Venere gelosa (1643)
L'Ulisse errante (1644)

Juan Hidalgo (1614–1685) (b. Madrid, Spain)
Fortunas de Androméda y Perseo (1653; attributed)
Celos aun del aire matan (1659: Cephalus and Procris)
La estatua de Prometeo (1670 or 1674)
Los Celos hacen estrellas (1672)
Los juegos Olímpico (1673)
Alfeo y Aretusa (?1674)
Endimión y Diana (1675)
Icaro y Dédalo (1684)
Apolo y Leucotea (1684)

Pietro Andrea Ziani (1616–1684) (b. Venice, Italy)
La guerriera spartana (1654)
Eupatra (1655)
La fortune di Rodope e Damira (1657)
L'incostanza trionfante, ovvero Il Theseo (1658)
L'Antigona delusa da Alceste (1660)
Annibale in Capua (1661)
Gli scherzi di Fortuna subordinato al Pirro (1662)
La fatiche d'Ercole per Deianira (1679)
Circe (1665)
Galatea (1667)
Ippolita reina della amazzoni (1670)

Heraclio (1671)
Attila (1672)
Candaule (1679)
Enea in Cartagine (1680)

Andrea Mattioli (c.1620–1679) (b. Faenza, Italy)
Il ratto di Cefalo (1650)
L'Antiopa (1653)
La Didone (1656)
La Filli di Tracia (1664)
Perseo (1665)

Matthew Locke (c.1622–1677) (b. Devon, England)
Cupid and Death (1653: Score for Jame's Shirley's masque)
Psyche (1675: Semi-opera)

Francesco Cirillo (1623–after 1667) (b. Grumo Nevano, Italy)
Orontea, regina d'Egitto (1654)
Il ratto d'Elena (1655)
Orontea (1656)

Jacopo Melani (1623–1676) (b. Pistoia, Italy)
Scipione in Cartagine (1657)
Ercole in Tebe (1661)
Il ritorno d'Ulisse (1669)
Enea in Italia (1670)

Antonio Cesti (bap. 1623–1669) (b. Arezzo, Italy)
Alessandro vincitor di se stesso (1651)
Il Cesare amante (1651–1652)
L'Argia (1655)
Orontea (1656)
La Dori (1657)
La magnanimità d'Alessandro (1662)
Il Tito (1666)
Nettuno e Flora (1666)
La Semirami (1667)
Il pomo d'oro (1668)

Giuseppe Tricarico (1623–1697) (b. Gallipoli, Italy)
L'Endimione (1655)
La generosità d'Alessandro (1662)
L'Edmiro creduto Uranio (1670)

Marco Giuseppe Peranda (c.1625–1675) (b. Rome or Macerata, Italy)
Dafne (1671)
Jupiter und Io (1673)

Giovanni Andrea Bontempi (1625–1705) (b. Perugia, Italy)
Il Paride (1662)
Dafne (1671)
Jupiter und Io (1673)

Wolfgang Carl Briegel (1626–1712) (b. Königsberg, Germany)
Das verbesserte Parisurteil (1674)
L'enchantement de Medée (1688)

Francesco Provenzale (c.1626–1704) (b. Naples, Italy)
Il Ciro (1653)
Xerse (1657)
Artemisia (?1658)
Il Theseo (1658)

Giovanni Legrenzi (bap. 1626–1690) (b. Clusone, Italy)
Achille in Sciro (1663)
Eteocle e Polinice (1675)
Adone in Cipro (1676)
Germanico sul Reno (1676)
Antioco il grande (1681)
Creso (1681)
Pausania (1681)
Lisimaco riamato de Alessandro (1682)
Ottaviano Cesare Augusto (1682)
I due cesari (1683)
Publio Elio Pertinace (1684)
Ifianassa e Melampo (1685)

Robert Cambert (c.1628–1677) (b. Paris, France)
Pomone (1671)
Ariane, ou Le mariage de Bacchus (1674)

Francesco Lucio (c.1628–1658) (b. Venice, Italy)
L'Orontea (1649)
Gl'amori di Alessandro Magno e di Rossane (1651)
Pericle effeminato (1653)
L'Euridamante (1654)

Domenico Freschi (c.1630–1710) (b. Bassano del Grappa, Italy)
Iphide greca (1671)
Helena rapita de Paride (1677)
Tullia superba (1678/9)
Sardanapalo (1679)
La Circe (1679/80)
Berenice vendicativa (1680)
Pompeo Magno in Cilicia (1681)
Olimpia vendicata (1681)
Giulio Cesare trionfante (1682)
Silla (1683)
L'incoronatione di Dario (1684)
Teseo trà le rivali (1685)

Antonio Sartorio (1630–1680) (b. Venice, Italy)
Gl'amori infruttuosi di Pirro (1661)
Il Seleuco (1666)

La prosperità di Elio Seiano (1667)
La caduta di Elio Seiano (1667)
L'Orfeo (1672)
Massenzio (1673)
Alcina (1674–1675, imperf.)
Giulio Cesare in Egitto (1676)
Antonino e Pompeiano (1677)
L'Anacreonte tiranno (1677)
Ercole sul Termodonte (1678)

Jean-Baptiste Lully (1632–1687) (Giovanni Battista Lulli, b. Rome, Italy)
Les fêtes de l'Amour et de Bacchus (1672)
Cadmus et Hermione (1673)
Alceste, ou Le triomphe d'Alcide (1674)
Thésée (1675)
Atys (1676)
Isis (1677)
Psyché (1678)
Bellérophon (1679)
Proserpine (1680
Persée (1682)
Phaëton (1683)
Acis et Galatée (1686)
Achille et Polyxène (1687)

Marc-Antoine Charpentier (1634–1704) (b. Paris, France)
Les Amours d'Acis et de Galatée (1678)
Orphée descendant aux enfers (1683)
Actéon (1683–1685)
Actéon changé en biche (1684–1685)
La descente d'Orphée aux enfers (1685–1686)
Médée (1693)
Philomèle (?1694)
Apothéose de Laodamus à la memoire de M le Maréchal duc de Luxembourg (1695–
       1696: divertissement)

Carlo Grossi (c.1634–1688) (b. Vicenza, Italy)
Artaxerse, ovvero L'Ormondo costante (1669)
Nicomede in Bitinia (1677)

Antonio Draghi (c.1634–1700) (b. Rimini, Italy)
Achille riconosciuto (1668)
Il Ciro vendicatore de se stresso (1668)
Achille in Sciro (1669)
Il Perseo (1669)
Atalanta (1669)
Le risa di Democrito (1670)
Leonida in Tegea (1670)
Iphide Greca (1670)
Penelope (1670)
L'avidità di Mida (1671)

La prosperità do Elia Sejano (1671)
Gl'atomi d'Epicuro (1672)
Sulpitia (1672)
La Tessalonica (1673)
La lanterna di Diogene (1674)
Il ratto delle Sabine (1674)
Il trionfatore de' centauri (1674)
Il fuoco eterno custodito dalle Vestali (1674)
La nascita di Minerva (1674)
I pazzi Abderiti (1675)
Pirro (1675)
Zaleuco (1675)
Turia Lucretia (1675)
Hercole acquisatore dell'immortalità (1677)
Il silentio di Harpocrate (1677)
Adriano sul Monte Casio (1677)
La conquista del vello d'oro (1678)
Leucippe Phestia (1678)
Il templo di Diana in Taurica (1678)
La monarchia latina trionfante (1678)
Enea in Italia (1678)
Curzio (1679)
I vaticini di Tiresia Tebano (1680)
La patienza di Socrate con due mogli (1680)
Temistocle in Persia (1681)
Achille in Tessaglia (1681)
L'albero del ramo d'oro (1681)
Il tempio di Apollo in Delfo (1682)
La chimera (1682)
Il tempio d'Apollo in Delfo (1682)
La lira d'Orfeo (1683)
Tullio Hostilio (1684)
Il Palladio in Roma (1685)
Le ninfe ritrose (1686)
Il ritorno di Teseo dal labirinto di Creta (1686)
La grotta di Vulcano (1686)
Pigmaleone in Cipro (1689)
Il Telemaco (1689)
La regina de' volsci (1690)
Scipione preservatore di Roma (1690)
La chioma di Berenice (1690)
Il pellegrinaggio delle Gratie all'Oracolo Dodoneo (1691)
L'attioni fortunate di Perseo (1691)
La varietá di fortuna in Lucio Iunio Bruto, l'autore della libertá romana (1692)
Il vincitor magnanimo Tito Quintio Flaminio (1692)
I'imprese dell'Achille di Roma (1693)
Pelopida Tebano in Tessaglia (1694)
L'industrie amorose in Filli di Tracia (1695)
La finta cecitá do Antioco il grande (1695)

La magnanimità di Marco Fabrizio (1695)
Timone misantropo (1696)
L'Arsace (1698)
Il delizioso ritiro di Lucullo (1698)
L'Alceste (1700)

Pietro Simone Agostini (1635–1680) (b. Forlì, Italy)
Ippolita reina delle amazzoni (1670)
Eliogabalo (1670)
Il ratto delle Sabine (1680)

Bernardo Pasquini (1637–1710) (b. Massa Valdinievole, Italy)
La Tessalonica (1683)
L'Arianna (1685)
Il silentio d'Arpocrate (1686)
I giochi Troiani (1688)
La caduta del regno dell'Amazzoni (1690)

Giovanni Paolo Colonna (1637–1695) (b. Bologna, Italy)
La contese di Pallade e Venere sopra il bando d'Amore (1666)
Pelope e Ippodamia (1678)
Amilcare di Cipro (1692)

Giovanni Maria Pagliardi (1637–1702) (b. Genoa, Italy)
Caligula delirante (1672)
Lisimaco (1673)
Il Numa Pompilio (1674)
Il tiranno di Colco (1687)
Il Greco in Troia (1689)
Attilio Regolo (1693)

Giovanni Buonaventura Viviani (1638–after 1692) (b. Florence, Italy)
Astiage (1682)
Scipione affricano (1678)
Mitilene, regina delle Amazoni (1681)

Alessandro Stradella (1639–1682) (b. Nepi, Italy)
Il Girello (1668)
Dormi, Titone, addio (1671)
Aita, numi, aita (1672)

Alessandro Melani (1639–1703) (b. Pistoia, Italy)
Il trionfo della continenza considerato in Scipione Africano (1677)

Giovanni Antonio Boretti (c.1640–1672) (b. Rome, Italy)
La Zenobia (1666)
Eliogabolo (1667)
Alessandro amante (1667)
Ercole in Tebe (1670)
Marcello in Siracusa (1670)
Dario in Babylonia (1671)

Claudio Cesare (1672)
Domitiano (1672)

Nicolaus Adam Strungk (1640–1700) (bap. Brunswick, Germany)
Alceste (1680)
Theseus (1683)
Antiope (1689)
Alceste (1693)
Nero (1693)
Syrinx (1694)

Carlo Pallavicino (c.1640–1688) (b. Salò, Italy)
Demetrio (1666)
Aureliano (1666)
Diocleziano (1674)
Enea in Italia (1675)
Galieno (1675)
Vespasiano (1678)
Nerone (1679)
Le amazone nell'isole fortunate (1679)
Messalina (1679)
Licinio imperatore (1683)
Ricimero re de' vandali (1683)
Penelope la casta (1685)
Didone delirante (1686)
L'amazone corsara, ovvero L'Avilda regina de' Goti (1686)
Antiope (1689)

Johann Wolfgang Franck (1644–c.1710) (b. Unterschwaningen, Germany)
Der errettete Unschuld, oder Andromeda und Perseus (1675)
Der verliebte Phöbus (1678)
Die Drey Töchter des Cecrops (1686)
Aeneas der trojanischen Fürsten Ankunft in Italien (1680)
Alceste (1680)
Hannibal (1681)
Semele (1681)
Vespasianus (1681)
Attila (1682)
Diocletianus (1682)
Semiramis (1683)

Tomás de Torrejón y Velasco (1644–1728) (b. ?Villarrobledo, nr Albacete, Spain)
La púrpura de la Rosa (1701: Venus and Adonis)

Johann Lohner (1645–1705) (b. Nüremberg, Germany)
Der gerechte Zaleukus (1687)
Theseus (1688)

Carlo Ambrogio Lonati (c.1645–c.1710/15) (b. Milan, Italy)
Enea in Italia (1686)
I due germani rivali (1686)

Scipione Africano (1692)
L'Aiace (1694)
Music in *Tullio Ostilio* (1694)

Giovanni Maria Capelli (1648–1726) (b. Parma, Italy)
Giulio Flavio Crispo (1722)
Mitridate (1723)

Antonio Giannettini (1648–1721) (b. Fano, Italy)
Medea in Atene (1675)
L'Aurora in Atene (1678)
Temistocle in bando (1682)
L'Ermione racquistata (1686)
L'ingresso alla gioventù di Claudio Nerone (1692)
Tito Manlio (1701)
Artaserse (1705)

Joseph-François Salomon (1649–1732) (b. Toulon, France)
Médée et Jason (1713)
Metamorphoses (1713)
Théonoé (1715)

Pascal Collasse (1649–1709) (b. Reims, France)
Achille et Polyxène (1687)
Thétis et Pélée (1689)
Enée et Lavinie (1690)
Astrée (1692)
Jason, ou La toison d'or (1696)
La naissance de Vénus (1696)
Canente (1700: Picus et Canente)
L'Amour et l'Hymen (1701)
Polyxène et Pyrrhus (1706)

Giuseppe Antonio Bernabei (?1649–1732) (b. Rome, Italy)
Enea in Italia (1679)
Giulio Cesare ricovrato all'ombra (1680)
L'Ermione (1680)
L'Ascanio in Alba (1686)
Diana amante (1688)
Il trionfo d'Imeneo (1688)
L'Eraclio (1690)

John Blow (1649–1708) (b. Newark, England)
Venus and Adonis (c.1683)

Theobaldo di Gatti (c.1650–1727) (b. ?Florence, Italy)
Scylla (1701)

Johann Georg Conradi (?–1699) (b. ?, Germany)
Die schöne und getreue Ariadne (1691)
Der wunderbar-vergnugte Pygmalion (1693)

Bernardo Sabadini (?–1718) (b. ?Venice, Italy)
Furio Camillo (1686)
Zenone il tiranno (1687)
Olimpia placata (1687)
L'Ercole trionfante (1688)
Teseo in Atene (1688)
Hierone tiranno di Siracusa (1688)
Teodora clemente (1689)
Il Vespasiano (1689)
Pompeo continente (1690)
Diomede punito da Alcide (1691)
La pace fra Tolomeo e Seleuco (1691)
Circe abbandonata da Ulisse (1692)
Talestri inamorata d'Alessandro Magno (1693)
Demetrio tiranno (1694)
Furio Camillo (1697)
L'Aiace (1697)
A'Alarico (1698)
Il Domizio (1698)
L'Eraclea (1700)
Il Meleagro (1705)
Alessandro amante eroe (1706)
Annibale (1706)

Paolo Magni (c.1650–1737) (b. Milan, Italy)
Enea in Italia (1686)
Scipione africano (1692)
Endimione (1692)
L'Aiace (1694)
L'Amfione (1697)
Cleopatra regnante (1700)
Admeto re di Tessaglia (1702)
L'Agrippina (1703)
Il Meleagro (1705)
Tito Manlio (1710)

Petronio Franceschini (1650–1680) (b. Bologna, Italy)
L'Oronte di Menfi (1676)
Arsinoe (1676)
Apollo in Tessaglia (1679)
Dionisio (1681)

Theobaldo di Gatti (c.1650–1727) (b. ?Florence, Italy)
Scylla (1701)

Giuseppe Felice Tosi (fl. 1677–1693) (b. Bologna, Italy)
Atide (1679)
Traiano (1684)
Il Giunio Bruto (1686)
Orazio (1688)
Amulio e Nimitore (1689)

L'incoronazione di Serse (1690)
Pirro e Demetrio (1690)

Pietro Torri (c.1650–1737) (b. Peschiera, Italy)
Enone (1705)
L'innocenza difesa dai numi (1715: Ismene)
Astianatte (1716: Andromache)
La Merope (1719)
Eumene (1720)
Lucio Vero (1720)
L'Epaminonda (1727)
Edippo (1729)
L'Ippolito (1731)
Ciro (1733)
Catone in Utica (1736)

Johann Philipp Förtsch (1652–1732) (b. Wertheim am Main, Germany)
Croesus (1684)
Alexander in Sidon (1688)
Xerxes in Abydos (1689)
Ancile Romanum (1690)
Die gross mächtige Thalestris, oder *Letzte Königin der Amazonen* (1690)

Carlo Francesco Pollarolo (c.1653–1723) (b. ?, Italy)
Venere travestita (1678)
Enea in Italia (1686)
Alacico, re de Gotti (1689)
Antonino e Pompeo (1689)
La pace fra Tolobeo e Seleuco (1691)
Marc'Antonio (1692)
Onorio in Roma (1693)
Ottone (1694)
Ercole in cielo (1696)
Gli Inganni felici (1696)
Tito Manlio (1696)
La clemenza d'Augusto (1697)
L'Oreste in Sparta (1697)
Circe abbandonata di Ulisse (1697)
Marzio Coriolano (1698)
L'Ulisse sconosciuto (1698)
Il repudio d'Ottavia (1699)
Il giudizio di Paride (1699)
Lucio Vero (1700)
L'inganno di Chirone (1700)
Catone Uticenze (1701)
Ascanio (1702)
L'eroico amore (1704: Alcibiades)
Il giorno di notte (1704: Noris)
Il Dafni (1705)
Filippo, re della Grecia (1706)

Publio Cornelio Scipione (1712)
Peribea in Salamina (1712)
Eraclio (1712)
Giulio Cesare nell'Egitto (1713)
Semiramide (1714)
Tetide in Sciro (1715)
L'Arminio (1722)

Marc'Antonio Ziani (c.1653–1715) (b. Venice, Italy)
La sciava fortunata (1674)
Leonida in Tegea (1676)
Alessandro Magno in Sidone (1679, rev. 1683)
Alcibiade (1680)
Tullo Ostilio (1685)
L'inganno regnante, ovvero L'Atanaglilda, regina di Gottia (1687)
Creonte (1690)
L'amante eroe (1695: Alexander)
La finta pazzia d'Ulisse (1696)
Domizio (1696)
La ninfa bizarra (1697)
Eumene (1697)
Egisto re di Cipro (1698)
Temistocle (1701)
Gli ossequi della notte (*Cupeda*) (1701)
Romolo (1702)
Esopo (1703)
Caio Popilio (1704)
Ercole vincitor dell'Invidia (1706)
Flora (1706)
Meleagro (1706)
Atenaide (1714)
Andromeda (1714)

Agostino Steffani (1654–1728) (b. Castelfranco, Italy)
Marco Aurelio (1681)
Solone (1685)
Alarica il Baltha (1687)
Servio Tullio (1686)
Niobe, regina di Tebe (1688)
La lotta d'Hercole con Acheloo (1689)
La superbia d'Alessandro (1690)
Il Turno (1693–1697)
Baccanali (1695)
Arminio (1707)

Giovanni Porta (c.1655–1755) (b. Venice, Italy)
Numitore (1720)
L'Arianna nell'isola di Nasso (1723)
Antigone (1724)
La caduta de' Decemviri (1724)

Agide re di Sparta (1725)
Ulisse (1725)
Siroe re di Persia (1726)
Il trionfo di Flavio Olibrio (1726)
Doriclea ripudiata da Creso (1729)
Lucio Papirio dittatore (1732)
L'Issipile (1732)
La Semiramide (1733)
Adriano in Siria (1737)
Ifigenia in Aulide (1738)
Der Traum des Scipio (1744)

Pietro Porfirii (fl. 1687–1709) (b. Italy)
Zenocrate ambasciatore a'Macedoni (1687)
Il Vespasiano (1692)
L'Isifile amazzone di Lenno (1697)
La Leucippe (1709)

Marin Marais (1656–1728) (b. Paris, France)
Alcide (1693)
Ariane et Bacchus (1696)
Alcyone (1706)
Sémélé (1709)

Philipp Heinrich Erlebach (1657–1714) (b. Essens, Germany)
Die Plejades, oder Das Siebengestirne (1697)

Michel-Richard de Lalande (1657–1726) (b. Paris, France)
Adonis (1696)

Giovanni Battista Bassani (c.1657–1716) (b. Padua, Italy)
L'amorosa Preda di Paride (1683)
Falaride, tiranno d'Agrigento (1683)
L'Alarico, rè di Goti (1685)
Vitige (1686)
Il trionfo di Venere in Ida (1688)
Il coceio Nerva (1691)

Francesco Antonio Massimiliano Pistocchi (c.1659–1726) (b. Palermo, Sicily)
Il Leandro (1679)
Il Narciso (1697)
Le risa di Democrito (1700)

Henry Purcell (?1659–1695) (b. London, England)
Dido and Aeneas (1689)
Dioclesian (1690)
Incidental Music for Plays:
Amphitryon, or *The Two Sosias* (1690)
Circe (1685)
Cleomenes, The Spartan Hero (1692)
Oedipus (1692)
Pausanias, the Betrayer of His Country (1695)

Regulus (1692)
Sophonisba, or Hannibal's Overthrow (1685?)
Theodosius, or *The Force of Love* (1680)
Timon of Athens (1694)

Francesco Ballarotti (c.1660–1712) (b.?, Italy)
Enea in Italia (1686)
Ottaviano in Sicilia (1692)
L'Aiace (1694)
Ariovisto (1699)
La caduta dei Decemviri (1699)
Esione (1699)
Alciade (1709)

Giuseppe Fabbrini (?–1708) (b. ?Siena, Italy)
Coriolano (1706)

André Campra (bap. 1660–1744) (b. Aix-en-Provence, France)
L'Europe galante (1697)
Vénus, feste galante (1698)
Hésione (1700)
Les muses (1703)
Iphigénie en Tauride (1704)
Télémaque (1704)
Alcine (1795)
Hippodamie (1708)
Idomenée (1712)
Les amours de Vénus et de Mars (1712)
Télèphe (1713)
Enée et Didon (1714)
Camille, reine des volsques (1717)
Achille at Deidamie (1735)
Les noces de Vénus (1740)

Jean-Baptiste Matho (c.1660–1746) (b. Brittany, France)
Tircis et Célimène (1687)
Coronis (1699)
Philémon et Baucis (1703)
L'hôte de Lemnos (1707)
Arion (1714)

Johann Joseph Fux (c.1660–1741) (b. Hirtenfeld, Austria)
La clemenza d'Augusto (1702)
Julo Ascanio, re d'Alba (1708)
Dafne in Lauro (1714)
Orfeo ed Euridice (1715)
Diana placata (1717)
Psiche (1720)
Le nozze di Aurora (1722)
Giunone placata (1725)

La corona d'Arianna (1726)
Enea negli Elisi (1731)

Johann Sigismund Kusser (1660–1727) (b. Pressburg, Germany)
Cleopatra (1690)
Julia (1690)
Narcissus (1692)
Andromeda (1692)
Ariadne (1692)
Jason (1692)
Porus (1694)
Der grossmütige Scipio Africanus (1694)
Pyramus und Thisbe (1694)
L'Apollon enjoué (1700, lost)

Clemente Monari (?c.1660–after 1729) (b. Bologna, Italy)
Il Muzio Scevola (1692)
L'Aretusa (1703)
L'amazone corsara (1704)
L'Atalanta (1710)
Il Pirro (1719)

Gottfried Finger (c.1660–1730) (b. ?Olomouc, Moravia)
The Virgin Prophetess, or *The Fate of Troy* (1701)

Sebastián Durón (1660–1716) (b. Brihuega, Spain)
Apolo y Dafne (no date)
Acis y Galatea (no date)

Teofile Orgiani (?–1725) (b. Vicenza, Italy)
Il Dioclete (1687)
Euridice (1712)

Alessandro Scarlatti (1660–1725) (b. Palermo, Italy)
Diana ed Endimione (c.1680–1685)
Pompeo (1683)
La Psiche, o vero Amore innamorato (1683)
Olimpia vendicata (1685)
Clearco in Negroponte (1686)
L'Amazzone corsara (1689)
La Statira (1690)
L'humanità nelle fiere, o vero il Lucullo (1691)
Gerona tiranno di Siracusa (1692)
Il Pirro e Demetrio (1694)
Nerone fatto Cesare (1695)
Massimo Puppieno (1695)
Penelope la casta (1696?)
La Didone delirante (1696)
Comodo Antonino (1696)
La caduta de' Decemviri (1697)
Anacreonte (1698)

L'Eraclea (1700)
Dafni (1700)
Laodicea e Berenice (1701)
Il pastore di Corinto (1701)
Tito Sempronio Gracco (1702)
Tiberio imperatore d'Oriente (1702)
Il Flavio Cuniberto (1702?)
Arminio (1703)
Turno Aricino (1704)
Lucio Manilio l'imperioso (1706)
Il Mitridate eupatore (1707)
Il Teodosio (1709)
Giunio Bruto, o vero La caduta dei Tarquinii (1711)
Il Ciro (1712)
Scipio nelle Spagne (1714)
Il Tigrane (1715)
Telemaco (1718)
Il Cambise (1719)
Marco Attilio Regolo (1719)

Francesco Gasparini (1661–1727) (b. Camaiore, Italy)
Bellerofonte (1690)
Aiace (1697)
Girone Tiranno di Siracusa (1700)
Tibirio imperator d'Oriente (1702)
Alarico (1705)
Antioco (1705)
Statira (1706)
Anfitrione (1707)
Flavio Anicio Olibrio (1708)
Alciade (1709)
Atenaide (1709)
Sesostri re d'Egitto (1710)
La ninfa Apollo (1710)
Merope (1712)
Eraclio (1712)
Lucio Papirio (1714)
Eumene (1714)
Amor vince l'odio, ovvero Timocrate (1715)
Ciro (1716)
Pirro (1717)
Democrito (1718)
Astianatte (1719)
Lucio Vero (1719)
Tigranes (1719)
Nino (1720)
La pace fra Seleuco e Tolomeo (1720)
Tigrena (1724)

Henry Desmarets (1661–1741) (b. Paris, France)
Endymion (1686)
Didon (1693)
Circé (1694)
Vénus et Adonis (1697)
Iphigénie en Tauride (1704)
Le temple d'Astrée (1709)
Diane et Endymion (1711: lost)
Le temple d'Astrée (1709)

Giacomo Antonio Perti (1661–1756) (b. Bologna, Italy)
Atide (1679)
Marzio Coriolano (1683)
Oreste in Argo (1685)
L'incoronazione di Dario (1686)
La Flavia (1686)
Dionisio Siracusano (1689)
Brenno in Efeso (1690)
Il Pompeo (1691)
Furio Camillo (1692)
Nerone fatto cesare (1693)
Laodicea e Berenice (1694)
Penelope la casta (1696)
Perseo (1697)
Apollo geloso (1698)
Lucio Vero (1700)
Astianatte (1701)
Berenice regina d'Egitto (1709)

Giuseppe Vignola (1662–1712) (b. Naples, Italy)
Il Tullo Ostilio (1707)

Luigi Mancia (c.?1665–after 1708) (b. ?Brescia, Italy)
Paride in Ida (1687)
Flavio Cuniberto (1696)
Tito Manlio (1698)
Partenope (1699)
Alessandro in Susa (1708)

Carlo Francesco Cesarini (1666–after 1741) (b. San Martino, Italy)
Il Clearco in Negroponte (1695)
Giunio Bruto (1711)

Jean-Féry Rebel (bap. 1666–1747) (b. Paris, France)
Ulysse (1703)

Elisabeth-Claude Jacquet de la Guerre (1666–1729) (b. Paris, France)
Céphale et Procris (1694)

Attilio Ariosti (1666–1729) (b. Bologna, Italy)
Erifile (1697)
Tito Manlio (1717)

Caio Marzio Coriolano (1723)
Il Vespasiano (1724)
Aquilio consolo (1724)
Artaserse (1724)
Dario (1725)
Lucio Vero (1727)

Antonio Lotti (1667–1740) (b. Hanover or Venice, Italy)
Sidonio (1706)
Achille placato (1707)
La ninfa Apollo (1710)
Porsenna (1713)
Polidoro (1715)
Ciro in Babilonia (1716)
Alessandro Severo (1717)
Giove in Argo (1717)
Ascanio (1718)
Teofane (1719)

Johann Christoph Pepusch (1667–1752) (b. Berlin, Germany)
Thomyris, Queen of Scythia (1709)
Venus and Adonis (1715)
Apollo and Daphne (1716)
The Death of Dido (1716)
The Prophetess, or The History of Dioclesian (1724)

Jean-Claude Gillier (1667–1737) (b. Paris, France)
Amphion (1696)
Les plaisirs de l'amour et de Bacchus (1697)
Circé (1705)
Arlequin Thétis (1713)
Arlequin défenseur d'Homère (1715)
La ceinture de Vénus (1715)
Télémaque (1715)
Le Pharaon (1717)
Le jugement de Paris (1718)
L'île des Amazones (1720)
La statue merveilleuse (1720)
Le forêt de Dodone (1721)
Arlequin Emdymion (1721)
La Pénélope moderne (1728)
Les amours de Protée (1728)

John Eccles (?1668–1735) (b. London, England)
The Judgment of Paris (1701)
Semele (not performed until 1972)

Giovanni Bononcini (1670–1747) (b. Modena, Italy)
Eraclea, ovvero Il ratto delle Sabbine (1692)
Xerse (1694)
Tullo Ostilio (1694)

Muzio Scevola (1695)
Il trionfo di Camilla (1696)
La clemenza d'Augusto (1697)
Temistocle in bando (1698)
Cefalo (1702)
Polifemo (1702)
Endimione (1706)
Etearco (1707)
Turno Aricino (1707)
Mario fuggitivo (1708)
Caio Gracco (1710)
Crispo (1721)
Muzio Scevola (1721)
Calfurnia (1724)
Astianatte (1727)
Alessandro in Sidone (1737)
Zenobia (1737)

Giuseppe Boniventi (?1670–1727) (b. Venice, Italy)
Il gran Macedone (1690)
La Partenope (1709)
Endimione (1709)
Circe delusa (1711)
Arianna abbandonata (1719)
Filippo re di Macedonia (1720)

Antonio Caldara (c.1670–1736) (b. Venice, Italy)
La Partenope (1701)
Paride sull'Ida: Gl'amori di Paride con Enone (1704)
L'Arminio (1705)
Sofonisba (1708)
L'Atenaide (1709, 1714)
Giunio Bruto, overo La caduta de' Tarquinii (1711) (unfinished)
Tito e Berenice (1714)
Caio Marzio Coriolano (1717)
Il Tiridate, overo La verità nell'inganno (1717)
Ifigenia in Aulide (1718)
Dafne (1719)
Lucio Papirio dittatore (1719)
Apollo in cielo (1720)
Psiche (1720)
Scipione nelle Spagne (1722)
Euristeo (1724)
Andromaca (1724)
Semiramide in Ascalone (1725)
L'Etarco (1726)
Imeneo (1727)
Mitridate (1728)
Enone (1729)
Caio Fabbrizio (1729)

La pazienza di Socrate con due mogli (1731)
Il Demetrio (1731)
Livia (1731)
Adriano in Siria (1732)
L'Olimpiade (1733)
Demofoonte (1733)
La clemenza di Tito (1734)
Il natale di Minerva Tritonia (1735)
Scipione Africano il maggiore (1735)
Achille in Sciro (1736)
Ciro riconosciuto (1736)
Il Temistocle (1736)

Johann Hugo von Wilderer (1670/71–1724) (b. Bavaria, Germany)
Giocasta (1696)
Quinto Fabio Massimo (1697)

Charles-Hubert Gervais (1671–1744) (b. Paris, France)
Méduse (1697)
Penthée (1705 or 1709)
Hypermnestre (1716)
Les amours de Protée (1720)

Giuseppe Antonio Vincenzo Aldrovandini (1671–1707) (b. Bologna, Italy)
Dafne (1696)
Ottaviano (1696)
Cesare in Alessandria (1699)
Le due Auguste (1700)
Semiramide (1701)
Mitridate in Sebastia (1701)
Turno Aricino (1702)
Pirro (1704)
L'incoronazione di Dario (1705)

Tomaso Giovanni Albinoni (1671–1751) (b. Venice, Italy)
Il Tigrane, re d'Armenia (1697)
Diomede punito da Alcide (1700)
La prosperità di Elio Sejano (1707)
Ciro (1710)
Lucio Vero (1713)
Eumene (1717)
Meleagro (1718)
Cleomene (1718)
Antigono, tutore di Filippo, re di Macedonia (1724)
Scipio nelle Spagne (1724)
Laodice (1724)
Didone abbandonata (1725)
Merope (1731)
Candalide (1734)
Artamene (1741)

André Cardinal Destouches (1672–1749) (b. Paris, France)
Issé (1697)
Amadis de Grèce (1699)
Marthésie, reine des Amazones (1699)
Omphale (1701)
Callirhoé (1712)
Télémaque et Calypso (1714)
Sémiramis (1718)

Francesco Mancini (1672–1737) (b. Naples, Italy)
[Lucio] Silla (1703)
Alessandro il Grande in Sidone (1706)
Hydaspes (1710)
La Semele (1711)
Artaserse, re di Persia (1713)
Alessandro Severo (1718)
Trajano (1723)
L'Oront[e]a (1729)
Alessandro nell'Indie (1732)
Demofoonte (1735)

Carlo Agostino Badia (1672–1678) (b. ?Venice, Italy)
L'amazone corsara, ovvero L'Alvida, regina de' goti (1692)
La ninfa Apollo (1692)
Bacco, vincitore dell'India (1697)
Imeneo trionfante (1699)
Il Narciso (1699)
Cupido fuggitivo da Venere e ritrovato a'piedi della Sacra Reale Maestà d'Amalia
    (1700)
Diana rappacificata con Venere e con Amore (1700)
La costanza d'Ulisse (1700)
Enea negli Elisi (1702)
L'Arianna (1702)
La Psiche (1703)
Ercole, vincitore di Gerione (1708)
Gli amori di Circe con Ulisse (1709)

Georg Caspar Schürmann (1672/3–1751) (b. Idensen, Germany)
Endimione (1700)
Telemaque (1706)
Giasone (1707)
Die schöne Psyche (1708)
Procris und Cephalus (1714)
Die Plejades, oder Das Siebengestirn (1716)
Atis, oder Der Stumme Verliebte (1717)
Porsenna (1718)
Tiridate (1718)
Ixion (1722)
Hannibal in Capua (1726)

Orpheus (1727)
Magnus Torquatus (1730)

Antonio de Literes (?1673–1747) (b. Artá, Mallorca, Spain)
Júpiter y Danae (1700)
Acis y Galatea (1708)

Reinhard Keiser (1674–1739) (b. Teuchern, Germany)
Basilius (1694)
Procris und Cephalus (1694)
Clelia (1695)
Circe, oder Des Ulysses erster Theil (1696)
Penelope, oder Des Ulysses anderer Theil (1696)
Adonis (1697)
Orpheus (1698)
Der güldene Apfel (1698)
Janus (1698)
Iphigenia (1699)
Hercules und Hebe (1699)
Die Wiederkehr der güldnen Zeit (1699)
Endymion (1700)
Psyche (1701)
Pomona (1702)
Claudius (1703)
Minerva (1703)
Octavia (1705)
Lucretia (1705)
Helena (1709)
Heliates und Olympia (1709)
Arsinoe (1713)
Aurora (1710)
Julius Caesar (1710)
Croesus (1711)
Cato (1711)
Diana (1712)
Heraclius (1712)
Artemisia (1715)
Achilles (1716)
Julia (1717)
Trajanus (1717)
Jobates und Bellerophon (1717)
Psyche (1722)
Augustus (1722)
Ulysses (1722)
Ariadne (1722)
Lucius Verus (1728)
Circe (1734)

Louis de Lacoste (c.1675–before 1753) (b. ?, France)
Philomèle (1705)
Creuse l'athénienne (1712)
Télégone (1725)
Orion (1728)
Pomone (lost)

Giuseppe Maria Orlandini (1676–1760) (b. Florence, Italy)
Artaserse (1706)
La Merope (1717)
Lucio Papirio (1717)
Antigona (1718)
Le amazone vinte da Ercole (1718)
Ifigenia in Tauride (1719)
Paride (1720)
Nerone (1721)
Nino (1722)
Alessandro severo (1723)
Berenice (1725)
Berenice (1728)
Ifigenia in Aulide (1732)
Il Temistocle (1737)
L'Olimpiade (1737)
Le nozze di Perseo e d'Andromeda (1738)

Antonio Pollarolo (1676–1746) (b. Brescia, Italy)
Demetrio e Tolomeo (1702)
Leucippo e Teonoe (1719)
Lucio Papirio dittatore (1721)
Turia Lucrezia (1726)
Sulpizia fedele (1729)

John Weldon (1676–1736) (b. Chichester, England)
The Judgment of Paris (1701)

Antonio Maria Bononcini (1677–1726) (b. Modena, Italy)
Tigrane, re d'Armenia (1710)
Sesostri, re di Egitto (1716)
La conquista del vello d'oro (1717)
Astianatte (1718)
Nino (1720)
Merope (1721)
Endimione (1721)

Nicola Fago (1677–1745) (b. Taranto, Italy)
Radamisto (1707)
La Cassandra indovina (1711)
Lo Massilo (1712)

Nicola Francesco Haym (1678–1729) (b. Rome, Italy)
Camilla (1706)
Pyrrhus and Demetrius (1711)
Etearco (1711)
Creso, re di Lidia (1714)
Lucio Vero, imperatore di Roma (1715)

Antonio Vivaldi (1678–1741) (b. Venice, Italy)
Ottone in villa (1713)
Nerone fatto Cesare (1715)
L'incoronazione di Dario (1717)
Artabano, re de' Parti (1718)
Tito Manlio (1719, 1720)
La Candace (1720)
Filippo re di Macedonia (1720)
Ercole su'l Termodonte (1723)
Ipermestra (1727)
Dorilla in Tempe (1726)
Siroe re di Persia (1727)
L'Atenaide (1728)
Argippo (1730)
Semiramide (1732)
La fida ninfa (1732)
L'Olimpiade (1734)
Catone in Utica (1737)

Manuel de Zumaya (ca. 1678–1756) (b. Mexico)
La Partenope (1711)

Johann Christian Schieferdecker (1679–1732) (b. Teuchern, Germany)
Medea (1700)

Domenico Natale Sarro (1679–1744) (b. Trani, Apulia, Italy)
Candaule re di Lidia (1706)
Il Vespasiano (1707)
Arsace (1718)
Alessandro Severo (1719)
Endimione (1721)
Lucio Vero (1722)
La Partenope (1722)
Didone abbandonata (1724)
Tito Sempronio (1725)
Siroe re di Persia (1727)
Artemisia (1731)
Berenice (1732)
Demofoonte (1735)
Achille in Sciro (1737)
Le nozze di Teti e di Peleo (1739)
Ezio (1741)
Alessandro nell'Indie (1743)

Antonio Orefice (fl.1708–1734)
La Camilla (1710)
Circe delusa (1713)
La Caligola delirante (1714)
Lo finto Armenio (1717)

Pietro Vincenzo Chiocchetti (1680–1753) (b. Lucca, Italy)
Partenope (1726)
Andromaca (1726)
?Arteserse (1730)
La clemenza di Tito (1735)
Demofoonte (1735)
Solone (1741)

Giuseppe Porsile (1680–1750) (b. Naples, Italy)
Il ritorno di Ulisse alla patria (1707)
Alceste (1718)
Spartaco (1726)
La clemenza di Cesare (1727)
Telesilla (1729)
Scipione Africano (1730)
Sesostri, re d'Egitto (1737)
Psiche (no date)

Jean-Baptiste Stuck (1680–1755) (b. ?Florence, Italy)
Méléagre (1709)
Polidore (1720)
Orion (1725)

Toussaint Bertin de la Doué (1680–1743) (b. Paris, France)
Cassandre (1706)
Diomède (1710)
Ajax (1716)
Le jugement de Paris: pastorale héroïque (1718)

Agostino Bonaventura Coletti (c.1680–1752) (b. Lucca, Italy)
Bruto e Cassio (1699)
Paride in Ida (1706)
Ifigenia (1707)
Muzio Scevola (1723)
Codro re d'Atene (1726)
Timoleonte cittadino di Corinto (1729)

Giacomo Rampini (1680–1760) (b. Padua, Italy)
Marco Attilio Regolo (1713)
Ercole sul Termodonte (1715)

Georg Philipp Telemann (1681–1767) (b. Hamburg, Germany)
Der lachende Democritus (1703)
Cajus Caligula (1704)
Adonis (1708)
Narcissus (?1701)

Mario (1709)
Jupiter und Semele (1716)
Die Satyren in Arcadien (1719)
Der geduldige Socrates (1721)
Omphale (1724)
Orpheus (1726)
Calypso (1727)
Aesopus bei Hofe (1729)

Francesco Bartolomeo Conti (1681–1732) (b. Florence, Italy)
Circe fatta saggia (1713)
Alba Cornelia (1714)
Il Ciro (1715)
Teseo in Creta (1715)
Cloris und Thyrsis (1719)
Galatea vendicata (1719)
Alessandro in Sidone (1721)
Archelao (1722)
Pallade trionfante (1722)
Creso (1723)
Penelope (1724)
Meleagro (1724)
Issipile (1732)

Johann Mattheson (1681–1764) (b. Hamburg, Germany)
Die Plejades, oder Das Sieben-Gestirne (1699)
Der edelmüthige Porsenna (1704)
Cleopatra (1704)
Le retour du siècle d'or, das ist Die Wiederkehr der güldnen Zeit (1705)

Jean-Joseph Mouret (1682–1738) (b. Avignon, France)
Les fêtes, ou Le triomphe de Thalie (1714)
Ariane (1717)
Pirithous (1723)
Les amours des dieux (1727)
Les grâces (1735)
Le temple de Gnide (1742)

Rogue Ceruti (ca. 1683–1760) (b. Lima, Peru)
El mejor escudo de Perseo (1708)

Christoph Graupner (1683–1760) (b. Kirchberg, Saxony, Germany)
Dido, Königin von Carthago (1707)
Bellerophon (1708)
Berenice und Lucilla (1710)
Telemach (1711)

Francois Bouvard (1683–1760) (b. Lyons, France)
Médus, roi des Mèdes (1702)
Cassandre (1706)
Ariane et Bacchus (1729)

Johann David Heinichen (1683–1729) (b. Krossüln, Germany)
Hercules (c.1709)
Paris und Helene (1710)
Mario (1713)
Flavio Crispo (1720)

Giuseppe Vignati (?–1768) (b.?Bologna, Italy)
Porsena (1719)
Aquilio in Siracusa (1720)
Nerone (1724)

Jean-Phillippe Rameau (1683–1764) (b. Dijon, France)
Hippolyte et Aricie (1733)
Castor et Pollux (1737)
Les Fêtes d'Hébé, ou les talens liriques (1739)
Dardanus (1739)
Les Fêtes de Polymnie (1745)
Platée (1745)
Les Fêtes de Polymnie (1745)
Le Temple de la Gloire (1745)
Les fêtes de l'Hymen et de l'Amour, ou Les Dieux d'Egypte (1747)
Pigmalion (1748)
Les Surprises de l'Amour (1748)
Naïs (1749)
Acante et Céphise, ou La sympathie (1751)
Linus (1752)
Acante et Céphise (1751)
Daphnis et Eglé (1753)
Lysis et Délie (1753)
Les sibarites (1753)
Anacréon (1754, 1757)
Abaris, ou Les Boréades (1763)
Nélée et Myrthis (1754)
Zéphyre (no date)
Io (before 1745)

George Frederick Handel (1685–1759) (b. Halle, Germany)
Nero (1705)
Agrippina (1709)
Il pastor fido (1712, with ballet *Terpsichore* 1734)
Teseo (1712)
Silla (1714)
Acis and Galatea (1718)
Muzio Scevola (1721)
Ottone, re di Germania (1723)
Giulio Cesare in Egitto (1724)
Scipione (1726)
Alessandro (1726)
Admeto, re di Tessaglia (1727)
Siroe, re di Persia (1728)

Tolomeo, re di Egitto (1728)
Partenope (1730)
Poro, re dell'Indie (1731)
Ezio (1732)
Sosarme, re di Media (1732)
Arianna in Creta (1734)
Oreste (1734)
Atalanta (1736)
Arminio (1737)
Giustino (1737)
Berenice (1737)
Alessandro Severo (1738)
Serse (1738)
Giove in Argo [*Jupiter in Argos*] (1739)
Imeneo (1740)
Deidamia (1741)
Semele (1744)
Hercules (1745)

Pietro Giuseppe Sandoni (1685–1748) (b. Bologna, Italy)
Artaserse (1709)
Olimpiade (1733)
Adriano in Siria (1734)
Issipile (1735)

Domenico Scarlatti (1685–1757) (b. Naples, Italy)
L'Ottavia ristituita al trono (1703)
Tolomeo et Alessandro, overto La corona disprezzata (1711)
Tetide in Sciro (1712)
Ifigenia in Aulide (1713)
Ifigenia in Tauri (1713)
Amor d'un ombra e gelosia d'un aura (1714: Narciso)
Berenice, regina d'Egitto (1718)

Andrea Stefano Fiorè (1686–1732) (b. Milan, Italy)
La casta Penelope (1707)
Atenaide (1709)
Ercole in cielo (1710)
Il trionfo di Camilla (1713)
Merope (1716)
Sesostri, rè d'Egitto (1717)
Il trionfo di Lucilla (1718)
Publio Cornelio Scipione (1718)
Elena (1725)
Siroe, rè di Persia (1729)

Fortunato Chelleri (c.1686–1757) (b. Parma, Italy)
Alessandro il grande (1708)
Zenobia in Palmira (1709)
Atalanta (1713)
La caccia in Etolia (1715)

Ircano innamorata (1715)
Alessandro fra gli Amazzoni (1715)
Penelope la casta (1716)
Alessandro Severo (1718)
Amalassunta, regina di Goti (1718)
Arsacide (1721)
Il Temistocle (1721)

Nicola Porpora (1686–1768) (b. Naples, Italy)
Agrippina (1708)
Flavio Anicio Olibrio (1711)
Serenata a 3 (1712: Deianeira, Iole, Ercole)
Arianna e Teseo (1714; 2nd version, 1727)
Berenice regina d'Egitto (1718)
Temistocle (1718)
Eumene (1721)
Flavio Anicio Olibrio (1722)
Imeneo (1726)
Semiramide regina dell'Assyria (1724)
Didone abbandonata (1725)
Siroe re di Persia (1727)
Ezio (1728)
Mitridate (1730)
Annibale (1731)
Germanico in Germania (1732)
Issipile (1733)
Arianna in Nasso (1733)
Enea nel Lazio (1734)
Polifemo (1735)
Ifigenia in Aulide (1735)
Mitridate (1736)
La festa d'Imeneo (1736)
Lucio Papirio (1737)
Tiridate (1740)
Giasone (1742)
Statira (1742)
Partenope (1742)
Temistocle (1743)
Le nozze d'Ercole e d'Ebe (1744)
Filandro-Philander (1747)
Il trionfo di Camilla (1760)
Tolomeo re d'Egitto (no date)

John Ernest Galliard (1687–1749) (b. Celle, Germany)
Calypso and Telemachus (1712)

Luca Antonio Predieri (1688–1767) (b. Bologna, Italy)
La Partenope (1720)
Lucio Papirio (1714)
Merope (1718)

Tito Manlio (1721)
Sofonisba (1722)
Scipione (1724)
Cesare in Egitto (1728)
Astianatte (1729)
Ezio (1730)
Scipione il giovane (1731)
Alessandro nell'Indie (1731)
Il sogno di Scipione (1735)
Perseo (1738)
Astrea placata (1739)
Zenobia (1740)

Joseph Bodin de Boismortier (1689–1785) (b. Thionville, France)
Daphnis et Chloe (1747)
Daphné (no date)

Giovanni Maria Ruggieri (c.1689–1720) (b. ?Venice, Italy)
La saggia pazzia di Giunio Bruto (1698)
Milziade (1699)
Arato in Sparta (1710)
Arsinoe vendicata (1712)

Francesco Maria Veracini (1690–1768) (b. Florence, Italy)
Adriano in Siria (1735)
La clemenza di Tito (1737)
Partenio (1738)

Giovanni Antonio Giai (1690–1764) (b. Turin, Italy)
Sosostri, rè d'Egitto (1717)
Publio Cornelio Scipione (1725)
Mitridate (1730)
Demetrio (1732)
Eumene (1737)
Adriano in Siria (1740)
Le tre dee riunite (1750)

François Collin de Blamont (1690–1760) (b. Versailles, France)
Les festes grecques et romaines (1723)
Le retour des dieux sur la terre (1725)
Le Caprice d'Erato (1730)
Diane et Endymion (1731)
Jupiter, vainqueur des Titans (1745)
Les fetes de Thétis (1750)

Francesco Ciampi (c.1690–after 1764) (b. ?Massa or Pisa, Italy)
Sofonisba (1715)
Timocrate (1716)
Ciro (1726)
Lucio Vero (1726)
Zenobia (1726)

Onorio (1729)
Demofoonte (1735)

Gottfried Heinrich Stölzel (1690–1749) (b. Grünstadtel, Germany)
Narcissus (1711)
Valeria (1712)
Artemisia (1713)
Orion (1713)
Venus and Adonis (1715–1717)
Acis and Galathea ((1715–1717)
Diomedes (1718)
Die Musenberg (1723)
Hercules Prodicius (1725)
Endymion (1740)

Francesco Feo (1691–1761) (b. Naples, Italy)
L'amor tirannico, ossia Zenobia (1713)
Ipermestra (1728)
Arianna (1728)
Andromaca (1730)
L'Issipile (1733)
Arsace (1740)

Antonio Palella (1692–1761) (b. San Giovanni a Teduccio, Italy)
Tigrane (1745)

Giacomo Griffini (fl.1692–1697) (b. Italy)
Endimione (1692)

Geminiano Giacomelli (c.1692–1740) (b. Piacenza, Italy)
Ipermestra (1724)
Scipione in Cartagine nuova (1728)
Lucio Papirio dittator (1729)
Semiramide riconosciuta (1730)
Annibale (1731)
Epaminonda (1732)
Alessandro Severo (1732)
Adriano in Siria (1733)
La caccia in Etolia (1733)
Merope (1734)
Cesare in Egitto (1735)
Arsace (1736)
Demetrio (1737)
Achille in Aulide (1739)

Giovanni Alberto Ristori (1692–1753) (b. ?Bologna, Italy)
Pallide trionfante in Arcadia (1713)
Euristeo (1714)
Pigmalione (1714)
Cleonice (1718)
Didone abbandonata (1737)

Temistocle (1738)
Adriano in Siria (1739)
Diana vindicata (1746)
La liberalità di Numa Pompilio (2746)
Trajano (1746)
Il lamenti di Orfeo (1749)

Leonardo Leo (1694–1744) (b. San Vito degli Schiavi, now San Vito dei Normanni,
    Italy)
Il Pisistrato (1714)
Eumene (1714)
Sofonisba (1718)
Caio Greco (1720)
Arianna e Teseo (1721)
Timocrate (1723)
Turno Aricino (1724)
Zenobia in Palmira (1725)
Il trionfo di Camilla (1726)
Catone in Utica (1729)
Semiramide (1730)
Il Demetrio (1732, second version 1735, third version 1741)
Nitocri, regina d'Egitto (1733)
Il castello d'Atlante (1734)
Il Medo (1734)
Demofoonte (1735)
La clemenza di Tito (1735)
Lucio Papirio (1735)
L'Olimpiade (1737)
Sesostri re d'Egitto (1738)
Semiramide (1739)
Il Ciro riconosciuto (1739)
Achille in Sciro (1740)
Scipione nella Spagne (1740)
L'Alessandro (1741)
Andromaca (1742)
Issipile (1742)
Vologeso re de' Parti (1744)
La caduta di Germanico (no date)

Maurice Greene (1696–1755) (b. London, England)
The Judgment of Hercules (before 1740)
Phoebe (1755)

Leonardo Vinci (c.1696–1730) (b. Strongoli, Calabria, Italy)
Publio Cornelio Scipione (1722)
Eraclea (1724)
Ifigenia in Tauride (1725)
Il trionfo di Camilla (1725)
Astianatte ((1725)
Didone abbandonata (1724)

Ifigenia in Tauride (1725)
Siroe re di Persia (1726)
La caduta de'Decemviri (1727)
Catone in Utica (1728)
Medo (1728)
Flavio Anicio Olibrio (1728)
Semiramide riconosciuta (1729)
Alessandro nell'Indie (1730)
Artaserse (1730)

Jean-Marie LeClair (1697–1764) (b. Lyons, France)
Scylla et Glaucus (1746)

Giuseppe de Majo (1697–1771) (b. Naples, Italy)
Arianna e Teseo (1747)
Semiramide riconosciuta (1751)

Pietro Auletta (c.1698–1771) (b. San Angelo, Italy)
Ezio (1728)
Orazio (1737)
Caio Fabricio (1743)
Didone (1759)

Gaetano Maria Schiassi (1698–1754) (b. Bologna, Italy)
Il Demetrio (1732)
Alessandro nelle Indie (1734)
Il Demofoonte (1735)
Didone abbandonata (1735)
Artaserse (1737)

Antonio Bioni (1698–after 1739) (b. Venice, Italy)
Climene (1721)
Caio Mario (1722)
Mitridate (1722)
Endimione (1727)
Lucio Vero (1727)
Attalo ed Arsinoe (1728)
Artebano re dei Parti (1728)
Andromaco (1729/30)
Ercole su'l Termodonte (1730)
Adone (1731)
Lucio Papirio (1732)
Siroe (1732)
Demetrio (1732)
Issipile (1732)
Alessandro Severo (1733)
Alessandro nell'Indie (1733)
Artaserse (1733)

François Francoeur (1698–1787) (b. Paris, France)
Pirame et Thisbé (1726)
Ismène (1747)

Nicola Bonifacio Logroscino (1698–1765/7) (b. Bitonto, Italy)
Il Quinto Fabio (1738)
Il Leandro (1744)
Giunio Bruto (1748)
Olimpiade (1753)
Il natale di Achille (1760)
Perseo (1762)

Johann Adolf Hasse (1699–1783) (b. Bergedorf, Germany)
Antioco (1721)
Antonio e Cleopatra (1725)
Il Sesostrate (1726)
La Semele (1726)
Gerone tiranno di Siracusa (1727)
Enea in Caonia (1727)
Attalo, re di Bitinia (1728)
Tigrane (1729)
Artaserse (1730)
Arminio (1730, second version 1745)
Ezio (1730)
Cleofide [Alessandro nell'Indie] (1731)
Catone in Utica (1731)
Cajo Fabricio (1732)
Demetrio (1732)
Euristeo (1732)
Issipile (1732)
Siroe re di Persia (1733)
Tito Vespasiano (1735)
Senocrita (1737)
Atalanta (1737)
Numa Pompilio (1741)
Lucio Papirio (1742)
Didone abbandonata (1742)
Endimione (1743)
Antigono (1743)
Ipermestra (1744)
Semiramide riconosciuta (1744)
La spartana generosa, ovvero Archidamia (1747)
Leucippo (1747)
Demoofonte (1748)
Il natal di Giove (1749)
Attilio Regolo (1750)
Ciro riconosciuto (1751)
Adriano in Siria (1752)
Artemisia (1754)
Il re pastore (1762)
L'Olimpiade (1756)
Il sogno di Scipione (1758)
Achille in Sciro (1759)

Alcide al bivio (1760)
Zenobia (1761)
Il trionfo di Clelia (1762)
Egeria (1764)
Romolo ed Ersilia (1765)
Partenope (1767)
Piramo e Tisbe (1770)

Giovanni Francesco Brusa (?1700–after 1768) (b. Venice, Italy)
Arsace (1725)
Medea e Giasone (1726)
Semiramide riconosciuta (1756)
Adriano in Siria (1757)
Le statue (1757)
Olimpiade (1766)

Giacomo Maccari (c.1700–after 1744) (b. Rome, Italy)
Ottaviano trionfante di Marc'Antonio (1735)

Giuseppe Sellitto (1700–1777) (b. Naples, Italy)
L'Oronte (1730)
Drusilla e Strabone (1735)
Sesostri re d'Egitto (1742)
Orazio Curiazio (1746)

Giovanni Verocai (c.1700–1745) (b. Venice, Italy)
Penelope (1740)
Demofoonte (1742)
Zenobia und Radamistus (1742)
Cato (1743)
Hissifile (1743)
Sesostri (1744)
Il Ciro riconosciuto (1746)
Achille in Sciro (1746)
Apollo fra i pastori (1746)
Temistocle in bando (1747)

Francesco Corradini (c.1700–1769) (b. Venice, Italy)
Templo y monte de Filis y Demofonte (1731)
Eco y Narcisco (1734)
Trajano en Dacia (1735)
El anillo de Giges (1740)
La Briseida (1746)
La clemencia de Tito (1747)
El Polifemo (1748)

Giovanni Battista Mele (?1701–after 1752) (b. Naples, Italy)
La clemencia de Tito (1747)
El Polifemo (1748)

François Rebel (1701–1775) (b. Paris, France)
Pirame et Thisbé (1726)

John Frederick Lampe (c.1702–1751) (b. Saxony, Germany)
Aurora's Nuptials (1734)
Pyramus and Thisbe (1745)

Francesco Corselli (c.1702–1778) (b. Piacenza, Italy)
Venere placata (1731)
Nino (1732)
La Cautela en la amistad y el robo de las Sabinas (1735)
Alessandro nelle Indie (1738)
Achille in Sciro (1744)
La clemenza di Tito (1747)
Il Polifemo (1748)

Giuseppe Carcani (1703–1778) (b. Crema, Italy)
Demetrio (1742)
Alcibiade (1746)
Artaserse (1748)
Alcuni avvenimenti di Telemaco (1749)
Il Tigrane (1750)
Olimpiade (1757)
Arianna e Teseo (1759)

Carl Heinrich Graun (1703/4–1759) (b. Wahrenbrück, Germany)
Polydorus (1726/8)
Iphigenia in Aulis (1728)
Scipio Africanus (1732)
Pharao Tubaetes (1735)
Venere e Cupido (1742)
Cesare e Cleopatra (1742)
Artaserse (1743)
Catone in Utica (1744)
La festa del Imeneo (1744)
Alessandro e Poro (1744)
Lucio Papirio (1745)
Adriano in Siria (1746)
Demofoonte, re di Tracia (1746)
Cajo Fabricio (1746)
Il re pastore (1747)
Cinna (1748)
L'Europa galante (1748)
Ifigenia in Aulide (1748)
Coriolano (1749)
Il Mitridate (1750)
Britannico (1751)
L'Orfeo (1752)
Il giudizio di Paride (1752)
Silla (1753)
Semiramide (1754)
Ezio (1755)

I fratelli nemici (1756)
La Merope (1756)

Giovanni Battista Pescetti (c.1704–1766) (b. Venice, Italy)
Nerone detronato (1725)
Siroe re di Persia (1731)
Alessandro nelle Indie (1732)
Demetrio (1732)
La conquista del velo d'oro (1740)
Diana e Endimione (1739)
Busiri (1740)
Ezio (1747)
Arianna e Teseo (1750)
Artaserse (1751)
Zenobia (1761)
Andimione (no date)

Joseph-Nicolas-Pancrace Royer (c.1705–1755) (b. Turin, Italy)
Pyrrhus (1730)
Prométhée et Pandore (1744–1754)

Antonio Gaetano Pampani (c.1705–1775) (b. Modena, Italy)
Artaserse Longimani (1737)
Siroe (1738)
La caduta d'Amulio (1747)
La clemenza di Tito (1748)
Adriano in Siria (1750)
Andromaca (1753)
Astianatte (1755)
Artaserse 1756)
Antigono (1756)
Demofoonte (1757)
L'Olimpiade (1766)
Demetrio (1768)

Filippo Finazzi (?1706–1776) (b. Bergamo, Italy)
Temistocle (1746)

Andrea Bernasconi (1706–1784) (b. ?Marseilles, France)
Flavio Anicio Olibrio (1737)
Alessandro Severo (1738)
Temistocle (1740)
Demofoonte (1741)
Didone abbandonata (1741)
Endimione (1742)
La ninfa Apollo (1743)
Germanico (1744)
Antigono (1745)
Artaserse (1746)
Ezio (1749)
Adriano in Siria (1755)

Olimpiade (1764)
Semiramide riconosciuta (1765)
La clemenza di Tito (1768)
Demetrio (1772)

Baldassare Galuppi (1706–1785) (b. Burano, Italy)
La ninfa Apollo (1734)
Elisa regina di Tiro (1736)
Issipile (1737; second version 1750)
Alessandro nell'Indie (1738; second version 1754; third version 1755)
Adriano in Siria (1740; second version 1758)
Didone abbandonata (1740; second version 1765)
Oronte rè de' sciti (1740)
Berenice (1741)
Penelope (1741)
Scipione in Cartagine (1742)
Arsace (1743)
Ciro riconosciuto (1745, second version 1759)
Scipione nelle Spagne (1746)
L'Arminio (1747)
L'Olimpiade (1747)
Vologeso (1748)
Demetrio (1748; second version 1761)
Semiramide riconosciuta (1749)
Artaserse (1749)
Demofoonte (1749; second version 1758)
Antigona (1751)
Dario (1751)
Lucio Papirio (1751)
Artaserse (1751)
Sofonisba (1753; second version 1764)
Siroe (1754)
Attalo (1755)
Idomeneo (1756)
Ezio (1757)
Sesostri (1757)
Ipermestra (1758)
La clemenza di Tito (1760)
Antigono (1762)
Il Muzio Scevole (1762)
Il rè pastore (1762)
Arianna e Teseo (1763; second version 1769)
Cajo Mario (1764)
Ifigenia in Tauride (1768)

Domenico Paradies (1707–1791) (b. Naples, Italy)
Alessandro in Persia (1738)

Carlo Goldoni (1707–1793) (b. Venice, Italy)
Aristide (1735)

Il finto pazzo (1741)
Oronte re de' sciti (1741)
Tigrane (1741)

Egidio Duni (1708–1775) (b. Matera, Basilicata, Italy)
Nerone (1735)
Adriano in Siria (1735)
Demophontes, King of Thrace (1737)
La Didone abbandonata (1739)
Catone in Utica (1740)
Artaserse (1744)
Ipermestra (1748)
Ciro riconosciuto (1748)
Olimpiade (1755)

Matteo Capranica (1708–after 1776) (b. ?Amatrice, Rieti, Italy)
Alcibiade (1746)
L'Emilia (1747)
L'Aurelio (1748)
Merope (1751)

Giovanni Battista Lampugnani (1708–1788) (b. ?Milan, Italy)
Candace (1732)
Antigono (1736)
Arianna e Teseo (1737)
Ezio (1737)
Demofoonte (1738)
Didone abbandonata (1739)
Adriano in Siria (1740)
Semiramide riconosciuta (1741)
Arsace (1741)
Alceste (1744)
Semiramide (1745)
Tigrane (1747)
L'Olimpiade (1748)
Andromaca (1748)
Artaserse (1749)
Alessandro sotto le tende di Dario (1751)
Vologeso, re de' Patri (1752)
Vologeso (1753)
Siroe, re di Persia (1755)
Il re pastore (1758)
Enea in Italia (1763)

Francesco Araia (1709–1770) (b. Naples, Italy)
Berenice (1730)
Ciro reconosciuto (1731)
Il Cleomene (1731)
Lucio Vero (1735)
Artaserse (1738)
Seleuco (1744)

Scipione (1745)
Mitridate (1747)
Bellerofonte (1750)
Tsefal i Prokris (1755)
Alessandro nell'Indie (1755)

Antonio Aurisicchio (1710–1781) (b. Naples, Italy)
Andromaca (1753)
Eumene (1754)

Giovanni Battista Pergolesi (1710–1736) (b. Iesi, Italy)
Salustia (1732)
Adriano in Siria (1734)
L'Olimpiade (1735)
Il Flaminio (1735)

Charles-Simon Favart (1710–1792) (b. Paris, France)
Pyrame et Thisbé (1740)
Hippolyte et Aricie (1742)
Thésée (1745)

Thomas Augustine Arne (1710–1778) (b. London, England)
Dido and Aeneas (1734)
The Fall of Phaeton (1736)
The Judgment of Paris (1740)
Oedipus, King of Thebes (1740)
Lethe, or Aesop in the Shades (1749)
The Muses' Looking Glass (1749)
Artaxerxes (1762)
The Birth of Hercules (1763)
L'Olimpiade (1765)
Achilles in Petticoats (1773)
Caractacus (1776)

Pietro Pulli (c.1710–1759 or later) (b. Naples, Italy)
Vologeso re dei Parti (1741)
Caio Marzio Coriolano (1741)
Zenobia (1748)
Il Demetrio (1749)
Olimpiade (1751)
Andimione (no date)

Arvid Niclas Höpken (1710–1778) (b. Stockholm, Sweden)
Il re pastore (1752)
Catone in Utica (1753)

Giovanni Battista Ferrandini (c.1710–1791) (b. Venice, Italy)
Gordio (1727)
Berenice (1730)
Scipio nella Spagna (1732)
Ipermestra (1736)
Adriano in Siria (1737)

Demofoonte (1737)
Artaserse (1739)
Catone in Utica (1753)
Diana placata (1755)
Demetrio (1758)

Bernardo Aliprandi (?1710–?1792) (b. ?Milan, Italy)
Mitridate (1738)
Semiramide riconosciuta (1740)
Apollo trà le muse in Parnasso (1737)
Iphigenia in Aulide (1739)

Rinaldo da Capua (c.1710–c.1780) (b. Capua or Naples, Italy)
Ciro riconosciuto (1737)
Vologeso, re de' Parti (1739)
Catone in Utica (1740)
Didone abbandonata (1741)
Ipermestra (1741)
Turno Heredonio Aricino (1743)
Mario in Numidia (1749)
Attalo (1754)
Adriano in Siria (1758)

Ignaz Holzbauer (1711–1783) (b. Vienna, Austria)
Lucio Papirio dittatore (1737)
L'Issipile (1754)
Le nozze d'Arianna (1756)
La clemenza di Tito (1757)
Alessandro nell'Indie (1759)
Ippolito ed Aricia (1759)
Adriano in Siria (1768)
La morte di Didone (1779)

David Perez (1711–1778) (b. Naples, Italy)
Il Siroe (1740)
Demetrio (1741; second version 1766)
L'eroismo di Scipione (1741)
Alessandro nell'Indie (1744)
Merope (1744)
Leucippo (1744)
Medea (1744)
Artaserse (1748)
La clemenza di Tito (1749)
Andromaca (1750)
Semiramide (1750)
Vologeso (1750)
Ezio (1751)
La Zenobia (1751)
La Didone abbandonata (1751)
Adriano in Siria (1752)
Demofoonte (1752)

Olimpiade (1753)
Andromeda (1753)
L'Ipermestra (1754)
Lucio Vero (1754)
Alessandro nell'Indie (1755)
Enea in Italia (1759)
Arminio (1760)
La Berenice (1762)
Giulio Cesare (1762)
Creusa in Delfo (1774)
Il ritorno di Ulisse in Itaca (1774)

Giuseppe Bonno (1711–1788) (b. Vienna, Austria)
Trajano (1736)
Alessandro Severo (1737)
La pietà di Numa (1738)
Il natale di Numa Pompilio (1739)
La generosa Spartana (1740)
Il natale di Giove (1740)
Danae (1744)
Ezio (1749)
Il rè pastore (1751)
Didone abbandonata (1752)
L'Atenaide (no date)
Il sogno di Scipione (1763)

William Boyce (1711–1779) (b. London, England)
Peleus and Thetis (1740)
The Shepherd's Lottery (1751)

Gaetano Latilla (1711–1788) (b. Bari, Italy)
L'Ottavio (1733)
Temistocle (1737)
Demofoonte (1738)
Romolo (1729)
Siroe (1740)
Zenobia (1742)
Catone in Utica (1747)
Adriano in Siria (1747)
Olimpiade (1752)
Alessandro nell'Indie (1753)
Antigona (1753)
Tito Manlio (1755)
Ezio (1761)
Merope (1763)
Antigono (1775)

Jean-Joseph Cassanéa de Mondonville (1711–1772) (b. Narbonne, France)
Bacchus et Erigone (1747)
Vénus et Adonis (1752)
Titon et l'Aurore (1753)

Daphnis et Alcimadure (1754)
Thésée (1765)

John Christopher Smith (1712–1795) (b. Ansbach, England)
Ulysses (1733)
Issipile (1743)
Il Ciro riconosciuto (1745)
Dario (1746)
Artaserse (?1748)
Medea (1760–1761)

Paolo Scalabrini (1713–1803) (b. ?Lucca, Italy)
Artaserse (1742)
Oronte re de sciti (1742)
Cajo Fabricio (1743)
Siroe re di Persia (1744)
Antigono (1744)
Catone in Utica (1744)
Didone (1746)
Adriano (1749)
Alessandro nell'Indie (1749)

Antoine Dauvergne (1713–1797) (b. Moulins, France)
Les amours de Tempé (1752)
La sibylle (1753)
Enée et Lavinie (1758)
Les fêtes d'Euterpe (1758)
Canente (1760)
Hercule mourant (1761)
Polyxène (1763)
La mort d'Orfée (unperf.)
Sémiramis (no date)

Domènech Terradellas (1713–1751) (b. Barcelona, Spain)
Romolo (1739)
Cerere (1740)
Merope (1743)
Artaserse (1744)
Semiramide riconosciuta (1746)
Mitridate (1746)
Bellerophonte (1747)
Didone abbandonata (1750)
Imeneo in Atene (1750)
Sesostri re d'Egitto (1751)

Giuseppe Arena (1713–1784) (b. Malta)
Achille in Sciro (1738)
La clemenza di Tito (1738)
Artaserse (1741)
Tigrane (1741)
Alessandro in Persia (1741)

Cristoph Willibald Gluck (1714–1787) (b. Ersbach, near Weidenwang, Austria)
Artaserse (1741)
Demetrio (1742)
Demofoonte (1743)
Il Tigrane (1743)
La Sofonisba (1744)
Ipermestra (1744)
Poro (1744)
Ippolito (1745)
La caduta dei Giganti (1746)
Artamene (1746)
La nozze d'Ercole e d'Ebe (1747)
La Semiramide riconosciuta (1748)
La contesa de' numi (1749)
Ezio (1750; second version 1763)
Issipile (1752)
La clemenza di Tito (1752)
Antigono (1756)
Il rè pastore (1756)
Cythère assiégée (1759) and (1775)
Tetide (1760)
Orfeo e Euridice (1762, *azione teatrale*)
Il trionfo di Clelia (1763)
Il Parnaso confuso (1765)
Telemaco, ossia L'isola di Circe (1765)
Alceste (1767) and (1776)
Le feste d'Apollo (1769)
Paride ed Elena (1770)
Iphigénie en Aulide (1774)
Orphée et Eurydice (1774)
Alceste (1776)
Iphigénie en Tauride (1778)
Echo et Narcisse (1779)
Iphigenie auf Tauris (1781)

Niccolò Jommelli (1714–1774) (b. Aversa, Italy)
Astianatte (1741)
Ezio (1741, second version 1748, third version 1758, fourth version 1771)
Merope (1741)
Tito Manlio (1742, second version 1746, third version 1758)
Semiramide (1742; second version 1753; third version 1762)
Eumene (1742; second version 1747)
Ciro riconosciuto (1743; second version 1749)
Demofoonte (1743; second version 1753; third version 1764; fourth version 1770)
Alessandro nell'Indie (1743; second version 1760)
Antigono (1744)
Sofonisba (1745)
Caio Mario (1751)
Didone abbandonata (1747; second version 1749; third version 1763)

Artaserse (1749, second version 1756)
Demetrio (1749)
Achille in Sciro (1749; second version 1771)
Ifigenia in Aulide (1751)
Ipermestra (1751)
Attilio Regolo (1753)
La clemenza di Tito (1753; second version 1765)
Lucio Vero (1754)
Catone in Utica (1754)
Pelope (1755)
Creso (1757)
Temistocle (1757; second version 1765)
Endimione (1759)
Caio Fabrizio (1760)
L'Olimpiade (1761)
Il re pastore (1764)
Imeneo in Atene (1765)
Enea nel Lazio (1755: lost; second version 1767)
Vologeso (1766)
Fetonte (1768)
Le avventure di Cleomede (1771)
Ifigenia in Tauride (1771)
Cerere placata (1772)
Il trionfo di Clelia (1774)

Giovanni Battista Casali (c.1715–1792) (b. Rome, Italy)
Candaspe regina de' Sciti (1740)
Antigona (1752)
Arianna e Teseo (no date)

Francesco Maggiore (c.1715–?1782) (b. ?Naples, Italy)
Il Demetrio (1742)
Il Temistocle (1743)
Caio Marzio Coriolano (1744)
Artaserse (1747)

Daniel Dal Barba (1715–1801) (b. Verona, Italy)
Il Tigrane (1744)
Lo starnuto d'Ercole (c.1748)
Ciro in Armenia (1750)
Artaserse (1751)
Alessandro nell'Indie (1761)

Georg Christophe Wagenseil (1715–1777) (b. Vienna, Austria)
La clemenza di Tito (1746)
Demetrio (1746)
Alessandro nell'Indie (1748)
Il Siroe (1748)
L'Olimpiade (1749)
Antigono (1750)
Prometeo assoluto (1762)

Gennaro Manna (1715–1779) (b. Naples, Italy)
Tito Manlio (1742)
Siroe re di Persia (1743)
Artaserse (1743)
Achille in Sciro (1745)
Lucio Vero (1745)
Arsace (1746)
La clemenza di Tito (1747)
Adriano placato (1748)
Lucio Papirio dittatore (1748)
Eumene (1750)
Didone abbandonata (1751)
Demofoonte (1754)
Temistocle (1761)

Ignazio Fiorillo (1715–1787) (b. Naples, Italy)
L'egeste (1733)
Partenope nell'Adria (1738)
Volgeso (1742)
L'Olimpiade (1745)
Il finto pazzo (1748)
Astige re di Medi (1749)
Demofoonte (1750)
Didone abbandonata (1751)
Alessandro nell'Indie (1752)
Demetrio (1753)
Ciro riconosciuto (1753)
Endimione (1754)
Ipermestra (1759)
Artaserse (1765)
Andromeda (1771)

Girolamo Abos (1715–1760) (b. La Valetta, Italy)
Artaserse (1746)
Pelopida (1747)
Alessandro nelle Indie (1747)
Arianna e Teseo (1748)
Adriano in Siria (1750)
Tito Manilio (1751)
Erifile (1752)
Lucio Vero o sia Il vologeso (1752)
Il Medo (1753)

Hinrich Philip Johnsen (1716–1779) (b. Gottorf, Germany)
Aeglé (1774)
Neptun och Amphitrite (1775)

Felice de Giardini (1716–1796) (b. Turin, Italy)
Enea e Lavinia (1764)
Il re pastore (1765)
Sappho (1778)

Pasquale Cafaro (1716–1787) (b. San Pietro in Galatina, Italy)
La disfatta di Dario (1756)
L'incendio di Troia (1757)
Ipermestra (1761)
Arianna e Teseo (1766)
Creso, Ultimo rè della Lidia (1768)
L'Olimpiade (1769)
Antigono (1770)

Paul-César Gibert (1717–1787) (b. Versailles, France)
Deucalion et Pyrrha (1772)

Antonio Mazzoni (1717–1785) (b. Bologna, Italy)
Siroe, re di Persia (1746)
Issipile (1748)
Didone abbandonata (1752)
Demofoonte (1754)
Achille in Sciro (1754)
La clemenza di Tito (1755)
Antigono (1755)
Ifigenia in Tauride (1756)
Il re pastore (1757)
Arianna e Teseo (1758)
Eumene (1759)
Adriano in Siria (1760)

François-Joseph Giraud (?–1788) (b. France)
Deucalion et Pyrrha (1755)

Joseph Aloys Schmittbaur (1718–1809) (b. Bamberg, Germany)
Herkules auf dem Oeta (1771)
Lindor und Ismene (1779)
Endymion (1774)

Nicola Conforto (1718–after 1788) (b. Naples, Italy)
Antigono (1750)
Siroe (1752)
Ezio (1754)
Adriano in Siria (1754)
Livia Claudia vestale (1755)
La ninfa smarrita (1756)

Antonio Ferradini (?1718–1779) (b. Naples, Italy)
Artaserse (1752)
Ezio (1752)
Antigono (1758)
Demofoonte (1758)
Didone (1760)

Giuseppe Scarlatti (1718–1777) (b. Naples, Italy)
Merope (1740)
Dario (1741)

Arminio in Germania (1741)
Siroe (1742)
Pompeo in Armenia (1744)
Ezio (1744)
Olimpade (1745)
Artaserse (1747)
Partenope (1749)
Semiramide riconosciuta (1751)
Adriano in Siria (1752)
Demetrio (1752)
Alessandro nell'Inde (1753)
Caio Mario (1755)
Antigona (1756)
La clemenza di Tito (1760)
L'Issipile (1760)
Pelopida (1763)

Vincenzo Ciampi (?1719–1762) (b. Piacenza, Italy)
La Flaminia (1743)
L'Arminio (1744)
Artaserse (1747)
L'Adriano (1748)
Il trionfo de Camilla (1750)
Didone (1754)
Catone in Utica (1756)
La clemenza di Tito (1756–1757)
Arsinoe (1758)
Antigona (1762)

Giuseppe Scolari (?1720–after 1774) (b. ?Lisbon, Portugal)
L'Olimpiade (1746–1747)
Il vello d'oro (1748–1749)
Alessandro nell'Indie (1749)
Didone abbandonata (1752)
Adriano in Siria (1753–1754)
Cajo Fabricio (1755)
Statira (1756)
L'Andromaca (1757)
Artaserse (1757)
Cajo Mario (1765)
Antigono (1766)
Giulia Mammea (no date)

Maria Teresa Agnesi-Pinottini (1720–1795) (b. Milan, Italy)
Ciro in Armenia (1753)
Il rè pastore (1756)
Sofonisba (1765)

Johann Friedrich Agricola (1720–1774) (b. Dobitschen, Saxe-Altenburg, Germany)
Cleofide (1754)
Achille in Sciro (1765)

Amor e psiche (1767)
Il re pastore (1770)
Oreste e Pilade (1772), rev. as *I greci in Tauride*

Michelangelo Valentini (c.1720–after 1768) (b. Naples, Italy)
Il Demetrio (1745)
La clemenza di Tito (1753)
Adriano in Siria (1753)
Andromaca (1754)

Johann Georg Schürer (c.1720–1786) (b. Raudnitz, Bohemia)
Astraea placata (1746)
La Galatea (1746)
L'Ercole sul Termodonte (1747)
Doris (1747)
Calandro (1748)

João Cordeiro da Silva (fl. 1756–1808) (b. Portugal)
Il natal di Giove (1778)
Edalide e Cambise (1780)
Il ratto di Proserpina (1784)
Archelao (1785)
Telemaco nell'isola di Calipso (1787)
Megara tebana (1788)
Bauce e Palemone (1789)
Lindane e Dalmiro (1789)

Giuseppe Ponzo (fl. 1755–1791) (b. ?Naples, Italy)
Demetrio (1759)
Arianna e Teseo (1762)
Artaserse (1766)

Andrea Adolfati (1721–1760) (b. Venice, Italy)
Didone abbandonata (1747)
Arianna (1750)
Adriano in Siria (1751)
Ifigenia (1751)
Ipermestra (1752)
Vologeso (1752)
La clemenza di Tito (1753)
Sesostri re d'Egitto (1755)

Francisco António de Almeida (fl. 1722–1752) (b. Portugal)
La pazienza di Socrate (1733)
La finta pazza (1735)
L'Ippolito (1752)

Georg Anton Benda (1722–1795) (b. Staré Benátky, Prussia)
Ariadne auf Naxos (1775)
Medea (1775)
Theone (1778)
Pygmalion (1779)

Gregorio Sciroli (1722–after 1781) (b. Naples, Italy)
Ulisse errante (1749)
Sesostri re d'Egitto (1759)
Bellerofonte (1760)
Olimpiade (1760)
Merope (1761)
Alessandro nelle Indie (1764)

Giovanni Marco Rutini (1723–1797) (b. Florence, Italy)
Alessandro nell'Indie (1750)
Semiramide (1752)
Ezio (1763)
Vologeso re de' Parti (1775)

Francesco Antonio Baldassare Uttini (1723–1795) (b. Bologna, Italy)
Alessandro nelle Indie (1743)
Astianatte (1748)
Demofoonte (1750)
Siroe (1752)
L'Olimpiade (1753)
Zenobia (1754)
La Galatea (1755)
Il re pastore (1755)
Adriano in Siria (1757)
Cythère assiégée (1762)
Il sogno di Scipione (1764)
Psyché (1766)
Thetis och Pelée (1773)
Aeglé (1774)

Antonio Rodriguez de Hita (?1724/5–1787) (b. Valverde, Madrid, Spain)
La Briseida (1768)
Scipion en Cartagena (1770)

Domenico Fischietti (c.1725–after 1810) (b. Naples, Italy)
Artaserse (1754)
Olimpiade (1763)
Alessandro nell'Indie (1764)
Arianna e Teseo (1777)

Ferdinando Bertoni (1725–1813) (b. Saló, Italy)
Orazio e Curiazio (1746)
Didone abbandonata (1748)
Ipermestra (1748)
Antigono (1752)
Antigona (1756)
Lucio Vero (1757)
Ifigenia in Aulide (1762)
Achille in Sciro (1764)
L'Olimpiade (1765)
Ezio (1767)

Scipione nelle Spagne (1768)
Alessandro nell'indie (1769)
Il trionfo di Clelia (1769)
Andromaca (1771)
Orfeo ed Euridice (1776)
Creonte (1776)
Artaserse (1776)
Telemaco ed Eurice nell'isola di Calipso (1776)
Medonte re d'Epira (1777)
Quinto Fabio (1778)
Artaserse (1779)
Cajo Mario (1781)
Eumene (1783)

François-André Danican Philidor (1726–1795) (b. Dreux, France)
Persée (1780)
Thémistocle (1785)

Pasquale Anfossi (1727–1797) (b. Taggia, Italy)
La clemenza di Tito (1769)
Caio Mario (1770)
Quinto Fabio (1771)
Alessandro nell'Indie (1772)
Demofoonte (1773)
Antigono (1773)
Achille in Sciro (1774)
Lucio Silla (1774)
Olimpiade (1774)
Didone abbandonata (1775)
Adriano in Siria (1777)
Ezio (1778)
Cleopatra (1779)
Tito nelle Gallie (1780)
Il trionfo d'Arianna (1781)
Issipile (1784)
Creso (1787)
La maga Circe (1788)
Artaserse (1788)
Zenobia di Palmira (1789)

Tommaso Traetta (1727–1779) (b. Bitonto, Italy)
Ezio (1754)
Didone abbandonata (1757)
Olimpiade (1758)
Demofoonte (1758)
Ippolito ed Aricia (1759)
Enea nel Lazio (1760)
I Tindaridi, o Castore e Polluce (1760)
Enea e Lavinia (1761)
Zenobia (1761)

Alessandro nell'Indie (1762)
Sofonisba (1762)
Ifigenia in Tauride (1763)
Antigono (1764)
Semiramide (1765)
Siroe, re di Persia (1767)
Fetonte (1768)
Astrea Placata (1770)
Antigona (1772)
Amore e Psiche (1773)
Lucio Vero (1774)
La Merope (1776)
Telemaco (1777)
La disfatta di Dario (1778)
Gli eroi di Campi Elisi (1779)

Pierre-Montan Berton (1727–1780) (b. Maubert-Fontaine, France)
Deucalion et Pyrrha (1755)
Silvie (1765)
Erosine (1765)
Théonis, ou Le toucher (1767)

Anton Bachschmidt (1728–1797) (b. Eichstatt, Austria)
Il rè Pastore (1774)
La clemenza di Tito (1776)
Antigono (1778)

Franz Asplmayr (1728–1786) (b. Linz, Austria)
Pygmalion (1772)
Orpheus und Euridice (1779–1780)

Giacomo Insanguine (1728–1795) (b. Monopoli, Italy)
Demetrio (1759)
La Didone abbandonata (1770)
Eumene (1771)
Merope (1772)
Arianna e Teseo (1773)
Adriano in Siria (1773)
Eumene (1778)
Medonte (1779)
Calipso (1782)

Pietro Alessandro Guglielmi (1728–1804) (b. Massa, Italy)
L'Ottavio (1760)
Tito Manlio (1763)
L'Olimpiade (1763)
Siroe re di Persia (1764)
Adriano in Siria (1765)
Sesostri (1766)
Demofoonte (1766)
Antigono (1767)

Il re pastore (1767)
Ifigenia in Aulide (1768)
Alceste (1768)
Ezio (1770)
Demetrio (1772)
Merope (1775)
Vologeso (1775)
La Semiramide riconosciuta (1776)
Artaserse (1777)
Narcisso (1779)
Diana amante (1781)
Enea e Lavinia (1785)
Arsace (1788)
Alessandro nell'Indie (1789)
La lanterna di Diogene (1793)
Admeto (1794)
Il trionfo di Camilla (1795)
La morte di Cleopatra (1796)
Ippolito (1798)

Hermann Friedrich Raupach (1728–1778) (b. Stralsund, Germany)
Al'testa (1758: *Alcestes*)
Siroe, re di Persia (1760)

Niccolò Piccinni (1728–1800) (b. Bari, Italy)
Zenobia (1756)
Caio Mario (1757)
Alessandro nelle Indie (1758; second version 1774)
Ciro riconosciuto (1759)
Siroe re di Persia (1759)
Il re pastore (1760)
Olimpiade (1761; second version 1768)
Tigrane (1761)
Demofoonte (1761)
Artaserse (1762)
Antigono (1762)
Demetrio (1769)
Didone Abbandonata (1770)
Cesare in Egitto (1770)
Catone in Utica (1770)
Ipermestra (1772)
Scipione in Cartagena (1772)
Enea in Cuma (1775)
Phaon (1778)
Atys (1780)
Iphigénie en Tauride (1781)
Didon (1783)
Diane et Endymion (1784)
Pénélope (1785)
Clytemnestre (1787)

Ercole al Termedonte (1793)
I Decemviri (no date)

Pietro Pompeo Sales (c.1729–1797) (b. Brescia, Italy)
L'Antigona in Tebe (1767)
Antigono (1769)
Achille in Sciro (1774)
Il re pastore (no date)

Florian Leopold Gassmann (1729–1774) (b. Brüx, now Most, Czechoslovakia)
Merope (1757)
Issipile (1758)
Catone in Utica (1761)
Ezio (1762)
L'Olimpiade (1764)
Achille in Sciro (1766)
Amore e Psiche (1767)

Pierre-Alexandre Monsigny (1729–1817) (b. Fauquembergues, France)
Philémon et Baucis (1766)

Giuseppe Sarti (1729–1802) (b. Faenza, Italy)
Pompeo in Armenia (1752)
Il re pastore (1752, second version 1771)
Vologeso (1765)
Antigono (1754)
Ciro riconosciuto (1754)
Demofoonte (1755, second version 1771, third version 1782)
Sesostri (1755)
Arianna e Teseo (1756)
Achille in Sciro (1759)
Artaserse (1760)
Astrea Placata (1760)
Andromaca (1760)
Issipile (1761)
Alessandro nell'Indie (1761)
Semiramide (1762)
Didone abbandonata (1762, second version 1782)
Narciso (1763)
Cesare in Egitto (1763)
Il nefragio di Cipro (1764)
Ipermestra (1766)
Tronfølgen i Sidon (1771)
La clemenza di Tito (1771)
Il re pastore (1771)
Deucalion og Pyrrha (1772)
Aglae, eller Stotten (1774)
Ifigenia [in Aulide] (1777)
Medonte, re d'Epiro (1777)
Scipione (1778)
Adriano in Siria (1778)

Olimpiade (1778, second version 1783)
Achille in Sciro (1779)
Mitridate a Sinope (1779)
Siroe (1779)
Giulio Sabino (1781)
Alessandro e Timoteo (1782)
Atallo, re di Bitinia (1782)
Erifile (1783)
Castore e Polluce (1786)
Alessandro nell'Indie (1787)
Cleomene (1788)
Andromeda (1798)
Enea nel Lazio (1799)
Les amours de Flore et de Zéphire (1800)

Marcello Bernardini (c.1730–1799) (b. ?Capua, Italy)
Li tre Orfei (1784)
Il pazzo glorioso (1790)
Achille in Sciro (1794)

Tommaso Giordano (c.1730–1806) (b. Naples, Italy)
Il re pastore (1778)
Orfeo ed Euridice (1784)
Calypso, or Love and Enchantment (1785)

Antonio Sacchini (1730–1786) (b. Florence, Italy)
Olimpia tradita (1758)
Andromaca (1761)
Alessandro Severo (1763)
Alessandro nell'Indie (1763)
Olimpiade (1763)
Eumene (1764)
Semiramide riconosciuta (1764)
Lucio Vero (1764)
Il Creso (1765)
Artaserse (1768)
Scipione in Cartagena (1770)
Calliroe (1770)
Adriano in Siria (1771)
Ezio (1771)
Vologeso (1772)
Perseo (1774)
Erifile (1778)
Enea e Lavinia (1779)
Mitridate (1781)
Dardanus (1784)
Oedipe à Colonne (1786)

Gaetano Pugnani (1731–1798) (b. Turin, Italy)
Aurora (1775)
Adone e Venere (1784)

Achille in Sciro (1785)
Demofoonte (1787)
Demetrio a Rodi (1789)

Giuseppe Colla (1731–1806) (b. Parma, Italy)
Adriano in Siria (1762)
Tigrane (1766–1767)
Enea in Cartagine (1769)
Licida e Mopso (1769)
Vologeso (1770)
Andromeda (1771)
Didone (1773)
Tolomeo (1773)

Ignazio Celoniati (c.1731–1784) (b. Turin, Italy)
Ecuba (1769)
Didone abbandonata (1769)

Franz Joseph Haydn (1732–1809) (b. Rohrau, Lower Austria)
Philemon und Baucis, oder Jupiters Reise auf die Erde (1773)
Dido (1776)
La fedeltà premiata (1781)
L'Anima del Filosofo ossia Orfeo ed Euridice (1791)

Gian Francesco de Majo (1732–1770) (b. Naples, Italy)
Cajo Fabrizio (1760)
Artaserse (1762)
Catone in Utica (1763)
Demofoonte (1763)
Alcide negli orti esperidi (1764)
Ifigenia in Tauride (1764)
Alessandro [nell'Indie] (1766)
Antigono (1767)
Antigona (1768)
Ipermestra (1768)
Adriano in Siria (1769)
Didone abbandonata (1770)
Eumene (1771)

Giacomo Tritto (1733–1824) (b. Altamura, Italy)
L'Arminio (1786)
Apelle e Campaspe (1795)
La morte di Cesare (1798)
Cesare in Egitto (1805)
Elpinice e Vologeso (1806)
Andromaca e Pirro (1807)
Marco Albino in Siria (1810)

François-Joseph Gossec (1734–1829) (b. Vergnies, France)
Les agréments d'Hylas et Silvie (1768)
Sabinus (1773)

Aléxis et Daphné (1775)
Philémon et Baucis (1775)
Thésée (1782)

Franz Ignaz Beck (1734–1809) (b. Mannheim, Germany)
Le combat des Muses (1762)
Le jugement d'Apollon (1780)
Pandore (1789)

Luciano Xavier Santos (1734–1808) (b. Lisbon, Portugal)
Ercole sul Tago (1765)
Il natal di Giove (1766)
Il sogno di Scipione (1768)
Il Paladio conservato (1771)
Alcide al bivio (1778)
Palmira di Tebe (1781)
Esione (1784)
Il re pastore (1797)
La Galatea (unperf.)

Jean-Benjamin de La Borde (1734–1794) (b. Paris, France)
Les trois déesses rivalles (1760)
Ismène et Isménias, ou La fête de Jupiter (1763)
Thétis et Pelée (1765)
Pandore (1767)
Amphion (1767)

Carlo Monza (c.1735–1801) (b. Milan, Italy)
Olimpiade (1758)
Achille in Sciro (1764)
Temistocle (1766)
Oreste (1766)
Demetrio (1769)
Adriano in Siria (1769)
Germanico in Germania (1770)
Antigono (1772)
Alessandro nell'Indie (1775)
Cleopatra (1775)
Demofoonte (1776)
Caio Mario (1777)
Ifigenia in Tauride (1784)
Enea in Cartagine (1784)
Erifile (1785)

Johann Christian Bach (1735–1782) (b. Leipzig, Germany)
Artaserse (1760)
Catone in Utica (1761)
Alessandro nell'Indie (1762)
Orione, ossia Diana vendicata (1763)
Adriano in Siria (1765)
Carrataco (1767)

Endimione (1772)
Temistocle (1772)
Lucio Silla (1775)
La clemenza di Scipione (1778)

Mattia Vento (1735–1776) (b. Naples, Italy)
Demofoonte (1765)
Sofonisba (1766)
Artaserse (1771)
La vestale (1776)

Anton Schweitzer (1735–1787) (b. Coburg, Germany)
Elysium (1770)
Apollo unter den Hirten (1770)
Pygmalion (1772)
Aurora (1772)
Ariadne auf Naxos (1772–1773)
Alceste (1773)
Die Wahl des Hercules (1773)
Polyxena (1775)

Ernst Wilhelm Wolf (1735–1792) (b. Grossen Behringen, Germany)
Alceste (1786)

Bernardo Ottani (1736–1827) (b. Bologna, Italy)
Calipso (1776)
Catone in Utica (1777)
La Didone (1779)
Arminio (1781)
La clemenza di Tito (1798)

Antonio Tozzi (c.1736–after 1812) (b. Bologna, Italy)
Tigrane (1762)
Andromaca (1763)
Il re pastore (1766–1767)
Siroe (1766–1767)
Adriano in Siria (1770)
Zenobia (1773)
Orfeo ed Euridice (1775)

Salvatore Rispoli (c.1736/45–1812) (b. Naples, Italy)
Ipermestra (1785)

Michael Haydn (1737–1806) (b. Rohrau, Austria)
Andromeda e Perseo (1788)

Mysliveček, Josef (1737–1781) (b. Prague, Czechoslovakia)
Semiramide (1765)
Il Belerofonte (1767)
Il trionfo di Clelia (1767)
Il Demofoonte (1769; second version 1775)
L'Ipermestra (1769)

Il Demetrio (1773; second version 1779)
Romolo ed Ersilia (1773)
La clemenza di Tito (1773)
Erifile (1773)
Antigona (1774)
Atide (1774)
Artaserse (1774)
Ezio (1775)
Adriano in Siria (1776)
La Calliroe (1778)
L'Olimpiade (1778)
La Circe (1779)
Medonte (1780)
Antigono (1780)

Vincenzo Manfredini (1737–1799) (b. Pistoia, Italy)
Semiramide riconosciuta (1760)
Olimpiade (1762)
Artaserse (1772)

Brizio Petrucci (1737–1828) (b. Massalombarda, Italy)
Ciro riconosciuto (1765)
Demofoonte (1765)

Giuseppe Millico (1737–1802) (b. Terlizzi, Italy)
Ipermestra (1781)

Francesco Zannetti (1737–1788) (b. Volterra, Italy)
L'Antigono (1765)
La Didone abbandonata (1766)
Artaserse (1782)

Antonio Boroni (1738–1792) (b. Rome, Italy)
Demofoonte (1761)
Sofonisba (1764)
Siroe (1764)
Artaserse (1767)
Didone (1768)
Enea nel Lazio (1778)

Giovanni Battista Borghi (1738–1796) (b. Camerino, Italy)
Adriano in Siria (1759)
Merope (1768)
Alessandro in Armenia (1768)
Siroe (1771)
Il trionfo di Clelia (1773)
Artaserse (1775)
Creso, re di Lidia (1777)
Eumene (1777)
Tito Manlio (1780)
Quinto Fabio (1781)

Arbace (1782)
Piramo e Tisbe (1783)
Olimpiade (1784)
La morte di Semiramide (1791)

Giuseppe Sigismondo (1739–1826) (b. Naples, Italy)
Endimione (?1764/5)
Demetrio (no date)

Karl Ditters von Dittersdorf (1739–1788) (b. Vienna, Austria)
Il tribunale di Giove (1774)
Democrito correto (1787)
Gott Mars, oder Der eiserne Mann (1795)

Johann Gottfried Schwanenberger (c.1740–1804) (b. Wolfenbüttel, Germany)
Adriano in Siria (1762)
Il Temistocle (1762)
La Galatea (1763)
Ezio (1763)
La Didone abbandonata (1765)
Zenobia (1765)
L'Issipile (1766)
Antigono (1768)
L'Olimpiade (1782)
Recits in *Il Creso* (1760)

Francesco Piticchio (fl.1760–1800) (b. ?Palermo, Sicily)
Didone abbandonata (1780)
La vendetta di Medea (1798)

Giovanni Paisiello (1740–1816) (b. Roccaforzata, Italy)
Lucio Papirio dittatore (1767)
Olimpia (1768)
Demetrio (1771; second version 1779)
Annibale in Torino (1771)
Artaserse (1771)
La Semiramide in villa (1772)
La Dardané (1772)
Alessandro nell'Indie (1773)
Andromeda (1774)
Demofoonte (1775)
Socrate immaginario (1775)
La disfatta di Dario (1776)
Achille in Sciro (1778)
Alcide al bivio (1780)
Antigono (1785)
La grotta di Trofonio (1785)
Olimpiade (1786)
Pirro (1787)
Giunone Lucina (1787)
Fedra (1788)

Catone in Utica (1789)
Zenobia in Palmira (1790)
Ipermestra (1791)
Didone abbandonata (1794)
Andromaca (1797)
Proserpine (1803)

Victor Pélissier (c.1740/50–c.1820) (b. ?Paris, France)
Ariadne Abandoned by Theseus in the Isle of Naxos (1797)

Luigi Gatti (1740–1817) (b. Castro Lacizzi, Italy)
Alessandro nell'Indie (1768)
Olimpiade (1775)
Antigono (1781)
Demofoonte (1787)

Louis Granier (1740–1800) (b. Toulouse, France)
Théonis (1767)

Hieronymus Mango (c.1740–1790) (b.?Italy)
Ciro riconosciuta (1767)
Adriano in Siria (1768)

Jean-Paul-Egide Martini (1741–1816) (b. Freystadt, Bavaria, Germany)
Sapho (1794)

Johann Gottlieb Naumann (1741–1801) (b. Blasewitz, Germany)
L'Achille in Sciro (1767)
Alesandro nelle Indie (1768)
La clemenza di Tito (1769)
Ipermestra (1774)
Amphion (1778)
Orpheus og Eurydike (1786)
Medea in Colchide (1788)
Protesilao (1789)
Aci e Gallatea (1801)

André-Ernest-Modeste Grétry (1741–1813) (b. Liège, Belgium)
Céphale et Procris (1773)
Le jugement de Midas (1778)
Andromaque (1780)
Electre (1781–1782)
Les colonnes d'Alcide (1782)
Oedipe à Colonne (1785)
Amphitryon (1786)
Aspasie (1789)
Diogène et Alexandre (1794)
Anacréon chez Polycrate (1797)
Delphis et Mopsa (1803)

Giacomo Rust (1741–1786) (b. Rome, Italy)
Alessandro nell'Indie (1775)

Il Socrate immaginario (1776)
Calliroe (1776)
Il Giove di Creta (1776)
Il Parnaso confuso (1778)
Vologeso re de' Parti (1778)
Demofoonte (1780)
Artaserse (1781)
Adriano in Siria (1781)
Berenice (1786)

François Hippolyte Barthelemon (1741–1808) (b. Bordeaux, France)
Pelopida (1766)
Orpheus (1768)
The Judgment of Paris (1768)

Marc-Antoine Désaugiers (1742–1793) (b. Fréjus, France)
Le petit Oedipe (1779)
Erixène (1780)

Alessandro Felici (1742–1772) (b. Florence, Italy)
Antigono (1769)

Carlo Franchi (?1743–after 1779) (b. ?Naples, Italy)
Ifigenia in Aulide (1766)
La clemenza di Tito (1766)
Arsace (1768)
Siroe re di Persia (1770)

Giuseppe Gazzaniga (1743–1818) (b. Verona, Italy)
Ezio (1772)
L'isola di Alcina (1772)
Perseo ed Andromeda (1775)
L'isola di Calipso (1775)
Gli errori di Telemaco (1776)
Antigono (1781)
Tullo Ostilio (1784)
Circe (1786)
La Didone (1787)
Gli Argonauti in Colco (1790)
Idomeneo (1790)

John Abraham Fisher (1744–1806) (b. Dunstable or London, England)
The Court of Alexander (1770)
The Syrens (1776)

Pierre Joseph Candeille (1744–1827) (b. Estaires, France)
Les saturnales, ou Tibulle et Délie (1777)
Castor et Pollux (1791)

Karl Siegmund von Seckendorff (1744–1785) (b. Erlangen, Germany)
Proserpina (1778)

Luigi Marescalchi (1745–after 1805) (b. Bologna, Italy)
Alessandro nell'Indie (1778)
Andromeda e Perseo (1784)

João de Sousa Carvalho (1745–1798) (b. Estremoz, Portugal)
L'Eumene (1773)
Perseo (1779)
Testoride argonauta (1780)
Seleuco, re di Siria (1781)
Penelope nella partenza da Sparta (1782)
L'Endimione (1783)
Adrasto rè degli Argivi (1784)
Nettuno ed Eglé (1785)
Alcione (1787)
Numa Pompilio Il re de Romani (1789)

Gennaro Astarita (c.1745–1803) (b. ?Naples, Italy)
La Didone abbandonata (1780)
Ipermestra (1789)

Friedrich Benda (1745–1814) (b. Postdam, Germany)
Orpheus (1785)
Alceste (1786)

Nicolas-Jean Le Froid de Méreaux (1745–1797) (b. Paris, France)
Alexandre aux Indes (1783)
Oedipe et Jocaste (1791)
Fabius (1793)

Joseph Willibald Michl (1745–1816) (b. Neumarkt, Germany)
Il trionfo di Clelia (1776)
Regulus, der Patriot (1781)

Charles Dibdin (1745–1814) (b. Southampton, England)
Damon and Phillida (1768)
The Ephesian Matron, or the Widow's Tears (1769)
Interlude in *Amphitryon, or The Two Sosias* (1769)
Poor Vulcan (1778)
Jupiter and Alcmena (1781)
The Graces (1782)
Pandora (1783)

Barnaba Bonesi (1745–1824) (b. Paris, France)
Pigmalion (1780)
Amasis (1788)

James Hook (1746–1827) (b. Norwich, England)
Dido (1771)
Cupid's Revenge (1772)
Apollo and Daphne (1773)
The Feast of Anacreon (1788)

Domenico Corri (1746–1825) (b. Rome, Italy)
Alessandro nell'Indie (1774)

Giovanni Masi (c.1730–after 1776) (b. Florence, Italy)
Muzio Scevola (1760)
La disfatta di Dario (1774)
Vologeso re dei Parti (1776)

Venanzio Rauzzini (1746–1810) (b. Camerino, Italy)
Piramo e Tisbe (1775)
Didone abbandonata (1775)
Ezio (1781)
Creusa in Delfo (1783)
La vestale (1787)

Gian Francesco Fortunati (1746–1821) (b. Parma, Italy)
Ipermestra (1773)

Jean-Baptiste Rochefort (1746–1819) (b. Paris, France)
Daphnis et Florise (1782)
Ariane (1788)

Felice Alessandri (1747–1798) (b. ?Rome, Italy)
Ezio (1767)
Arianna e Teseo (1768)
Argea (1773)
Creso (1774)
Medonte re d'Epiro (1774)
Alcone e Ruggero (1775)
Calliroe (1778)
Adriano in Sirio (1779)
Erifile (1780)
Attalo re di Bitinia (1780)
Demofoonte (1783)
Artaserse (1783)
Il ritorno di Ulysse a Penelope (1790)
Dario (1791)
Virginia (1793)

Joseph Schuster (1748–1812) (b. Dresden, Germany)
La Didone abbandonata (1776)
Demofoonte (1776)
Creso in Media (1779)
Amor e Psyche (1780)

Etienne Joseph Floquet (1748–1785) (b. Aix-en-Provence, France)
Le triomphe d'Alcide (1783)

Theodor (1748–1823) (b. Strasbourg, Alsace)
Calypso abbandonata (1784)
Artaserse (1785)

Joachim Albertini (1748–1812) (b. Pesaro, Italy)
Circe und Ulisses (1785)
Scipione africano (1789)
La virgine vestale (1803)

Louis Joseph Saint-Amans (1749–1820) (b. Marseilles, France)
La mort de Didon (1776)
Daphnis et Thémire (1778)
Psyché et l'Amour (1778)
Aspasie (1795)

Georg Joseph Vogler (1749–1814) (b. Würzburg, Germany)
Castore e Polluce (1787)

Domenico Cimarosa (1749–1801) (b. Aversa, Italy)
Caio Mario (1780)
Alessandro nell'Indie (1781)
Giunio Bruto (1781)
La Circe (1783)
Oreste (1783)
L'Olimpiade (1784)
Artaserse (1784)
La Cleopatra (1789)
Penelope (1795)
Gli Orazi ed i Curiazi (1796)
Achille all'assedio di Troia (1797)
Artemisia regina di Caria (1797)

Prosper-Didier Deshayes (c.1750–1815) (b. France)
Le défaite du serpent Python par Apollon (1786)
Delie (1787)
La chute de Phaëton (1788)
Le petit Orphée (1793)

Gaetano Monti (c.1750–?1816) (b. Naples, Italy)
L'Adriano in Siria (1775)

Mathias Stabinger (c.1750–1815) (b. Germany)
Calipso abbandonata (c.1777)
Pigmalion (1787)

Antonio Salieri (1750–1825) (b. Legnago, Italy)
L'Europa riconosciuta (1778)
Semiramide (1782)
Les Danaïdes (1784)
La grotta di Trofonio (1785)
Les Horaces (1786)
Il pastor fido (1789)
Catalina (1792)
Eraclito e Democrito (1795)
Palmira, regina di Persia (1795)
Cesare in Farmacusa (1800)

Annibale in Capua (1801)
La vestale (1768) (doubtful)

Giuseppe Calegari (c.1750–1812) (b. Padua, Italy)
La Zenobia in Palmira (1779)
Artemisia (1782)
Il natal d'Apollo (1783)

Alessio Prati (1750–1788) (b. Ferrara, Italy)
L'Ifigenia in Aulide (1784)
La vendetta di Nino (1786)
Olimpia (1786)
Demofoonte (1786)

Louis Raymond (fl.1785–1806) (b. France)
Anacréon (1785)

Michele Mortellari (c.1750–1807) (b. Palermo, Sicily)
Didone abbandonata (1772)
Arsace (1775)
Antigona (1776)
Ezio (1777)
Antigono (1778)
Alessandro nell'Indie (1778)
Troia distrutta (1778)
Lucio Silla (1778)
Medonte (1780)
Semiramide (1784)

Francesco Salari (1751–1828) (b. Bergamo, Italy)
Ifigenia in Aulide (1776)

Dmitry Stepanovich Bortnyansky (1751–1825) (b. Glukhov, Ukraine)
Creonte (1776)
Quinto Fabio (1778)
Alcide (1778)

Giuseppe Giordani (1751–1798) (b. Naples, Italy)
Demetrio (1780)
Erifile (1780)
Il ritorno d'Ulisse (1782)
Tito Manlio (1784)
La vestale (1785)
Ifigenia in Aulide (1786)
Alciade e Telesia (1787)
Caio Ostilio (1788)
Scipione (1788)
La disfatta di Dario (1789)
Cajo Mario (1789)
Aspasia (1790)
Nicomede (1790)

Medonte, re di Epiro (1791)
Atalanta (1792)

Ferdinand Kauer (1751–1831) (b. Klein-Thaya, Austria)
Telemach Prinz von Ithaka (1801)
Der travestirte Telemach (1805)
Antiope und Telemach (1805)
Orpheus und Eurydice (1813)
Antonius und Kleopatra (1814)
Die Amazonen im Böhmen (1815)
Amor und Psyche (1817)

Jean-Baptiste Lemoyne (1751–1796) (b. Eymet, France)
Electre (1782)
Phèdre (1786)
Silvius Nerva (1792)
Miltiade à Marathon (1793)
Toute la Grèce (1794)
L'île des femmes (1796)

Carl David Stegmann (1751–1826) (b. Staucha, Germany)
Philemon und Baucis (1777)

Carl Stenborg (1752–1813) (b. Stockholm, Sweden)
Petis och Thelée (1779)

Justin Heinrich Knecht (1752–1817) (b. Biberach, Germany)
Scipio vor Karthago (1789)

Johann Friedrich Reichardt (1752–1814) (b. Königsberg, Germany)
Cephalus und Prokris (1777)
Ino (1779)
Panthée (1786)
Andromeda (1788)
Protesilao (1789)
L'Olimpiade (1791)
Hercules Tod (1802)

Giuseppe Francesco Bianchi (c.1752–1810) (b. Cremona, Italy)
Giulio Sabino (1772)
Demetrio (1774)
Eurione (1775)
Erifile (1779)
Castore e Polluce (1779)
Arbace (1781)
Venere e Adone (1781)
La Zemira (1781)
Olimpiade (1781)
Piramo e Tisbe (1783)
Briseide (1783)
Cajo Mario (1784)
Alessandro nell'Indie (1785)

Mesenzio, re d'Etruria (1786)
Artaserse (1787)
Scipione africano (1787)
La morte di Cesare (1788)
Arminio (1790)
Caio Ostilio (1791)
Deifile (1791)
Seleuco, re di Siria (1791)
Aci e Galatea (1792)
Antigona (1796)
Merope (1797)
Cinna (1798)
La morte di Cleopatra (1801)
Le triomphe d'Alcide à Athènes (1806)

Niccolò Antonio Zingarelli (1752–1837) (b. Naples, Italy)
Antigono (1786)
Ifigenia in Aulide (1787)
Artaserse (1789)
Antigone (1790)
La morte di Cesare (1790)
Pirro, re d'Epiro (1791)
Annibale in Torino (1792)
Atalanta (1792)
Apelle (1793)
Quinto Fabio (1794)
Gli Orazi e i Curiazi (1795)
Andromeda (1796)
La morte di Mitridate (1797)
Meleagro (1798)
Il ratto delle Sabine (1799)
Clitennestra (1800)
Edipo a Colono (1802)
Il ritorno di Serse (1808)
Berenice, regina d'Armenia (1811)

Giuseppe Moneta (1754–1806) (b. Florence, Italy)
Il Meleagro (1785)
La vendetta di Medea (1787)
Orfeo negli Elisi (1788)
Il sacrifizio d'Ifigenia (1789)
Oreste (1798)

Vicente Martín y Soler (1754–1806) (b. Valencia, Italy)
Ifigenia in Aulide (1779)
Ipermestra (1780)
Andromaca (1780)
Partenope (1782)
Vologeso (1783)
L'arbore di Diana (1787)

Franz Anton Hoffmeister (1754–1812) (b. Rothenburg am Neckar, Austria)
Der Königssohn aus Ithaka (1795)

Luigi Caruso (1754–1823) (b. Naples, Italy)
Artaserse (1774)
Scipione in Cartagena (1779)
Giunio Bruto (1785)
Demetrio (1790)

Gaetano Isola (1754–1813) (b. Genoa, Italy)
Medonte (1785)
Lisandro (1790)
Le danaidi (1792)

Gaetano Marinelli (1754–1820) (b. Naples, Italy)
Il trionfo d'Arianna (1785–1786)
Lucio Papirio (1791)
La vendetta di Medea (1792)
Arminio (1792)
Attalo, re di Bitinia (1793)
Issipile (1796)
La morte di Cleopatra (1800)
Alessandro in Efeso (1810)

Peter Winter (1754–1825) (b. Mannheim, Germany)
Helena und Paris (1782)
Bellerophon (1785)
Circe (1788)
Medea und Jason (1789)
Psyche (1790)
Catone in Utica (1791)
Antigona (1791)
Il sacrifizio di Creta, ossia Arianna e Teseo (1792)
I fratelli rivali (1793)
Babylons Pyramiden (1797)
Das Labyrinth, oder Der Kampf mit den Elementen (1798)
La Grotte di Calipso (1807)
Il ratto di Proserpina (1815)

David August von Apell (1754–1832) (b. Kassel, Germany)
La clemenza di Tito (1787)
Anacreon (1803)

Antoine-Frederic Gresnick (1755–1799) (b. Liège, Belgium)
Alceste (1786)
Eponine et Sabinus (1796)
Léonidas, ou les Spartiates (1799)

Giuseppe Antonio Capuzzi (1755–1818) (b. Breno, Brescia, Italy)
Cefalo e Procri (1792)
Eco e Narciso (1793)

Gabriele Prota (1755–1843) (b. Naples, Italy)
Ezio (1784)

Gaetano Andreozzi (1755–1826) (b. Aversa, Italy)
Arbace (1781)
Olimpiade (1782)
Medonte, re d'Epiro (1783)
Didone abbandonata (1784)
Giasone e Medea (1785)
Catone in Utica (1786)
Virginia (1787)
Agesilao, re di Sparta (1788)
Arminio (1788)
Artaserse (1789)
La morte di Giulio Cesare (1790)
Arsinoe (1795)
Il trionfo di Arsace (1796)
Argea (1799)
Sesostri (1802)
Il trionfo di Alessandro (1803)
Piramo e Tisbe (1803)
Il trionfo di Alessandro Magno il Macedone (1815)

Olof Åhlström (1756–1835) (b. Åletorp, Värdinge, Sweden)
Den bedragne Bachan (1789)

Wolfgang Amadeus Mozart (1756–1791) (b. Salzburg, Austria)
Apollo et Hyacinthus seu Hyacinthi Metamorphosis (1767)
Mitridate, Re di Ponto (1770)
Ascanio in Alba (1771)
Il sogno di Scipione (1772)
Lucio Silla (1772)
Il re pastore (1775)
Thamos, Konig in Aegypten (1780)
Idomeneo, re di Creta (1781)
La clemenza di Tito (1791)

Vincenzo Righini (1756–1812) (b. Bologna, Italy)
Antigono (1788)
Alcide al bivio (1790)
Enea nel Lazio (1793)
Il trionfo d'Arianna (1793)
Atalante e Meleagro (1797)
Tigrane (1800)

Joseph Martin Kraus (1756–1792) (b. Miltenberg am Main, Germany)
Proserpin (1781)
Aeneas i Cartago eller Dido och Aeneas (1782)
Oedip (1785 [lost])

Johann Christoph Vogel (1756–1788) (b. Nurenberg, Germany)
La toison d'or (1786 revived as *Médée de Colchos*, 1788)
Démophon (1789)

Antonio Calegari (1757–1828) (b. Padua, Italy)
Alessandro nell'Indie (1779)
Deucalione e Pirra (1781)
Telemaco in Sicilia (1792)

Antonio Leal Moreira (1758–1819) (b. Abrantes, Portugal)
Bireno ed Olimpia (1782)
Ascanio in Alba (1785)
Artemisia, regina di Caria (1787)
Gli eroi spartani (1788)

Bernardo Porta (1758–1829) (b. Rome, Italy)
Agricole Viala, ou le héros de 13 ans (1793)
L'oracle (1797)
Les Horaces (1800)

Alphonse-Toussaint-Joseph-Andre-Marie Marseille Fortia de Piles (1758–1826)
        (b. Marseilles, France)
Vénus et Adonis (1784)

Johann Christian Friedrich Haeffner (1759–1833) (b. Oberschönau, Thuringia)
Electra (1787)
Alcides inträde i världen (1793)

Johann Christoph Kaffka (1759–after 1803) (b. Regensburg, Germany)
Antonius und Cleopatra (1779)

Francesco Gardi (1760/5–c.1810) (b. ?)
Enea nel Lazio (1786)
Apollo esule (1793)

Maria Luigi Carlo Zanobi Salvator Cherubini (1760–1842) (b. Florence, Italy)
Il Quinto Fabio (1779, second version 1783)
Adriano in Siria (1782)
Mesenzio, re d'Etruria (1782)
Olimpiade (1783)
L'Alessandro nell'Indie (1784)
Demetrio (1785)
Il Giulio Sabino (1786)
Ifigenia in Aulide (1788)
Démophon (1788)
Médée (1797)
Epicure (1800)
Anacréon ou l'amour fugitif (1803)
Pimmalione (1809)

Jean-François Le Sueur (1760–1837) (b. Drucat-Plessiel, France)
Télémaque (1796)

Le triomphe de Trajan (1807)
Alexandre a Babylone (1814)

Giuseppe Maria Curcio (fl. 1780–1809) (b. Naples, Italy)
Il trionfo di Scipione in Cartagine (1795)
Giulio Cesare in Egitto (1796)
Ifigenia in Aulide (1799)
Argea (1799)
Roma liberata (1800)

Angelo Tarchi (c.1760–1814) (b. Naples, Italy)
Ademira (1783)
Bacco ed Arianna (1784)
Mitridate re di Ponto (1785)
L'Arminio (1785)
Ifigenia in Aulide (1785)
Virginia (1785)
Ariarate (1786)
Ifigenia in Tauride (1786)
Demofoonte (1786)
Il trionfo di Clelia (1786)
Melite riconosciuta (1787)
Antioco (1788)
Demetrio (1788)
Artaserse (1788)
Alessandro nelle Indie (1788)
Ezio (1789)
Giulio Sabino (1790)
L'apoteosi d'Ercole (1790)
Tito Manilio (1791)
L'Olimpiade (1792)
Adrasto re d'Egitto (1792)
La morte di Nerone (1792)
Le Danaidi (1794)
Ciro riconosciuto (1796)

Yevstigney Ipat'yevich Fomin (1761–1800) (b. St. Petersburg, Russia)
Orfey i Evridika (1791: Melodrama)
Klorida i Milon (1800: Chloris and Milo)
Zolotoye yabloko ("The Golden Apple": on *Daphnis and Chloe*, 1803)

Vittorio Trento (c.1761–1833) (b. Venice, Italy)
Orfeo negli Elisi (1789)
La morte di Semiramide (1794)
Lidia (1800)
Il retorno di Serse (1800)
Ifigenia in Aulide (1804)
Andromeda (1805)
Climene (1811)
Giulio Sabino in Langres (1824)

Giambattista Cimador (1761–1805) (b. Venice, Italy)
Ati e Cibele (1789)
Pimmalione (1790)
Il ratto di Proserpine (1791)

Stephen Storace (1762–1796) (b. London, England)
The Cave of Trophonius (1791)
Dido, Queen of Carthage (1792)

Giuseppe Nicolini (1762–1842) (b. Piacenza, Italy)
Artaserse (1795)
La clemenza di Tito (1797)
Bruto (1798)
I baccanali di Roma (1801)
I Manlii (1801)
Fedra (1803)
La selvaggia del messico (1804)
Peribea e Telamone (1804)
Traiano in Dacia (1807)
Coriolano (1808)
Dario Istaspe (1810)
Abradate e Dircea (1811)
Quinto Fabio (1811)
L'ira di Achille (1814)
Giulio Cesare nelle Gallie (1819)
Annibale in Bitinia (1821)
Aspasia e Agide (1824)

Marcos António Portugal (1762–1830) (b. Lisbon, Portugal)
Il Cinna (1793)
Demofoonte (1794)
Il ritorno di Serse (1797)
Alceste (1798)
Idante (1800)
Adrasto re d'Egitto (1800)
Il trionfo di Clelia (1802)
La Sofonisba (1803)
La Merope (1804)
La morte di Mitridate (1806)
Artaserse (1806)

Simon Mayr (1763–1845) (b. Mendorf, Germany)
Saffo (1794)
Telemaco nella isola di Calipso (1797)
Lauso e Lidia (1798)
Adriano in Siria (1798)
Argene (1801)
Ercole in Lidia (1803)
Il ritorno di Ulisse (1809)
Alcide al bivio (1809)
Il sacrifizio d'Ifigenia (1811; revised as *Ifigenia in Aulide*, 1820)

Medea in Corinto (1813)
Mennone e Zemira (1817)
Ifigenia in Tauride (1817)
La danaide (1819)
Fedra (1821)
Demetrio (1824)

Franz Ignaz Danzi (1763–1826) (b. Schwetzingen, Germany)
Cleopatra (1780)
Der Sylphe (1788)
Iphigenie in Aulis (1807)
Dido (1811)

Etienne-Nicolas Méhul (1763–1817) (b. Givet, Ardennes, France)
Adrien, empereur de Rome (1790–1791; second version 1800; third version 1801)
Horatius Coclès (1794)
Epicure (1800)
Bion (1800)
Héléna (1803)
Les amazones, ou La fondation de Thèbes (1811)
Sésostris (incomplete)

Peter Ritter (1763–1846) (b. Mannheim, Germany)
Alexander in Indien (1811)
Das Kind des Herkules (1812)

Stanislaus Spindler (1763–1819) (b. Steingaden, Germany)
Pyramus und Thisbe (1785)

Valentino Fioravanti (1764–1837) (b. Rome, Italy)
I tre Orfei (1787)
Camilla (1804)
Il giudizio di Paride (1808)
Didone abbandonata (1810)

Luigi Piccinni (1764–1827) (b. Rome, Italy)
Hippomène et Atalante (1810)

Vincenzo Federici (1764–1826) (b. Pesaro, Italy)
L'Olimpiade (1789)
L'usurpator innocente (1790)
Castore e Polluce (1803)
Oreste in Tauride (1804)
Sofonisba (1805)
Idomeneo (1806)
Ifigenia in Aulide (1809)

Pietro Terziani (1765–1831) (b. Rome, Italy)
Creso (1788)

Anton Eberl (1765–1807) (b. Vienna, Austria)
Pyramus und Thisbe (1794)

Daniel Steibelt (1765–1823) (b. Berlin, Germany)
Phèdre (1818)
Le jugement de Midas (c.1823)

Rodolphe Kreutzer (1766–1831) (b. Versailles, France)
Flaminius à Corinthe (1801)
Astyanax (1801)
Harmodius et Aristogiton (1804)
Aristippe (1808)
La fête de Mars (1809)
L'oriflamme (1814)
La princesse de Babylone (1815)
Les dieux rivaux (1816)

Franz Xaver Süssmayr (1766–1803) (b. Schwanenstadt, Austria)
Piramo e Tisbe (c.1793)
Alcidoro e Dalisa, o sia Gli amanti in Tempe (one scene) (no date)

Luigi Capotorti (1767–1842) (b. Molfetta, Italy)
Enea in Cartagine (1800)
Gli Orazi i Curiazi (1800)
Ciro (1805)
Marco Curzio (1813)

Henri-Montan Berton (1767–1844) (b. Paris, France)
L'oriflamme (1814)
Les dieux rivaux, ou les fêtes de Cythère (1816)
Virginie, ou Les décemvirs (1823)

Andreas Jakob Romberg (1767–1821) (b. Vechta, Germany)
Die Grossmut des Scipio (1816)

Bernard Heinrich Romberg (1767–1841) (b. Dinklage, Germany)
Ulysses und Circe (1807)

Franceso Basili (1767–1850) (b. Loreto, Italy)
Il ritorno di Ulisse (1798)
Achille all'assedio di Troia (1798)
Antigona (1799)
L'ira di Achille (1817)

Sebastiano Nasolini (?1768–1798/9) (b. Piacenza or Venice, Italy)
Il Catone in Utica (1789)
Adriano in Siria (1789)
Andromaca (1790)
La morte de Semiramide (1790)
Teseo e Stige (1790)
Ercole al Termodonte (1791)
La morte di Cleopatra (1791)
La Calliroe (1792)
Tito e Berenice (1793)
Epponina (1794)

Merope (1796)
La morte di Mitridate (1797)
Timoleone (1798)
Il trionfo di Clelia (1798)

Carl Bernhard Wessely (1768–1826) (b. Berlin, Germany)
Psyche (1789)

Bonifazio Asioli (1769–1832) (b. Corregio, Italy)
Cinna (1792)
Pigmalione (1796)

Louis-Luc Loiseau de Persuis (1769–1819) (b. Metz, France)
Léonidas, ou Les Spartiates (1799)
Le triomphe de Trajan (1807)
Les dieux rivaux, ou Les fêtes de Cythère (1816)

Francesco Gnecco (c.1769–1810/11) (b. Genoa, Italy)
Alessandro nell'Indie (1800)
Arsace e Semiramide (1804)

Giuseppe Farinelli (1769–1836) (b. Este, Italy)
Antioco in Egitto (1798)
La caduta della nuova Cartagine (1803)
Climene (1806)
Calliroe (1807)
Annibale in Capua (1810)
Idomeneo (1811)
Lauso e Lidia (1813)
Partenope (1814)
Scipione in Cartagena (1815)

Antoine Reicha (1770–1836) (b. Prague, Czechoslovakia)
Télémaque (1800–1801)
Philoctète (before 1822)
Sapho (1822)

Ferdinando Paer (1771–1839) (b. Parma, Italy)
Orphée et Euridice (1791)
Circe (1792)
Laodicea (1793)
Idomeneo (1794)
Ero e Leandro (1794)
Il Cinna (1795)
Camilla, ossia il sotterraneo (1799)
Achille (1801)
Sofonisba (1805)
Numa Pompilio (1808)
Cleopatra (1808)
Diana e Endimione, ossia Il ritardo (1811)
La Didone (1810)

I Baccanti (1813)
L'oriflamme (1814)

Gottlob Benedict Bierey (1772–1840) (b. Dresden, Germany)
Pyramus und Thisbe (1811)

Giovanni Liverati (1772–1846) (b. Bologna, Italy)
Enea in Cartagine (1796)
La presa d'Egea (1809)
The Nymph of the Grotto (1829)
Amore e Psiche (1831)

Giuseppe Mosca (1772–1839) (b. Naples, Italy)
Ifigenia in Aulide (1799)
Sesostri (1803)

Karl Jacob Wagner (1772–1822) (b. Darmstadt, Germany)
Pygmalion (1797)
Adonis (1815)
Chimene (1822)

Josef Triebensee (1772–1846) (b. Wittingau, Bohemia)
Telemach auf der Insel Ogygia (1824)

Nicolas Isouard (1773–1818) (b. Malta)
Artaserse re di Persia (1794)
Flaminius à Corinthe (1801)

Gaspare Spontini (1774–1851) (b. Maiolati, Italy)
Olimpie (1819; second version 1821 as *Olimpia*; third version 1826)
Il Teseo riconosciuto (1798)
Le vestale (1807)
Les dieux rivaux ou Les fêtes de Cythère (1816)

Ferdinando Orlandi (1774–1848) (b. Parma, Italy)
Nino (1804)
Fedra (1820)

François-Adrien Boieldieu (1775–1834) (b. Rouen, France)
Télémaque (1806)

Felice Alessandro Radicati (1775–1820) (b. Turin, Italy)
Coriolano (1809)
Fedra (1811)
Castore e Polluce (1815)

E.T.A. Hoffmann (1776–1822) (b. Nancy, France)
Aurora (1812)
Thassilo (1815)

Janos Fusz (1777–1819) (b. Tolna, Hungary)
Pyramus es Thisbe (c.1801)
Romulus und Remus (1816)

Charles-Louis Hanssens (1777–1852) (b. Ghent, Belgium)
Alcibiade (1829)

Vincenza Pucitta (1778–1861) (b. Civitavecchia, Italy)
Andromaca (1806)
La vestale (1810)
Boadicea (1813)
Aristodemo (1814)

Sigismund Neukomm (1778–1858) (b. Salzburg, Austria)
Alexander am Indus (1804)
Niobé (1809)

Anton Fischer (1778–1808) (b. Ried, Swabia)
Theseus und Ariadne (1809)

Friedrich August Kanne (1778–1833) (b. Delitzsch, Saxony)
Anakreon und Sappho (1805)
Orpheus (1807)

Stefano Pavesi (1779–1850) (b. Casaletto Vaprio, Italy)
Andromaco (1804)
La vedetta di Medea (1804)
Trionfo d'Emilia (1805)
I Baccanali di Roma (1806)
Aristodemo (1807)
Ippolita, regina delle amazzoni (1809)
Arminia (1810)
Aspasia e Cleomene (1812)
Le Danaide romane (1816)
Il gioventù di Cesare (1817)
Arminio (1821)
Antigona e Lauso (1822)

Louis Alexandre Piccinni (1779–1850) (b. Paris, France)
Alcibiade solitaire (1814)

Victor-Charles-Paul Dourlan (1780–1864) (b. Dunkirk, France)
Philoclès (1806)

Conradin Kreutzer (1780–1849) (b. Messkirch, Baden, Germany)
Aesop in Phrygien (1816)
Orestes (1818)

Felice Blangini (1781–1841) (b. Turin, Italy)
Trajano in Dacia (1814)

Carlo Coccia (1782–1873) (b. Naples, Italy)
Teseo e Medea (1815)

Daniel-François-Esprit Auber (1782–1871) (b. Caen, France)
Actéon (1836)
La sirène (1844)

Johann Nepomuk Poissl (1783–1865) (b. Haukenzell, Germany)
Antigonus (1808)
Ottaviano in Sicilia (1812)
Issipile (1818)

Giacomo Cordella (1786–1846) (b. Naples, Italy)
Annibale in Capua (1809)
Alcibiade (1825)
Partenope (1840)

Sir Henry Rowley Bishop (1786–1855) (b. London, England)
Artaxerxes (1813)
Telemachus (1815)

Pietro Raimondi (1786–1853) (b. Rome, Italy)
L'oracolo di Delfo (1811)
Ciro in Babylonia (1820)
Argia (1823)
Berenice in Roma (1824)

Michele Carafa (1787–1872) (b. Naples, Italy)
Ifigenia in Tauride (1817)
Berenice in Siria (1818)

Ramon Carnicer (1789–1855) (b. Lérida, Spain)
Ipermestra (1843)

Nicola Antonio Manfroce (1791–1813) (b. Palmi Calabro, Italy)
Ecuba (1812)

Peter Joseph von Lindpaintner (1791–1856) (b. Koblenz, Germany)
Demophoon (1811)
Die Amazone (1831)

Mlle. Guenin de Presles (1791–?) (b. France)
Daphnis et Amanthée (1807)

Gioachino Rossini (1792–1868) (b. Pesaro, Italy)
Ciro in Babilonia (1812)
Aureliano in Palmira (1813)
Ermione (1819)

Pietro Coppola (1793–1877) (b. Castrogiovanni, Italy)
Achille in Sciro (1828)

Saverio Mercadante (1795–1870) (b. Altamura, Italy)
L'apoteosi d'Ercole (1819)
Anacreonti in Samo (1820)
Scipione in Cartagine (1820)
Andronico (1821)
Didone abbandonata (1823)
Le nozze di Telemaco ed Antiope (1824)
Ipermestra (1824–1825)
Ezio (1827)

Adriano in Siria (1828)
La vestale (1840)
Medea (1851)

Giovanni Battista Gordigiani (1795–1871) (b. Modena, Italy)
Pygmalione (1845)

Heinrich August Marschner (1795–1861) (b. Zittau, Germany)
La clemenza di Tito (1816)
Lucretia (1820–1826)

Wilhelm Mangold (1796–1875) (b. Darmstadt, Germany)
Merope (1823)

Giovanni Pacini (1796–1867) (b. Catania, Italy)
Cesare in Egitto (1821)
Temistocle (1824)
Alessandro nelle Indie (1824)
Niobe (1826)
Furio Camillo (1839)
Saffo (1840)
Medea (1845)
Merope (1848)

Franz Schubert (1797–1828) (b. Vienna, Austria)
Adrast (1819–1820)
Die Verschworenen (*Der Häusliche Krieg*, after Aristophanes' *Lysistrata* and
    Ecclesiazusae, 1861)

Domenico Gaetano Maria Donizetti (1797–1848) (b. Bergamo, Italy)
Il Pigmalione (1816)
L'ira d'Achille (1817)
L'esule di Roma, ossia Il proscritto (1828)
Poliuto (1848)

Karl Gottlieb Reissiger (1798–1859) (b. Belzig, Germany)
Didone abbandonata (1824)

Fromental Halévy (1799–1862) (b. Paris, France)
Marco Curzio (1822)
Pygmalion (c.1824)
Erostrate (1825)

Giuseppe Persiani (c.1799/1805–1869) (b. Recanati, Italy)
Danao re d'Argo (1827)

Vincenzo Bellini (1801–1835) (b. Catania, Sicily)
Norma (1831)

Hector Berlioz (1803–1869) (b. Paris, France)
Les Troyens (1860)

Adolphe Adam (1803–1856) (b. Paris, France)
Die Hamadryaden (1840)

Ignaz Lachner (1807–1895) (b. Rain am Lech, Germany)
Zenobia vor der Romerschlacht (1830)

Lauro Rossi (1812–1885) (b. Macerata, Italy)
Le Sabine (1852)
La sirena (1855)
Cleopatra (1876)

Richard Wagner (1813–1883) (b. Leipzig, Germany)
Rienzi, der Letzte der Tribunen (1842)
Achilleus (1850: incomplete)

Carlo Pedrotti (1817–1893) (b. Verona, Italy)
Antigone (without a date)

Charles-François Gounod (1818–1893) (b. Paris, France)
Sapho (1851)
Philémon et Baucis (1860)
Polyeucte (1878)

Jacques Offenbach (1819–1880) (b. Cologne, Germany)
Orphée aux enfers (1858; second version 1874)
La Belle Hélène (1864)

Franz Suppé (1819–1895) (b. Spalato, Austria)
Die Schöne Galathee (1865)

Giovanni Bottesini (1821–1889) (b. Crema, Italy)
Ero e Leandro (1879)

Victor Massé (1822–1884) (b. Lorrient, France)
Galathée (1852)
La Petite Soeur d'Achille (unperf. 1872)
Une nuit de Cléopâtre (1885)

Ernest Reyer (1823–1909) (b. Marseilles, France)
Erostrate (1862)
Salammbô (1890)

Hervé (Florimond Ronger) (1825–1892) (b. France)
Agamemnon (1856)
Le Retour d'Ulysse (1862)
Les Troyens en Champagne (1863)
Les Sphinx (1879)
Bacchanale (1892)

Anton Grigor'yevich Rubinstein (1829–1894) (b. Vïkhvatintsï on the Dnestr, Ukraine)
Néron (1879)

José Angel Montero (1832–1881) (b. Caracas, Venezuela)
Virginia (1873)

Camille Saint-Saëns (1835–1921) (b. Paris, France)
Proserpine (1887)
Ascanio (1890)

Phryné (1893)
Hélène (1904)
Déjanire (1911)

Max Zenger (1837–1911) (b. Germany)
Eros und Psyche (1901)

Théodore Dubois (1837–1924) (b. Rosnay, Marne, France)
L'enlèvement de Proserpine (1879)

Melesio Morales (1838–1908) (b. Mexico City, Mexico)
Cleopatra (1891)

Modest Petrovich Mussorgsky (1839–1881) (b. Karevo, Russia)
Salammbô (1880)

Emmanuel Chabrier (1841–1894) (b. Ambert, Puy-de-Dome, France)
Briséïs, ou Les amants de Corinth (1888–1891)

Arrigo Boito (1842–1918) (b. Padua, Italy)
Nerone (1924)

Henri Maréchal (1842–1924) (b. Paris, France)
Déidamie (1893)
Daphnis et Chloé (1899)

Jules Massenet (1842–1912) (b. Montaud, France)
Méduse (1870)
Thaïs (1894)
Sapho (1897)
Ariane (1906)
Bacchus (1909)
Roma (1912)
Cléopâtre (1915)

Mykola Vitaliyovych Lysenko (1842–1912) (b. Hrynky, Ukraine)
Sappho (1896–1900)
Eneída (1910)

Gabriel Fauré (1845–1924) (b. Parmiers, Ariège, France)
Prométhée (1900) (demi-opera)
Pénélope (1913)

August Bungert (1845–1915) (b. Mülheim an der Ruhr, Germany)
Die Odyssee:
Kirke (1898)
Odysseus' Heimkehr (1896)
Nausicaa (1901)
Odysseus' Tod (1903)
Zygmunt Noskowski (1846–1909) (b. Warsaw, Poland)
Livia Quintilla (1898)

Arthur Coquard (1846–1910) (b. Paris, France)
Cassandre (1881)
Pompée (1888)

Gaston Salvayre (1847–1916) (b. Toulouse, France)
Calypso (1872)
Myrto (no date)

Luigi Mancinelli (1848–1921) (b. Orvieto, Italy)
Ero e Leandro (1896)

Zdenek Fibich (1850–1900) (b. Vseborice, Bohemia)
Medea (1863 Lost)
Hippodamia (1888–1891)

Vincent d'Indy (1851–1931) (b. Paris, France)
La rêve de Cinyras (1922)

Raoul Pugno (1852–1913/14) (b. Montrouge, France)
Le retour d'Ulysse (1889)
La vocation de Marius (1890)

Sergey Ivanovich Taneyev (1856–1915) (b. Vladimir, Russia)
Oresteya (1895)

Ruggero Leoncavallo (1857–1919) (b. Naples, Italy)
Edipo re (1920)
Prometeo (no date)

Isidore De Lara (1858–1935) (b. London, England)
Messaline (1899)

August Enna (1859–1939) (b. Nakskov)
Agleia (1884)
Areta (1884)
Kleopatra (1894)
Afrodites Praestinde (1925)

Raoul Gunsbourg (1859–1955) (b. Bucharest, Romania)
Lysistrata (1923)

Dionyssios Lavrangas (1860/4–1941) (b. Argostolion, Greece)
Galatea (1887)
Dido (1909)
Ikaros (1930)

Alberto Franchetti (1860–1942) (b. Turin, Italy)
Germania (1902)
Giove a Pompei (1921)
Glauco (1922)

George W.L. Marshall-Hall (1862–1915) (b. London, England)
Dido and Aeneas (?before 1890)
Alcestis (1898)
Aristodemus (1902)

Marie François Maurice Emmanuel (1862–1938) (b. Bar-sur-Aube, France)
Prométhée enchaîné (1916–1918)
Salamine (1921–1923)

Camille Erlanger (1863–1919) (b. Paris, France)
Aphrodite (1906)
Bacchus triomphant (1909)

Xavier Leroux (1863–1919) (b. Velletri, Italy)
Vénus et Adonis (1897)
Nausithoé (1920)

Hugo Kaun (1863–1932) (b. Berlin, Germany)
Sappho (1917)
Menandra (1926)

Pietro Mascagni (1863–1945) (b. Livorno, Italy)
Iris (1898)
Nerone (1935)

Paul Felix Weingartner (1863–1942) (b. Zara, Dalmatia)
Orestes: Agamemnon, Das Totenopfer, Die Erinyen (1902)

Alberto Nepomuceno (1864–1920) (b. Fortaleza, Brazil)
Artémis (1898)
Abul (1899–1905)
Incidental music for *Electra* (no date)

Richard Strauss (1864–1949) (b. Munich, Germany)
Elektra (1909)
Ariadne auf Naxos (1912)
Die ägyptische Helena (1928, rev. 1933)
Daphne (1938)
Die Liebe der Danae (1952)
Settings and revisions:
Iphigénie auf Tauris (Gluck) (1890)
Die Ruinen von Athen (Beethoven) (1924)
Idomeneo (Mozart) (1931)

Vladimir Ivanovich Rebikov (1866–1920) (b. Krasnoyarsk, Siberia)
Tea: Boginya (1904: Thea, the Goddess)
Nartsiss (1913: Narcissus)
Arakhne (1915: Arachne)

Learmont Drysdale (1866–1909) (b. Edinburgh, Scotland)
The Plague (1896)
The Oracle (1897)
Hippolytus (1905)

Umberto Giordano (1867–1948) (b. Foggia, Italy)
Giove a Pompei (1921)

Claude Terrasse (1867–1923) (b. France)
Les Travaux d'Hercule (1901)

Pierre Maurice (1868–1936) (b. Allaman, Switzerland)
Andromède (1912)
Le vengeance du pharaon (1934–1935)

Albert Roussel (1869–1937) (b. Tourvoing, France)
La Naissance de la lyre (1925)

Pietro Canonica (1869–1959) (b. Turin, Italy)
Medea (1953)

Henry Hadley (1871–1937) (b. Somerville, Mass., USA)
The Atonement of Pan (1912)
Cleopatra's Night (1920)

Alexander Zemlinsky (1871–1942) (b. Vienna, Austria)
Der König Kandaules (1935–1936)
Circe (1939)

Déodat de Séverac (1872–1921) (b. St. Félix de Caraman en Lauragais, France)
Héliogabale (1910)

William Henry Bell (1873–1946) (b. St. Albans, England)
Hippolytus (1910–1914)

Reynaldo Hahn (1874–1947) (b. Caracas, Venezuela)
Nausicaa (1919)

Sir Donald Francis Tovey (1875–1940) (b. London, England)
The Bride of Dionysus (1932)

Havergal Brian (1876–1972) (b. Dresden, Staffordshire, England)
Agamemnon (1957)

Raoul Laparra (1876–1943) (b. Bordeaux, France)
Amphitryon (1929)

Manuel de Falla (1876–1946) (b. Cádiz, Spain)
Atlántida (1961)

Vittorio Gnecchi (1876–1954) (b. Milan, Italy)
Cassandra (1905; second version 1909)

Vincenzo Tommasini (1878–1950) (b. Rome, Italy)
Medea (1902–1904)

Rutland Boughton (1878–1960) (b. Aylesbury, England)
Alkestis (1922)

Ildebrando Pizzetti (1880–1968) (b. Parma, Italy)
Aeneas (1904–1907: prol. and sketches)
Fedra (1915)
Ifigenia (1950)
Clitennestra (1965)

Theodore Pease Stearns (1880–1935) (b. Berea, Ohio, USA)
Endymion (1895)
Atlantis (1926)

Paul Le Flem (1881–1984) (b. Lézardrieux, France)
Endymion et Sémélé (1903)

George Enescu (1881–1955) (b. Liveni-Virnav, Romania)
Oedipe (Tragédie Lyrique) (1936)

Karol Szymanowski (1882–1937) b. Tymoszówka, Ukraine)
Król Roger [adapted from Euripides' *Bacchae*] (1926)

Gian Francesco Malipiero (1882–1973) (b. Venice, Italy)
Orfeo (1919–1920)
L'Orfeide (1925)
Le aquile di Aquileia (1928)
Favola d'Orfeo (1932)
Giulio Cesare (1934–1935)
Antonio e Cleopatra (1936–1937)
Ecuba (1938–1940)
Vergilii Aeneis (1946)

Igor Stravinsky (1882–1971) (b. Oranienbaum, now Lomonosov, Russia)
Oedipus Rex (1927)
Perséphone (1933–1934)

Theofrastos Sakellaridis (1883–1950) (b. Athens, Greece)
Ymenaeos (1901)
Apollo (1923)
Iro ke Leandros (1927)

Alfredo Casella (1883–1947) (b. Turin, Italy)
La Favola di Orfeo (1932)

Juan Manén (1883–1971) (b. Barcelona, Spain)
Acté (1908)
Nerón i Acté (1928)

Felipe Boero (1884–1958) (b. Buenos Aires, Argentina)
Ariana y Dionysos (1920)
Las Bacantes (1925)

Ludomir Rozycki (1884–1953) (b. Warsaw, Poland)
Meduza (1912)
Eros i Psyche (1914)

Giuseppe Mulè (1885–1951) (b. Termini Imerese, Sicily)
Dafni (1928)

André-Charles Samson Gailhard (1885–1966) (b. Paris, France)
Amaryllis (1906)
La fille du soleil (1909)

Egon Wellesz (1885–1974) (b. Vienna, Austria)
Alkestis (1924)
Die Bakchantinnen (1931)

Dimitrie Cuclin (1885–1978) (b. Galati, Romania)
Traian and Dochia (1921)
Agamemnon (1922)

Bellerophon (1925)
Meleagridele (1930)

Othmar Schoeck (1886–1957) (b. Brunnen, Switzerland)
Venus (1922)
Penthesilea (1927)

Nicolae Bretan (1887–1968) (b. Nasaud, Romania)
Arald (1942)

Lucile Crews (1888–?) (b. USA)
Ariadne-Dionysus (?1926)

Georgios Sklavos (1888–1976) (b. Braila, Romania)
Niove (1920)
Amphitryon (1955–1960)

Colin Macleod Campbell (1890–1953) (b. Britain)
Thais and Talmaae (1921)

Bohuslav Martinu (1890–1959) (b. Policka, east Bohemia)
Alexandre (1937)
Ariane (1961)

Guido Guerrini (1890–1965) (b. Faenza, Italy)
Enea (1953)

Jacques Ibert (1890–1962) (b. Paris, France)
Persée et Andromède (1921)

Arthur Bliss (1891–1975) (b. London, England)
The Olympians (1949)

Alberto Savinio (1891–1952) (b. Athens, Greece)
La mort de Niobé (1913)
Orfeo vedovo (1950)

Darius Milhaud (1892–1974) (b. Aix-en-Provence, France)
Les malheurs d'Orphée (1926)
L'enlèvement d'Europe (1927)
L'abandon d'Ariane (1928)
La délivrance de Thésée (1928) (The last three are parts 1, 2, and 3 of a trilogy.)
Médée (1939)
Agamemnon, Les choéphores, and *Les euménides* (1913–1922) (music for the *Oresteia*
    from Claudel's translation)

Giorgio Federico Ghedini (1892–1965) (b. Cuneo, Italy)
Le Baccanti (1941–1944)

Hendrik Andriessen (1892–1981) (b. Haarlem, Holland)
Philomela (1950)

Arthur Honegger (1892–1955) (b. Le Havre, France)
Antigone (1927)

John Laurence Seymour (1893–1986) (b. Los Angeles, Calif., USA)
Antigone (1920)

Paul Dessau (1894–1979) (b. Hamburg, Germany)
Orpheus (1931)
Das verhör des Lukullus (1951; reworked as *Die Verurteilung des Lukullus* 1951)

Carl Orff (1895–1985) (b. Munich, Germany)
Klage der Ariadne (1925; second version 1940)
Orpheus (1929)
Carmina Burana (1937) (*cantiones profanae*)
Catulli Carmina (1943) (*Ludi Scaenici*)
Antigonae (1949) (*Ein Trauerspiel des Sophokles von Hölderlin*)
Trionfo di Afrodite (1953) (*Concerto Scenico*)
Oedipus der Tyrann (1959) (*Ein Trauerspiel des Sophocles von Hölderlin*)
Prometheus (1967)
Arrangements of Monteverdi's *Orfeo, Lamento di Arianna,* and
    L'Incoronazione di Poppea (1920s)

Mario Castelnuovo-Tedesco (1895–1968) (b. Florence, Italy)
Bacco in Toscano (1925–1926)

Juan José Castro (1895–1968) (b. Avellaneda, Buenos Aires province, Argentina)
Proserpina y el extranjero (1952)

Max Brand (1896–1980) (b. Lemberg, Austria)
Kleopatra (c.1932–1938)

Roger Sessions (1896–1985) (b. Brooklyn, New York, USA)
The Trial of Lucullus (1947)

Erich Wolfgang Korngold (1897–1957) (b. Brno, Czechoslovakia)
Der Ring des Polykrates (1916)

Marcel Mihalovici (1898–1985) (b. Bucharest, Romania)
L'intransigeant Pluton (1928)
Phèdre (1950)
Les jumeaux (1962: Plautus' *Menaechmi*)

Emmanuel Bondeville (1898–1987) (b. Rouen, France)
Antoine et Cléopâtre (1974)

Salvatore Allegra (1898–1993) (b. Palermo, Italy)
Romulus (1946)

Francis Poulenc (1899–1963) (b. Paris, France)
Les mamelles de Tirésias

Hans Haug (1900–1967) (b. Basel, Switzerland)
Orfée (1954)
Le miroir d'Agrippine (1953–1954)
L'îlot des sirènes (without date)

Ernst Krenek (1900–1991) (b. Vienna, Austria)
Orpheus und Eurydike (1926)

Leben des Orest (1928–1929)
Cefalo e Procri (1933)
La Incoronazione de Poppea by Monteverdi (adaptation) (1937)
Tarquin (1940)
Pallas Athene weint (1952–1955)

Henri Tomasi (1901–1971) (b. Marseilles, France)
Ulysse, ou Le beau périple (1962)

Harry Partch (1901–1974) (b. Oakland, Calif., USA)
King Oedipus (Music Dance Drama, after W.B. Yeats, 1952)
Revelation in the Courthouse Park (1961: *Bacchae*)
Delusion of the Fury (Ritual of Dream and Delusion, 1969)

Federico Ghisi (1901–1975) (b. Shanghai, China)
Piramo e Tisbe (1941–1943)

Werner Egk (1901–1983) (b. Auchsesheim, Germany)
Circe (1945)

Stefan Wolpe (1902–1972) (b. Berlin, Germany)
Zeus and Elida: Musikaische Groteske (1928)

Hans Chemin-Petit (1902–1981) (b. Potsdam, Germany)
Die Klage der Ariadne (1971)

William Walton (1902–1983) (b. Oldham, England)
Troilus and Cressida (1954)

Rudolf Wagner-Régeny (1903–1969) (b. Szász-Régen, Transylvania)
Moschopulos (1928)
Prometheus (1958)

Lennox Berkeley (1903–1989) (b. Boars Hill, England)
Castaway [on Odysseus and Nausicaa] (1967)

Luigi Dallapiccola (1904–1975) (b. Pisino d'Istria, Italy)
Ulisse (1968)

Isa Krejčí (1904–1968) (b. Prague, Czechoslovakia)
Antigona (1934)

Walter Leigh (1905–1942) (b. London, England)
The Frogs (1936)

Marc Blitzstein (1905–1964) (b. Philadelphia, Penn., USA)
The Harpies (1931)
Juno (1959)

Inglis Gundry (1905–) (b. London, England)
The Return of Odysseus (1938)

Michael Tippett (1905–) (b. London, England)
King Priam (1962)

Boris Papandopulo (1906–1991) (b. Honnef, Germany)
Amfitrion (1936)

Elisabeth Lutyens (1906–1983) (b. London, England)
Penelope (1950)
Isis and Osiris (1976)

Louise Talma (1906–) (b. Archachon (US))
The Alcestiad (1962)

Henk Badings (1907–1987) (b. Bandung, Java)
Orestes (1954)
Asterion (1957)

Roberto Lupi (1908–1971) (b. Milan, Italy)
La nuova Euridice (1957)
Persefone (1970)

Edward Staempfli (1908–) (b. Bern, Switzerland)
Medea (1954)
Caligula (1981)

Marin Goleminov (1908–) (b. Kyustendil, Bulgaria)
Trakiiski idoli [Thracian Idols] (1981)

Jean Kurt Forest (1909–1975) (b. Darmstadt, Germany)
Sisyphos und Polyander (1974)

Heinz Röttger (1909–1977) (b. Herford, Germany)
Phaeton (1957)

Samuel Barber (1910–1981) (b. West Chester, Penn., USA)
Anthony and Cleopatra (1966)

Rolf Lieberman (1910–) (b. Zurich, Switzerland)
Penelope (1954)
Freispruch für Medea (1995)

Heinrich Sutermeister (1910–) (b. Feuerthalen, Switzerland)
Niobe (1946)

Erik Bergman (1911–) (b. Finland)
The Singing Tree (1988)

Peggy Glanville-Hicks (1912–1990) (b. Melbourne, Australia)
Nausicaa (1961)
Sappho (1965)

Hugo Weisgall (1912–1997) (b. Ivançice, Bohemia)
The Gardens of Adonis (1959)

Cesar Bresgen (1913–1988) (b. Florence, Italy)
Das Urteil des Paris (1943)
Ercole (1956)

Benjamin Britten (1913–1976) (b. Lowestoft, England)
The Rape of Lucretia (1946)
Realizations of Henry Purcell—*Dido and Aeneas; Orpheus Britannicus*

Maurice Ohana (1914–) (b. Casablanca, Morocco)
Syllabaire pour Phèdre (1968)

Helmut Eder (1916–) (b. Linz, Austria)
Oedipus (1960)

Lou Harrison (1917–) (b. Portland, Ore., USA)
Young Caesar (1971)

Tauno Pylkkanen (1918–1980) (b. Helsinki, Finland)
Ikaros (1960)

Bruno Maderna (1920–1973) (b. Venice, Italy)
Hyperion (1964)
Satyricon (1973)

Paul Kont (1920–) (b. Vienna, Austria)
Lysistrate (1961)
Plutos (1977)

Gerard Victory (1921–) (b. Dublin, Ireland)
Circe (1971–2)

Peter Wishart (1921–1984) (b. Crowborough, England)
Clytemnestra (1974)

Felix Werder (1922–) (b. Berlin, Germany)
The Agamemnon of Aeschylus (1967)
Medea (1985)

Iain Hamilton (1922–) (b. Glasgow, Scotland)
Agamemnon (1967–1969, 1987, 1989)
Pharsalia (1969)
The Catiline Conspiracy (1974)

Harold Blumenfeld (1923–) (b. Seattle, Wash., USA)
Amphitryon 4 (1962)

Flavio Testi (1923–) (b. Florence, Italy)
La furore di Oreste (1956)

Arghyris Kounadis (1924–) (b. Constantinople, Turkey)
The Return (1961: *The Way to Colonos*)
Teiresias (1975)
Lysistrate (1983)

Luigi Nono (1924–1990) (b. Venice, Italy)
Prometeo (1984)

Mikis Theodorakis (1925–) (b. Smyrna, Turkey)
Kostas Kariotakis, The Metamorphosis of Dionysus (1987).
Medea (1991) "Hommage à Verdi"

Elektra (1996) "Hommage à Puccini"
Antigone (1999) "Hommage à Bellini"
Music and songs for Michael Cacoyannis' *Elektra* (1961); *The Trojan Women* (1970);
  Iphigenia (1976)

Yasushi Akutagawa (1925–1989) (b. Tokyo, Japan)
Hiroshima no Orufe (1967)

Gabriel Charpentier (1925–) (b. Richmond, Quebec, Canada)
Orphée (1969; *Orphée* II 1972)

Claude Prey (1925–) (b. Fleury sur Andelle, France)
Métamorphose d'Echo (1967)

Antoine Duhamel (1925–) (b. Valmondois, France)
Les travaux d'Hercule (1981)

Charles Chaynes (1925–) (b. Toulouse, France)
Jocaste (1993?)

Hans Werner Henze (1926–) (b. Gütersloh, Germany)
The Bassarids (1966)

Ton de Leeuw (1926–) (b. Rotterdam, Netherlands)
Alceste (1963)
Antigone (1991)

Betsy Jolas (1926–) (b. Paris, France)
Le Cyclope (1986)

Meyer Kupferman (1926–) (b. New York, USA)
Antigonae (1973)
Prometheus (1978)

Karel Kupka (1927–1985) (b. Rychvald, Czechoslovakia)
Lysistrata (1958)
Opus Odysseus (1984)

John Joubert (1927–) (b. Cape Town, South Africa)
Antigone (1954)

Wilhelm Killmayer (1927–) (b. Munich, Germany)
La tragedia di Orfeo (1961)

Pascal Bentoiou (1927–) (b. Bucharest, Romania)
Jertfirea Iphigeniei (1968: *Iphigeneia's Sacrifice*)

Margaret Garwood (1927–) (b. Haddonfield, N.J., USA)
The Trojan Women (1967, rev. 1979)

John Buller (1927–) (b. London, England)
Bakhai (1992)

William Russo (1928–) (b. Chicago, Ill., USA)
Antigone (1967)
Aesop's Fables (1971, rev. 1972)

Jean-Michel Damase (1928–) (b. Bordeaux, France)
Eurydice (1972)

Thea Musgrave (1928–) (b. Barnton, Midlothian, Scotland)
The Voice of Ariadne (1974)

Sylvano Bussotti (1931–) (b. Florence, Italy)
Fedra (1988)

Jonathan Elkus (1931–) (b. San Francisco, Calif., USA)
Medea (1970)
Helen in Egypt (1970)

Alexander Goehr (1932–) (b. Berlin, Germany)
Arianna (1995)

Doru Popovici (1932–) (b. Resita, Romania)
Prometheu (1958)

Marvin David Levy (1932–) (b. Passaic, N.J., USA)
Mourning Becomes Electra (1967)

Aurel Stroe (1932–) (b. Bucharest, Romania)
Les Choéphores (1978)
Agamemnon (1983)
Eumenides (1986)

Per Nørgård (1932–) (b. Gentofte, Denmark)
Labyrinten (1967)

Bernadetta Matuszczak (1933/37–) (b. Torun, Poland)
Prometheus (1981–1982)

Harrison Birtwistle (1934–) (b. Accrington, England)
Nenia: The Death of Orpheus (1970)
Meridian (1971, on Orpheus)
The Fields of Sorrow (1971, on Orpheus)
The Oresteia (1981)
The Mask of Orpheus (1986)

Peter Zinovieff (1934–) (b. Accrington, England)
The Mask of Orpheus (1986)

John C. Eaton (1935–) (b. Bryn Mawr, Penn., USA)
Heracles (1964)
The Lion and Androcles (1974)
The Cry of Clytaemnestra (1980)

Bent Lorentzen (1935–) (b. Stenvad, Denmark)
Euridice (1965)

Josep Soler Sardà (1935–) (b. Vilafranca del Penedès, Spain)
Agamemnon (1960)
Edipo y Yocasta (1972)
Nerón (1985)

Peter Schickele [P.D.Q. Bach] (1935–) (b. Ames, Iowa, USA)
Oedipus Tex (1988)

Theodore Antoniou (1935–) (b. Athens, Greece)
Clytemnestra (1967)
Cassandra (1969)
Periander (1977–1979)

Raymond Pannell (1935–) (b. London, England)
Circe (1977)

Philip Glass (1937–) (b. Baltimore, Md., USA)
Akhnaten (1984)

Lee Breuer (1937–) (b. New York, USA), with Bob Telson (USA)
Gospel at Colonus (1982)

Einojuhani Rautavaara (1938–) (b. Helsinki, Finland)
Apollo ja Marsyas (1973)

Louis Andriessen (1939–) (b. Utrecht, Netherlands)
Orpheus (1977)

Jörns Helge (1941–)
Europa und der Stier (1988)

Joanna Bruzdowicz (1943–) (b. Warsaw, Poland)
Les Troyennes (1972)

Gavin Bryars (1943–) (b. Goole, England)
Medea (1984)

Daniel Börtz (1943–) (b. Hässleholm, Sweden)
Backanterna (1991)

André Bon (1946–) (b. France)
Le rapt de Perséphone (1987)

Adriano Guarnieri (1947–) (b. Sustinente, near Mantua)
Medea (1991)

Salvatore Sciarrino (1947–) (b. Palermo, Sicily)
Amore e Psiche (1973)
Perseo e Andromeda (1991)

Renaud Gagneux (1947–) (b. Paris, France)
Orphée (1989)

Conrad Cummings (1948–) (b. San Francisco, Calif., USA)
Eros and Psyche (1983)
Cassandra (1984–1985)

Stephen Oliver (1950–1992) (b. Chester, England)
Euridice (1981)
Timon of Athens (1991)

Param Vir (1952–) (b. Delhi, India)
Ion (2000)

Wolfgang Rihm (1953–) (b. Karlsruhe, Germany)
Oedipus (1987)

Robert Convery (1954–) (b. Wichita, Kans., USA)
Pyramus and Thisbe (1982)

Richard Blackford (1954–) (b. London, England)
Metamorphoses (1983)

Beat Furrer (1954–) (b. Austria)
Narcissus (1994)

Pascal Dusapin (1955–) (b. France)
Medeamaterial (1992)

Mark-Anthony Turnage (1960–) (b. Grays, England)
Greek (1988)

Michael John LaChiusa (1961–) (b. Chappaqua, New York, USA)
Marie Christine (1999)

John Fisher (1963–) (b. San Francisco, Calif., USA)
Medea, The Musical (1995)

Index

About the Author

MARIANNE McDONALD is Professor of Theatre and Classics at the University of California, San Diego, and a member of the Royal Irish Academy. She was a Fulbright professor in 1999 and in addition to her post at UCSD, is adjunct professor at Trinity College, Dublin and a fellow at the National University of Ireland. With over 140 publications, she is the author of *Terms for Happiness in Euripides*, *Euripides in Cinema*, *Ancient Sun/Modern Light*, and *Star Myths*.